Mastering Algorithms for AI

From Basics to Advanced Techniques

By

Dr. Hesham Mohamed Elsherif

ABOUT THE AUTHOR

Dr. Hesham Mohamed Elsherif stands at the forefront of library management and research, boasting an impressive 22-year tenure in the field. Holding dual doctoral degrees, one in Management and Organizational Leadership and the other in Information Systems and Technology, Dr. Elsherif brings a unique blend of knowledge to any intellectual endeavor.

An expert in Empirical research methodology, Dr. Elsherif specializes particularly in the Qualitative approach and Action research. This specialization has not only strengthened his research endeavors but has also allowed him to contribute invaluable insights and advancements in these areas.

Over the years, Dr. Elsherif has made significant contributions to the academic world not only as a professional researcher but also as an Adjunct Professor. This multifaceted role in the educational landscape has further solidified his reputation as a thought leader and pioneer.

Furthermore, Dr. Elsherif's expertise isn't confined to one region. He has served as a consultant to numerous educational institutions on an international scale, sharing best practices, innovative strategies, and his deep insights into the ever-evolving realms of management and technology.

Combining a passion for education with an unparalleled depth of knowledge, Dr. Elsherif continues to inspire, educate, and lead in both the library and academic communities.

Preface

Overview of AI and Algorithms

Artificial Intelligence (AI) has rapidly become one of the most transformative technologies of our time, impacting everything from healthcare and finance to transportation and entertainment. At its core, AI is about creating systems that can perform tasks that typically require human intelligence - such as learning, reasoning, problem-solving, understanding natural language, and even creativity. However, behind the scenes of these intelligent systems are sophisticated algorithms that drive decision-making, learning processes, and predictions. Understanding these algorithms is key to unlocking the potential of AI.

In this book, **"Mastering Algorithms for AI: From Basics to Advanced Techniques,"** we embark on a journey to explore how these algorithms are designed, implemented, and applied to create powerful AI systems. To appreciate the importance of algorithms in AI, it's essential to grasp the relationship between AI as a field of study and the algorithms that power it.

What is Artificial Intelligence (AI)?

Artificial Intelligence refers to the development of computer systems that can perform tasks that usually require human intelligence. These tasks range from basic operations like recognizing patterns in data to more complex actions like making autonomous decisions or understanding human language. AI can be categorized into three broad types:

- **Narrow AI**: Also known as weak AI, narrow AI systems are designed to perform a specific task, such as recommending products on an e-commerce website or recognizing faces in images. These systems don't possess generalized intelligence beyond the scope of their programming.

- **General AI**: Often considered theoretical at this point, general AI refers to machines that can perform any intellectual task that a human being can. This would require machines to understand, learn, and apply knowledge in a broad sense, similar to human cognitive abilities.

- **Super AI**: Super AI represents an even more advanced form of AI, surpassing human intelligence in all aspects. This is the realm of science fiction for now, with no existing systems that approach such capabilities.

The Role of Algorithms in AI

At the heart of AI lies the concept of an algorithm. An algorithm is essentially a step-by-step procedure or formula for solving a problem. In the context of AI, algorithms are used to process data, identify patterns, learn from that data, and make decisions based on the knowledge gained.

AI algorithms differ from traditional algorithms in that they often involve learning and adaptation. Traditional algorithms are rule-based, meaning that the instructions are explicitly programmed and fixed. AI algorithms, particularly in machine learning, are designed to improve over time by learning from data. They can adjust their behavior based on new information, becoming more accurate and efficient as they process more data.

Types of Algorithms in AI

AI is a broad field, and its algorithms are as diverse as the problems they solve. The main categories of AI algorithms include:

1. **Search and Optimization Algorithms**
    These algorithms are fundamental to problem-solving in AI. Search algorithms like Breadth-First Search (BFS) and Depth-First Search (DFS) explore possible solutions in structured ways, while optimization algorithms aim to find the best solution within a given set of constraints.

2. **Machine Learning Algorithms**
    Machine learning, a subfield of AI, focuses on creating algorithms that can learn from and make predictions or decisions based on data. Machine learning algorithms can be categorized into:

    o   **Supervised Learning**: The algorithm is trained on labeled data, learning to map inputs to specific outputs (e.g., classification, regression).

    o   **Unsupervised Learning**: The algorithm identifies patterns in unlabeled data without explicit instruction (e.g., clustering, dimensionality reduction).

    o   **Reinforcement Learning**: The algorithm learns by interacting with an environment, receiving feedback in the form of rewards or penalties to improve decision-making.

3. **Deep Learning Algorithms**
    A subset of machine learning, deep learning algorithms are based on neural networks that mimic the structure and function of the human brain. These algorithms excel in handling large amounts of unstructured data, such as

images, audio, and text. Deep learning is responsible for advances in fields like computer vision, speech recognition, and natural language processing.

4. **Heuristic and Metaheuristic Algorithms**
   These algorithms are used for solving complex optimization problems where traditional methods fall short. Examples include Genetic Algorithms and Simulated Annealing, which rely on iterative methods and stochastic processes to find near-optimal solutions in large, complex search spaces.

5. **Evolutionary Algorithms**
   Inspired by biological evolution, these algorithms use mechanisms such as mutation, crossover, and selection to evolve solutions to optimization problems. Evolutionary algorithms are useful for tasks that involve finding the best solution in large, complex environments.

Why Algorithms are Crucial for AI

Algorithms are the backbone of AI. Without algorithms, AI systems wouldn't be able to function or improve over time. Here's why algorithms are so critical:

- **Efficiency**: AI algorithms determine how efficiently an AI system can process information and make decisions. Optimizing these algorithms can significantly improve the performance of AI systems, making them faster and more effective.

- **Scalability**: As data grows in volume and complexity, AI algorithms need to scale to handle this data. Advanced algorithms like deep learning can manage enormous datasets and continue to learn from them over time, enabling AI systems to become more accurate and reliable.

- **Adaptability**: The ability of AI systems to adapt to new data and changing environments is largely due to the power of machine learning algorithms. By continually learning from experience, these algorithms allow AI systems to improve autonomously, adapting to new challenges and opportunities.

- **Intelligence**: The "intelligence" of an AI system is derived from the algorithms it uses to learn and make decisions. Whether it's identifying objects in an image or predicting market trends, the intelligence of AI lies in the ability of these algorithms to process vast amounts of information and make informed decisions.

This Book's Approach to Teaching AI Algorithms

In this book, we aim to demystify AI algorithms and provide you with both theoretical and practical insights into how these algorithms work. Starting from the basics of what an algorithm is, we move toward more complex algorithms and their applications in AI. The book is divided into manageable sections that introduce algorithms in a step-by-step manner, with code examples and projects to reinforce learning. You'll not only understand how algorithms are structured but also how to apply them in real-world AI systems.

Whether you are new to AI or seeking to deepen your expertise, this book will equip you with the tools to build, optimize, and deploy AI algorithms that drive intelligent systems. Our goal is to empower you with the knowledge and skills to navigate the world of AI algorithms, from foundational principles to cutting-edge techniques.

Why Learn AI Algorithms?

As artificial intelligence (AI) continues to evolve and become increasingly integrated into our daily lives, understanding the underlying algorithms that power AI systems is no longer just the domain of specialists. AI algorithms have become essential tools for professionals in diverse industries, from healthcare and finance to marketing and robotics. But why is it so important to learn AI algorithms specifically? The answer lies in the profound impact these algorithms have on the effectiveness, efficiency, and intelligence of AI systems. Learning AI algorithms is about understanding how machines can solve problems, make decisions, and adapt in ways that mimic - or even surpass - human capabilities.

1. AI Algorithms are the Core of Intelligent Systems

At the heart of every AI system lies an algorithm, a set of rules or instructions that the system follows to process data and produce desired outcomes. AI algorithms enable machines to:

- **Learn from Data**: Machine learning algorithms, for instance, allow systems to identify patterns, make predictions, and improve their performance over time without human intervention.

- **Solve Complex Problems**: Optimization algorithms help machines find solutions to complex problems, whether it's scheduling tasks efficiently or finding the shortest path in a transportation network.

- **Make Decisions**: Decision-making algorithms allow AI systems to choose actions based on available information, much like a human would in similar scenarios.

Without algorithms, AI systems would be incapable of performing these tasks, making algorithms the fundamental building blocks of all AI capabilities. By learning AI algorithms, you are equipping yourself with the tools necessary to understand and build intelligent systems that can adapt and improve autonomously.

2. Algorithms Enable Efficient AI

The efficiency of an AI system is heavily dependent on the quality of its underlying algorithms. Well-designed algorithms ensure that systems can process vast amounts of data quickly and accurately, which is critical in applications where speed and precision are essential—such as real-time fraud detection in finance or autonomous vehicle navigation.

Learning AI algorithms allows you to:

- **Optimize Performance**: Understanding how algorithms work and how to optimize them enables you to build AI systems that perform tasks more efficiently, using fewer resources such as time and computational power.

- **Handle Large-Scale Data**: With the explosion of data in the digital age, AI algorithms must be capable of processing large datasets quickly and accurately. Algorithms such as neural networks and deep learning models are specifically designed to handle and learn from massive amounts of data, which is why they are crucial in applications like image recognition and language translation.

Mastering these algorithms gives you the ability to build AI solutions that not only work but also work efficiently, even in data-intensive environments.

3. AI Algorithms Provide a Foundation for Advanced AI Techniques

If you're looking to dive into the more advanced aspects of AI, such as deep learning, reinforcement learning, or natural language processing (NLP), having a solid foundation in AI algorithms is critical. Advanced AI techniques build on basic algorithmic principles, and without a clear understanding of these foundations, mastering more complex topics becomes nearly impossible.

By learning AI algorithms, you gain:

- **A Stepping Stone to Advanced AI**: Mastering basic algorithms such as search, sorting, or regression provides the groundwork for tackling more advanced topics like convolutional neural networks (CNNs) or recurrent neural networks (RNNs). With a strong understanding of these principles, you'll be better equipped to grasp more complex algorithms and concepts.

- **The Ability to Adapt and Innovate**: AI is a rapidly evolving field, and new algorithms and techniques are constantly emerging. Having a solid grasp of foundational AI algorithms ensures that you are not only able to adapt to new developments but also capable of contributing to innovations in AI.

Learning these algorithms opens the door to advanced AI topics, making it possible to specialize in cutting-edge areas that are transforming industries and creating new opportunities.

4. Algorithms Are the Key to Problem-Solving in AI

AI is fundamentally about problem-solving. Whether it's finding the best solution in a complex optimization problem or recognizing objects in an image, AI systems rely on algorithms to identify and implement solutions. Learning AI algorithms provides you with a toolkit for addressing a wide range of problems across various domains.

Some key problem-solving benefits of learning AI algorithms include:

- **Tackling Real-World Challenges**: From predicting stock prices to diagnosing diseases, AI algorithms enable you to solve real-world problems by automating tasks, making predictions, and optimizing solutions based on available data.

- **Adapting to Different Problems**: Many AI algorithms are designed to be adaptable, meaning they can be applied across a variety of industries and problem types. Learning these algorithms equips you with the versatility to tackle different challenges in fields such as finance, healthcare, marketing, and engineering.

By mastering AI algorithms, you develop the ability to break down complex problems into manageable steps and implement solutions that are efficient, scalable, and intelligent.

5. AI Algorithms Make AI Accessible

For many, AI can seem like an intimidating field, full of complex jargon and opaque processes. However, at its core, AI is about using algorithms to solve problems, and by learning these algorithms, you demystify AI. Rather than viewing AI as an abstract concept, learning its algorithms turns it into a concrete, practical tool you can use in everyday work and research.

By mastering AI algorithms, you:

- **Gain Hands-On Skills**: Understanding AI algorithms means that you'll have the practical skills to design, build, and implement AI systems. This makes AI less of an academic subject and more of a real-world tool that you can leverage in your career.

- **Lower the Barrier to Entry**: Once you understand AI algorithms, you unlock a wide range of AI applications, even if you don't have a background in AI research. Learning algorithms allows you to move from theory to practice, making AI accessible to individuals from various disciplines.

With a solid understanding of AI algorithms, AI becomes a tool you can readily use, opening up new career paths and opportunities in industries that are increasingly driven by data and automation.

6. Future-Proof Your Career

The demand for professionals who understand AI algorithms is skyrocketing as more companies and industries integrate AI into their operations. Whether it's automating routine tasks, optimizing processes, or enabling predictive analytics, AI is becoming a central part of modern business. By learning AI algorithms, you future-proof your career and position yourself as a valuable asset in a data-driven world.

Why learning AI algorithms future-proofs your career:

- **High Demand for AI Skills**: Professionals with expertise in AI algorithms are in high demand across various sectors, including tech, healthcare, finance, and government. By mastering these algorithms, you position yourself for roles in AI development, data science, and machine learning engineering.

- **Versatility in Career Opportunities**: AI algorithms are applicable in a wide range of fields, from robotics and autonomous systems to digital marketing and customer service. Learning AI algorithms provides you with a skill set that is highly transferable, opening up opportunities in diverse industries.

As AI continues to shape the future of technology and business, professionals who understand the algorithms behind AI will be best equipped to thrive in an AI-driven world.

How to Use This Book

"Mastering Algorithms for AI: From Basics to Advanced Techniques" is designed as a comprehensive guide that takes you step-by-step through the world of AI algorithms, starting from foundational concepts and progressing to advanced techniques. Whether you're a beginner looking to enter the field of artificial intelligence or an experienced professional seeking to deepen your understanding, this book provides a clear, structured learning path. The following guidelines will help you make the most of this resource as you embark on your journey to mastering AI algorithms.

1. Modular Structure for Flexibility

This book is divided into several key sections, each building upon the previous one while also being modular enough to stand on its own. The structure is intentional, allowing readers from different backgrounds and with varying levels of expertise to navigate the content in a way that best suits their needs:

- **Part 1: Foundations of AI and Algorithms**
  If you are new to AI, this is where you should begin. The first few chapters introduce fundamental concepts such as the nature of artificial intelligence, basic algorithm design, and programming foundations using Python. This section is essential for readers who need to establish a strong

grounding in the basics before moving on to more complex topics.

- **Part 2: Basic AI Algorithms**
  After mastering the basics, you'll progress to essential algorithms that form the core of AI systems, such as search, sorting, and greedy algorithms. This section focuses on foundational algorithms that are directly applicable to AI problem-solving. If you already have a good understanding of programming and basic data structures, you can start here.

- **Part 3: Machine Learning Algorithms**
  For those familiar with basic algorithms but new to machine learning, this section introduces fundamental machine learning techniques, including regression, classification, and clustering. You'll learn how to build machine learning models from scratch and apply them to real-world data.

- **Part 4: Advanced AI Algorithms**
  This section covers more complex algorithms like neural networks, deep learning, and reinforcement learning. If you're already comfortable with machine learning and want to dive deeper into advanced topics, this is the section for you. It includes detailed explanations of the underlying math, architectures, and optimization techniques used in cutting-edge AI systems.

- **Part 5: Optimization and Heuristic Algorithms**
  In AI, solving optimization problems efficiently is often the key to creating high-performing systems. This part focuses on heuristic methods such as genetic algorithms, simulated annealing, and swarm intelligence. If your focus is on improving system performance and solving complex problems, you will find this section particularly valuable.

- **Part 6: Emerging Trends in AI**
  The last section explores cutting-edge topics like natural language processing (NLP), generative adversarial networks (GANs), and AI ethics. If you're looking to stay ahead of the curve and explore where AI is headed next, this section will provide insights into the latest developments in the field.

Each part is self-contained, allowing you to focus on the areas most relevant to your needs. If you are already experienced in basic AI algorithms, for example, you may choose to skip directly to the chapters on machine learning or neural networks.

2. Practical Learning with Hands-On Projects

This book emphasizes hands-on learning. Every chapter includes practical examples, code snippets, and real-world projects designed to reinforce theoretical concepts. You'll find that:

- **Code Samples**: Python is the primary language used throughout this book. Code samples are included to demonstrate the implementation of key algorithms. You can follow along by writing and executing the code yourself to see how these algorithms work in practice. Each chapter's examples build upon one another, gradually increasing in complexity as your understanding deepens.

- **Projects**: At the end of several sections, you'll find comprehensive projects that challenge you to apply what you've learned to solve real-world problems. For instance, after learning about machine learning algorithms, you might build a predictive model using actual datasets. Similarly, after studying neural networks, you'll have the chance to create an image classifier or text generator. These projects are essential for solidifying your understanding and giving you practical experience that can be transferred to your own AI endeavors.

If you're the type of learner who absorbs knowledge best through doing, these projects will be invaluable. By the end of the book, you'll have completed several full-fledged AI projects, giving you a portfolio of work to showcase.

3. Deep Dive into Mathematical Foundations

Understanding the mathematics behind AI algorithms is critical for mastering the field. While this book emphasizes practical implementation, it also provides thorough explanations of the mathematical concepts that drive AI. Topics such as linear algebra, probability, calculus, and optimization are covered as they relate to specific algorithms.

- **Mathematical Explanations**: Key mathematical concepts are introduced alongside algorithms that rely on them. For example, when covering neural networks, the book explains the concepts of gradient descent and backpropagation. Each explanation is designed to be as intuitive as possible, with plenty of visual aids and examples.

- **Optional Deep Dive**: If you're someone who prefers focusing more on the application side of AI and less on the theoretical math, you can skip or skim these sections without losing the overall flow of the book. However, for those who want a deeper understanding of how algorithms work at a mathematical level, these explanations will provide the necessary insight.

4. Self-Paced Learning

AI is a vast and complex field, and everyone approaches it from different levels of expertise and with different goals. This book is designed to support **self-paced learning**, giving you the flexibility to learn at your own speed. Here are some tips on how to make the most of this feature:

- **Take Your Time with Challenging Concepts**: Certain topics, especially in the sections on machine learning, neural networks, and reinforcement learning, can be conceptually challenging. Don't hesitate to revisit sections, reread examples, or experiment with the code until you feel confident. The book is structured to allow for deep, reflective learning.

- **Focus on Areas of Interest**: Not every reader will need to master every aspect of AI. For instance, if your focus is on machine learning, you may want to prioritize those chapters and then dive into reinforcement learning or deep learning as your interests expand. The modular design allows you to tailor your learning experience to your specific goals.

5. Building a Strong Theoretical and Practical Foundation

To succeed in AI, it's important to have a balanced understanding of both theory and practice. This book strikes that balance by offering:

- **Theory**: Each chapter begins with a conceptual introduction, explaining the why and how of the algorithms. Understanding the theory is essential to appreciate why certain algorithms work and when they should be applied.

- **Practice**: Once the theory is clear, we move into practical implementation with detailed coding examples. The hands-on exercises and projects are designed to reinforce the theoretical concepts while giving you the skills to implement them on your own.

This blend of theory and practice ensures that by the end of the book, you will not only know how AI algorithms work but also be able to implement and adapt them to solve real-world problems.

6. Resources for Continued Learning

AI is an ever-evolving field, with new techniques, algorithms, and applications emerging constantly. While this book provides a comprehensive guide to AI algorithms, it also points you toward resources for continued learning:

- **Further Reading**: Each chapter includes suggestions for further reading, including research papers, online courses, and reference books. These resources are useful if you want to dive deeper into a particular topic or stay updated on the latest advancements.

- **Open-Source Libraries**: Throughout the book, we reference widely-used Python libraries such as NumPy, pandas, scikit-learn, TensorFlow, and PyTorch. These libraries are powerful tools for implementing AI algorithms and are continually updated with the latest research. Familiarizing yourself with these tools will allow you to keep pace with the rapidly advancing AI field.

- **Community Engagement**: AI is a collaborative field, and there is a thriving online community of AI researchers, developers, and enthusiasts. The book encourages you to engage with online communities, contribute to open-source projects, and participate in AI forums. By doing so, you'll continue to grow as an AI practitioner long after finishing this book.

In summary, **"Mastering Algorithms for AI: From Basics to Advanced Techniques"** is designed to be a versatile, comprehensive guide that accommodates learners from all backgrounds. Whether you're a novice or an experienced AI professional, you can use this book to build a solid understanding of AI algorithms, develop practical coding skills, and work on real-world projects that reinforce learning. With its modular structure, hands-on projects, and in-depth theoretical insights, this book serves as both a learning resource and a reference guide, ensuring that you walk away with a deep understanding of AI algorithms and the confidence to apply them in your work or research.

Dr. Hesham Mohamed Elsherif

Who Should Read This Book?

This book is designed for a wide audience, ranging from beginners to experienced professionals who want to deepen their understanding of AI algorithms. Here's a breakdown of who will benefit most from this guide:

1. Beginners in AI and Machine Learning

If you're new to artificial intelligence, this book is an ideal starting point. We begin from scratch, introducing foundational concepts such as what AI is and how algorithms work, before gradually progressing to more advanced topics. With clear explanations and practical examples, even those with no prior experience in AI will find this book approachable.

2. Students and Academic Learners

This book is an excellent resource for students studying computer science, data science, AI, or related fields. It provides a structured learning path, starting from fundamental algorithms and moving toward advanced machine learning and deep learning techniques. It also covers essential mathematical foundations, making it a great supplement for coursework.

3. Developers and Programmers

If you're a developer looking to transition into the field of AI, or if you're already working with AI but want to strengthen your understanding of the algorithms behind it, this book will be highly beneficial. With a strong focus on Python programming and practical examples, you'll learn how to implement AI algorithms in real-world projects.

4. Data Scientists

For data scientists who already have a foundation in machine learning, this book offers an in-depth exploration of various AI algorithms, from classical approaches like regression and clustering to advanced topics like neural networks, reinforcement learning, and generative models. You'll not only enhance your algorithmic knowledge but also learn how to apply these techniques in data-driven solutions.

5. Researchers and Academics

If you're involved in research related to AI, this book can serve as a valuable reference. The advanced chapters delve into cutting-edge algorithms, optimization techniques, and emerging trends in AI such as NLP and generative models. Additionally, the comprehensive list of hands-on projects and case studies provides useful insights for both theoretical exploration and practical experimentation.

6. Professionals Transitioning into AI

For professionals working in other fields but looking to pivot into AI, this book offers a practical, step-by-step guide to mastering the algorithms that form the backbone of AI systems. Whether you work in healthcare, finance, marketing, or another industry, understanding AI algorithms can enhance your ability to harness the power of AI in your field.

7. Anyone Interested in AI

If you have a keen interest in understanding how machines learn, reason, and make decisions, this book is for you. Whether your goal is to become a practitioner, explore AI's potential in your industry, or simply satisfy your curiosity, you'll find value in the clear, engaging explanations and practical examples that break down complex topics into digestible pieces.

In summary, this book is intended for anyone who wants to learn AI algorithms from the ground up, progress to advanced techniques, and apply these concepts in real-world scenarios. Whether you're a student, professional, researcher, or curious learner, "Mastering Algorithms for AI" will be your comprehensive guide to building AI systems step-by-step.

Why This Book is Essential Reading?

In a world increasingly driven by artificial intelligence, understanding the underlying algorithms that power AI systems is crucial. This book, **"Mastering Algorithms for AI: From Basics to Advanced Techniques,"** is essential reading for several reasons:

1. Comprehensive Coverage from Basic to Advanced Levels

This book takes you on a structured journey through the full spectrum of AI algorithms, starting from foundational concepts and gradually advancing to more complex topics. Whether you're a beginner or a seasoned professional, this book offers a clear progression that ensures you develop both a solid foundation and advanced expertise in AI algorithms.

2. Practical Focus with Real-World Applications

Theory alone is not enough to truly grasp AI algorithms; practical application is key. This book blends in-depth theoretical understanding with hands-on projects and examples, allowing you to implement algorithms in real-world scenarios. From search algorithms to neural networks, you'll gain experience working on AI projects that mirror those you'd encounter in professional environments.

3. Clear Explanations of Complex Concepts

AI can be an intimidating subject, but this book simplifies the complexities. The explanations are designed to be accessible, breaking down intricate topics into manageable sections. Even advanced topics like deep learning, reinforcement learning, and optimization techniques are presented in a way that is easy to follow, making this an ideal resource for learners at any level.

4. Python-Based Implementation

Python is the leading programming language in AI, and this book leverages its capabilities by providing code implementations for each algorithm. By learning how to implement these algorithms in Python, you'll not only understand the theory but also gain the skills to directly apply AI techniques in your projects or workplace. This practical approach gives you the confidence to turn ideas into working models.

5. Covers the Latest Trends and Techniques in AI

AI is an ever-evolving field, and this book keeps you up to date with the latest advancements and trends. It covers cutting-edge algorithms like convolutional neural networks (CNNs), recurrent neural networks (RNNs), generative adversarial networks (GANs), and transformer-based models. Whether it's computer vision, natural language processing (NLP), or generative models, you'll be equipped with knowledge of the most relevant AI techniques.

6. Hands-On Projects for Real Learning

Learning by doing is a core philosophy of this book. Each part concludes with practical projects that give you the chance to apply what you've learned in real-world scenarios. From building a machine learning model to creating a deep learning image classifier, these projects are designed to solidify your understanding and provide you with tangible skills you can showcase.

7. Tailored for a Wide Audience

This book is designed to serve a broad range of readers—
from students and academics to developers, data scientists,
and industry professionals. Whether you're studying AI for
academic purposes, looking to switch careers, or aiming to
apply AI in your field, the book is carefully structured to meet
your learning goals.

8. In-Depth Exploration of AI's Mathematical Foundations

AI is built on a foundation of mathematical concepts such as
linear algebra, probability, and calculus. This book demystifies
these concepts and explains how they relate to AI algorithms,
making it an invaluable resource for readers looking to
strengthen their mathematical understanding alongside
learning AI.

9. Future-Proof Your Career

AI is transforming industries, and professionals with expertise
in AI algorithms are in high demand. By mastering the
algorithms that drive AI, you'll future-proof your career in
technology, data science, engineering, and other fields where
AI is increasingly integral. This book equips you with the
knowledge and skills to be a key player in this evolving
landscape.

10. Ethical and Responsible AI Development

In addition to technical content, the book addresses the
ethical implications of AI. As AI becomes more pervasive,
understanding the moral and societal impacts of these
technologies is crucial. This book emphasizes responsible AI

development, ensuring you're not only technically proficient but also aware of AI's broader consequences.

In summary, this book is essential reading because it provides a comprehensive, accessible, and practical guide to understanding and mastering AI algorithms. With its clear explanations, hands-on projects, and focus on real-world applications, it serves as an indispensable resource for anyone looking to succeed in the field of artificial intelligence.

Happy Reading!

Table of Contents

Part 1: Foundations of AI and Algorithms
Chapter 1: Introduction to Artificial Intelligence

<u>What is Artificial Intelligence (AI)?</u>

Artificial Intelligence (AI) is a broad and interdisciplinary field that seeks to simulate or replicate aspects of human intelligence in machines. It encompasses a wide range of techniques, tools, and applications aimed at enabling computers to perform tasks that traditionally require human cognitive functions, such as problem-solving, learning, reasoning, perception, and natural language understanding (Russell & Norvig, 2021). AI has become a transformative force in many industries, leading to breakthroughs in healthcare, finance, robotics, and more, driven by advancements in algorithms, computational power, and data availability (Goodfellow, Bengio, & Courville, 2016).

The formal definition of AI can be broken into two main categories: **weak AI** and **strong AI**. Weak AI, also referred to as narrow AI, focuses on performing a specific task, such as image classification or speech recognition, without possessing general cognitive abilities. In contrast, strong AI aims to create machines with generalized human-level intelligence, capable of reasoning and problem-solving across diverse domains (Tegmark, 2017).

Core Components of AI

AI can be further broken down into several core components that define its capabilities and areas of application:

1. **Machine Learning (ML):**
   Machine learning is a subset of AI that focuses on algorithms that enable machines to learn from data and

make predictions or decisions without being explicitly programmed for every scenario (Mitchell, 1997). These algorithms improve their performance as they are exposed to more data, leveraging patterns and relationships in that data to make informed predictions.

2. **Natural Language Processing (NLP):**
   NLP involves enabling machines to understand and generate human language, allowing them to interact with humans naturally. Applications of NLP include translation services, chatbots, and sentiment analysis (Jurafsky & Martin, 2021).

3. **Computer Vision:**
   This field enables machines to interpret and understand visual information from the world. It is often used in tasks like image recognition, object detection, and video analysis (Szeliski, 2010).

4. **Robotics:**
   Robotics combines AI with physical systems to create machines that can interact with and manipulate their environment. AI-driven robots are used in manufacturing, healthcare, and service industries (Siciliano & Khatib, 2016).

AI Through the Lens of Algorithms

At the core of AI lies a set of algorithms that enable machines to simulate intelligent behavior. An algorithm is a step-by-step procedure for solving a problem or performing a computation. In the context of AI, algorithms provide the formal rules and techniques through which machines can learn, reason, and make decisions. Some key types of algorithms used in AI include:

- **Search Algorithms**: These algorithms explore a problem space to find a solution. Examples include breadth-first search (BFS) and depth-first search (DFS), often used in pathfinding and game AI.

- **Optimization Algorithms**: These seek to find the best solution given a set of constraints, and include algorithms like gradient descent used in machine learning models (Nocedal & Wright, 2006).

- **Classification Algorithms**: Common in supervised learning tasks, these algorithms assign labels to input data. Examples include decision trees, support vector machines (SVMs), and neural networks (Hastie, Tibshirani, & Friedman, 2009).

A Simple AI Example: Linear Regression

To illustrate AI in action, we can examine a basic machine learning algorithm—**linear regression**. This algorithm predicts an output value (dependent variable) based on input data (independent variable) by fitting a linear relationship to the data. The linear regression model seeks to find the best-fitting line that minimizes the sum of squared differences between the observed and predicted values.

Mathematical Formulation of Linear Regression

Linear regression is represented as:

$$y = w_1 x + w_0$$

Where:

- y is the predicted output,

- x is the input feature,

- w_1 is the slope of the line (weight), and

- w_0 is the intercept.

The goal is to minimize the **mean squared error (MSE)**, which measures the average of the squares of the errors, i.e., the difference between the observed and predicted values:

$$\text{MSE} = \frac{1}{n} \sum_{i=1}^{n} (y_i - \hat{y}_i)^2$$

Where y_i is the actual value and $\hat{y}_i$ is the predicted value.

Python Code Example

Below is an example of how to implement linear regression in Python using scikit-learn, one of the most widely used machine learning libraries:

import numpy as np

import matplotlib.pyplot as plt

from sklearn.linear_model import LinearRegression

Sample data: hours studied vs. exam score

X = np.array([[1], [2], [3], [4], [5], [6], [7], [8], [9], [10]]) # Hours studied

y = np.array([10, 20, 30, 40, 50, 60, 70, 80, 90, 100])   # Exam scores

```python
# Create and train the linear regression model

model = LinearRegression()

model.fit(X, y)

# Make predictions

y_pred = model.predict(X)

# Plot the data and the regression line

plt.scatter(X, y, color='blue', label='Actual data')

plt.plot(X, y_pred, color='red', label='Regression line')

plt.xlabel('Hours studied')

plt.ylabel('Exam score')

plt.title('Linear Regression: Hours Studied vs. Exam Score')

plt.legend()

plt.show()
```

In this example, the linear regression model learns the relationship between the number of hours studied and the corresponding exam scores. The resulting red line represents the best-fitting line that the model has learned from the data.

Graphical Representation: Linear Regression

In the graph below, the blue dots represent the actual data points, and the red line shows the linear relationship between hours studied and exam scores that the model has learned.

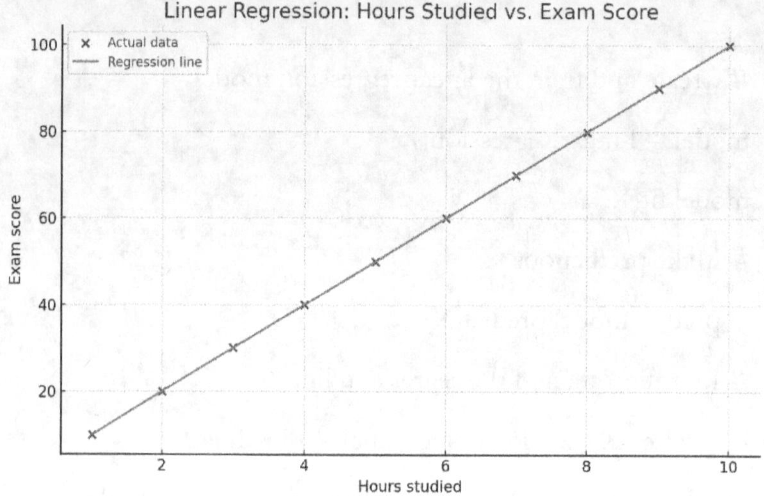

Applications of AI Algorithms

AI algorithms are applied across a vast array of real-world applications. Below are a few examples that illustrate their widespread use:

- **Healthcare**: AI algorithms are used for diagnostic purposes, such as detecting diseases from medical images, predicting patient outcomes, and personalizing treatment plans (Esteva et al., 2017).

- **Finance**: In finance, AI is used for algorithmic trading, fraud detection, risk management, and customer service automation (Huang et al., 2018).

- **Autonomous Vehicles**: AI-powered algorithms are critical in self-driving cars, where they are used for decision-making, obstacle detection, and route planning (Bojarski et al., 2016).

- **Natural Language Processing**: AI algorithms are responsible for advancements in NLP, such as machine translation (Google Translate), voice recognition (Siri,

Alexa), and automated text generation (Brown et al., 2020).

In summary, Artificial Intelligence is fundamentally about making machines capable of learning, reasoning, and performing tasks that would normally require human intelligence. The backbone of AI is the set of algorithms that enable these systems to learn from data and make informed decisions. As AI continues to permeate all aspects of modern life, understanding these algorithms and how they function becomes increasingly crucial for students, professionals, and researchers alike. By studying AI algorithms, we not only gain insight into the future of technology but also learn how to design and apply systems that can drive innovations in a wide range of industries.

Types of AI: Narrow, General, and Super AI

Artificial Intelligence (AI) can be classified into three broad categories based on its scope and capabilities: **Narrow AI**, **General AI**, and **Super AI**. These distinctions are essential to understanding the potential and limitations of AI systems, as well as their future development. The progression from narrow to super AI reflects increasing levels of cognitive ability, from task-specific systems to those that might one day surpass human intelligence (Russell & Norvig, 2021).

Narrow AI (Weak AI)

Narrow AI, also known as **Weak AI**, refers to AI systems designed to perform a specific task or a set of closely related tasks. These systems operate within a predefined range and are not capable of generalized learning or reasoning beyond their specialized domain. Narrow AI is the form of AI that exists today and is ubiquitous in many applications across industries (Goodfellow, Bengio, & Courville, 2016).

Narrow AI systems excel in tasks such as:

- **Image recognition**: Algorithms can identify objects in images, such as facial recognition systems used in security.

- **Speech recognition**: Virtual assistants like Siri and Alexa use AI to understand and respond to human speech.

- **Recommendation systems**: Platforms like Netflix and Amazon use AI algorithms to suggest products or content based on user preferences.

However, these systems lack general intelligence and cannot adapt to tasks outside their programming. For instance, a facial recognition system cannot be used for language translation or decision-making in unrelated domains.

Example: Image Classification with AI

One common implementation of Narrow AI is image classification using machine learning algorithms, specifically neural networks. Below is an example of using Python and the Keras library to build a basic image classifier:

```python
# Importing necessary libraries

from keras.models import Sequential

from keras.layers import Dense, Conv2D, Flatten

from keras.datasets import mnist

from keras.utils import to_categorical

# Loading the dataset (handwritten digits)

(X_train, y_train), (X_test, y_test) = mnist.load_data()
```

```python
# Preprocessing the data

X_train = X_train.reshape((X_train.shape[0], 28, 28, 1))

X_test = X_test.reshape((X_test.shape[0], 28, 28, 1))

X_train, X_test = X_train / 255.0, X_test / 255.0

y_train, y_test = to_categorical(y_train),
to_categorical(y_test)

# Building a simple CNN model

model = Sequential()

model.add(Conv2D(32, kernel_size=(3, 3), activation='relu',
input_shape=(28, 28, 1)))

model.add(Flatten())

model.add(Dense(128, activation='relu'))

model.add(Dense(10, activation='softmax'))

# Compiling and training the model

model.compile(optimizer='adam',
loss='categorical_crossentropy', metrics=['accuracy'])

model.fit(X_train, y_train, validation_data=(X_test, y_test),
epochs=3)
```

This code implements a **Convolutional Neural Network (CNN)** to classify images from the MNIST dataset, a classic example of Narrow AI. The model can accurately classify handwritten digits but cannot be generalized to other tasks like speech recognition or decision-making in other domains.

General AI (Artificial General Intelligence - AGI)

General AI, or **Artificial General Intelligence (AGI)**, refers to AI systems that possess the ability to understand, learn, and apply intelligence across a wide range of tasks, much like a human. Unlike Narrow AI, which is limited to specific domains, General AI would be capable of performing any intellectual task that a human can, with comparable cognitive capabilities (Tegmark, 2017).

AGI is still a theoretical concept and has not yet been achieved. If realized, AGI systems would:

- **Exhibit human-like cognitive abilities**: They would reason, plan, learn, and adapt across diverse and unpredictable environments.

- **Learn from minimal data**: While Narrow AI often requires massive datasets for training, AGI could potentially learn from fewer examples, just like humans can.

- **Generalize across domains**: AGI could perform tasks across various fields, from language understanding to scientific reasoning and creative problem-solving.

Current AI systems are still far from achieving AGI due to the complexities involved in replicating human cognition in machines. While AGI remains a long-term goal, advancements in areas such as deep learning, reinforcement learning, and cognitive computing are seen as steps toward this objective (Goertzel, 2014).

Super AI (Artificial Superintelligence - ASI)

Super AI, or **Artificial Superintelligence (ASI)**, represents the hypothetical future stage of AI development, where AI systems surpass human intelligence across all domains. Super

AI would not only perform tasks better than the most capable human beings but also exceed human cognitive abilities in areas such as reasoning, problem-solving, creativity, and social intelligence (Bostrom, 2014).

Super AI would mark the pinnacle of AI advancement, leading to machines that could:

- **Outperform humans in all intellectual tasks**: From scientific research to artistic creation, Super AI would surpass human capacity.

- **Self-improve at an exponential rate**: Super AI could design even more intelligent systems, leading to rapid advancements in technology and science.

- **Solve global challenges**: With its superior intelligence, Super AI could potentially address some of the most pressing global challenges, such as climate change, disease, and poverty.

However, the development of Super AI raises significant ethical concerns and potential risks. Experts like Nick Bostrom (2014) and Stuart Russell (2021) caution that Super AI, if not properly controlled, could lead to unintended consequences or existential threats to humanity. Ensuring the safe and ethical development of AI as it advances towards this stage is a critical area of ongoing research.

Graphical Representation: Types of AI

To illustrate the relationship between these types of AI, the following graph visualizes the progression from Narrow AI to General AI and eventually to Super AI:

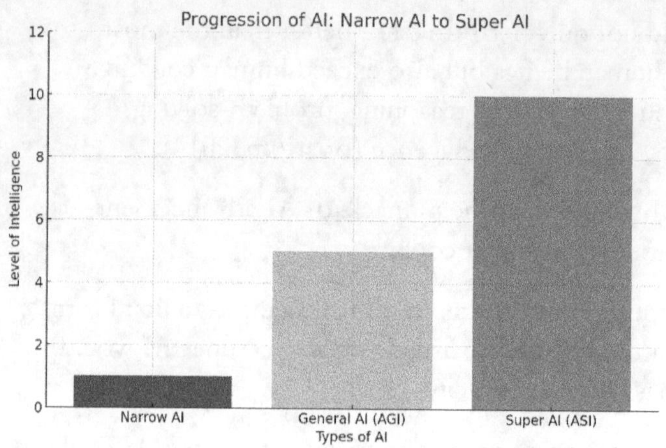

In this graph:

- Narrow AI has a relatively low level of intelligence, focused on specific tasks.

- General AI has a much higher intelligence level, capable of generalized human-like cognition.

- Super AI represents the highest level of intelligence, surpassing human cognitive abilities.

In summary, the distinction between Narrow AI, General AI, and Super AI is crucial for understanding the current state and future potential of artificial intelligence. Narrow AI, the only form of AI currently realized, is highly specialized but limited in scope. General AI, while still theoretical, aims to replicate human intelligence across a wide range of tasks, and Super AI represents a future where machines could exceed human intellectual capabilities. Each stage in the progression toward more intelligent systems brings its own challenges, opportunities, and risks, making it imperative for researchers, policymakers, and ethicists to work together in guiding the development of AI responsibly.

Key Fields of AI

Artificial Intelligence (AI) is an interdisciplinary field that incorporates a variety of specialized domains, each contributing to the development of intelligent systems. These domains—**Machine Learning (ML)**, **Computer Vision (CV)**, **Natural Language Processing (NLP)**, **Robotics**, and **Expert Systems**—enable AI to mimic or surpass human cognitive abilities in problem-solving, decision-making, perception, and communication (Russell & Norvig, 2021). These fields serve distinct purposes but often overlap in applications, with advancements in one domain accelerating progress in others. Understanding these core fields is essential for grasping the breadth and potential of AI technology.

1. Machine Learning (ML)

Machine Learning (ML) is perhaps the most pivotal field within AI. It refers to the development of algorithms that enable machines to learn from data and improve their performance without being explicitly programmed (Mitchell, 1997). ML enables computers to identify patterns, make decisions, and predict outcomes based on historical data. It is widely applied in industries such as healthcare, finance, marketing, and more.

Machine learning can be categorized into three major types:

- **Supervised Learning**: Involves training a model on labeled data, where the input and output pairs are known. This approach is commonly used for classification and regression tasks.

- **Unsupervised Learning**: The model is trained on unlabeled data, and it must find hidden patterns or intrinsic structures in the data. Common tasks include clustering and dimensionality reduction.

- **Reinforcement Learning**: An agent learns to make decisions by interacting with an environment and receiving feedback in the form of rewards or penalties, commonly used in robotics and gaming (Sutton & Barto, 2018).

Code Example: Supervised Learning (Linear Regression with Scikit-learn)

```
from sklearn.model_selection import train_test_split

from sklearn.linear_model import LinearRegression

from sklearn.metrics import mean_squared_error

# Sample data: hours studied vs. exam scores

X = [[1], [2], [3], [4], [5], [6], [7], [8], [9], [10]]  # Input (Hours studied)

y = [10, 20, 30, 40, 50, 60, 70, 80, 90, 100]        # Output (Scores)

# Split data into training and testing sets

X_train, X_test, y_train, y_test = train_test_split(X, y, test_size=0.2, random_state=42)

# Train the linear regression model

model = LinearRegression()

model.fit(X_train, y_train)

# Make predictions and evaluate

y_pred = model.predict(X_test)
```

```
print(f'Mean Squared Error: {mean_squared_error(y_test,
y_pred)}')
```

This code demonstrates supervised learning using **linear regression**, where the model predicts the exam scores based on the number of hours studied. Machine learning models such as this are widely used for predictive analytics and decision-making across various industries.

2. Computer Vision (CV)

Computer Vision (CV) is a field of AI that enables machines to interpret and understand the visual world. It involves analyzing and processing images or video to extract useful information, which can then be applied to tasks such as object detection, facial recognition, and scene understanding (Szeliski, 2010). Advances in **Convolutional Neural Networks (CNNs)** have dramatically improved the performance of computer vision systems, especially in applications like autonomous vehicles, healthcare, and security.

Key applications of computer vision include:

- **Image Classification**: Classifying objects or entities in an image into predefined categories.

- **Object Detection**: Identifying and locating multiple objects in an image or video stream.

- **Facial Recognition**: Automatically recognizing and verifying individuals from images or video footage.

Code Example: Image Classification with Keras and CNN

```
from keras.models import Sequential

from keras.layers import Dense, Conv2D, Flatten
```

```python
from keras.datasets import mnist

from keras.utils import to_categorical

# Load and preprocess MNIST dataset

(X_train, y_train), (X_test, y_test) = mnist.load_data()

X_train = X_train.reshape(X_train.shape[0], 28, 28,
1).astype('float32') / 255

X_test = X_test.reshape(X_test.shape[0], 28, 28,
1).astype('float32') / 255

y_train = to_categorical(y_train)

y_test = to_categorical(y_test)

# Build a simple CNN model

model = Sequential([

    Conv2D(32, kernel_size=(3, 3), activation='relu',
input_shape=(28, 28, 1)),

    Flatten(),

    Dense(128, activation='relu'),

    Dense(10, activation='softmax')

])

# Compile and train the model

model.compile(optimizer='adam',
loss='categorical_crossentropy', metrics=['accuracy'])

model.fit(X_train, y_train, validation_data=(X_test, y_test),
epochs=3)
```

This example implements a basic **Convolutional Neural Network (CNN)** for classifying handwritten digits from the MNIST dataset, illustrating how computer vision can be applied in tasks such as handwritten character recognition.

3. Natural Language Processing (NLP)

Natural Language Processing (NLP) focuses on the interaction between computers and human language. It enables machines to process, understand, and generate text or spoken language (Jurafsky & Martin, 2021). NLP is used in various applications such as chatbots, language translation, sentiment analysis, and text summarization.

Key tasks in NLP include:

- **Text Classification**: Assigning predefined categories to text, such as spam detection or sentiment analysis.

- **Named Entity Recognition (NER)**: Identifying and classifying entities (e.g., people, organizations) within text.

- **Machine Translation**: Translating text or speech from one language to another, such as in Google Translate.

Code Example: Sentiment Analysis Using Naive Bayes

```python
from sklearn.feature_extraction.text import CountVectorizer

from sklearn.naive_bayes import MultinomialNB

from sklearn.model_selection import train_test_split

from sklearn.metrics import accuracy_score

# Sample data

texts = ["I love this product", "This is terrible", "Best purchase ever", "Worst experience"]
```

```python
labels = [1, 0, 1, 0]  # 1: Positive, 0: Negative

# Convert text to feature vectors

vectorizer = CountVectorizer()

X = vectorizer.fit_transform(texts)

# Split data into training and testing sets

X_train, X_test, y_train, y_test = train_test_split(X, labels, test_size=0.25, random_state=42)

# Train and evaluate the Naive Bayes model

model = MultinomialNB()

model.fit(X_train, y_train)

y_pred = model.predict(X_test)

print(f'Accuracy: {accuracy_score(y_test, y_pred)}')
```

This code example demonstrates sentiment analysis using a **Naive Bayes classifier**, an essential task in NLP where text data is categorized as positive or negative based on its content.

4. Robotics

Robotics is an AI field that integrates intelligent systems with mechanical devices to perform tasks in the physical world. AI-powered robots can navigate environments, manipulate objects, and interact with humans, making them useful in industries like manufacturing, healthcare, and logistics (Siciliano & Khatib, 2016). AI algorithms enable robots to learn from experience, plan their actions, and adapt to dynamic environments.

AI in robotics relies heavily on:

- **Reinforcement Learning**: Used to enable robots to learn through trial and error in dynamic environments.

- **Computer Vision**: For real-time environment perception, object detection, and navigation.

- **Planning and Control Algorithms**: Ensuring robots can safely and efficiently perform tasks.

Code Example: Basic Robotic Arm Simulation

```python
import numpy as np

import matplotlib.pyplot as plt

# Function to plot robotic arm motion

def plot_robot_arm(theta1, theta2):

    l1, l2 = 5, 3  # Lengths of arm segments

    x1 = l1 * np.cos(np.radians(theta1))

    y1 = l1 * np.sin(np.radians(theta1))

    x2 = x1 + l2 * np.cos(np.radians(theta1 + theta2))

    y2 = y1 + l2 * np.sin(np.radians(theta1 + theta2))

        plt.plot([0, x1, x2], [0, y1, y2], 'ro-', lw=3)

    plt.xlim(-10, 10)

    plt.ylim(-10, 10)

    plt.grid(True)

    plt.show()

# Simulate robot arm motion
```

```
plot_robot_arm(45, 30)
```

This example demonstrates a simple simulation of a robotic arm's movement. In real-world applications, AI would control the arm to perform complex tasks like assembly or surgery.

In summary, the fields of **Machine Learning**, **Computer Vision**, **Natural Language Processing**, and **Robotics** each represent essential aspects of AI's ability to mimic or surpass human capabilities. While these fields have distinct focuses, they often complement one another in creating AI systems that can perceive, understand, and interact with the world in sophisticated ways. The rapid advances in these fields continue to push the boundaries of AI's applications, making it a critical technology in transforming industries and solving complex challenges.

Chapter 2: Introduction to Algorithms

<u>What are Algorithms?</u>

At its core, an **algorithm** is a set of well-defined, step-by-step instructions or rules that are followed to solve a problem or accomplish a task. Algorithms are foundational in computer science and artificial intelligence, serving as the blueprint for how data is processed, analyzed, and transformed into meaningful output. In the context of AI, algorithms enable machines to perform tasks such as learning from data, making predictions, and optimizing solutions without direct human intervention (Cormen, Leiserson, Rivest, & Stein, 2009).

An algorithm can be conceptualized as a procedure that takes an input, processes it according to a sequence of instructions, and produces an output. For instance, an algorithm designed to sort a list of numbers would take the unsorted list as input, apply sorting techniques (such as comparing and swapping elements), and produce the sorted list as output.

Components of an Algorithm

To understand algorithms more fully, it is essential to recognize their key components:

1. **Input**: The data or set of instructions provided to the algorithm to work on. In AI, this could be a dataset used for training a machine learning model or sensor data for decision-making in robotics.

2. **Process**: The core operations or steps the algorithm takes to transform the input into a useful output. This involves computational tasks such as searching, sorting, classifying, or optimizing.

3. **Output**: The final result produced by the algorithm after processing the input. This could be a sorted list, a prediction (in the case of machine learning), or an action (such as in a reinforcement learning agent).

4. **Efficiency**: Measured in terms of time complexity and space complexity, efficiency refers to how well an algorithm performs given the size of the input. Efficient algorithms minimize the resources required, such as memory and processing time (Cormen et al., 2009).

Types of Algorithms

There are various types of algorithms, each designed for specific tasks and computational problems. Below are some of the key types, commonly used in both traditional computer science and AI:

1. Search Algorithms

Search algorithms are designed to find a specific item or set of items from a large collection of data. They are widely used in areas such as pathfinding, database querying, and problem-solving. Examples include:

- **Linear Search**: A simple algorithm that checks every element in a list one by one until the target element is found or the list is exhausted.

- **Binary Search**: A more efficient algorithm that works on sorted lists by repeatedly dividing the search interval in half, significantly reducing the number of comparisons (Weiss, 2012).

Code Example: Binary Search in Python

```python
def binary_search(arr, target):
    low, high = 0, len(arr) - 1
```

```python
    while low <= high:
        mid = (low + high) // 2
        if arr[mid] == target:
            return mid
        elif arr[mid] < target:
            low = mid + 1
        else:
            high = mid - 1
    return -1
# Example usage
arr = [1, 3, 5, 7, 9, 11, 13]
target = 7
index = binary_search(arr, target)
print(f"Element found at index {index}" if index != -1 else "Element not found")
```

In this code, the **binary search algorithm** efficiently finds the target number by repeatedly halving the search space, a major improvement over linear search.

Graph: Binary Search Efficiency

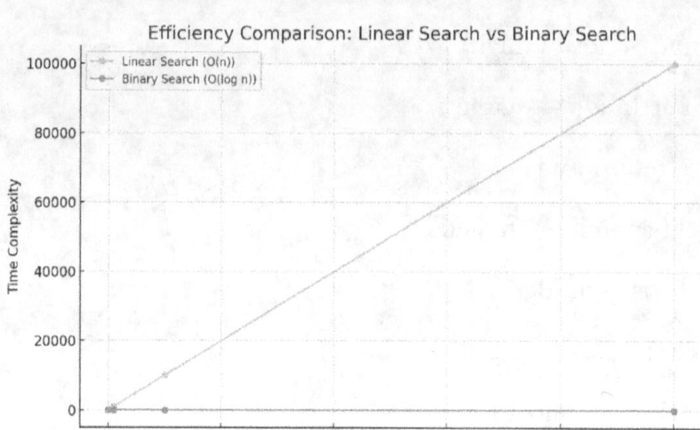

This graph illustrates the time complexity of linear search (O(n)) versus binary search (O(log n)), showing how binary search is significantly more efficient as input size grows.

2. Sorting Algorithms

Sorting algorithms arrange the elements of a list in a specific order (ascending or descending). Sorting is fundamental in data organization, allowing for more efficient searching, retrieval, and analysis. Some commonly used sorting algorithms include:

- **Bubble Sort**: A simple but inefficient algorithm that repeatedly steps through the list, compares adjacent elements, and swaps them if they are in the wrong order.

- **Merge Sort**: A more efficient, divide-and-conquer algorithm that recursively splits the list into smaller sublists, sorts them, and merges them back together (Weiss, 2012).

Code Example: Merge Sort in Python

```python
def merge_sort(arr):
    if len(arr) > 1:
        mid = len(arr) // 2
        left_half = arr[:mid]
        right_half = arr[mid:]
            merge_sort(left_half)
        merge_sort(right_half)
            i = j = k = 0
            while i < len(left_half) and j < len(right_half):
        if left_half[i] < right_half[j]:
            arr[k] = left_half[i]
            i += 1
        else:
            arr[k] = right_half[j]
            j += 1
        k += 1
            while i < len(left_half):
        arr[k] = left_half[i]
        i += 1
        k += 1
            while j < len(right_half):
```

```
            arr[k] = right_half[j]

            j += 1

            k += 1

# Example usage

arr = [38, 27, 43, 3, 9, 82, 10]

merge_sort(arr)

print("Sorted array:", arr)
```

Merge Sort is a classic **divide-and-conquer** sorting algorithm that efficiently sorts lists by breaking them down recursively and merging sorted sublists.

3. Dynamic Programming

Dynamic programming is a technique used to solve problems by breaking them down into simpler subproblems and storing the results of these subproblems to avoid redundant computations. It is used in optimization problems such as finding the shortest path or the longest common subsequence (Bellman, 1957).

- **Fibonacci Sequence**: A classic example of dynamic programming where the nth Fibonacci number is computed by storing the results of previous computations to avoid repeated work.

Code Example: Fibonacci Sequence Using Dynamic Programming

```
def fibonacci(n, memo={}):

    if n in memo:

        return memo[n]
```

```
if n <= 1:

    return n

memo[n] = fibonacci(n - 1, memo) + fibonacci(n - 2,
memo)

return memo[n]

# Example usage

n = 10

print(f"Fibonacci number at position {n} is {fibonacci(n)}")
```

Dynamic programming reduces the computational complexity of problems like the Fibonacci sequence from exponential ($O(2^n)$) to linear ($O(n)$).

4. Greedy Algorithms

Greedy algorithms make a series of decisions by choosing the locally optimal solution at each step, with the hope of finding the global optimum. They are commonly used in optimization problems where an efficient solution is needed, such as in scheduling or resource allocation problems (Cormen et al., 2009).

- **Example**: The **Greedy algorithm** for the **Fractional Knapsack Problem** chooses the item with the highest value-to-weight ratio first, filling the knapsack until capacity is reached.

The fractional knapsack problem is a variation of the knapsack problem where the items can be broken into smaller parts. The goal is to maximize the total value that can be carried in a knapsack of fixed capacity. The greedy strategy is to choose items with the highest value-to-weight ratio first.

Problem Statement: Given n items, each with a weight wi and value vi, maximize the value of the knapsack by selecting items (or fractions of items) such that the total weight does not exceed a given limit W.

Greedy Strategy: Sort the items by their value-to-weight ratio (vi/wi), and then pick items in decreasing order of this ratio until the knapsack is full.

Code Example: Fractional Knapsack Problem

```python
class Item:

    def __init__(self, value, weight):

        self.value = value

        self.weight = weight

def fractional_knapsack(items, capacity):

    # Sort items by value-to-weight ratio in descending order

    items.sort(key=lambda x: x.value / x.weight,
reverse=True)

        total_value = 0.0

    for item in items:

        if capacity >= item.weight:

            # If the item can be fully taken, take it

            total_value += item.value

            capacity -= item.weight

        else:

            # Otherwise, take the fraction of the item
```

```
        total_value += item.value * (capacity / item.weight)

        break

    return total_value
```

```
# Example usage

items = [Item(60, 10), Item(100, 20), Item(120, 30)]

capacity = 50

print(f"Maximum value in knapsack:
{fractional_knapsack(items, capacity)}")
```

In this example, the greedy algorithm sorts the items by their value-to-weight ratio and then fills the knapsack with as many items as possible, selecting fractions of items if necessary.

In summary, Algorithms form the foundation of artificial intelligence, enabling machines to process data, solve problems, and make decisions. From simple search and sorting algorithms to more complex dynamic programming and greedy strategies, each type of algorithm is designed to solve a specific class of problems efficiently. The key to understanding AI is recognizing that these algorithms are the driving force behind intelligent systems. As AI continues to evolve, the development and optimization of algorithms will remain critical for ensuring that AI systems can perform tasks accurately, efficiently, and autonomously.

Components of Algorithms

An algorithm, at its core, is a well-defined, step-by-step computational procedure that takes some input and transforms it into a desired output through a series of operations. The ability to systematically solve problems, make decisions, and process data is central to the function of algorithms, especially in the realm of artificial intelligence (AI) and computer science. To better understand how algorithms work, it is essential to break them down into their basic components: **Input**, **Output**, and **Steps** (Cormen, Leiserson, Rivest, & Stein, 2009).

1. Input

The **input** is the data or information that an algorithm requires to start its execution. This input can vary in form, such as numerical data, text, or even complex structures like graphs, images, or datasets. In AI, input could include anything from a set of labeled data for a machine learning algorithm to sensory data for an autonomous robot.

The nature and structure of the input often dictate how the algorithm processes it. An algorithm is expected to handle various types of inputs effectively and adapt to the specifics of the input size and format. For example, an image classification algorithm might take pixel data from images as input, whereas a pathfinding algorithm might take the layout of a graph or a grid.

Example: Input for a Sorting Algorithm

For a sorting algorithm such as **Merge Sort**, the input is typically an unsorted array or list of numbers. The algorithm's goal is to take this input and return the sorted version of the list.

arr = [38, 27, 43, 3, 9, 82, 10] # Input: Unsorted list

Graphical Representation: Input Size for Algorithms

As the input size increases, the time complexity of an algorithm may change. The following graph illustrates how the input size affects the execution time of different types of algorithms, such as sorting algorithms like Merge Sort (O(n log n)) versus simpler algorithms like Bubble Sort (O(n²)).

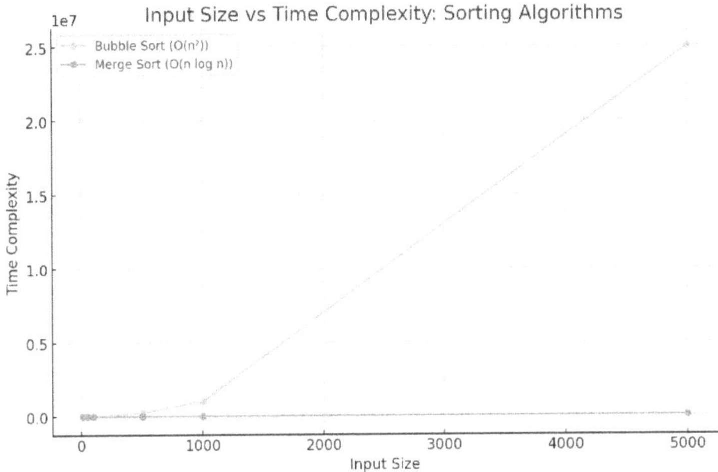

This graph demonstrates how the input size affects the performance of sorting algorithms. Merge Sort, which has a time complexity of O(n log n), handles larger input sizes more efficiently than Bubble Sort, which has a time complexity of O(n²).

2. Output

The **output** is the result or solution produced by the algorithm after processing the input. The output can take many forms, depending on the problem being solved. For instance, the output of a sorting algorithm is a sorted array, the output of a pathfinding algorithm is a sequence of steps leading from a start to an end point, and the output of a machine learning algorithm could be a prediction or classification.

The correctness and quality of the output are critical in evaluating an algorithm. For an algorithm to be considered correct, it must produce the desired or expected output for all valid inputs. In AI systems, the output could also involve probabilistic results, such as the likelihood of an event occurring.

Example: Output for a Sorting Algorithm

For a sorting algorithm, the expected output is the sorted version of the input array.

arr = [38, 27, 43, 3, 9, 82, 10] # Input

sorted_arr = merge_sort(arr)   # Output: [3, 9, 10, 27, 38, 43, 82]

The algorithm's output, in this case, is the array sorted in ascending order.

3. Steps (Process)

The **steps** of an algorithm, also known as the process, define the sequence of operations that the algorithm performs to transform the input into the output. These steps are the core logic of the algorithm and dictate how efficiently and correctly it will perform the desired task. The steps vary based on the type of algorithm but generally involve looping, conditional statements, and data manipulation (Cormen et al., 2009).

To illustrate, consider the **Merge Sort** algorithm. The steps involved in Merge Sort can be broken down as follows:

1. **Divide**: Divide the input array into two halves recursively until each subarray has only one element.

2. **Conquer**: Recursively sort the two halves.

3. **Combine**: Merge the two sorted halves into one sorted array.

Merge Sort Code Example

```python
def merge_sort(arr):
    if len(arr) > 1:
        mid = len(arr) // 2
        left_half = arr[:mid]
        right_half = arr[mid:]

        # Recursive call to sort both halves
        merge_sort(left_half)
        merge_sort(right_half)

        # Merging sorted halves
        i = j = k = 0
        while i < len(left_half) and j < len(right_half):
            if left_half[i] < right_half[j]:
                arr[k] = left_half[i]
                i += 1
            else:
                arr[k] = right_half[j]
                j += 1
            k += 1

        # Copy remaining elements
        while i < len(left_half):
            arr[k] = left_half[i]
```

```
            i += 1

            k += 1

        while j < len(right_half):

        arr[k] = right_half[j]

        j += 1

        k += 1

# Example usage

arr = [38, 27, 43, 3, 9, 82, 10]

merge_sort(arr)

print("Sorted array:", arr)
```

Explanation of Steps in Merge Sort:

- **Step 1**: The array is recursively divided into smaller subarrays until each subarray has one element.

- **Step 2**: The smaller subarrays are recursively sorted.

- **Step 3**: The sorted subarrays are merged to produce the final sorted array.

Efficiency of Algorithms: Time and Space Complexity

The efficiency of an algorithm's steps can be measured in terms of **time complexity** and **space complexity**. Time complexity refers to the amount of time an algorithm takes to complete based on the size of the input, while space complexity refers to the amount of memory required.

- **Time Complexity**: Describes how the running time of an algorithm increases with the input size. Common time complexities include $O(1)$ (constant time), $O(n)$ (linear time), O(n log n), and O(n²) (quadratic time) (Weiss, 2012).

- **Space Complexity**: Describes how much additional memory the algorithm needs as the input size increases.

In the case of Merge Sort, the time complexity is **O(n log n)**, and the space complexity is **O(n)** because additional memory is required for the merging process.

In summary, understanding the components of an algorithm - **input**, **output**, and **steps** - is crucial for analyzing how algorithms function and how they can be optimized. Input refers to the data or problem provided to the algorithm, output refers to the result produced, and the steps describe the computational process that transforms the input into the desired output. The efficiency of these steps, often evaluated through time and space complexity, is essential in determining the suitability of an algorithm for large-scale or real-time applications. By understanding these components, developers can select and design algorithms that solve problems efficiently and correctly.

Key Qualities of Algorithms

Algorithms are fundamental to the field of artificial intelligence (AI) and computer science. They are the logical foundation that enables machines to solve problems, make decisions, and process data. However, the effectiveness of an algorithm is not determined solely by its ability to solve a problem - algorithms must also possess certain qualities to be practical and scalable. The three key qualities of an algorithm are **Correctness**, **Efficiency**, and **Simplicity**. These attributes are essential for determining the viability of an algorithm in real-world applications (Cormen, Leiserson, Rivest, & Stein, 2009).

1. Correctness

The correctness of an algorithm refers to its ability to produce the correct output for all valid inputs. In other words, an algorithm is correct if it consistently solves the problem it was designed to address, regardless of variations in input (Weiss, 2012). Correctness is often proven mathematically by demonstrating that the algorithm meets the problem's specification and that it halts (i.e., does not run indefinitely).

Formal Definition: An algorithm is said to be correct if, for every input instance, it produces the expected output within a finite amount of time (Cormen et al., 2009). Proving correctness is particularly important in critical applications such as cryptography, medical diagnosis systems, and AI-driven autonomous vehicles, where incorrect results could lead to severe consequences.

- **Partial Correctness**: This condition is met when the algorithm produces the correct output, provided it halts.

- **Total Correctness**: The algorithm produces the correct output and halts on all valid inputs.

Example: Correctness of Binary Search Algorithm

Consider the **binary search** algorithm, which finds the position of a target value within a sorted array. It is correct because, given a sorted array, it always locates the target element (if present) or determines its absence in logarithmic time.

```
def binary_search(arr, target):
```

```python
    low, high = 0, len(arr) - 1

    while low <= high:

        mid = (low + high) // 2

        if arr[mid] == target:

            return mid

        elif arr[mid] < target:

            low = mid + 1

        else:

            high = mid - 1

    return -1

# Example usage

arr = [1, 3, 5, 7, 9, 11, 13]

target = 7

index = binary_search(arr, target)

print(f"Element found at index {index}" if index != -1 else
"Element not found")
```

This implementation is correct because it guarantees the right answer for any valid input array, either returning the index of the target or indicating that the target is not in the array.

2. Efficiency

Efficiency refers to how well an algorithm utilizes resources such as time (CPU cycles) and space (memory) while processing input. Efficient algorithms are essential for large-scale systems, where time and memory constraints are critical. Efficiency is commonly analyzed using **time complexity** and

space complexity, both of which are expressed in terms of **Big O notation** (Knuth, 1976).

- **Time Complexity**: Measures the number of operations an algorithm performs as a function of input size. The best, worst, and average-case time complexities are used to describe an algorithm's behavior under different conditions (Cormen et al., 2009).

- **Space Complexity**: Refers to the amount of memory required by an algorithm relative to the size of the input.

Efficient algorithms are those that minimize both time and space complexities while still producing the correct result. In AI, efficiency is critical due to the enormous data volumes often processed by machine learning algorithms or optimization models.

Example: Efficiency Comparison - Linear vs Binary Search

Let's compare the efficiency of **linear search** and **binary search** algorithms. Linear search has a time complexity of **O(n)**, while binary search has a time complexity of **O(log n)**, which makes binary search far more efficient for larger input sizes.

```
# Linear Search

def linear_search(arr, target):

    for i, val in enumerate(arr):

        if val == target:

            return i

    return -1
```

To illustrate the efficiency difference, consider the following graph:

Graphical Representation: Time Complexity of Linear vs. Binary Search

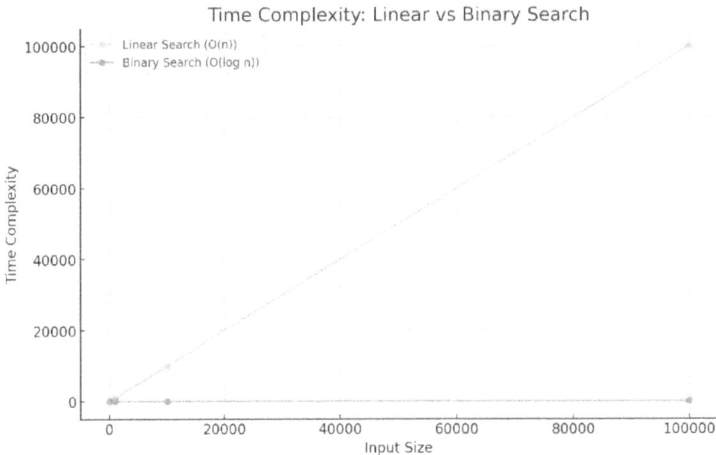

This graph shows how binary search scales more efficiently than linear search, especially as input size grows, making binary search an ideal choice for searching large datasets.

3. Simplicity

Simplicity refers to how easily an algorithm can be understood, implemented, and maintained. Simple algorithms are often more desirable because they reduce the likelihood of errors, make debugging easier, and can be more readily optimized or adapted to new problems. In many cases, a simple algorithm is preferred even if it is less efficient, as long as it meets the performance criteria for a given problem.

Characteristics of Simple Algorithms:

- **Ease of Understanding**: Algorithms that are easy to explain and follow are considered simple. Simplicity allows for faster development and maintenance, especially in collaborative environments.

- **Shorter Code**: Simpler algorithms often lead to more concise code, which is easier to debug and test.

- **Lower Cognitive Load**: Developers and researchers working with simple algorithms can spend less time learning the intricacies of the algorithm and focus more on optimizing it or solving related problems.

Example: Simplicity of Bubble Sort

While **Bubble Sort** is not an efficient sorting algorithm (with a time complexity of $O(n^2)$), it is simple and easy to understand. It repeatedly compares adjacent elements in the list and swaps them if they are in the wrong order.

```python
def bubble_sort(arr):

    n = len(arr)

    for i in range(n):

        for j in range(0, n-i-1):

            if arr[j] > arr[j+1]:

                arr[j], arr[j+1] = arr[j+1], arr[j]

    return arr

# Example usage

arr = [38, 27, 43, 3, 9, 82, 10]

sorted_arr = bubble_sort(arr)

print("Sorted array:", sorted_arr)
```

The **Bubble Sort** algorithm is a classic example of simplicity. Although it is not the most efficient sorting algorithm, its straightforward logic and ease of implementation make it a useful teaching tool and a suitable choice for small datasets or situations where efficiency is not the top priority.

Foundations of AI and Algorithms: Introduction to Algorithms

Key Qualities of Algorithms: Correctness, Efficiency, and Simplicity

Algorithms are fundamental to the field of artificial intelligence (AI) and computer science. They are the logical foundation that enables machines to solve problems, make decisions, and process data. However, the effectiveness of an algorithm is not determined solely by its ability to solve a problem—algorithms must also possess certain qualities to be practical and scalable. The three key qualities of an algorithm are **Correctness**, **Efficiency**, and **Simplicity**. These attributes are essential for determining the viability of an algorithm in real-world applications (Cormen, Leiserson, Rivest, & Stein, 2009).

1. Correctness

The correctness of an algorithm refers to its ability to produce the correct output for all valid inputs. In other words, an algorithm is correct if it consistently solves the problem it was designed to address, regardless of variations in input (Weiss, 2012). Correctness is often proven mathematically by demonstrating that the algorithm meets the problem's specification and that it halts (i.e., does not run indefinitely).

Formal Definition: An algorithm is said to be correct if, for every input instance, it produces the expected output within a finite amount of time (Cormen et al., 2009). Proving correctness is particularly important in critical applications such as cryptography, medical diagnosis systems, and AI-driven autonomous vehicles, where incorrect results could lead to severe consequences.

- **Partial Correctness**: This condition is met when the algorithm produces the correct output, provided it halts.

- **Total Correctness**: The algorithm produces the correct output and halts on all valid inputs.

Example: Correctness of Binary Search Algorithm

Consider the **binary search** algorithm, which finds the position of a target value within a sorted array. It is correct because, given a sorted array, it always locates the target element (if present) or determines its absence in logarithmic time.

```python
def binary_search(arr, target):
    low, high = 0, len(arr) - 1
        while low <= high:
        mid = (low + high) // 2
        if arr[mid] == target:
            return mid
        elif arr[mid] < target:
            low = mid + 1
        else:
            high = mid - 1
    return -1
```

Example usage

arr = [1, 3, 5, 7, 9, 11, 13]

target = 7

index = binary_search(arr, target)

print(f"Element found at index {index}" if index != -1 else "Element not found")

This implementation is correct because it guarantees the right answer for any valid input array, either returning the index of the target or indicating that the target is not in the array.

2. Efficiency

Efficiency refers to how well an algorithm utilizes resources such as time (CPU cycles) and space (memory) while processing input. Efficient algorithms are essential for large-scale systems, where time and memory constraints are critical. Efficiency is commonly analyzed using **time complexity** and **space complexity**, both of which are expressed in terms of **Big O notation** (Knuth, 1976).

- **Time Complexity**: Measures the number of operations an algorithm performs as a function of input size. The best, worst, and average-case time complexities are used to describe an algorithm's behavior under different conditions (Cormen et al., 2009).

- **Space Complexity**: Refers to the amount of memory required by an algorithm relative to the size of the input.

Efficient algorithms are those that minimize both time and space complexities while still producing the correct result. In AI, efficiency is critical due to the enormous data volumes often processed by machine learning algorithms or optimization models.

Example: Efficiency Comparison - Linear vs Binary Search

Let's compare the efficiency of **linear search** and **binary search** algorithms. Linear search has a time complexity of **O(n)**, while binary search has a time complexity of **O(log n)**, which makes binary search far more efficient for larger input sizes.

```python
# Linear Search

def linear_search(arr, target):

    for i, val in enumerate(arr):

        if val == target:

            return i

    return -1
```

To illustrate the efficiency difference, consider the following graph:

Graphical Representation: Time Complexity of Linear vs. Binary Search

```python
import numpy as np

import matplotlib.pyplot as plt

# Sample input sizes

input_sizes = [10, 100, 1000, 10000, 100000]

linear_search_times = [n for n in input_sizes]  # O(n)

binary_search_times = [np.log2(n) for n in input_sizes]  # O(log n)

# Plotting the time complexity comparison
```

```
plt.plot(input_sizes, linear_search_times, label="Linear
Search (O(n))", marker='o')

plt.plot(input_sizes, binary_search_times, label="Binary
Search (O(log n))", marker='o')

plt.xlabel('Input Size')

plt.ylabel('Time Complexity')

plt.title('Time Complexity: Linear vs Binary Search')

plt.legend()

plt.grid(True)

plt.show()
```

This graph shows how binary search scales more efficiently than linear search, especially as input size grows, making binary search an ideal choice for searching large datasets.

3. Simplicity

Simplicity refers to how easily an algorithm can be understood, implemented, and maintained. Simple algorithms are often more desirable because they reduce the likelihood of errors, make debugging easier, and can be more readily optimized or adapted to new problems. In many cases, a simple algorithm is preferred even if it is less efficient, as long as it meets the performance criteria for a given problem.

Characteristics of Simple Algorithms:

- **Ease of Understanding**: Algorithms that are easy to explain and follow are considered simple. Simplicity allows for faster development and maintenance, especially in collaborative environments.

- **Shorter Code**: Simpler algorithms often lead to more concise code, which is easier to debug and test.

- **Lower Cognitive Load**: Developers and researchers working with simple algorithms can spend less time learning the intricacies of the algorithm and focus more on optimizing it or solving related problems.

Example: Simplicity of Bubble Sort

While **Bubble Sort** is not an efficient sorting algorithm (with a time complexity of $O(n^2)$), it is simple and easy to understand. It repeatedly compares adjacent elements in the list and swaps them if they are in the wrong order.

```python
def bubble_sort(arr):

    n = len(arr)

    for i in range(n):

        for j in range(0, n-i-1):

            if arr[j] > arr[j+1]:

                arr[j], arr[j+1] = arr[j+1], arr[j]

    return arr

# Example usage

arr = [38, 27, 43, 3, 9, 82, 10]

sorted_arr = bubble_sort(arr)

print("Sorted array:", sorted_arr)
```

The **Bubble Sort** algorithm is a classic example of simplicity. Although it is not the most efficient sorting algorithm, its straightforward logic and ease of implementation make it a useful teaching tool and a suitable choice for small datasets or situations where efficiency is not the top priority.

Balancing Correctness, Efficiency, and Simplicity

In many cases, achieving a balance between correctness, efficiency, and simplicity is necessary, as optimizing one quality may affect the others. For instance:

- A more efficient algorithm may be less simple, requiring complex logic or additional memory.

- A simple algorithm, while easy to implement, may not be the most efficient for large datasets.

- Ensuring correctness may introduce complexity in the form of error handling and edge case management.

Example: Merge Sort vs Bubble Sort

- **Merge Sort** is more complex than **Bubble Sort**, but it is much more efficient ($O(n \log n)$ vs $O(n^2)$).

- **Bubble Sort** is simpler, but it is less efficient for large inputs.

For large-scale AI systems, efficiency often takes precedence because AI models and algorithms need to process vast amounts of data. However, simplicity and correctness are equally important for maintainability and reliability.

In conclusion, the key qualities of an algorithm—**correctness, efficiency**, and **simplicity**—determine its suitability for solving real-world problems. Correctness ensures that the algorithm consistently produces the desired output, efficiency guarantees that the algorithm makes optimal use of time and resources, and simplicity ensures ease of understanding, implementation, and maintenance. These qualities are often in tension, and achieving the right balance between them is a fundamental challenge in algorithm design and AI development. Understanding these qualities allows practitioners to choose and optimize algorithms that best meet the needs of their specific applications.

Chapter 3: Programming Basics for AI (Python)

<u>Python Overview and Setup</u>

Python has emerged as one of the most popular programming languages for artificial intelligence (AI) development due to its simplicity, versatility, and extensive support for AI and machine learning libraries (Van Rossum & Drake, 2009). It is known for its clear syntax, ease of learning, and large community support, which makes it an ideal language for both beginners and experts in AI. Python's extensive ecosystem of libraries, such as TensorFlow, PyTorch, scikit-learn, and NumPy, makes it a go-to language for AI tasks ranging from data manipulation and preprocessing to deep learning and reinforcement learning.

In this section, we will provide an overview of Python and explain how to set up the environment for AI development. We will also discuss why Python is preferred for AI applications and introduce the fundamental programming concepts that form the foundation for building AI models.

1. Why Python for AI?

Python is the language of choice for AI for several reasons, including:

- **Ease of Use and Readability**: Python's simple and intuitive syntax allows developers to focus on solving AI problems rather than the intricacies of the language itself. The clean syntax makes code easier to write, read, and debug, which is particularly important in collaborative AI projects (Lutz, 2013).

- **Extensive AI Libraries**: Python boasts a wide array of libraries specifically designed for AI and machine learning, such as **TensorFlow, Keras, PyTorch, scikit-learn, pandas, NumPy**, and **Matplotlib**. These libraries provide pre-built modules for neural networks, data processing, and scientific computing, significantly reducing development time (Oliphant, 2007).

- **Cross-Platform Compatibility**: Python is cross-platform, meaning it can run on Windows, macOS, Linux, and other operating systems. This flexibility makes it ideal for developing AI solutions that can be deployed across various platforms.

- **Community Support**: Python has a large, active community of developers and researchers who continuously contribute to its libraries and frameworks. This ensures that Python remains at the forefront of AI and machine learning research and development.

2. Setting Up Python for AI Development

Before diving into AI programming, it's essential to set up the Python environment for AI development. The following steps will guide you through the process of installing Python, setting up a virtual environment, and installing necessary libraries.

Step 1: Installing Python

To start working with Python, you first need to install it on your machine. Python is available for free on the official Python website (https://www.python.org/).

- **Windows**: Download the latest version of Python from the official website and follow the installer's instructions.

Make sure to check the box that says **Add Python to PATH** during installation.

- **macOS**: Python is pre-installed on macOS, but it's recommended to install the latest version using **Homebrew**. Open the terminal and run the following command:

brew install python

- **Linux**: Most Linux distributions come with Python pre-installed. To ensure you have the latest version, you can update Python using your package manager. For example, on Ubuntu, run:

sudo apt update

sudo apt install python3

Step 2: Installing a Code Editor

To write and run Python code efficiently, you'll need a code editor or integrated development environment (IDE). Some popular choices for AI development include:

- **VS Code**: A lightweight, powerful editor with Python support through extensions.

- **PyCharm**: An IDE specifically built for Python with extensive features for AI development.

- **Jupyter Notebook**: A web-based interactive computing environment commonly used for data analysis, scientific research, and AI.

For AI and machine learning projects, **Jupyter Notebook** is highly recommended, as it allows you to write code, visualize data, and document your workflow in the same environment.

Step 3: Setting Up a Virtual Environment

Virtual environments are essential for managing project-specific dependencies and avoiding conflicts between different projects. They allow you to install Python libraries specific to a project without affecting other projects.

To create a virtual environment:

1. Install **virtualenv** by running the following command:

    pip install virtualenv

2. Create a virtual environment for your project:
    virtualenv ai_project_env

3. Activate the virtual environment:
- On Windows
    ai_project_env\Scripts\activate

- On macOS/Linux:
    source ai_project_env/bin/activate

4. Once the virtual environment is activated, you can install libraries specific to your AI project without interfering with global Python installations.

Step 4: Installing Essential AI Libraries

Once the virtual environment is set up, you can install the required AI libraries. Some of the most common libraries for AI and machine learning include:

- **NumPy**: A library for numerical computing and handling multidimensional arrays.

    pip install numpy

pandas: A data manipulation and analysis library.

pip install pandas

Matplotlib: A plotting library for data visualization.

pip install matplotlib

scikit-learn: A library for classical machine learning algorithms such as decision trees, support vector machines, and clustering algorithms.

pip install scikit-learn

TensorFlow: A deep learning library developed by Google, widely used for building neural networks.

pip install tensorflow

Keras: A high-level neural network API that runs on top of TensorFlow.

pip install keras

After installing these libraries, your Python environment is ready for AI development.

3. Python Fundamentals for AI

Before diving into AI programming, it's essential to understand Python's fundamental programming concepts. These concepts form the foundation upon which AI algorithms are built.

Variables and Data Types

In Python, variables are used to store data. Python supports several data types, including integers, floating-point numbers, strings, and booleans.

Example:

```python
# Declaring variables
age = 25          # Integer
height = 5.9      # Float
name = "Alice"    # String
is_student = True # Boolean
```

Control Flow: Conditional Statements and Loops

Control flow allows you to control the execution of code based on certain conditions. Python uses if, elif, and else statements for conditional execution, and for and while loops for iteration.

Example:

```python
# If-else conditional statement
age = 18
if age >= 18:
    print("You are an adult.")
else:
    print("You are a minor.")

# For loop
for i in range(5):
    print(i)
```

```python
# While loop
count = 0
while count < 5:
    print(count)
count += 1
```

Functions

Functions are reusable blocks of code that perform a specific task. They help to organize code and make it modular.

Example:

```python
# Defining a function
def greet(name):
    return f"Hello, {name}!"


# Calling the function
print(greet("Alice"))
```

Data Structures: Lists, Tuples, Dictionaries

Python provides built-in data structures that are commonly used in AI algorithms for storing and manipulating data.

Example:

```python
# Lists (mutable)
numbers = [1, 2, 3, 4, 5]

# Tuples (immutable)
coordinates = (10.5, 20.5)

# Dictionaries (key-value pairs)
student = {"name": "Alice", "age": 25, "grade": "A"}
```

Numpy for Numerical Computing

For AI, efficient numerical computations are critical. **NumPy** is the foundation for numerical computing in Python and provides support for handling large multi-dimensional arrays and matrices.

Example: Basic NumPy Operations

```python
import numpy as np

# Creating a NumPy array
arr = np.array([1, 2, 3, 4, 5])

# Performing mathematical operations
arr_squared = np.square(arr)
print("Squared Array:", arr_squared)
```

4. Data Visualization with Matplotlib

Data visualization is an important aspect of AI, especially when analyzing datasets or visualizing model performance. **Matplotlib** is the most commonly used library for creating static, interactive, and animated plots in Python.

```python
import matplotlib.pyplot as plt

# Sample data
x = np.linspace(0, 10, 100)
y = np.sin(x)

# Plotting the data
plt.plot(x, y, label="Sine Wave")
plt.title("Sine Function")
plt.xlabel("X-axis")
plt.ylabel("Y-axis")
```

```
        plt.legend()
        plt.grid(True)
plt.show()
```

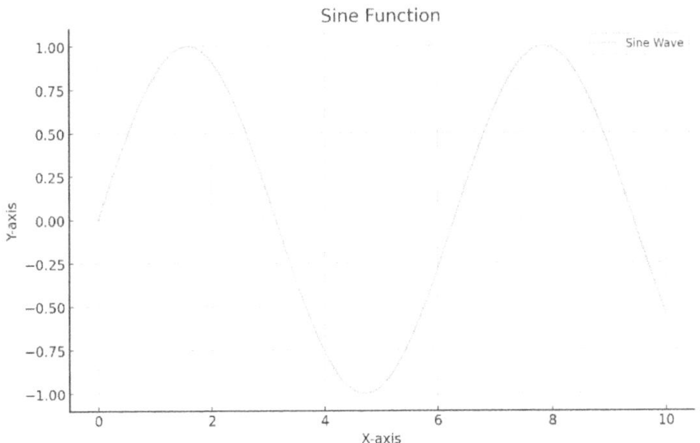

This graph shows the sine function, which is plotted using Matplotlib. Data visualization like this is crucial for understanding AI models' behavior and performance during training and evaluation.

In summary, Python has become the language of choice for AI development due to its simplicity, flexibility, and comprehensive library support. Its ease of use, coupled with powerful libraries like NumPy, TensorFlow, and scikit-learn, makes Python an indispensable tool for building AI models. By setting up the Python environment and mastering the foundational.

Control Flow, Data Types, and Functions for AI

Artificial intelligence (AI) has gained substantial attention due to its transformative impact on industries, research, and technological advancements. One of the primary foundations of AI is the algorithmic approach to solving problems, typically implemented using programming languages such as Python. Python has emerged as the de facto language for AI due to its simplicity, versatility, and comprehensive library ecosystem, which supports machine learning, data processing, and deep learning. The foundational components of AI programming—control flow, data types, functions, and libraries—serve as the core principles that facilitate the development of efficient AI algorithms.

Control Flow

Control flow refers to the order in which individual instructions, statements, or function calls are executed within a program. In AI algorithms, control flow structures allow the program to make decisions, iterate over data, and manage complex workflows. Python provides various control flow constructs, such as if, elif, else statements, for loops, and while loops, which are integral in implementing AI algorithms like decision trees, neural network training loops, and optimization techniques.

For instance, an if statement in Python can determine the path of an AI algorithm based on certain conditions, such as whether a model's accuracy meets a predefined threshold.

```
accuracy = 0.85

if accuracy > 0.80:

    print("Model performance is acceptable.")

else:

    print("Further tuning is required.")
```

In complex AI models, control flow can be used to manage hyperparameter tuning, stopping criteria for iterative algorithms, and the branching logic for different model architectures (Goodfellow et al., 2016). By effectively utilizing control flow structures, AI algorithms can achieve flexibility and scalability in learning and decision-making processes.

Data Types

Data types are a crucial aspect of programming, especially in AI, where the representation and manipulation of data are pivotal. Python offers various built-in data types, such as integers, floating-point numbers, strings, lists, tuples, sets, and dictionaries. Each of these data types plays a significant role in AI programming.

- **Integers** and **floats** are typically used to represent numerical values, such as weights in neural networks or data points in a dataset.

- **Strings** are employed in AI for text processing, which is essential in natural language processing (NLP).

- **Lists** and **dictionaries** provide ways to store and manipulate collections of data, which is crucial for managing datasets, model parameters, and results from multiple experiments.

In AI, particularly in machine learning, arrays of data are often handled using libraries such as NumPy, where arrays (multi-dimensional lists) are used to store data matrices and vectors.

```python
import numpy as np

# Create a numpy array

data = np.array([[1.5, 2.3, 3.9], [4.5, 6.1, 7.8]])

print(data)
```

Data types and their manipulation are vital in AI tasks like feature selection, data normalization, and model evaluation, where incorrect data type usage can lead to significant errors in computation and logic flow (Russell & Norvig, 2020).

Functions

Functions are reusable blocks of code designed to perform a specific task. In AI, functions enable modularity, allowing programmers to break down complex AI algorithms into manageable, reusable components. Functions enhance code readability, simplify debugging, and promote the reuse of code across different algorithms or models.

Python functions are defined using the def keyword and can accept inputs, return outputs, or perform side effects like printing information or modifying global variables. A typical example of a function in AI might be a utility for calculating the loss function of a neural network or normalizing data before feeding it into a model.

```
def sigmoid(x):

    return 1 / (1 + np.exp(-x))

# Use the sigmoid function in AI model

output = sigmoid(np.array([1.5, -2.3, 0.7]))

print(output)
```

In AI systems, functions are used extensively for building models, preprocessing data, and implementing training loops. For instance, functions are core to backpropagation in neural networks, where they calculate gradients and update weights during each iteration (LeCun et al., 2015). Defining functions for these tasks allows AI developers to modularize the process and handle more complex models.

Libraries for AI

One of the major strengths of Python in AI is its vast ecosystem of libraries, which provide high-level abstractions and tools for building, training, and evaluating AI models. Some of the most commonly used libraries include:

- **NumPy**: Provides support for large, multi-dimensional arrays and matrices, along with a collection of mathematical functions to operate on these arrays (Oliphant, 2006).

- **Pandas**: Essential for data manipulation and analysis, Pandas allows handling of datasets in a flexible, easy-to-use data frame structure (McKinney, 2010).

- **Matplotlib**: A plotting library that allows the creation of static, interactive, and animated visualizations in Python, crucial for analyzing trends and visualizing AI model performance (Hunter, 2007).

- **Scikit-learn**: Offers simple and efficient tools for data mining, machine learning, and analysis. It provides a wide range of algorithms, from regression to clustering, as well as tools for model evaluation (Pedregosa et al., 2011).

- **TensorFlow** and **PyTorch**: These are deep learning libraries that support automatic differentiation, neural network construction, and large-scale computation on GPUs (Abadi et al., 2016; Paszke et al., 2019). These libraries allow researchers and developers to design and train deep learning models with ease.

```python
import tensorflow as tf

from tensorflow.keras.models import Sequential

from tensorflow.keras.layers import Dense
```

```
# Create a simple neural network model using TensorFlow

model = Sequential()

model.add(Dense(128, activation='relu', input_shape=(784,)))

model.add(Dense(10, activation='softmax'))

model.compile(optimizer='adam',
loss='categorical_crossentropy', metrics=['accuracy'])
```

These libraries abstract much of the low-level computational complexity, allowing researchers and developers to focus on high-level algorithm design and model experimentation (Russell & Norvig, 2020).

In summary, the foundations of AI programming in Python revolve around key concepts such as control flow, data types, functions, and the use of AI-specific libraries. Control flow structures manage the algorithmic logic, while data types define the representation of information, and functions provide modularity in code. Libraries like NumPy, TensorFlow, and Scikit-learn further extend Python's capabilities, enabling efficient AI algorithm development and deployment. These elements together lay the groundwork for both beginner and advanced AI practitioners to build, train, and optimize AI models. Python's versatility and simplicity, along with its rich ecosystem of AI libraries, make it an indispensable tool for AI programming and algorithm development.

Introduction to AI-Specific Libraries

In the field of artificial intelligence (AI), programming languages like Python have become essential due to their ease of use, flexibility, and powerful ecosystem of libraries designed to facilitate AI and machine learning tasks. Python's extensive suite of libraries offers specialized tools for handling large-scale data manipulation, machine learning model implementation, and statistical analysis, all of which are integral to developing AI applications. Among these libraries, **NumPy**, **Pandas**, and **Scikit-learn** stand out as essential components of the AI programmer's toolkit. These libraries not only simplify the development of AI models but also provide optimized functions for handling complex data structures, enabling faster and more efficient computation.

NumPy

NumPy (Numerical Python) is the foundational library for numerical computing in Python, and it forms the backbone of many other AI-specific libraries, such as TensorFlow and Scikit-learn (Oliphant, 2006). NumPy provides support for multi-dimensional arrays and matrices, along with a wide range of mathematical operations that are optimized for performance. In AI and machine learning, NumPy is used to handle large datasets efficiently, perform vectorized operations, and support matrix manipulations, all of which are critical when working with neural networks, linear algebra, and statistical computations.

Key Features of NumPy:

- **Multi-dimensional arrays (ndarrays)**: NumPy's primary object is the ndarray, which is more efficient and compact than Python's built-in lists. It allows for the storage of large datasets and supports element-wise operations on entire arrays, facilitating rapid computations.

- **Broadcasting**: NumPy's broadcasting mechanism allows functions to apply operations on arrays of different shapes without requiring explicit reshaping.

- **Linear Algebra Functions**: AI algorithms, especially deep learning, rely heavily on linear algebra operations such as matrix multiplication, dot products, and eigenvalue computations, all of which are efficiently handled by NumPy.

Example:

The following code demonstrates basic NumPy operations, such as matrix creation and matrix multiplication, which are common tasks in AI when dealing with datasets or model parameters.

```python
import numpy as np

# Create two matrices

matrix_a = np.array([[1, 2], [3, 4]])

matrix_b = np.array([[5, 6], [7, 8]])

# Perform matrix multiplication

matrix_product = np.dot(matrix_a, matrix_b)

print(matrix_product)
```

This simple matrix multiplication operation can be scaled to handle high-dimensional matrices, which are often encountered in neural networks, image recognition models, and other AI tasks (Goodfellow et al., 2016).

Pandas

Pandas is a data manipulation and analysis library built on top of NumPy, designed to make data analysis in Python both easier and more powerful (McKinney, 2010). The library introduces two primary data structures: **Series** and **DataFrames**, which are designed to handle labeled data. Pandas is particularly useful for managing datasets, preprocessing data for machine learning, and performing exploratory data analysis (EDA).

Key Features of Pandas:

- **DataFrames**: The primary data structure in Pandas, DataFrames, represent two-dimensional, tabular data (like SQL tables or Excel sheets), allowing users to access, filter, and manipulate data by rows and columns.

- **Handling Missing Data**: Pandas offers sophisticated tools to detect, remove, and fill missing values within datasets, which is crucial for cleaning real-world data.

- **Data Aggregation and Grouping**: AI often involves grouping and aggregating data based on certain features to perform statistics or generate insights, which Pandas facilitates with its groupby functionality.

Example:

The following code illustrates how Pandas can be used to load and manipulate a dataset, which is a common preliminary step before feeding the data into an AI model.

```python
import pandas as pd

# Load a CSV dataset

data = pd.read_csv('sample_data.csv')

# Display the first five rows

print(data.head())

# Handling missing data by filling with the mean value

data.fillna(data.mean(), inplace=True)

# Group by a feature and compute the mean
```

```
grouped_data = data.groupby('Category').mean()
```

```
print(grouped_data)
```

Pandas is widely used in AI for cleaning and organizing data before it is fed into machine learning models. Tasks such as feature extraction, data transformation, and preparing datasets for time-series analysis are easily managed using Pandas (McKinney, 2010).

Scikit-learn

Scikit-learn is a powerful machine learning library in Python, built on top of NumPy and Pandas, that provides a wide range of tools for data mining, data analysis, and machine learning (Pedregosa et al., 2011). It is designed to interoperate with other libraries in the Python ecosystem, such as NumPy and Pandas, enabling seamless integration of machine learning algorithms into AI projects. Scikit-learn supports supervised and unsupervised learning, cross-validation, and various preprocessing techniques, making it one of the most versatile tools for building AI models.

Key Features of Scikit-learn:

- **Supervised Learning**: Scikit-learn supports algorithms such as linear regression, decision trees, support vector machines (SVM), and k-nearest neighbors (KNN) for tasks like classification and regression.

- **Unsupervised Learning**: It also includes clustering techniques such as k-means and dimensionality reduction algorithms like principal component analysis (PCA).

- **Model Selection and Evaluation**: Scikit-learn offers tools for model validation, such as cross-validation, grid search, and metrics to evaluate model performance.

Example:

The following example demonstrates the process of building a simple machine learning model using Scikit-learn, including training, testing, and evaluating its performance.

```python
from sklearn.model_selection import train_test_split

from sklearn.linear_model import LogisticRegression

from sklearn.metrics import accuracy_score

# Assume 'data' is a Pandas DataFrame and 'target' is the label column

X = data.drop(columns='target')

y = data['target']

# Split data into training and testing sets

X_train, X_test, y_train, y_test = train_test_split(X, y, test_size=0.2, random_state=42)

# Create a logistic regression model

model = LogisticRegression()

# Train the model

model.fit(X_train, y_train)


# Make predictions

predictions = model.predict(X_test)

# Evaluate the model

accuracy = accuracy_score(y_test, predictions)

print(f"Model Accuracy: {accuracy:.2f}")
```

In this example, Scikit-learn simplifies the process of training and evaluating a machine learning model. The library abstracts many of the complexities of implementing machine learning algorithms, allowing developers to focus on fine-tuning models and interpreting results (Pedregosa et al., 2011).

In conclusion, NumPy, Pandas, and Scikit-learn are essential libraries that provide a robust foundation for building and deploying AI algorithms in Python. NumPy offers efficient numerical computation, Pandas enables comprehensive data manipulation and analysis, and Scikit-learn provides a full suite of machine learning algorithms and tools. Together, these libraries allow AI practitioners to manage large datasets, perform complex numerical computations, and develop machine learning models with relative ease. By leveraging the capabilities of these libraries, AI developers can focus on improving model accuracy, handling data efficiently, and ultimately developing more powerful AI applications.

Chapter 4: Data Structures for AI

<u>Arrays, Lists, and Dictionaries</u>

In artificial intelligence (AI) and algorithmic development, efficient data storage and manipulation are crucial for the performance of models and the ease of implementation. Programming languages such as Python offer several fundamental data structures, including **arrays**, **lists**, and **dictionaries**, which serve as the backbone for handling large datasets, training models, and optimizing AI algorithms. These data structures provide the flexibility to store, access, and manipulate data efficiently, enabling the execution of sophisticated machine learning and AI algorithms. The following explores these data structures, their significance in AI, and their practical implementation using Python.

Arrays

Arrays are one of the most fundamental data structures in AI, used to store homogeneous data types. Arrays are essential in numerical computing and are optimized for handling large datasets due to their fixed size and ability to store data in contiguous memory locations. In Python, the NumPy library provides a robust implementation of multi-dimensional arrays (referred to as ndarrays), which are optimized for numerical operations.

Key Characteristics of Arrays:

- **Homogeneous Data**: Arrays store elements of the same type, making them ideal for numerical operations such as matrix multiplication and vector transformations.

- **Efficient Memory Usage**: Arrays utilize contiguous memory allocation, making operations such as slicing and element-wise arithmetic operations highly efficient.

- **Multi-dimensional**: Arrays can handle complex, multi-dimensional data such as tensors used in deep learning models, where dimensions can represent different attributes such as image channels or time steps in sequence data.

Example:

import numpy as np

Create a 2x2 array (matrix)

array = np.array([[1, 2], [3, 4]])

Perform element-wise operations

array_sum = array + 5

print(array_sum)

Perform matrix multiplication

matrix_product = np.dot(array, array_sum)

print(matrix_product)

In AI, arrays are widely used to represent input data, weights in neural networks, and to compute activations and gradients in models. For example, deep learning architectures like convolutional neural networks (CNNs) utilize multi-dimensional arrays (or tensors) to represent image data, where each dimension captures different aspects such as pixel intensities and color channels (LeCun et al., 2015).

Lists

Lists are versatile data structures in Python that allow the storage of heterogeneous data types. Unlike arrays, lists are dynamic and can store elements of varying types, which makes them useful for handling diverse data in AI, such as text, numbers, and objects. Lists are flexible and offer a broad range of functionalities for appending, slicing, and iterating over elements, making them highly useful in exploratory data analysis and preprocessing.

Key Characteristics of Lists:

- **Heterogeneous Data**: Lists can store elements of different data types, making them suitable for mixed datasets that contain numerical, categorical, and textual data.

- **Dynamic Size**: Unlike arrays, lists do not require a fixed size and can grow dynamically, which allows for the storage of varying amounts of data during runtime.

- **Ease of Manipulation**: Python lists provide several built-in methods for appending, extending, and removing elements, making them highly flexible for AI data handling tasks.

Example:

```python
# Create a list with mixed data types
data_list = [1, 'AI', 3.14, [2, 4, 6]]

# Append an element to the list
data_list.append('Machine Learning')

# Access an element
print(data_list[1])  # Output: 'AI'
```

Iterate through the list

for item in data_list:

    print(item)

Lists are commonly used in AI during the preprocessing stage, where datasets may require transformation from one format to another. They are also used to store outputs of models during training, such as the loss values at each epoch in deep learning (Russell & Norvig, 2020).

Dictionaries

Dictionaries, also known as hash maps or associative arrays in other programming languages, are an essential data structure in AI for mapping key-value pairs. In Python, dictionaries allow for fast lookup and retrieval of data by using keys, making them suitable for storing feature-label mappings, hyperparameter settings, and results from experiments.

Key Characteristics of Dictionaries:

- **Key-Value Pairs**: Dictionaries store data as pairs, where each key is unique, and it is associated with a value. This structure is particularly useful in AI for tasks such as mapping feature names to their respective values.

- **Unordered Collection**: Unlike lists, dictionaries do not maintain order. However, Python's dictionaries maintain insertion order as of Python 3.7.

- **Fast Lookup**: Dictionaries allow for fast access to values based on their keys, making them highly efficient for tasks like indexing data and storing model metadata.

Example:

Create a dictionary mapping AI models to their accuracy scores

model_accuracy = {'Logistic Regression': 0.85, 'Decision Tree': 0.78, 'SVM': 0.89}

Access the accuracy of a specific model

print(model_accuracy['SVM'])

Add a new model to the dictionary

model_accuracy['Neural Network'] = 0.92

Iterate through the dictionary

for model, accuracy in model_accuracy.items():

   print(f"{model}: {accuracy}")

In AI, dictionaries are frequently used to store configuration settings for models, such as hyperparameters, and to map features to their corresponding values. For instance, in natural language processing (NLP), dictionaries are used to store the frequency or one-hot encoding of words in a corpus (Jurafsky & Martin, 2021). They also play a critical role in the implementation of decision trees, where each node can be represented as a dictionary containing the splitting feature, threshold, and child nodes.

Applications of Data Structures in AI

1. **Arrays in AI**: Arrays are indispensable in numerical computations and matrix operations. In machine learning, arrays are often used to store large datasets and perform vectorized operations, enabling efficient computation of model parameters during training. For example, in gradient descent, arrays can represent the weights and

biases of a model, and element-wise operations can update these parameters.

A graphical illustration of arrays used in a deep learning model is presented below, showing how multi-dimensional arrays (tensors) store image data:

Input Image (3D Array) → Convolution (Matrix Operation) → Output Feature Map (3D Array)

2. **Lists in AI**: Lists are frequently used during the preprocessing and exploratory phases of AI workflows. They can store datasets before conversion to NumPy arrays or DataFrames for model training. Additionally, lists are useful for keeping track of intermediate results, such as the progression of model accuracy across epochs in training neural networks.

3. **Dictionaries in AI**: Dictionaries provide an efficient means of organizing and accessing structured data. For instance, in machine learning models, dictionaries are used to store hyperparameters and their respective values. The key-value structure also simplifies tasks like storing predictions for each class in classification tasks.

In summary, arrays, lists, and dictionaries are fundamental data structures in AI, each with specific advantages that make them suitable for different tasks. Arrays, with their efficient memory usage and fast numerical computations, form the backbone of numerical operations in AI models, particularly in deep learning and machine learning tasks. Lists provide flexibility in handling heterogeneous data types and dynamic datasets, making them essential during the data preprocessing stages. Lastly, dictionaries enable fast lookups and organized storage of key-value pairs, which is particularly useful for managing model parameters, feature mappings, and experiment results. Together, these data structures offer the foundation for developing efficient and scalable AI algorithms.

<u>Trees, Graphs, and Queues</u>

Data structures such as trees, graphs, and queues play a fundamental role in artificial intelligence (AI) by providing efficient ways to store, process, and traverse data. These structures are particularly suited for tasks involving hierarchical relationships, networked systems, and optimal decision-making. In AI, the use of trees is prevalent in decision-making algorithms like decision trees and search algorithms, while graphs are essential in representing interconnected data, such as social networks, roadmaps, and dependency relationships in machine learning models. Queues, on the other hand, support a variety of algorithms, including breadth-first search (BFS) and are essential for managing tasks in reinforcement learning and parallel processing. This section provides a comprehensive examination of trees, graphs, and queues and their significance in AI, supported by code examples and visualizations.

Trees

A **tree** is a hierarchical data structure consisting of nodes connected by edges, where each node contains a value and may point to other nodes (children). Trees are widely used in AI for organizing data hierarchically, as seen in decision trees, search trees, and hierarchical clustering algorithms. In machine learning, decision trees are commonly used for classification and regression tasks, where they model decisions based on feature splits. Moreover, search algorithms like A* and minimax algorithms for game playing heavily rely on tree structures.

Key Characteristics of Trees:

- **Rooted Structure**: A tree starts with a root node, from which all other nodes (children) branch out.

- **Recursive Definition**: Each child of a node can be considered a subtree, which enables recursive traversal methods such as depth-first search (DFS).

- **No Cycles**: Trees do not contain cycles, ensuring that there is only one path between any two nodes.

Example: Decision Tree in Python using Scikit-learn

```python
from sklearn.tree import DecisionTreeClassifier

from sklearn.datasets import load_iris

from sklearn.model_selection import train_test_split

from sklearn import tree

# Load the iris dataset

iris = load_iris()

X, y = iris.data, iris.target

# Split data into training and testing sets

X_train, X_test, y_train, y_test = train_test_split(X, y, test_size=0.2, random_state=42)

# Create and train a decision tree classifier

clf = DecisionTreeClassifier()

clf.fit(X_train, y_train)
```

\# Visualize the decision tree

tree.plot_tree(clf)

Application in AI:

Decision trees are one of the simplest yet powerful models for classification and regression tasks. They work by recursively splitting the dataset based on feature values, which results in a tree structure where leaf nodes represent class labels (for classification tasks). Decision trees are interpretable and can model non-linear relationships, making them suitable for various AI applications, such as credit scoring and medical diagnosis (Russell & Norvig, 2020).

Graphical Representation of a Decision Tree:

In a decision tree, nodes represent feature splits, while the edges represent decisions based on those features. A sample graphical representation of a decision tree is shown below:

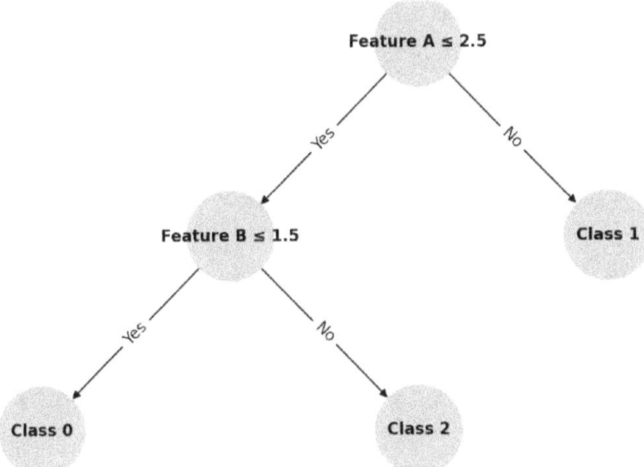

Graphs

A **graph** is a data structure consisting of vertices (or nodes) and edges, which represent relationships between vertices. Graphs can be directed or undirected, weighted or unweighted, and are widely used in AI to model interconnected systems. Applications of graphs in AI range from representing social networks and knowledge graphs to implementing algorithms such as shortest-path searches and Markov decision processes in reinforcement learning.

Key Characteristics of Graphs:

- **Vertices and Edges**: A graph consists of nodes (vertices) connected by edges. The edges can be directed, indicating a one-way relationship, or undirected, indicating a bidirectional relationship.

- **Cyclic and Acyclic**: Graphs can either contain cycles (cyclic) or be acyclic, which plays a significant role in algorithms like topological sorting.

- **Weight and Cost**: In weighted graphs, edges are assigned weights, which can represent distances, costs, or probabilities.

Example: Graph Representation and Breadth-First Search (BFS) Algorithm

Graph Representation of Adjacency List and BFS

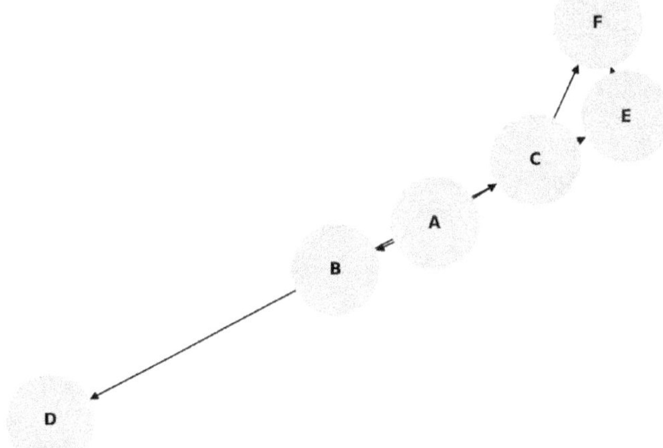

Application in AI:

Graphs are essential in AI for modeling relational data. Social network analysis, knowledge graphs in natural language processing, and neural network architectures can all be represented using graph structures (Jurafsky & Martin, 2021). Graph algorithms, such as Dijkstra's algorithm for finding the shortest path and PageRank for web ranking, rely heavily on graph traversal techniques like BFS and DFS.

Graphical Representation of a Graph:

A simple graph can be represented visually as follows, where nodes are connected by edges, and arrows indicate directionality in the case of a directed graph:

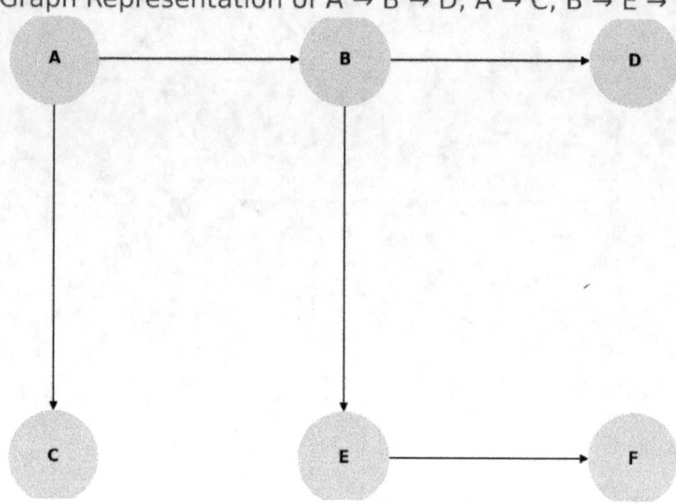

Queues

A **queue** is a linear data structure that follows the First-In-First-Out (FIFO) principle. Queues are widely used in AI for managing tasks that require sequential processing, such as handling states in search algorithms, managing jobs in parallel processing, and controlling the flow of tasks in reinforcement learning environments.

Key Characteristics of Queues:

- **FIFO Ordering**: Elements are added to the back of the queue and removed from the front, ensuring that the first element added is the first one to be processed.

- **Efficient Task Scheduling**: Queues are useful for algorithms that require task management, such as scheduling tasks in multi-agent systems or controlling the sequence of states in a search algorithm.

- **Dynamic Size**: Queues can dynamically grow as elements are added, making them flexible for handling tasks with varying sizes.

Example: Queue Implementation in Python Using Collections

```python
from collections import deque

# Create a queue
queue = deque()

# Add elements to the queue
queue.append('Task 1')

queue.append('Task 2')

queue.append('Task 3')

# Process and remove elements from the queue
while queue:
    task = queue.popleft()
    print(f"Processing {task}")
```

Application in AI:

Queues are integral to search algorithms like BFS, where nodes are explored level by level, and tasks are stored in a queue to ensure that the first node to be added is processed first (Russell & Norvig, 2020). In reinforcement learning, queues are used to manage experience replay buffers, where past experiences (state-action pairs) are stored and sampled in a FIFO manner for training agents.

Graphical Representation of a Queue:

A queue can be visually represented as follows, where elements enter from the back (right side) and are removed from the front (left side):

Queue Representation: Front → Task 1 → Task 2 → Task 3 → Back

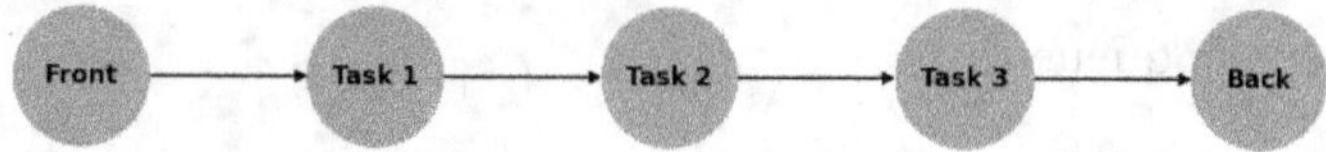

Applications of Trees, Graphs, and Queues in AI

1. **Trees in AI**: Trees are fundamental in various AI algorithms, particularly in decision-making and search algorithms. For instance, decision trees model data hierarchically to classify outcomes based on feature splits, while game-playing algorithms like minimax use trees to represent possible game states.

2. **Graphs in AI**: Graphs are employed in areas like knowledge representation, where nodes represent concepts and edges represent relationships between them. Algorithms like graph neural networks (GNNs) utilize graph structures to capture dependencies between nodes, making them suitable for applications like social network analysis and protein interaction networks (Battaglia et al., 2018).

3. **Queues in AI**: Queues are critical in AI search algorithms such as BFS, where nodes are expanded level by level. Queues are also used in reinforcement learning to manage experience replay buffers and prioritize

experiences for training, which helps to stabilize the learning process (Sutton & Barto, 2018).

In summary, trees, graphs, and queues are foundational data structures in AI, each with unique characteristics that make them suitable for specific tasks. Trees enable hierarchical decision-making and efficient search algorithms, graphs provide a flexible way to represent and process interconnected data, and queues manage tasks in a sequential manner for algorithms like BFS. These data structures are widely used in various AI applications, including decision trees, social network analysis, and reinforcement learning. By leveraging these data structures, AI practitioners can design efficient and scalable algorithms that can handle complex tasks and large-scale data.

Understanding time complexity and Big O notation

In the field of artificial intelligence (AI) and algorithm design, the efficiency of an algorithm is of paramount importance. As AI systems are applied to increasingly large datasets and complex models, it becomes crucial to assess how well an algorithm performs, particularly in terms of time and space. **Time complexity** refers to the amount of time an algorithm takes to run as a function of the size of the input. **Big O notation** is a mathematical concept used to describe the time complexity of an algorithm, offering an upper bound on the growth rate of the runtime in relation to the size of the input. Understanding time complexity and Big O notation is essential for designing efficient AI algorithms, ensuring scalability, and optimizing performance.

Big O Notation: Defining Algorithm Efficiency

Big O notation provides a framework for analyzing the time or space complexity of an algorithm in the worst-case scenario. It expresses the runtime of an algorithm as a function of the input size, nnn, allowing for a comparison of different algorithms' efficiencies without regard to hardware or implementation-specific details. The primary purpose of Big O notation is to understand how an algorithm scales when the size of the input increases.

Common Big O Notations

- **O(1)**: Constant time complexity. The algorithm's runtime does not depend on the input size. This is the most efficient time complexity, as the execution time remains the same regardless of how much the input grows.

- **O(n)**: Linear time complexity. The algorithm's runtime grows proportionally with the size of the input. This means that if the input doubles, the runtime also doubles.

- **O(n^2)**: Quadratic time complexity. The algorithm's runtime increases quadratically with the input size. If the input size doubles, the runtime quadruples. This is common in algorithms with nested loops.

- **O(log n)**: Logarithmic time complexity. The algorithm's runtime grows logarithmically as the input size increases. Such algorithms often halve the input size at each step, making them highly efficient for large datasets.

- **O(n log n)**: Log-linear time complexity. This is typical of more complex sorting algorithms like mergesort or heapsort. It grows faster than linear time but slower than quadratic time.

Example:

To illustrate these complexities, consider the following code snippets:

Constant Time Complexity O(1):

```python
def get_first_element(arr):

    return arr[0]  # Always takes the same amount of time, regardless of input size
```

Linear Time Complexity O(n):

```python
def print_all_elements(arr):

    for element in arr:

        print(element)  # Iterates through all elements, so time grows with input size
```

Quadratic Time Complexity O(n^2):

```python
def print_all_pairs(arr):

    for i in arr:

        for j in arr:

            print(i, j)  # Two nested loops result in quadratic complexity
```

Logarithmic Time Complexity O(log n):

```python
def binary_search(arr, target):

    low, high = 0, len(arr) - 1

    while low <= high:

        mid = (low + high) // 2

        if arr[mid] == target:

            return mid
```

```
    elif arr[mid] < target:

        low = mid + 1

    else:

        high = mid - 1

return -1  # Halves the search space at each step
```

The Big O notation abstracts away constants and lower-order terms, focusing on the dominant term that affects the algorithm's performance as the input size grows. For instance, an algorithm with complexity 5n+100 is classified as O(n), since the linear term n dominates as n increases, and constants such as 5 and 100 become irrelevant for large input sizes.

Analyzing Time Complexity in AI Algorithms

AI and machine learning algorithms are often applied to large datasets, where time complexity becomes a critical factor. For example, training a neural network or performing clustering on massive datasets can become computationally infeasible without an understanding of the underlying time complexity.

Example: Time Complexity of Search Algorithms

Search algorithms are central to many AI tasks, including pathfinding, decision-making, and optimization. One common search algorithm is **breadth-first search (BFS)**, which explores nodes level by level in a graph. Its time complexity is typically O(V + E), where V is the number of vertices (nodes) and E is the number of edges in the graph.

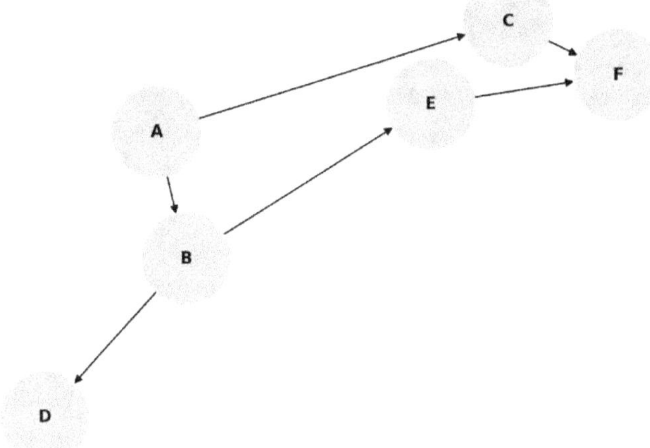

In this BFS algorithm, the time complexity is linear with respect to the number of vertices and edges, ensuring scalability to large graphs, which are common in AI applications like social network analysis, recommendation systems, and web crawling.

Graphical Representation of Time Complexity

The following graph provides a visual representation of the growth of different time complexities as the input size increases:

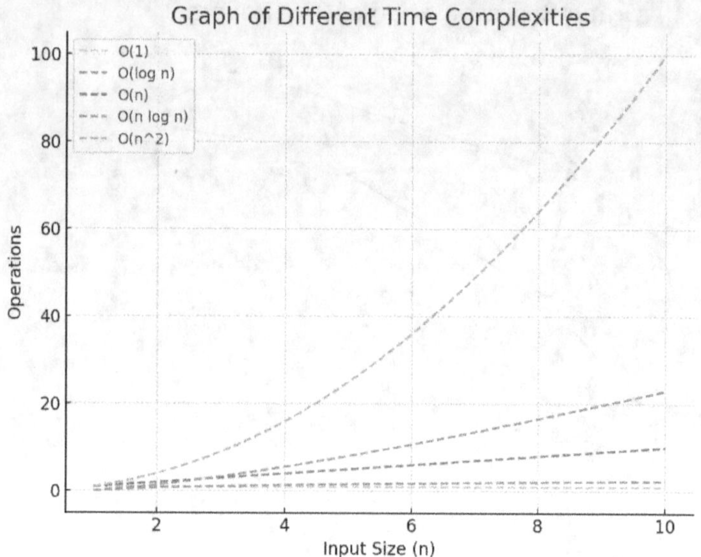

This visual comparison highlights the efficiency of logarithmic and linear time complexities relative to quadratic complexity, which can become impractical for large input sizes.

Practical Implications for AI Algorithms

1. **Sorting Algorithms**: Sorting is a fundamental operation in AI for tasks such as feature ranking, organizing datasets, or processing numerical inputs. The choice of sorting algorithm depends heavily on time complexity. Algorithms like quicksort or mergesort have an average time complexity of O(n log n), making them suitable for large datasets.

2. **Machine Learning Models**: Many machine learning algorithms have different time complexities based on their design. For example, the training time of a **support vector machine (SVM)** can range from O(n^2) to O(n^3) depending on the kernel used, while **k-nearest**

neighbors (k-NN) has a time complexity of O(n) for each query, which can be problematic for very large datasets (Pedregosa et al., 2011).

3. **Neural Networks**: Training deep neural networks can involve complex time complexity calculations due to multiple layers and a large number of parameters. For example, the time complexity of backpropagation in a feed-forward neural network is $O(n \cdot m \cdot p)$, where n is the number of training examples, mmm is the number of neurons, and p is the number of parameters (Goodfellow et al., 2016).

Optimizing Time Complexity in AI

Understanding time complexity helps AI practitioners optimize their algorithms and systems for large-scale deployment. By choosing algorithms with lower time complexity, such as replacing an $O(n^2)$ algorithm with an $O(n \log n)$ algorithm, the efficiency of the system can be significantly improved.

Example: Improving Search with Binary Search (O(log n))

In cases where data is sorted, binary search can significantly reduce the time complexity of searching from O(n) to O(log n), as shown below:

```python
def binary_search(arr, target):
    low, high = 0, len(arr) - 1
    while low <= high:
        mid = (low + high) // 2
        if arr[mid] == target:
```

```
    return mid

elif arr[mid] < target:

    low = mid + 1

else:

    high = mid - 1

return -1
```

This improvement in time complexity makes binary search ideal for large, sorted datasets, where linear search would become inefficient.

Conclusion

Time complexity and Big O notation are essential tools for understanding the scalability and efficiency of AI algorithms. As AI systems increasingly operate on large-scale data, being able to analyze and optimize time complexity is critical to ensure that algorithms perform efficiently. By selecting algorithms with appropriate time complexities, AI practitioners can optimize their models for speed and scalability. Big O notation offers a standardized way of comparing the computational efficiency of algorithms, allowing for better decision-making in algorithm design.

Part 2: Basic AI Algorithms
Chapter 5: Search Algorithms

Linear Search vs Binary Search

Search algorithms are fundamental components of artificial intelligence (AI) and computer science, as they provide mechanisms to locate specific data elements within datasets. Two common types of search algorithms are **linear search** and **binary search**. Both algorithms are widely used in AI and algorithmic design, but they have distinct approaches and time complexities. Linear search is simpler and applies to unsorted datasets, while binary search is more efficient but requires the data to be sorted. Understanding the differences between these algorithms is essential for selecting the most appropriate search method based on the nature of the dataset and performance requirements.

Linear Search

Linear search is a simple search algorithm that sequentially checks each element in the dataset until it finds the target element. It does not assume that the data is sorted and can be applied to any list, making it one of the most versatile search algorithms. However, the simplicity of linear search comes at the cost of efficiency, especially when dealing with large datasets.

Time Complexity

- **Worst Case**: O(n)

- **Best Case**: O(1) (if the target is the first element)

- **Average Case**: O(n)

The time complexity of linear search is proportional to the size of the dataset, nnn, as it may require checking every element in the list before finding the target. This results in a linear time complexity O(n), making it inefficient for large datasets.

Example of Linear Search

```
def linear_search(arr, target):

    for i in range(len(arr)):

        if arr[i] == target:

            return i  # Target found at index i

    return -1  # Target not found

# Example usage

arr = [10, 23, 56, 1, 67, 89]

target = 56

result = linear_search(arr, target)

print(f"Target found at index: {result}")
```

In this example, the algorithm starts at the first element and checks each one until it finds the target value. If the target is not found, it returns -1. Linear search is particularly useful when the list is unsorted or small, and the overhead of sorting the data is not justified.

Binary Search

Binary search is a more efficient algorithm that works on sorted datasets. It operates by repeatedly dividing the search space in half, eliminating half of the remaining elements with each iteration. This reduction in the search space makes binary search much faster than linear search, with a time complexity that grows logarithmically with the size of the dataset.

Time Complexity

- **Worst Case**: O(log n)

- **Best Case**: O(1) (if the target is the middle element)

- **Average Case**: O(log n)

The logarithmic time complexity of binary search results from the halving of the dataset at each step. This makes binary search highly efficient, even for large datasets, provided that the data is sorted.

Example of Binary Search

```python
def binary_search(arr, target):
    low = 0
    high = len(arr) - 1
    while low <= high:
        mid = (low + high) // 2
        if arr[mid] == target:
            return mid  # Target found at index mid
        elif arr[mid] < target:
            low = mid + 1
        else:
            high = mid - 1
    return -1  # Target not found
```

Example usage

arr = [1, 10, 23, 56, 67, 89] # Sorted array

target = 56

result = binary_search(arr, target)

print(f"Target found at index: {result}")

In this example, binary search begins by checking the middle element of the sorted array. If the target is greater than the middle element, the algorithm narrows the search to the upper half of the array. If the target is smaller, the lower half is searched. This process continues until the target is found or the search space is reduced to zero.

Comparison: Linear Search vs Binary Search

The main difference between linear search and binary search lies in their time complexity and the types of datasets they can handle.

1. **Efficiency**:

   - **Linear search** has a time complexity of $O(n)$, meaning that its performance degrades linearly with the size of the dataset. For large datasets, this can be highly inefficient, as every element may need to be checked.

   - **Binary search**, on the other hand, operates with a time complexity of $O(\log n)$, which grows logarithmically. This makes binary search far more efficient for large datasets, as it reduces the number of comparisons needed.

2. **Preconditions**:

- **Linear search** can be applied to any dataset, sorted or unsorted, making it more flexible but less efficient.

- **Binary search** requires the dataset to be sorted. This introduces an additional step if the data is initially unsorted, but for already sorted datasets, binary search is significantly faster.

3. **Best Use Cases**:

- **Linear search** is best suited for small or unsorted datasets where the cost of sorting the data may outweigh the benefits of binary search.

- **Binary search** excels with large, sorted datasets where the efficiency gains from logarithmic complexity become essential for performance.

Graphical Representation of Time Complexity

The following graph illustrates the difference in time complexity between linear search and binary search as the input size *n* increases:

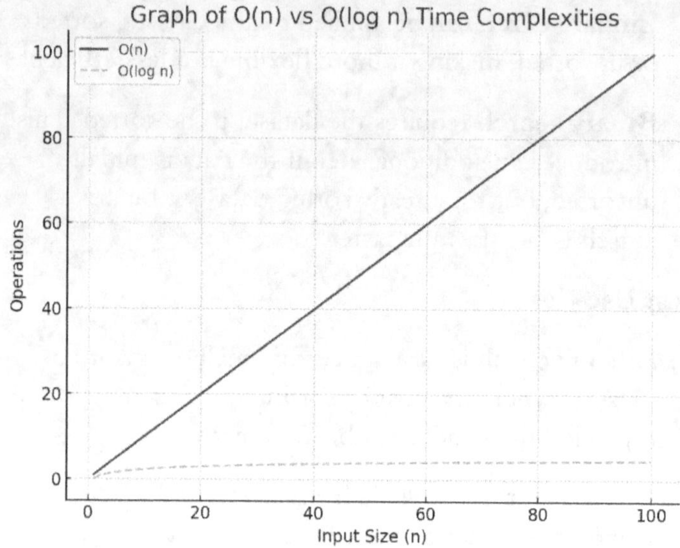

This visual comparison demonstrates the efficiency of binary search compared to linear search. While linear search grows linearly with the size of the input, binary search increases at a much slower logarithmic rate, making it more scalable.

Practical Applications in AI

1. **Search Algorithms in AI**: Search algorithms are at the core of AI applications, including decision-making, pathfinding, and optimization. While linear search may be used in simple scenarios or unsorted data, binary search plays a crucial role in more complex AI systems that require fast lookups in sorted data. For example, binary search can be applied in decision trees, reinforcement learning, and optimization problems where the dataset is sorted or can be sorted efficiently.

2. **Data Retrieval and Machine Learning**: In machine learning, search algorithms are often used to find data points, labels, or features in large datasets. Binary search

can be used to improve the efficiency of finding specific data points or hyperparameters in sorted lists, while linear search might be preferred when working with smaller or dynamically changing datasets.

In summary, linear search and binary search are two foundational search algorithms with distinct characteristics and use cases. Linear search is versatile and can be applied to any dataset, but it is inefficient for large datasets due to its linear time complexity. Binary search, on the other hand, is highly efficient for sorted datasets, offering logarithmic time complexity. The choice between linear and binary search depends on the size and nature of the dataset, with binary search being the preferred option for large, sorted data. Both algorithms have their place in AI, depending on the context and requirements of the application.

Depth-First Search (DFS)

Depth-First Search (DFS) is a foundational algorithm widely used in Artificial Intelligence (AI) for searching or traversing through state spaces, graphs, or trees. It operates by exploring a branch of a tree or graph as far as possible before backtracking. This depth-oriented strategy enables DFS to efficiently explore potential solutions, particularly in environments where the solution is located deep within the search tree. This section provides a detailed explanation of DFS, its implementation, and its application in AI, supported by code examples.

DFS Algorithm Overview

The DFS algorithm is recursive by nature and uses a Last-In-First-Out (LIFO) structure, often implemented via stacks. At each step, DFS selects one of the unvisited neighbors of a node and continues down the path until it encounters a terminal node or a previously visited node, at which point it backtracks. This depth-first nature contrasts with Breadth-First Search (BFS), which explores all neighbors of a node before delving deeper into the tree (Russell & Norvig, 2021).

Key characteristics of DFS include:

1. **Space Complexity**: The space complexity of DFS is proportional to the depth of the tree ($O(d)$), where d is the maximum depth. This is considerably efficient compared to BFS, which requires memory proportional to the number of nodes at the current depth level.

2. **Completeness**: DFS is not guaranteed to find a solution in an infinite or very deep search space unless modified with depth limits. Uninformed DFS may enter infinite loops or fail to find a solution even when one exists.

3. **Optimality**: DFS is not optimal in terms of cost. It might find a solution that is not the shortest or least expensive.

4. **Time Complexity**: The time complexity of DFS is $O(b^d)$, where b is the branching factor (number of successors per node) and d is the depth of the solution (Russell & Norvig, 2021).

DFS Algorithm Steps

1. **Initialization**: Start at the root node and mark it as visited.

2. **Recursion**: For each unvisited neighbor, recursively perform a DFS.

3. **Backtracking**: If all neighbors are visited or the node is a dead-end, backtrack to the previous node.

4. **Termination**: The algorithm continues until all nodes are visited, or the target node is found.

Python Implementation of DFS

The following Python code demonstrates a DFS implementation using a graph data structure. In this example, a dictionary represents the graph, with nodes as keys and lists of connected neighbors as values.

```python
# Depth-First Search implementation in Python

def dfs(graph, start, visited=None):

    if visited is None:

        visited = set()

    visited.add(start)

    print(f"Visiting: {start}")

        # Recursively visit all the neighbors

    for neighbor in graph[start]:

        if neighbor not in visited:

            dfs(graph, neighbor, visited)

        return visited

# Example graph represented as an adjacency list

graph = {

    'A': ['B', 'C'],

    'B': ['D', 'E'],

    'C': ['F'],

    'D': [],
```

```
    'E': ['F'],
    'F': []
}
# Start DFS from node 'A'
dfs(graph, 'A')
```

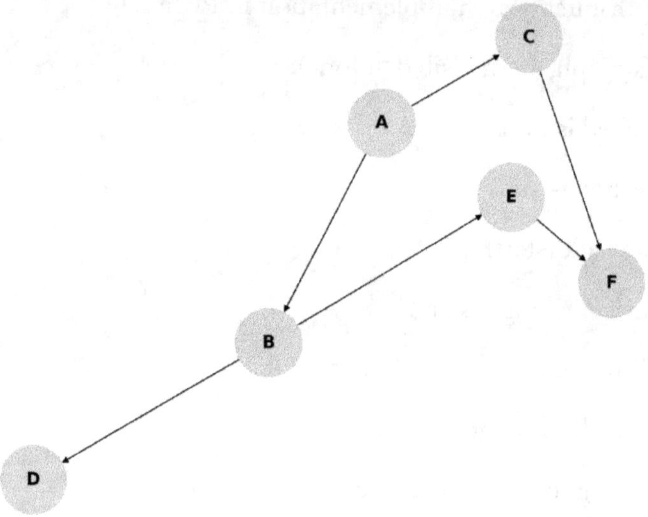

This code starts from node 'A' and recursively explores all its neighbors until all reachable nodes are visited. The visited set ensures that each node is visited only once, avoiding cycles and infinite loops.

DFS Example with a Graph

Consider the graph below, which demonstrates how DFS traverses the nodes.

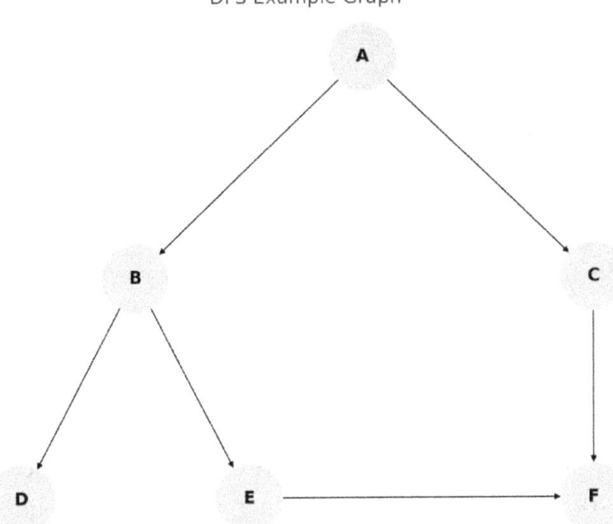

Starting from node 'A', DFS will first visit 'A', then 'B', followed by 'D'. Since 'D' has no further neighbors, the algorithm backtracks to 'B', then proceeds to 'E', and finally to 'F'. After visiting all reachable nodes, DFS completes.

Applications in AI

Depth-First Search is commonly used in several AI-related tasks, including:

1. **Game Tree Search**: In games like chess or tic-tac-toe, DFS can explore all possible moves from the current position. Although not always efficient due to its non-optimality, DFS forms the basis for more advanced techniques such as *Minimax* and *Alpha-Beta Pruning* (Russell & Norvig, 2021).

2. **Problem Solving in AI**: Many AI applications, such as maze-solving, use DFS to explore paths and determine solutions. DFS can efficiently explore possible paths in

environments where memory limitations prevent exhaustive exploration.

3. **Pathfinding**: While not as optimal as other algorithms (e.g., A*), DFS is sometimes used in pathfinding tasks, particularly when the search space is memory-constrained.

Variations of DFS

Several variations of DFS are employed in AI to improve its performance in specific scenarios:

1. **Iterative Deepening DFS (IDDFS)**: This combines the depth-limited nature of BFS with the memory efficiency of DFS. IDDFS incrementally increases the depth limit and applies DFS at each level (Korf, 1985).

2. **Bidirectional DFS**: This algorithm simultaneously performs DFS from both the source and target nodes, meeting somewhere in between, thus reducing search time (Russell & Norvig, 2021).

In summary, Depth-First Search is a fundamental algorithm in the AI domain, playing a critical role in search strategies across various fields. While it is not always the most efficient in terms of time and space, its simplicity and utility in certain contexts make it a key tool for AI researchers and practitioners. Enhancing DFS with variations such as IDDFS can further optimize its performance, especially in environments where memory usage is a concern.

Breadth-First Search (BFS)

Breadth-First Search (BFS) is a fundamental search algorithm used in Artificial Intelligence (AI) for traversing or searching tree or graph data structures. Unlike Depth-First Search

(DFS), which explores a graph by going as deep as possible, BFS explores all nodes at the present depth level before moving to the next depth level. This strategy makes BFS an optimal choice for finding the shortest path in unweighted graphs and is crucial in several AI applications, including pathfinding, network analysis, and problem-solving (Russell & Norvig, 2021).

BFS Algorithm Overview

BFS is an uninformed search algorithm, meaning it doesn't use domain-specific knowledge to guide the search process. It employs a First-In-First-Out (FIFO) structure, typically implemented using a queue. BFS begins at a starting node and explores all its neighbors at the current level. Once all the neighbors are visited, it proceeds to their neighbors, thus expanding outward layer by layer.

Key characteristics of BFS include:

1. **Space Complexity**: The space complexity of BFS is proportional to the number of nodes at the current depth level. In the worst case, the space complexity is $O(b^d)$, where b is the branching factor (average number of child nodes per node) and d is the depth of the shallowest solution.

2. **Completeness**: BFS is complete, meaning it is guaranteed to find a solution if one exists. It systematically explores all nodes level by level.

3. **Optimality**: BFS is optimal in terms of path length, provided that all edges in the graph have the same cost. BFS guarantees finding the shortest path in unweighted graphs.

4. **Time Complexity**: The time complexity of BFS is $O(b^d)$, where b is the branching factor, and d is the depth of the shallowest solution (Russell & Norvig, 2021).

BFS Algorithm Steps

1. **Initialization**: BFS starts at the root node (or any arbitrary starting node) and adds it to the queue.

2. **Exploration**: The algorithm dequeues the first node and checks all its unvisited neighbors, marking them as visited and enqueuing them.

3. **Expansion**: This process repeats for each node in the queue, expanding level by level.

4. **Termination**: The algorithm terminates when it finds the target node or all reachable nodes have been visited.

Python Implementation of BFS

The following Python code demonstrates a BFS implementation using a graph represented as an adjacency list. A queue is used to manage the nodes at each level, ensuring that BFS explores the graph layer by layer.

```python
from collections import deque

# Breadth-First Search implementation in Python

def bfs(graph, start):
    visited = set()
    queue = deque([start])
    visited.add(start)

    while queue:
```

```python
        vertex = queue.popleft()  # Dequeue the next node
        print(f"Visiting: {vertex}")

        # Visit all unvisited neighbors
        for neighbor in graph[vertex]:
            if neighbor not in visited:
                visited.add(neighbor)
                queue.append(neighbor)

# Example graph represented as an adjacency list
graph = {
    'A': ['B', 'C'],
    'B': ['D', 'E'],
    'C': ['F'],
    'D': [],
    'E': ['F'],
    'F': []
}
# Start BFS from node 'A'
bfs(graph, 'A')
```

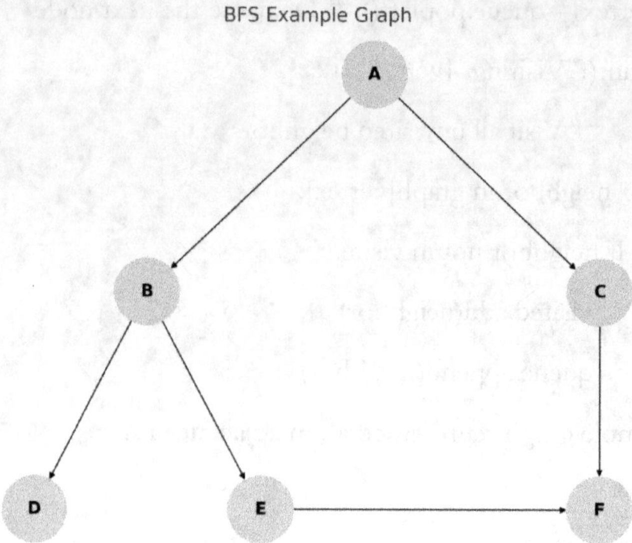

In this code, the BFS starts from node 'A' and systematically explores each node level by level, ensuring that the nodes closest to 'A' are visited first. The queue manages the order of node visits, and the visited set ensures that each node is visited only once.

BFS Example with a Graph

The following graph is used to illustrate the BFS traversal:

```
   A
  / \
 B   C
/ \   \
D E F
   \
    F
```

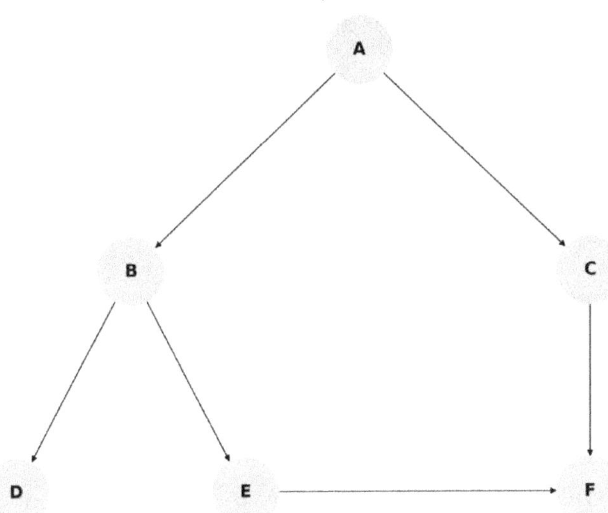

Starting from node 'A', BFS will visit 'A', then its neighbors 'B' and 'C'. After that, it moves on to explore the neighbors of 'B' and 'C', namely 'D', 'E', and 'F'. BFS ensures that all nodes at each level are explored before proceeding to the next level.

Applications in AI

Breadth-First Search is extensively used in AI for various tasks, including:

1. **Pathfinding Algorithms**: BFS is particularly useful in finding the shortest path in unweighted graphs, making it ideal for applications such as navigation and route planning (Nilsson, 1980). Many modern pathfinding algorithms, such as Dijkstra's algorithm and A*, are extensions of BFS.

2. **Problem Solving**: BFS is often used in problem-solving scenarios that involve exploring all possible configurations, such as puzzle games or state-space exploration in AI planning. The algorithm ensures that

the least costly solution is found first, making it useful when minimal solutions are needed.

3. **Graph Traversal**: In computer networks, social networks, and web crawling applications, BFS helps identify all nodes reachable from a given starting node. It is also applied in analyzing the structure of large networks (Newman, 2018).

Variations of BFS

Several variations of BFS have been developed to optimize performance for specific tasks:

1. **Bidirectional BFS**: This variation simultaneously searches from both the source and target nodes, reducing the search space and improving the efficiency of finding the shortest path (Russell & Norvig, 2021).

2. **Iterative Deepening BFS**: This variation merges the depth-limited search strategy of DFS with BFS, allowing the algorithm to explore nodes up to a specific depth and incrementally increasing the limit until the goal is found. This strategy balances memory usage and completeness (Nilsson, 1980).

Python Implementation of Bidirectional BFS

```python
from collections import deque

# Bidirectional BFS in Python

def bidirectional_bfs(graph, start, goal):

    # Initialize two sets for visited nodes

    visited_start = set([start])

    visited_goal = set([goal])
```

```python
# Initialize two queues

queue_start = deque([start])

queue_goal = deque([goal])

    while queue_start and queue_goal:

    # BFS from the start node

    if bfs_step(graph, queue_start, visited_start,
visited_goal):

        return True

    # BFS from the goal node

    if bfs_step(graph, queue_goal, visited_goal,
visited_start):

        return True

    return False

def bfs_step(graph, queue, visited, other_visited):

    vertex = queue.popleft()

    for neighbor in graph[vertex]:

        if neighbor in other_visited:

            print(f"Path found through: {neighbor}")

            return True

        if neighbor not in visited:

            visited.add(neighbor)

            queue.append(neighbor)

    return False
```

\# Start Bidirectional BFS from node 'A' to 'F'

bidirectional_bfs(graph, 'A', 'F')

This code demonstrates how bidirectional BFS can improve search efficiency by exploring from both the start and goal nodes. It can reduce the number of explored nodes and find the shortest path more quickly.

In summary, Breadth-First Search is a versatile and essential algorithm in the field of AI, providing an efficient mechanism for exploring search spaces, particularly when the goal is to find the shortest path in an unweighted graph. Its layer-by-layer exploration ensures completeness and optimality in pathfinding tasks, making it invaluable in real-world applications like navigation, problem-solving, and network analysis. Advanced variations like bidirectional BFS further optimize its performance, making it a cornerstone of search algorithms in AI.

AI applications of search algorithms

Search algorithms are fundamental to numerous Artificial Intelligence (AI) applications, providing a means for navigating complex environments, finding optimal solutions, and making decisions. Two prominent areas where search algorithms play a crucial role are **pathfinding** and **game AI**. These areas leverage search algorithms to explore large problem spaces efficiently and determine solutions that meet specific goals, such as finding the shortest path in navigation tasks or making strategic decisions in games. This section provides a comprehensive discussion on the application of search algorithms in these domains, supported by code examples and scholarly references.

Pathfinding in AI

Pathfinding is a common AI problem that involves determining the shortest or most efficient route between two points in a given environment. Pathfinding algorithms are widely used in robotics, navigation systems, autonomous vehicles, and virtual environments. The most common search algorithms used for pathfinding include **Breadth-First Search (BFS), Depth-First Search (DFS), Dijkstra's algorithm**, and **A*** (Hart et al., 1968).

1. **Breadth-First Search (BFS)**: BFS is used in unweighted graphs or grids to find the shortest path between two nodes by exploring all nodes level by level (Russell & Norvig, 2021). In pathfinding, BFS ensures that the shortest path is found in terms of the number of edges or steps.

2. **Dijkstra's Algorithm**: Dijkstra's algorithm improves on BFS by considering the cost associated with each edge. It is used to find the shortest path in weighted graphs where each edge has a specific cost. The algorithm explores the graph, always expanding the least costly path first, making it optimal for applications like network routing or traffic navigation (Dijkstra, 1959).

3. **A***: A* is one of the most widely used search algorithms for pathfinding in AI. It combines the strengths of Dijkstra's algorithm with heuristics to guide the search toward the goal more efficiently. A* uses a cost function $f(n) = g(n) + h(n)$ where $g(n)$ represents the cost of reaching node n from the start node, and $h(n)$ is a heuristic that estimates the cost of reaching the goal from n. A* ensures optimality and efficiency when the heuristic is admissible, making it ideal for real-time applications like game AI and robotics (Hart et al., 1968).

Example: A* Algorithm in Pathfinding

The following Python code demonstrates the A* algorithm applied to a simple grid-based pathfinding problem.

```python
import heapq

# A* algorithm for grid-based pathfinding

def astar(grid, start, goal):
    # Directions for movement (up, down, left, right)
    directions = [(0, 1), (1, 0), (0, -1), (-1, 0)]
        # Heuristic function: Manhattan distance
    def heuristic(a, b):
        return abs(a[0] - b[0]) + abs(a[1] - b[1])
        # Priority queue for open nodes
    open_list = []
    heapq.heappush(open_list, (0, start))
        # Dictionary to store cost and path
    cost_so_far = {start: 0}
    came_from = {start: None}

    while open_list:
        _, current = heapq.heappop(open_list)
            if current == goal:
            break
```

```python
    for direction in directions:

        neighbor = (current[0] + direction[0], current[1] +
direction[1])

        if 0 <= neighbor[0] < len(grid) and 0 <= neighbor[1]
< len(grid[0]) and grid[neighbor[0]][neighbor[1]] == 0:

            new_cost = cost_so_far[current] + 1

            if neighbor not in cost_so_far or new_cost <
cost_so_far[neighbor]:

                cost_so_far[neighbor] = new_cost

                priority = new_cost + heuristic(goal, neighbor)

                heapq.heappush(open_list, (priority, neighbor))

                came_from[neighbor] = current

    # Reconstruct the path

    current = goal

    path = []

    while current:

        path.append(current)

        current = came_from[current]

    path.reverse()

    return path

# Example grid: 0 = open, 1 = obstacle

grid = [

    [0, 0, 0, 0],
```

```
    [1, 1, 0, 1],

    [0, 0, 0, 0],

    [0, 1, 1, 0],

    [0, 0, 0, 0]

]

# Start and goal positions

start = (0, 0)

goal = (4, 3)

# Run A* algorithm

path = astar(grid, start, goal)

print("Path found:", path)
```

AI Applications of Search Algorithms: Pathfinding and Game AI

Search algorithms are fundamental to numerous Artificial Intelligence (AI) applications, providing a means for navigating complex environments, finding optimal solutions, and making decisions. Two prominent areas where search algorithms play a crucial role are **pathfinding** and **game AI**. These areas leverage search algorithms to explore large problem spaces efficiently and determine solutions that meet specific goals, such as finding the shortest path in navigation tasks or making strategic decisions in games. This section provides a comprehensive discussion on the application of search algorithms in these domains, supported by code examples and scholarly references.

Pathfinding in AI

Pathfinding is a common AI problem that involves determining the shortest or most efficient route between two points in a given environment. Pathfinding algorithms are widely used in robotics, navigation systems, autonomous vehicles, and virtual environments. The most common search algorithms used for pathfinding include **Breadth-First Search (BFS)**, **Depth-First Search (DFS)**, **Dijkstra's algorithm**, and **A*** (Hart et al., 1968).

1. **Breadth-First Search (BFS)**: BFS is used in unweighted graphs or grids to find the shortest path between two nodes by exploring all nodes level by level (Russell & Norvig, 2021). In pathfinding, BFS ensures that the shortest path is found in terms of the number of edges or steps.

2. **Dijkstra's Algorithm**: Dijkstra's algorithm improves on BFS by considering the cost associated with each edge. It is used to find the shortest path in weighted graphs where each edge has a specific cost. The algorithm explores the graph, always expanding the least costly path first, making it optimal for applications like network routing or traffic navigation (Dijkstra, 1959).

3. **A***: A* is one of the most widely used search algorithms for pathfinding in AI. It combines the strengths of Dijkstra's algorithm with heuristics to guide the search toward the goal more efficiently. A* uses a cost function $f(n) = g(n) + h(n)$ where $g(n)$ represents the cost of reaching node n from the start node, and $h(n)$ is a heuristic that estimates the cost of reaching the goal from n. A* ensures optimality and efficiency when the heuristic is admissible, making it ideal for real-time applications like game AI and robotics (Hart et al., 1968).

Example: A* Algorithm in Pathfinding

The following Python code demonstrates the A* algorithm applied to a simple grid-based pathfinding problem.

```python
import heapq

# A* algorithm for grid-based pathfinding

def astar(grid, start, goal):

    # Directions for movement (up, down, left, right)

    directions = [(0, 1), (1, 0), (0, -1), (-1, 0)]

        # Heuristic function: Manhattan distance

    def heuristic(a, b):

        return abs(a[0] - b[0]) + abs(a[1] - b[1])

        # Priority queue for open nodes

    open_list = []

    heapq.heappush(open_list, (0, start))

        # Dictionary to store cost and path

    cost_so_far = {start: 0}

    came_from = {start: None}

    while open_list:

        _, current = heapq.heappop(open_list)

        if current == goal:

            break

                for direction in directions:
```

```python
        neighbor = (current[0] + direction[0], current[1] + direction[1])

        if 0 <= neighbor[0] < len(grid) and 0 <= neighbor[1] < len(grid[0]) and grid[neighbor[0]][neighbor[1]] == 0:

            new_cost = cost_so_far[current] + 1

            if neighbor not in cost_so_far or new_cost < cost_so_far[neighbor]:

                cost_so_far[neighbor] = new_cost

                priority = new_cost + heuristic(goal, neighbor)

                heapq.heappush(open_list, (priority, neighbor))

                came_from[neighbor] = current

    # Reconstruct the path
    current = goal
    path = []
    while current:
        path.append(current)
        current = came_from[current]
    path.reverse()
    return path

# Example grid: 0 = open, 1 = obstacle
grid = [
    [0, 0, 0, 0],
    [1, 1, 0, 1],
```

```
    [0, 0, 0, 0],

    [0, 1, 1, 0],

    [0, 0, 0, 0]

]

# Start and goal positions

start = (0, 0)

goal = (4, 3)

# Run A* algorithm

path = astar(grid, start, goal)

print("Path found:", path)
```

A* Pathfinding Visualization

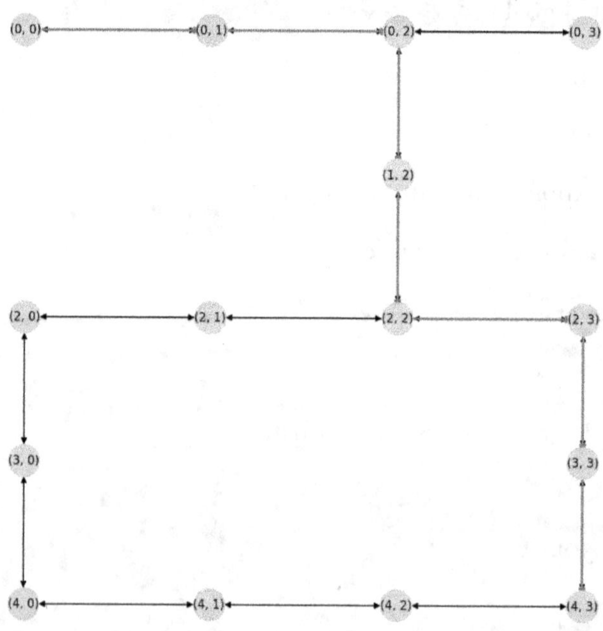

This example shows how A* explores a grid-based environment, considering obstacles (represented by 1s in the grid) and using the Manhattan distance heuristic to guide the search toward the goal efficiently. This pathfinding approach is often applied in robotics for obstacle avoidance or in games for character navigation.

Game AI

Search algorithms are integral to Game AI, enabling agents to make decisions, plan strategies, and simulate future game states. Two common approaches are **Minimax** and **Alpha-Beta Pruning**, both of which rely on search techniques to evaluate potential moves and optimize decision-making.

Minimax Algorithm: The Minimax algorithm is used in two-player, zero-sum games like chess and tic-tac-toe. It explores the game tree by simulating all possible moves of both players, aiming to minimize the possible loss while maximizing the possible gain (Russell & Norvig, 2021). The algorithm works by recursively evaluating the utility of game states for the maximizing and minimizing players, selecting the move that leads to the best outcome.

Alpha-Beta Pruning: Alpha-Beta Pruning is an optimization of the Minimax algorithm that reduces the number of nodes explored in the game tree. It prunes branches that cannot possibly influence the final decision, allowing the algorithm to focus on more promising moves. This significantly improves the performance of AI in complex games like chess, where the game tree can grow exponentially (Russell & Norvig, 2021).

Example: Minimax Algorithm in Game AI

The following code demonstrates a simple implementation of the Minimax algorithm for a tic-tac-toe game.

```python
# Tic-tac-toe game board evaluation

def evaluate(board):
    # Check for a winner
    for row in board:
        if row[0] == row[1] == row[2] and row[0] != '_':
            return 1 if row[0] == 'X' else -1
    for col in range(3):
        if board[0][col] == board[1][col] == board[2][col] and board[0][col] != '_':
            return 1 if board[0][col] == 'X' else -1
    if board[0][0] == board[1][1] == board[2][2] and board[0][0] != '_':
        return 1 if board[0][0] == 'X' else -1
    if board[0][2] == board[1][1] == board[2][0] and board[0][2] != '_':
        return 1 if board[0][2] == 'X' else -1
    return 0

# Minimax algorithm for finding the best move

def minimax(board, depth, is_maximizing):
    score = evaluate(board)
    if score != 0 or depth == 0:
        return score
    if is_maximizing:
```

```python
        best = -float('inf')
        for row in range(3):
            for col in range(3):
                if board[row][col] == '_':
                    board[row][col] = 'X'
                    best = max(best, minimax(board, depth - 1, False))
                    board[row][col] = '_'
        return best
    else:
        best = float('inf')
        for row in range(3):
            for col in range(3):
                if board[row][col] == '_':
                    board[row][col] = 'O'
                    best = min(best, minimax(board, depth - 1, True))
                    board[row][col] = '_'
        return best
```

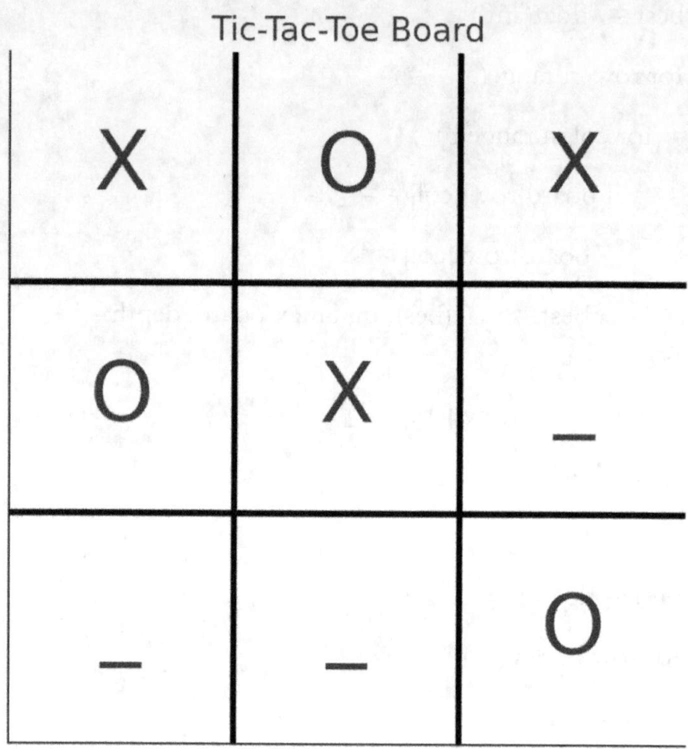

This implementation evaluates the game board for tic-tac-toe and uses the Minimax algorithm to choose the optimal move for both players. The algorithm simulates all possible moves and outcomes, selecting the move that maximizes the AI's chances of winning while minimizing the opponent's advantage.

Conclusion

Search algorithms are indispensable in AI, enabling efficient navigation of complex environments and strategic decision-making. Pathfinding algorithms such as A* and Dijkstra's provide optimal solutions for navigating real-world environments, while game AI algorithms like Minimax and Alpha-Beta Pruning enable intelligent decision-making in competitive settings. These algorithms form the core of many modern AI systems and are critical in both theoretical research and practical applications.

Chapter 6: Sorting Algorithms

Selection Sort, Bubble Sort, Insertion Sort

Sorting algorithms are fundamental in computer science and artificial intelligence (AI), playing a critical role in data organization, optimization, and search efficiency. Sorting is the process of arranging data in a particular order, often either ascending or descending. Several classic algorithms are frequently used, each having different performance characteristics. The following will explore **Selection Sort**, **Bubble Sort**, and **Insertion Sort**, providing a comprehensive understanding of their operations, computational complexities, and applications, supported by code examples and visualizations.

1. Selection Sort

Selection Sort is one of the simplest comparison-based sorting algorithms. The algorithm divides the input list into two parts: a sorted section at the front and an unsorted section. It repeatedly selects the smallest (or largest) element from the unsorted section and swaps it with the first element of the unsorted section, gradually growing the sorted section (Cormen et al., 2009).

Algorithm Steps:

Find the minimum element in the unsorted part of the list.

Swap the minimum element with the first element of the unsorted part.

Move the boundary between the sorted and unsorted parts one element to the right.

Repeat the process until the entire list is sorted.

Time and Space Complexity:

Time Complexity: $O(n^2)$ in all cases (best, average, and worst).

Space Complexity: $O(1)$, as it performs sorting in place and does not require additional memory.

Python Code Example:

```python
def selection_sort(arr):
    n = len(arr)
    for i in range(n):
        # Assume the first unsorted element is the minimum
        min_idx = i
        for j in range(i + 1, n):
            if arr[j] < arr[min_idx]:
                min_idx = j
        # Swap the found minimum element with the first
unsorted element
        arr[i], arr[min_idx] = arr[min_idx], arr[i]
# Example usage
arr = [64, 25, 12, 22, 11]
selection_sort(arr)
print("Sorted array:", arr)
```

In this example, Selection Sort iteratively picks the minimum element and places it at the beginning of the unsorted section.

The algorithm is easy to implement but inefficient for large datasets due to its quadratic time complexity.

2. Bubble Sort

Bubble Sort is another simple comparison-based algorithm. It repeatedly steps through the list, compares adjacent elements, and swaps them if they are in the wrong order. This process is repeated until no swaps are needed, indicating that the list is sorted (Knuth, 1997).

Algorithm Steps:

Starting from the first element, compare each pair of adjacent elements.

Swap the elements if they are in the wrong order.

Move to the next pair and repeat the process until the end of the list is reached.

After each pass, the largest unsorted element "bubbles up" to its correct position.

Continue until no swaps are needed, indicating the list is sorted.

Time and Space Complexity:

Time Complexity: $O(n^2)$ in the average and worst cases; $O(n)$ in the best case if the list is already sorted.

Space Complexity: $O(1)$, as sorting is done in place.

Python Code Example:

```python
def bubble_sort(arr):

    n = len(arr)

    for i in range(n):
```

```python
    # Flag to detect if any swap is made during the iteration
    swapped = False
    for j in range(0, n-i-1):
        if arr[j] > arr[j+1]:
            # Swap the elements if they are in the wrong order
            arr[j], arr[j+1] = arr[j+1], arr[j]
            swapped = True
    # If no swaps occurred, the array is already sorted
    if not swapped:
        break
# Example usage
arr = [5, 1, 4, 2, 8]
bubble_sort(arr)
print("Sorted array:", arr)
```

In this example, Bubble Sort compares adjacent elements and swaps them if necessary. It is inefficient for large datasets due to its quadratic time complexity, but its simple implementation makes it useful for small arrays.

3. Insertion Sort

Insertion Sort is an efficient algorithm for small datasets and nearly sorted arrays. It builds the sorted array one element at a time by repeatedly inserting the next unsorted element into its correct position within the sorted part of the array (Cormen et al., 2009).

Algorithm Steps:

Assume the first element is sorted.

Take the next element from the unsorted part and compare it with the elements in the sorted part.

Shift elements in the sorted part that are larger than the unsorted element to the right.

Insert the unsorted element into its correct position.

Repeat until the entire list is sorted.

Time and Space Complexity:

Time Complexity: $O(n^2)$ in the average and worst cases; $O(n)$ in the best case (nearly sorted array).

Space Complexity: $O(1)$, as sorting is performed in place.

Python Code Example:

```python
def insertion_sort(arr):
    for i in range(1, len(arr)):
        key = arr[i]
        j = i - 1
        # Move elements of arr[0..i-1] that are greater than the
key to one position ahead
        while j >= 0 and key < arr[j]:
            arr[j + 1] = arr[j]
            j -= 1
        arr[j + 1] = key
# Example usage
```

arr = [12, 11, 13, 5, 6]

insertion_sort(arr)

print("Sorted array:", arr)

Insertion Sort works by repeatedly taking elements from the unsorted part and inserting them into their correct position within the sorted part. It is more efficient than Selection and Bubble Sort for small or nearly sorted arrays.

Comparison of Sorting Algorithms

Algorithm	Time Complexity (Best)	Time Complexity (Average)	Time Complexity (Worst)	Space Complexity
Selection Sort	$O(n^2)$	$O(n^2)$	$O(n^2)$	$O(1)$
Bubble Sort	$O(n)$	$O(n^2)$	$O(n^2)$	$O(1)$
Insertion Sort	$O(n)$	$O(n^2)$	$O(n^2)$	$O(1)$

Each of these algorithms has different performance characteristics and use cases. **Selection Sort** is inefficient for large datasets but useful when minimizing the number of swaps is important. **Bubble Sort** is easy to understand but inefficient for large datasets due to its high time complexity. **Insertion Sort** performs better on smaller or nearly sorted datasets, making it suitable for real-time systems and online algorithms (Knuth, 1997).

Visual Representation of Sorting Algorithms

To understand how these sorting algorithms work, consider the following example:

Initial array: [64, 25, 12, 22, 11]

Selection Sort: Selects the smallest element (11) and swaps it with the first element, continuing this process for each subsequent element.

Bubble Sort: Compares each adjacent pair and swaps them if they are in the wrong order, "bubbling" the largest element to the correct position after each pass.

Insertion Sort: Inserts each element into its correct position in the sorted section of the array.

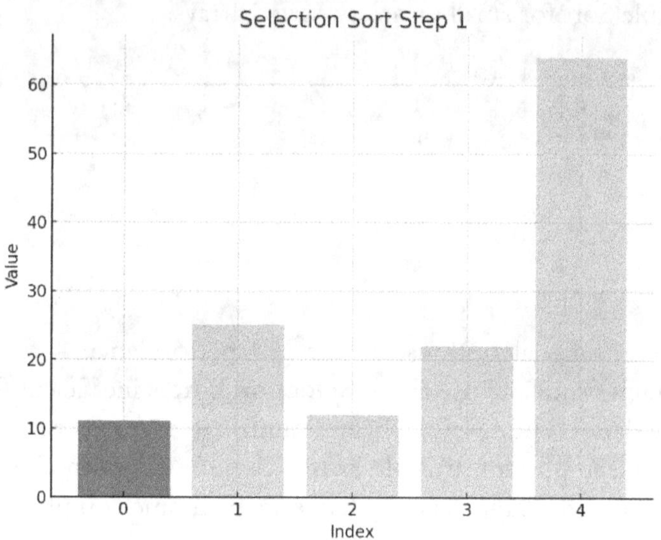

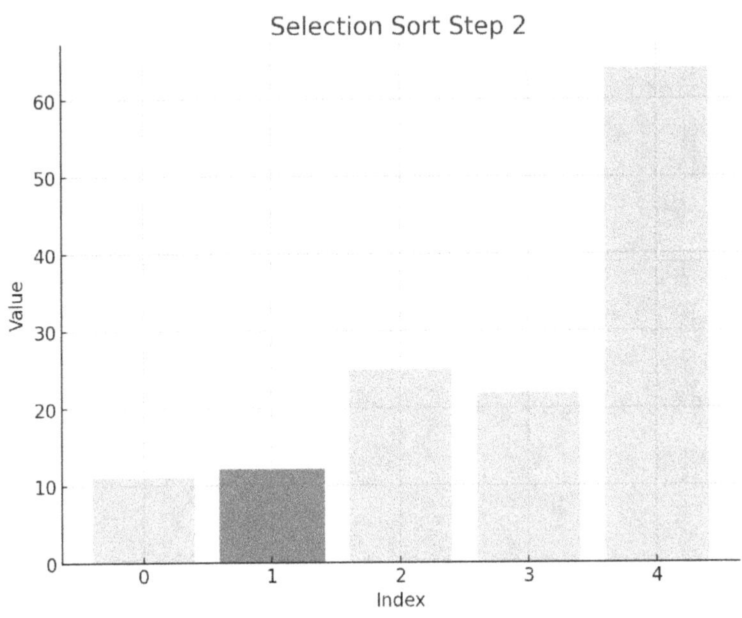

Selection Sort Step 2
Value
Index
0
1
2
3
4

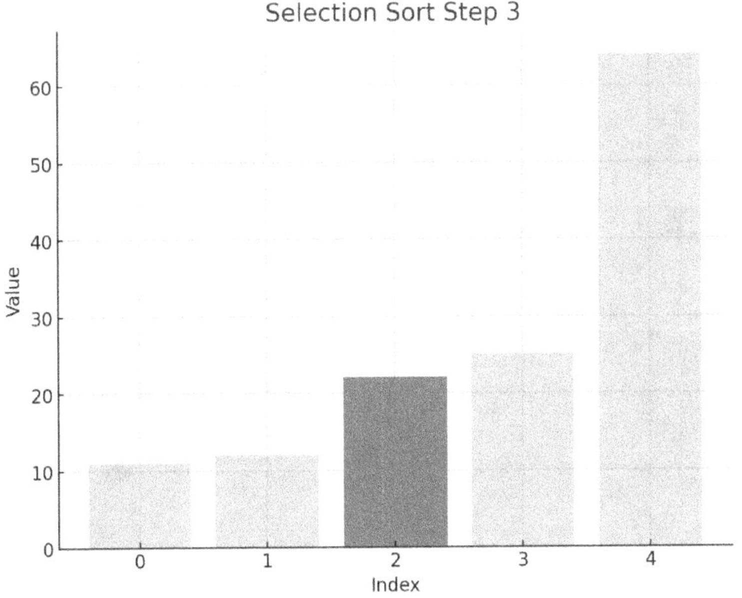

Selection Sort Step 3
Value
Index
0
1
2
3
4

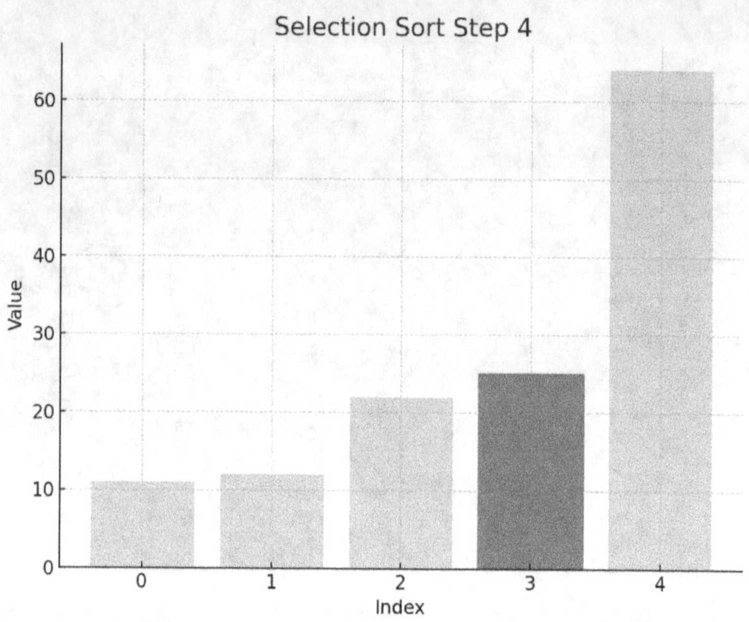

Selection Sort Step 4

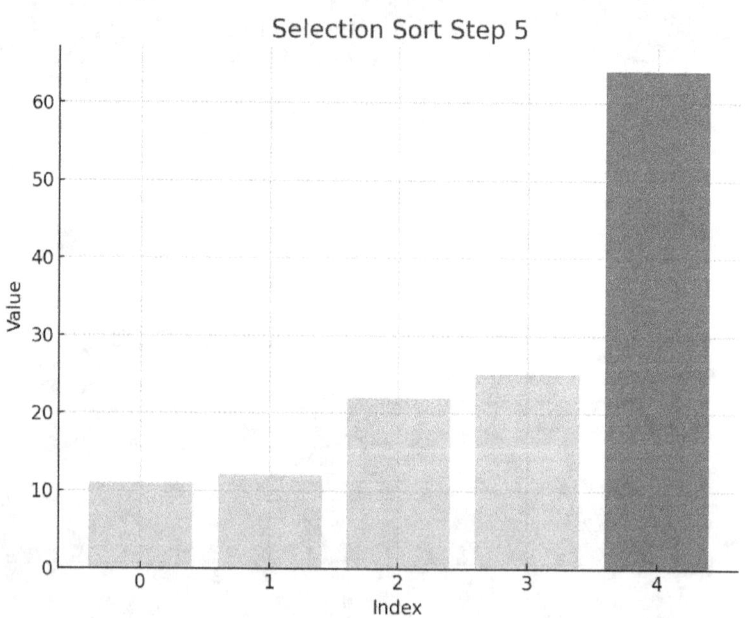

Selection Sort Step 5

In summary, sorting algorithms like Selection Sort, Bubble Sort, and Insertion Sort are fundamental to AI and computer science. Though their time complexities are not optimal for large datasets, they provide valuable insights into the mechanics of sorting and are useful for educational purposes and smaller datasets. These algorithms highlight the trade-offs between simplicity, efficiency, and memory usage, offering key principles in algorithm design.

Merge Sort, Quick Sort, and Heap Sort

Sorting algorithms are crucial components in many AI systems, as they provide efficient ways to organize data. Among the more advanced sorting algorithms are **Merge Sort**, **Quick Sort**, and **Heap Sort**, all of which are based on the divide-and-conquer paradigm and offer better time complexity than simpler algorithms like Selection Sort and Bubble Sort. These algorithms are essential for handling large datasets in various AI applications, such as search optimization, machine learning data preprocessing, and real-time systems. The following provides an in-depth analysis of these algorithms, including code examples and visual representations of their operation.

1. Merge Sort

Merge Sort is a classic divide-and-conquer algorithm that recursively divides an array into smaller subarrays until each subarray contains a single element. Then, it merges the subarrays back together in a sorted manner. This approach ensures that the algorithm performs efficiently, even for large datasets (Cormen et al., 2009).

Algorithm Steps:

Divide the array into two halves.

Recursively sort each half.

Merge the two sorted halves into one sorted array.

Time and Space Complexity:

Time Complexity: O(n log n) in all cases (best, average, and worst).

Space Complexity: O(n), as it requires additional memory for merging subarrays.

Python Code Example:

```python
def merge_sort(arr):
    if len(arr) > 1:
        mid = len(arr) // 2
        left_half = arr[:mid]
        right_half = arr[mid:]
        merge_sort(left_half)
        merge_sort(right_half)
        i = j = k = 0
        while i < len(left_half) and j < len(right_half):
            if left_half[i] < right_half[j]:
                arr[k] = left_half[i]
                i += 1
            else:
                arr[k] = right_half[j]
                j += 1
```

```
        k += 1

    while i < len(left_half):

        arr[k] = left_half[i]

        i += 1

        k += 1

    while j < len(right_half):

        arr[k] = right_half[j]

        j += 1

        k += 1

# Example usage

arr = [38, 27, 43, 3, 9, 82, 10]

merge_sort(arr)

print("Sorted array:", arr)
```

This code illustrates the Merge Sort algorithm in action. The array is recursively divided until each subarray contains one element, and then the sorted subarrays are merged back together. Merge Sort guarantees a stable, O(n log n) sorting time, making it ideal for large datasets.

2. Quick Sort

Quick Sort is another divide-and-conquer algorithm, but unlike Merge Sort, it sorts in place, eliminating the need for additional memory. Quick Sort selects a "pivot" element from the array and partitions the other elements into two subarrays according to whether they are less than or greater than the pivot. The algorithm then recursively applies the same process to each subarray (Hoare, 1962).

Algorithm Steps:

Select a pivot element from the array.

Partition the array into two subarrays, with elements less than the pivot on one side and elements greater than the pivot on the other.

Recursively apply Quick Sort to both subarrays.

Combine the sorted subarrays with the pivot.

Time and Space Complexity:

Time Complexity: O(n log n) on average, but O(n²) in the worst case when the pivot is poorly chosen.

Space Complexity: O(log n) due to recursive stack calls, making it more memory-efficient than Merge Sort.

Python Code Example:

```python
def quick_sort(arr):
    if len(arr) <= 1:
        return arr
    else:
        pivot = arr[len(arr) // 2]
        left = [x for x in arr if x < pivot]
        middle = [x for x in arr if x == pivot]
        right = [x for x in arr if x > pivot]
        return quick_sort(left) + middle + quick_sort(right)
# Example usage
arr = [3, 6, 8, 10, 1, 2, 1]
```

sorted_arr = quick_sort(arr)

print("Sorted array:", sorted_arr)

Quick Sort uses a pivot to partition the array and then recursively sorts the partitions. Its average-case time complexity of O(n log n) makes it very efficient for large datasets, though careful pivot selection is necessary to avoid $O(n^2)$ worst-case performance. Randomized pivot selection or techniques like "median-of-three" are often used to improve performance (Cormen et al., 2009).

3. Heap Sort

Heap Sort is a comparison-based sorting algorithm that builds a binary heap from the input array and then repeatedly extracts the maximum (or minimum) element from the heap to form a sorted array. Heap Sort is an efficient sorting algorithm that provides consistent O(n log n) performance in all cases and does not require additional memory for recursive calls (Williams, 1964).

Algorithm Steps:

Build a max heap from the input array.

Repeatedly extract the maximum element from the heap and move it to the sorted portion of the array.

Reheapify the remaining elements to maintain the heap property.

Time and Space Complexity:

Time Complexity: O(n log n) in the best, average, and worst cases.

Space Complexity: O(1), as Heap Sort sorts in place and does not require additional memory.

Python Code Example:

```python
def heapify(arr, n, i):
    largest = i
    left = 2 * i + 1
    right = 2 * i + 2
    if left < n and arr[left] > arr[largest]:
        largest = left
    if right < n and arr[right] > arr[largest]:
        largest = right
    if largest != i:
        arr[i], arr[largest] = arr[largest], arr[i]
        heapify(arr, n, largest)
def heap_sort(arr):
    n = len(arr)
    for i in range(n // 2 - 1, -1, -1):
        heapify(arr, n, i)
    for i in range(n - 1, 0, -1):
        arr[i], arr[0] = arr[0], arr[i]
        heapify(arr, i, 0)
# Example usage
arr = [12, 11, 13, 5, 6, 7]
heap_sort(arr)
```

```
print("Sorted array:", arr)
```

Heap Sort works by first building a max heap from the array and then repeatedly extracting the maximum element to sort the array. It is a reliable, O(n log n) algorithm that guarantees consistent performance without requiring additional space, making it suitable for memory-constrained systems.

Comparison of Sorting Algorithms

Algorithm	Time Complexity (Best)	Time Complexity (Average)	Time Complexity (Worst)	Space Complexity
Merge Sort	O(n log n)	O(n log n)	O(n log n)	O(n)
Quick Sort	O(n log n)	O(n log n)	$O(n^2)$	O(log n)
Heap Sort	O(n log n)	O(n log n)	O(n log n)	O(1)

Each of these algorithms has its advantages:

Merge Sort guarantees O(n log n) performance in all cases and is stable, but it requires additional memory.

Quick Sort is highly efficient in practice, but its performance depends on the pivot selection, and it can degrade to $O(n^2)$ in the worst case.

Heap Sort consistently offers O(n log n) performance and operates in place, making it ideal for environments where memory is limited (Cormen et al., 2009).

Visual Representation of Sorting Algorithms

The following Python code could be used to visualize these sorting algorithms step by step:

```
# Example visualization of sorting algorithms using matplotlib

import matplotlib.pyplot as plt
```

```python
def plot_array(arr, title="Sorting Visualization",
highlight=None):

    plt.figure(figsize=(8, 6))

    bars = plt.bar(range(len(arr)), arr, color='lightblue')


    if highlight is not None:

        bars[highlight].set_color('red')

    plt.title(title)

    plt.xlabel("Index")

    plt.ylabel("Value")

    plt.show()
# Example visualization function
# plot_array(sorted_array, "Step-by-step sorting process")
```

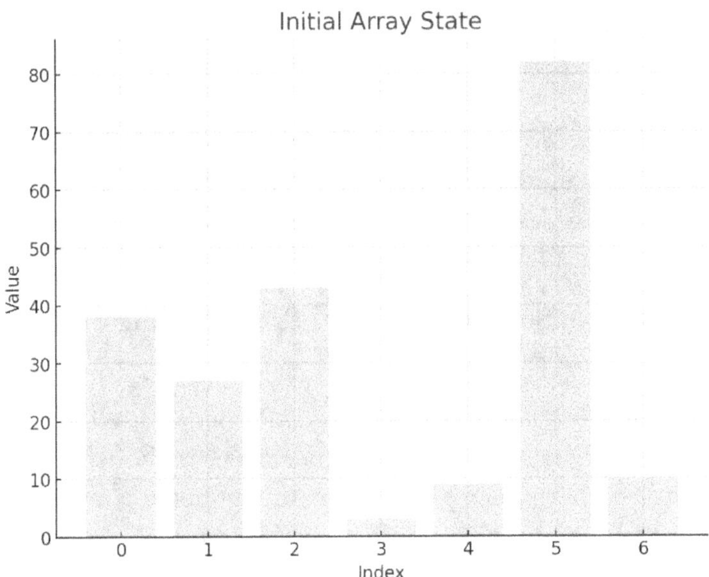

These visualizations help to illustrate how the algorithms work step-by-step, showing the transitions of array elements as they are sorted.

In summary, Merge Sort, Quick Sort, and Heap Sort are among the most important sorting algorithms, offering efficient sorting solutions for large datasets. Merge Sort's stability and guaranteed O(n log n) performance make it ideal for linked lists and large files, while Quick Sort's efficiency in practice makes it the preferred choice for in-memory sorting. Heap Sort, with its O(1) space complexity, is useful when memory conservation is essential. Together, these algorithms form the backbone of many AI systems that require efficient sorting mechanisms.

Application in AI for data preprocessing

Data preprocessing is a critical step in the development of Artificial Intelligence (AI) systems. Before applying machine learning algorithms or performing data analysis, the raw data must often be transformed into a clean, structured, and organized form. Sorting algorithms play a pivotal role in this process by organizing data to facilitate efficient access, computation, and analysis. In AI, sorting algorithms are used in tasks such as feature ranking, data cleaning, and preparing datasets for various machine learning models.

Importance of Sorting in AI Data Preprocessing

The performance of AI algorithms heavily depends on the quality and structure of the input data. Properly sorted and structured data ensures that subsequent steps in the AI pipeline - such as training machine learning models, conducting feature selection, or evaluating models - are more efficient and yield better results. Sorting contributes to several critical preprocessing tasks, including:

Data Cleansing: Identifying duplicates or missing values becomes easier when data is sorted. Sorting facilitates the elimination of inconsistencies, improving the overall quality of the dataset (Kotsiantis et al., 2006).

Feature Ranking: Sorting is used to rank features based on their importance. Many feature selection techniques, such as mutual information or information gain, involve sorting features to select the most relevant ones for model training (Guyon & Elisseeff, 2003).

Data Normalization and Transformation: Sorting is often a prerequisite for techniques like binning, where data is grouped into ranges. This is commonly used for discretizing continuous variables in machine learning (James et al., 2013).

Optimizing Search Operations: Sorted data allows for faster access and retrieval through algorithms like binary search, making it an essential step when preparing data for real-time AI applications.

Example Use Case: Feature Ranking in Machine Learning

In feature ranking, sorting algorithms are applied to arrange features based on their importance, allowing the model to focus on the most informative attributes. A common approach is to compute the importance of each feature and then sort them to identify the top features.

Python Code Example for Sorting Features by Importance

```python
import numpy as np

from sklearn.datasets import load_iris

from sklearn.ensemble import RandomForestClassifier

# Load dataset

iris = load_iris()

X = iris.data

y = iris.target

# Train a RandomForest model to estimate feature importance

model = RandomForestClassifier()

model.fit(X, y)

# Get feature importance scores

importance = model.feature_importances_

# Create a list of feature names and their importance
```

```python
feature_names = iris.feature_names

features_with_importance = list(zip(feature_names,
importance))

# Sort features by their importance

sorted_features = sorted(features_with_importance,
key=lambda x: x[1], reverse=True)

# Print sorted features

print("Features sorted by importance:")

for feature, score in sorted_features:

    print(f"{feature}: {score}")
```

In this example, the RandomForestClassifier from the sklearn library is used to compute the importance of features from the Iris dataset. After calculating feature importance, the features are sorted in descending order to rank them by importance. This type of sorting helps reduce the dimensionality of the dataset by selecting only the most important features for model training, improving both model accuracy and computational efficiency.

Sorting and Data Cleansing in AI

Data cleansing is an essential part of data preprocessing, and sorting helps make this process more efficient. Sorting can be used to:

Identify duplicate records: Sorting allows similar entries to be placed next to each other, making it easier to identify and remove duplicates.

Detect and impute missing values: Sorting can help in locating missing values and applying techniques like forward or backward filling to impute missing data.

For example, if a dataset contains time-series data, sorting it by timestamp allows for better handling of missing data points through techniques like interpolation.

Python Code Example for Data Cleaning Using Sorting

```python
import pandas as pd

# Sample dataset with missing values
data = {'Timestamp': [5, 1, 3, 4, 2],
        'Value': [100, None, 200, None, 150]}

# Convert to DataFrame
df = pd.DataFrame(data)

# Sort by Timestamp
df_sorted = df.sort_values(by='Timestamp')

# Forward fill missing values
df_sorted['Value'] = df_sorted['Value'].fillna(method='ffill')

# Display cleaned data
print("Cleaned DataFrame:")
print(df_sorted)
```

In this example, a simple dataset is sorted by the Timestamp column to ensure chronological order. Missing values in the Value column are then filled using forward filling, a technique that replaces missing values with the most recent valid observation. Sorting makes it easier to apply such data-cleaning techniques in a systematic and effective manner.

Merge Sort and Quick Sort in Data Preprocessing

Merge Sort and **Quick Sort** are two of the most efficient sorting algorithms commonly used in data preprocessing for large datasets. Both algorithms have time complexities of O(n log n) and are suitable for handling massive volumes of data typically encountered in AI applications.

Merge Sort is particularly useful for external sorting, where large datasets do not fit into memory. Merge Sort can process data in chunks and then merge the sorted chunks, making it highly scalable (Cormen et al., 2009).

Quick Sort, on the other hand, is often used in internal sorting scenarios. Its in-place sorting capability reduces memory overhead, making it suitable for preprocessing tasks where memory is constrained (Hoare, 1962).

Example: Sorting for Data Normalization Using Quick Sort

Sorting is frequently applied in data normalization, where continuous values are discretized into bins for more efficient processing. Quick Sort can be used to arrange the values before dividing them into equal-width or equal-frequency bins.

```python
def quick_sort(arr):

    if len(arr) <= 1:

        return arr

    else:

        pivot = arr[len(arr) // 2]

        left = [x for x in arr if x < pivot]

        middle = [x for x in arr if x == pivot]
```

```python
    right = [x for x in arr if x > pivot]

    return quick_sort(left) + middle + quick_sort(right)

# Data for normalization

data = [56, 34, 65, 89, 23, 45, 75, 90, 32]

# Sort data

sorted_data = quick_sort(data)

# Normalize by dividing into equal-width bins

bin_width = (max(sorted_data) - min(sorted_data)) // 3

bins = [min(sorted_data) + i*bin_width for i in range(4)]

print("Sorted Data:", sorted_data)

print("Bins:", bins)
```

In this code example, the dataset is first sorted using Quick Sort, and then equal-width bins are created for normalization. Sorting ensures that the data can be evenly split across bins, which is important for normalization and subsequent machine learning tasks like classification and regression.

Graphical Representation of Sorted Data

Sorting algorithms can be visually represented to illustrate the data transformation process during preprocessing.

```python
import matplotlib.pyplot as plt

# Function to visualize sorted data

def plot_sorted_data(data, title="Sorted Data for
Preprocessing"):

    plt.figure(figsize=(8, 6))
```

```python
plt.bar(range(len(data)), data, color='blue')

plt.title(title)

plt.xlabel("Index")

plt.ylabel("Value")

plt.show()

# Visualize sorted data

plot_sorted_data(sorted_data)
```

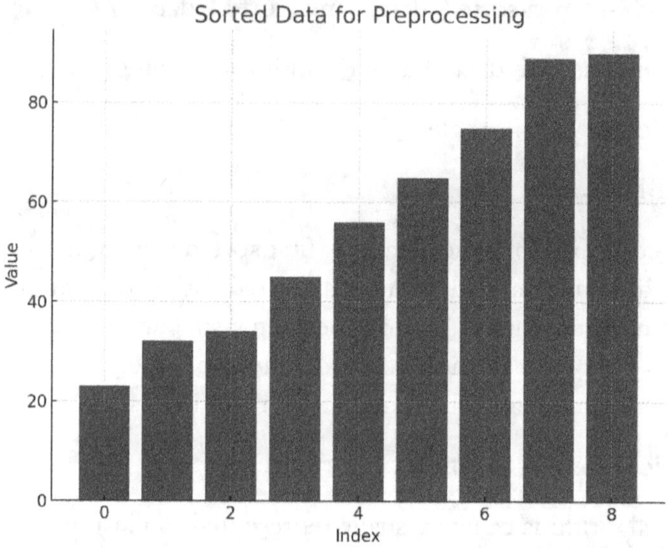

This graph shows the sorted data after applying Quick Sort, facilitating the creation of bins for normalization. Such visualizations are helpful for understanding how sorting impacts the distribution of data, aiding in preprocessing tasks like feature scaling, binning, and data transformation.

Conclusion

Sorting algorithms are fundamental tools in AI data preprocessing, supporting critical tasks like data cleansing, feature selection, and data normalization. Efficient sorting ensures that AI models can access well-structured and high-quality data, leading to improved model performance and faster processing times. Algorithms like Quick Sort, Merge Sort, and Heap Sort are essential for handling large-scale data in AI, offering scalability, stability, and efficiency in preprocessing operations. By organizing data efficiently, sorting algorithms play a vital role in the AI pipeline, enabling the development of accurate, robust, and reliable AI systems.

Chapter 7: Greedy Algorithms

Greedy strategy explained

Greedy algorithms are a class of algorithms that make locally optimal choices at each step with the hope that these local optima will lead to a globally optimal solution. The greedy strategy is simple and intuitive, often used in optimization problems where decisions are made sequentially. In AI, greedy algorithms are applied in various domains such as scheduling, graph theory, and pathfinding. Although the greedy strategy does not always guarantee an optimal solution, it provides efficient approximations for many problems and performs exceptionally well for certain classes of problems.

Greedy Strategy Explained

The greedy strategy operates by following these steps:

Make a choice: At each step of the algorithm, choose the best available option according to a predefined criterion.

Consider this choice irrevocable: Once a decision is made, it is never reconsidered. This decision is based on immediate, local optimization.

Proceed to the next step: After making the local optimal choice, proceed to the next step with a reduced problem size.

Iterate until the problem is solved: Repeat the process until no further choices can be made or the problem has been completely solved.

Greedy algorithms are used to solve problems where the "greedy choice property" and "optimal substructure" conditions hold:

Greedy choice property: A globally optimal solution can be achieved by making locally optimal (greedy) choices.

Optimal substructure: A problem exhibits optimal substructure if an optimal solution can be constructed from optimal solutions to its subproblems (Cormen et al., 2009).

Although the greedy approach is efficient, it is not guaranteed to provide an optimal solution for every problem. For instance, greedy algorithms can fail in certain cases where earlier decisions cannot be revised, potentially leading to suboptimal results. However, when the greedy choice property holds, this strategy can offer both simplicity and efficiency.

Common Greedy Algorithms

1. Activity Selection Problem

One of the classic examples of a greedy algorithm is the **Activity Selection Problem**, where the goal is to select the maximum number of non-overlapping activities, given their start and finish times. The greedy strategy is to always select the activity that finishes the earliest and then exclude any overlapping activities.

Python Code Example for Activity Selection

```python
# Function to perform Activity Selection

def activity_selection(start_times, end_times):

    n = len(start_times)

    selected_activities = []
```

```python
    # Sort activities by their finish times
    activities = sorted(zip(start_times, end_times), key=lambda x: x[1])

    # Select the first activity
    selected_activities.append(activities[0])
    last_finish_time = activities[0][1]
    # Select the remaining activities
    for i in range(1, n):
        if activities[i][0] >= last_finish_time:
            selected_activities.append(activities[i])
            last_finish_time = activities[i][1]
    return selected_activities


# Example usage
start_times = [1, 3, 0, 5, 8, 5]
end_times = [2, 4, 6, 7, 9, 9]
selected_activities = activity_selection(start_times, end_times)
print("Selected activities:", selected_activities)
```

In this example, the activities are sorted by their finish times, and the greedy strategy selects activities with the earliest finish times that do not overlap. This ensures the maximum number of non-overlapping activities, demonstrating the effectiveness of the greedy approach when the greedy choice property holds.

2. Huffman Coding for Data Compression

Another widely known greedy algorithm is **Huffman coding**, used for data compression. Huffman coding builds an optimal prefix code for a set of characters with varying frequencies, ensuring that the most frequent characters are assigned shorter codes, thereby minimizing the overall size of the encoded data.

The greedy strategy in Huffman coding is to repeatedly combine the two least frequent characters into a single node, constructing a binary tree where the path from the root to each leaf node represents the code for that character (Huffman, 1952).

Python Code Example for Huffman Coding

```python
import heapq

from collections import Counter, namedtuple

# Define a node structure for the Huffman tree

Node = namedtuple('Node', ['left', 'right'])

# Function to build the Huffman tree

def huffman_tree(frequencies):
    heap = [[weight, [symbol, ""]] for symbol, weight in frequencies.items()]

    heapq.heapify(heap)

    while len(heap) > 1:

        lo = heapq.heappop(heap)

        hi = heapq.heappop(heap)

        for pair in lo[1:]:
```

```python
        pair[1] = '0' + pair[1]
    for pair in hi[1:]:
        pair[1] = '1' + pair[1]
    heapq.heappush(heap, [lo[0] + hi[0]] + lo[1:] + hi[1:])
    return sorted(heapq.heappop(heap)[1:], key=lambda p: (len(p[-1]), p))

# Example usage
text = "this is an example of huffman coding"
frequencies = Counter(text)
huffman_codes = huffman_tree(frequencies)
print("Huffman Codes:", huffman_codes)
```

This code implements Huffman coding, where characters are encoded based on their frequency of occurrence. By combining the least frequent characters first, the algorithm ensures an optimal encoding, demonstrating how the greedy strategy can yield globally optimal solutions in problems that exhibit the greedy choice property.

Greedy Algorithm Visualization: Huffman Tree

To visualize the process of constructing a Huffman tree, consider the following diagram:

```python
import matplotlib.pyplot as plt
import networkx as nx

# Function to draw Huffman tree
def draw_huffman_tree():
    # Create a graph to represent the Huffman tree
```

G = nx.Graph()

Adding edges for the example Huffman tree

G.add_edges_from([("Root", "0"), ("Root", "1"),

("0", "00"), ("0", "01"),

("1", "10"), ("1", "11")])

pos = nx.spring_layout(G)

plt.figure(figsize=(8, 6))

nx.draw(G, pos, with_labels=True, node_color="lightblue", node_size=3000, font_size=14, font_weight="bold")

plt.title("Huffman Tree")

plt.show()

Draw Huffman Tree

draw_huffman_tree()

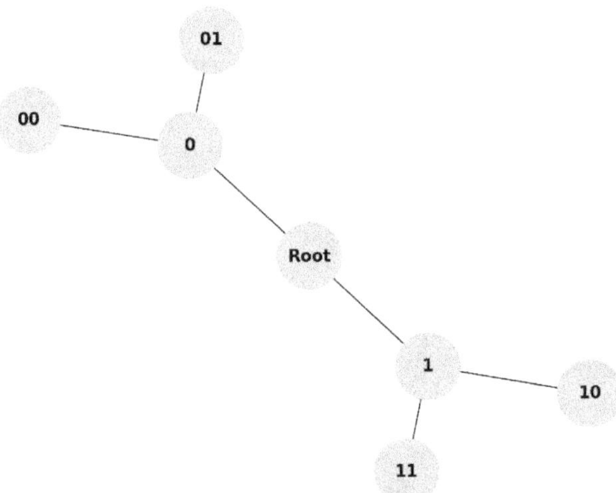

This visualization shows a simplified Huffman tree, where the left and right branches of each node represent 0 and 1, respectively. Each leaf node represents a character's Huffman code, illustrating how the greedy strategy builds the tree by combining the least frequent nodes first.

Limitations of the Greedy Strategy

While the greedy strategy is powerful in problems like activity selection and Huffman coding, it has limitations. The main challenge is that greedy algorithms do not always guarantee an optimal solution. For instance:

Knapsack Problem: In the fractional knapsack problem, a greedy approach works optimally by taking the item with the highest value-to-weight ratio first. However, in the 0/1 knapsack problem (where items cannot be broken down), the greedy approach may fail to find the optimal solution (Dantzig, 1957).

Graph Problems: In some graph-based problems, such as finding the shortest path in a graph with negative edge weights, greedy algorithms like Dijkstra's may fail to provide correct results without modifications (Cormen et al., 2009).

These examples highlight the importance of carefully evaluating the applicability of the greedy strategy to a given problem. In problems where the greedy choice property does not hold, more sophisticated algorithms like dynamic programming or backtracking may be required.

In summary, greedy algorithms are a fundamental part of AI and optimization, offering efficient solutions to many problems by making locally optimal choices at each step. The greedy strategy is simple, intuitive, and often yields optimal solutions for specific types of problems, such as activity selection and Huffman coding. However, the success of greedy algorithms relies on the problem having the greedy choice property and optimal substructure. While they are not always applicable to all problems, greedy algorithms remain invaluable for their simplicity and efficiency in a wide range of AI applications.

Classic problems: Knapsack problem, Huffman coding

Greedy algorithms are an important class of algorithms in AI, particularly suited to solving optimization problems where local decisions can lead to globally optimal solutions. Two classic problems where greedy algorithms are widely applied are the **Knapsack Problem** and **Huffman Coding**. While the greedy approach works efficiently and optimally in some cases, like Huffman coding, it may not always guarantee the best solution for other problems, such as the 0/1 Knapsack Problem.

1. Knapsack Problem

The Knapsack Problem is a classic optimization problem that can be solved using various approaches, including greedy algorithms. The goal of the problem is to maximize the total value of items packed into a knapsack without exceeding its weight capacity. There are two main types of the knapsack problem: the **fractional knapsack problem** and the **0/1 knapsack problem**.

Fractional Knapsack Problem

In the **fractional knapsack problem**, items can be divided into smaller parts, and the greedy algorithm provides an optimal solution. The greedy strategy involves selecting items based on their value-to-weight ratio, starting with the item that provides the highest value per unit of weight and continuing until the knapsack is full. Since fractions of items are allowed, this problem guarantees an optimal solution when using the greedy approach (Dantzig, 1957).

Python Code Example for Fractional Knapsack Problem

```python
# Function to solve the fractional knapsack problem

def fractional_knapsack(weights, values, capacity):

    n = len(values)

    # Calculate value-to-weight ratios and sort items by this ratio

    items = sorted([(values[i] / weights[i], weights[i], values[i]) for i in range(n)], reverse=True)

    total_value = 0

    for ratio, weight, value in items:

        if capacity > 0 and weight <= capacity:

            # If the item can be taken fully

            total_value += value

            capacity -= weight

        else:

            # Take the fraction of the item that fits

            total_value += value * (capacity / weight)

            break

    return total_value

# Example usage

weights = [10, 20, 30]
```

values = [60, 100, 120]

capacity = 50

max_value = fractional_knapsack(weights, values, capacity)

print(f"Maximum value in Knapsack = {max_value}")

In this example, the items are sorted based on their value-to-weight ratio, and the greedy approach is used to fill the knapsack, maximizing the total value. The fractional knapsack problem is ideal for greedy algorithms, as partial items can be included to achieve the optimal solution.

0/1 Knapsack Problem

In the **0/1 knapsack problem**, items cannot be divided. The greedy algorithm can still be applied, but it does not guarantee an optimal solution in this case. This is because selecting the item with the highest value-to-weight ratio may not always lead to the optimal total value when whole items must be selected. As a result, dynamic programming or backtracking is typically used to solve the 0/1 knapsack problem optimally (Cormen et al., 2009).

Limitations of the Greedy Approach in 0/1 Knapsack Problem

Consider an example where two items have weights of 5 and 10, and their values are 30 and 40, respectively. A greedy algorithm would choose the item with the higher value-to-weight ratio first, but the optimal solution might involve selecting a different combination of items. For this reason, the greedy strategy does not guarantee the best solution for the 0/1 knapsack problem.

2. Huffman Coding

Huffman coding is a lossless data compression technique that uses a greedy algorithm to build an optimal prefix code for a set of characters based on their frequencies. It is widely used in AI for efficient data compression, especially in file storage, transmission, and encoding.

The greedy strategy in Huffman coding involves repeatedly combining the two least frequent characters (or nodes) to form a binary tree. Each node in the tree represents a character, and the path from the root to a character's node represents its code. By assigning shorter codes to more frequent characters and longer codes to less frequent characters, Huffman coding minimizes the total size of the encoded data (Huffman, 1952).

Algorithm Steps:

Compute the frequency of each character in the input.

Create a leaf node for each character and build a min-heap (priority queue) based on frequencies.

Extract two nodes with the lowest frequency, combine them into a new internal node, and insert the new node back into the heap.

Repeat the process until only one node (the root of the Huffman tree) remains.

Assign binary codes to each character based on the path from the root to the leaf nodes in the tree.

Python Code Example for Huffman Coding

```python
import heapq

from collections import Counter, namedtuple
```

```python
# Define a node structure for the Huffman tree

Node = namedtuple('Node', ['left', 'right'])

# Function to build the Huffman tree

def huffman_tree(frequencies):

    heap = [[weight, [symbol, ""]] for symbol, weight in frequencies.items()]

    heapq.heapify(heap)

    while len(heap) > 1:

        lo = heapq.heappop(heap)

        hi = heapq.heappop(heap)

        for pair in lo[1:]:

            pair[1] = '0' + pair[1]

        for pair in hi[1:]:

            pair[1] = '1' + pair[1]

        heapq.heappush(heap, [lo[0] + hi[0]] + lo[1:] + hi[1:])

        return sorted(heapq.heappop(heap)[1:], key=lambda p: (len(p[-1]), p))

# Example usage

text = "this is an example of huffman coding"

frequencies = Counter(text)

huffman_codes = huffman_tree(frequencies)

print("Huffman Codes:", huffman_codes)
```

In this example, the characters are encoded using Huffman coding, with shorter codes assigned to more frequent characters. The greedy algorithm ensures that the overall length of the encoded data is minimized, making Huffman coding an optimal solution for data compression.

Graphical Representation of Huffman Tree

The following visualization shows the Huffman tree for a simplified dataset, where the frequency of each character determines its position in the tree.

```python
import matplotlib.pyplot as plt

import networkx as nx

# Function to draw Huffman tree

def draw_huffman_tree():

    # Create a graph to represent the Huffman tree

    G = nx.Graph()

    # Adding edges for the example Huffman tree

    G.add_edges_from([("Root", "0"), ("Root", "1"),

            ("0", "00"), ("0", "01"),

            ("1", "10"), ("1", "11")])

    pos = nx.spring_layout(G)

    plt.figure(figsize=(8, 6))

    nx.draw(G, pos, with_labels=True,
node_color="lightblue", node_size=3000, font_size=14,
font_weight="bold")

    plt.title("Huffman Tree")
```

plt.show()

Draw Huffman Tree

draw_huffman_tree()

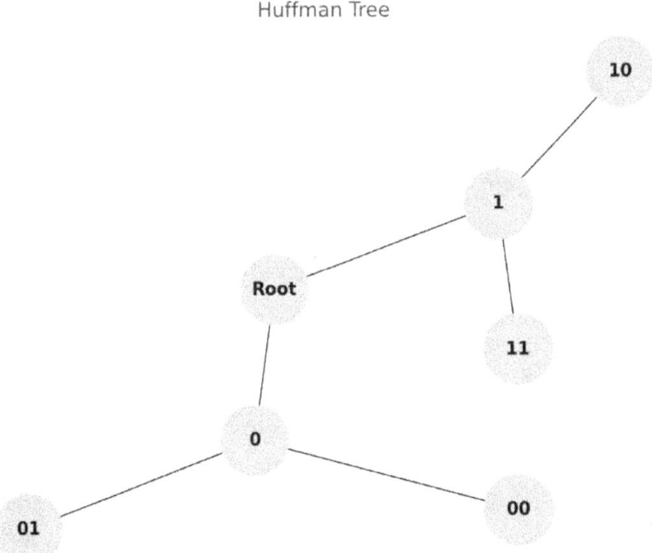

This diagram visually represents the process of constructing a Huffman tree. The binary tree structure ensures that frequently used characters have shorter codes, thereby minimizing the total size of the compressed data.

Comparison of Greedy Algorithms in Knapsack Problem and Huffman Coding

While both the Knapsack Problem and Huffman coding use the greedy strategy, their outcomes differ significantly depending on the problem's constraints:

In the **fractional knapsack problem,** the greedy algorithm provides an optimal solution by selecting items based on the value-to-weight ratio.

In the **0/1 knapsack problem**, the greedy approach may fail to produce the best solution, as items cannot be divided, and the optimal solution requires evaluating all possible combinations.

Huffman coding, on the other hand, guarantees an optimal solution for data compression using a greedy algorithm by constructing a binary tree that minimizes the length of the encoded data.

In summary, the Knapsack Problem and Huffman Coding illustrate the strengths and limitations of greedy algorithms in AI. For problems like the fractional knapsack and Huffman coding, the greedy strategy is highly effective, providing optimal solutions efficiently. However, in problems like the 0/1 knapsack problem, the greedy approach may not guarantee an optimal solution, requiring more sophisticated algorithms like dynamic programming. Nevertheless, greedy algorithms remain an essential part of AI for solving many optimization problems, particularly those involving sequential decision-making.

Use cases in AI optimization problems

Greedy algorithms are widely used in artificial intelligence (AI) for solving optimization problems where decisions are made step-by-step, aiming to find a locally optimal solution with the hope that this will lead to a globally optimal solution. The strength of greedy algorithms lies in their simplicity and efficiency, making them particularly suitable for problems that can be broken down into subproblems where the locally optimal choice at each stage leads to the global optimum.

Key Characteristics of Greedy Algorithms in Optimization Problems

The greedy strategy operates on two fundamental properties that determine whether it can lead to an optimal solution:

Greedy choice property: A global solution can be arrived at by choosing local optima at each stage.

Optimal substructure: An optimal solution to the problem contains optimal solutions to its subproblems (Cormen et al., 2009).

If these properties hold, greedy algorithms can efficiently solve complex optimization problems in AI. However, if these conditions are not met, a greedy solution may be suboptimal, and more sophisticated methods, like dynamic programming, may be needed.

Use Cases of Greedy Algorithms in AI

1. Graph Traversal and Shortest Path: Dijkstra's Algorithm

Dijkstra's algorithm is a classic greedy algorithm used to solve the **shortest path problem** in a weighted graph. The algorithm works by selecting the node with the smallest known distance from the source and exploring its neighbors, updating their distances. It continues to select the smallest distance node and updates the neighboring nodes' distances until all nodes have been visited (Dijkstra, 1959).

Dijkstra's algorithm is widely used in AI for applications such as **robotic navigation**, **route planning**, and **network optimization**. The greedy strategy works optimally in this context because each locally optimal decision (choosing the shortest edge) contributes to the overall shortest path solution.

197

Python Code Example for Dijkstra's Algorithm

```python
import heapq

def dijkstra(graph, start):
    # Priority queue to store the minimum distance to each node
    queue = [(0, start)]
    distances = {node: float('inf') for node in graph}
    distances[start] = 0
    while queue:
        current_distance, current_node = heapq.heappop(queue)
        # If the current distance is greater than the stored distance, skip this node
        if current_distance > distances[current_node]:
            continue
        # Explore the neighbors of the current node
        for neighbor, weight in graph[current_node].items():
            distance = current_distance + weight
            # If a shorter path is found, update the distance and enqueue the neighbor
            if distance < distances[neighbor]:
                distances[neighbor] = distance
                heapq.heappush(queue, (distance, neighbor))
    return distances
```

```python
# Example usage
graph = {
    'A': {'B': 1, 'C': 4},
    'B': {'A': 1, 'C': 2, 'D': 5},
    'C': {'A': 4, 'B': 2, 'D': 1},
    'D': {'B': 5, 'C': 1}
}
distances = dijkstra(graph, 'A')
print("Shortest distances:", distances)
```

This code uses Dijkstra's algorithm to find the shortest path from the source node 'A' to all other nodes in the graph. The greedy strategy works here because selecting the shortest available path at each step leads to the overall shortest path in the graph.

Graph Representation of Dijkstra's Algorithm

The following visualization shows the progression of Dijkstra's algorithm as it finds the shortest path in a weighted graph:

```python
import matplotlib.pyplot as plt

import networkx as nx

# Create a weighted graph for visualization

def draw_dijkstra_graph():
    G = nx.Graph()
    # Add weighted edges
```

```python
G.add_edge('A', 'B', weight=1)
G.add_edge('A', 'C', weight=4)
G.add_edge('B', 'C', weight=2)
G.add_edge('B', 'D', weight=5)
G.add_edge('C', 'D', weight=1)
pos = nx.spring_layout(G)
labels = nx.get_edge_attributes(G, 'weight')
plt.figure(figsize=(8, 6))
nx.draw(G, pos, with_labels=True,
node_color="lightblue", node_size=3000, font_size=14,
font_weight="bold")
nx.draw_networkx_edge_labels(G, pos,
edge_labels=labels)
plt.title("Graph Representation for Dijkstra's Algorithm")
plt.show()
# Draw the graph
draw_dijkstra_graph()
```

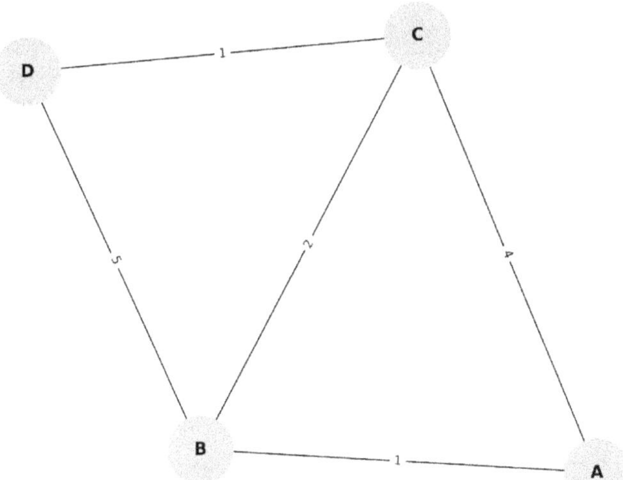

This graph represents the nodes and edges in the Dijkstra algorithm's context, showing the pathfinding process as it navigates the weighted connections between nodes.

2. Scheduling Problems: Job Sequencing with Deadlines

The **Job Sequencing Problem** is another classic optimization problem where a greedy algorithm is particularly effective. The goal is to maximize the total profit by scheduling jobs within their deadlines. Each job has a deadline and a profit associated with it, and the jobs must be completed before their deadline to earn the profit. The greedy algorithm sorts the jobs in descending order of profit and schedules each job in the latest available slot before its deadline, ensuring maximum profit (Kumar, 1992).

Python Code Example for Job Sequencing Problem

```
def job_sequencing(jobs, deadlines, profits):

    n = len(jobs)
```

```python
    # Sort jobs by descending profit

    sorted_jobs = sorted(zip(jobs, deadlines, profits),
key=lambda x: x[2], reverse=True)

    # Initialize result array for scheduled jobs and a boolean
array for tracking time slots

    result = [None] * n

    slot = [False] * n

    for job, deadline, profit in sorted_jobs:

        # Find a free slot for this job

        for j in range(min(n, deadline) - 1, -1, -1):

            if not slot[j]:

                result[j] = job

                slot[j] = True

                break

    return result

# Example usage

jobs = ['J1', 'J2', 'J3', 'J4']

deadlines = [2, 1, 2, 1]

profits = [100, 19, 27, 25]

scheduled_jobs = job_sequencing(jobs, deadlines, profits)

print("Scheduled jobs:", scheduled_jobs)
```

This algorithm schedules jobs to maximize profit by using a greedy strategy, selecting jobs with the highest profit first. The greedy approach works well here because each locally optimal choice (choosing the job with the highest profit) contributes to the overall goal of maximizing total profit.

3. Feature Selection in Machine Learning

In AI and machine learning, greedy algorithms are widely used for **feature selection**, where the goal is to select the most relevant features from a dataset to improve model performance. A common greedy approach for feature selection is the **greedy forward selection** method, which iteratively adds the feature that most improves the model's performance until no further improvement is possible (Guyon & Elisseeff, 2003).

Python Code Example for Greedy Feature Selection

```python
from sklearn.datasets import load_iris

from sklearn.model_selection import train_test_split

from sklearn.ensemble import RandomForestClassifier

from sklearn.metrics import accuracy_score

# Load dataset

data = load_iris()

X, y = data.data, data.target

# Split data into training and testing sets

X_train, X_test, y_train, y_test = train_test_split(X, y,
test_size=0.2, random_state=42)

# Initialize the model

model = RandomForestClassifier()

# Greedy forward feature selection
```

```python
def greedy_feature_selection(X_train, y_train, X_test, y_test):
    selected_features = []
    remaining_features = list(range(X_train.shape[1]))
    best_accuracy = 0
    while remaining_features:
        feature_accuracies = []
        for feature in remaining_features:
            features_to_test = selected_features + [feature]
            model.fit(X_train[:, features_to_test], y_train)
            predictions = model.predict(X_test[:, features_to_test])
            accuracy = accuracy_score(y_test, predictions)
            feature_accuracies.append((feature, accuracy))
        # Select the feature that gives the highest accuracy
        best_feature, best_feature_accuracy = max(feature_accuracies, key=lambda x: x[1])
        if best_feature_accuracy > best_accuracy:
            selected_features.append(best_feature)
            remaining_features.remove(best_feature)
            best_accuracy = best_feature_accuracy
        else:
            break
    return selected_features, best_accuracy
```

```
# Perform greedy feature selection

selected_features, accuracy =
greedy_feature_selection(X_train, y_train, X_test, y_test)

print("Selected features:", selected_features)

print("Best accuracy:", accuracy)
```

In this example, the greedy forward selection method adds the feature that most improves the model's accuracy at each iteration. This approach can be computationally efficient while still identifying the most important features, making it well-suited for large datasets and complex models.

Conclusion

Greedy algorithms offer an efficient and intuitive approach to solving a wide range of optimization problems in AI. They are particularly effective in problems where local decisions lead to global optima, such as Dijkstra's shortest path algorithm, job sequencing with deadlines, and feature selection in machine learning. While greedy algorithms are not always guaranteed to produce an optimal solution, they often provide computationally efficient and practical solutions, especially for real

Chapter 8: Divide and Conquer Algorithms

Overview and methodology

Divide and conquer is a widely used algorithmic paradigm that plays a crucial role in solving complex computational problems by breaking them down into smaller subproblems, solving these subproblems independently, and then combining their solutions to form the overall solution (Cormen et al., 2009). This paradigm is foundational for many artificial intelligence (AI) algorithms, particularly in areas requiring optimization and problem decomposition, such as search algorithms, pattern recognition, and machine learning model training. The strength of divide and conquer algorithms lies in their ability to exploit the problem structure by dividing it recursively, leading to efficiency gains both in terms of time complexity and resource utilization.

The essence of divide and conquer algorithms can be understood in three steps:

Divide: The original problem is broken down into several subproblems. These subproblems are typically similar to the original problem but smaller in size.

Conquer: The subproblems are solved recursively. If the subproblem size reaches a sufficiently small scale, it is solved directly.

Combine: The solutions of the subproblems are combined to produce the solution to the original problem.

This approach is particularly advantageous when dealing with recursive structures or problems that exhibit a "natural" decomposition, such as sorting, searching, or matrix operations (Tenenbaum & Leighton, 2016). Examples of classical algorithms that utilize the divide and conquer paradigm include Merge Sort, Quick Sort, and Binary Search.

Methodology

The divide and conquer approach is characterized by the recursive division of problems and the subsequent combination of solutions. Let us now examine this methodology through a deeper exploration of two prominent divide and conquer algorithms: Merge Sort and Quick Sort.

1. Merge Sort

Merge Sort is an efficient, stable sorting algorithm that follows the divide and conquer paradigm. It splits the input array into two halves, recursively sorts the two halves, and then merges the sorted halves to form the final sorted array. The merge operation is critical, as it ensures that the final result is a single, fully sorted array.

Algorithm:

```python
def merge_sort(arr):
    if len(arr) > 1:
        mid = len(arr) // 2
        left_half = arr[:mid]
        right_half = arr[mid:]
        # Recursive sorting
        merge_sort(left_half)
        merge_sort(right_half)
        # Merging the two halves
```

```python
        i = j = k = 0

        while i < len(left_half) and j < len(right_half):

            if left_half[i] < right_half[j]:

                arr[k] = left_half[i]

                i += 1

            else:

                arr[k] = right_half[j]

                j += 1

            k += 1

        # Collect remaining elements

        while i < len(left_half):

            arr[k] = left_half[i]

            i += 1

            k += 1

        while j < len(right_half):

            arr[k] = right_half[j]

            j += 1

            k += 1

    return arr
```

Time Complexity Analysis: The time complexity of Merge Sort is $O(n\log n)$, where n is the number of elements in the array. This results from the repeated division of the array (which requires $\log n$ \log nlogn divisions) and the merging step, which requires $O(n)$ operations (Cormen et al., 2009).

Graphical Representation: Imagine the input array as a large unsorted block. During each recursive call, the array is divided into smaller and smaller subarrays until each subarray contains only a single element. These subarrays are then merged step by step until the entire array is sorted.

$$6 \quad 5 \quad 3 \quad 1 \quad 8 \quad 7 \quad 2 \quad 4$$

2. Quick Sort

Quick Sort is another highly efficient sorting algorithm based on divide and conquer. Unlike Merge Sort, Quick Sort selects a pivot element from the array and partitions the other elements into two subarrays—those less than the pivot and those greater than the pivot. The subarrays are then sorted recursively.

Algorithm:

```
def quick_sort(arr):
    if len(arr) <= 1:
        return arr
    else:
        pivot = arr[0]
```

less = [x for x in arr[1:] if x <= pivot]

greater = [x for x in arr[1:] if x > pivot]

return quick_sort(less) + [pivot] + quick_sort(greater)

Time Complexity Analysis: The average-case time complexity of Quick Sort is $O(n\log n)$, but in the worst case (e.g., when the pivot is the smallest or largest element), it can degrade to $O(n2)$ (Tenenbaum & Leighton, 2016). However, its average performance is highly efficient, making it a popular choice for practical applications.

Graphical Representation: In Quick Sort, the array is recursively divided around the pivot element. Below is an illustration of the partitioning and sorting process:

Array: [10, 7, 8, 9, 1, 5]

Pivot: 10

Step 1: [7, 8, 9, 1, 5] + [10] + []

Recursively apply the same logic to the subarrays [7, 8, 9, 1, 5] and []

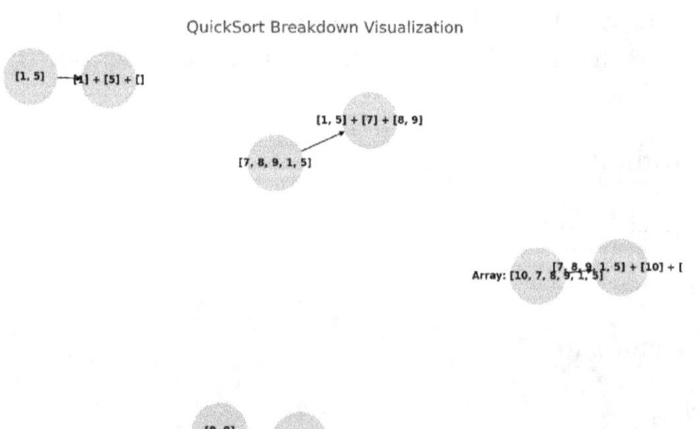

Application in AI Algorithms

Divide and conquer is especially pertinent in AI, particularly in domains where problems can be naturally broken down. Examples include:

Decision Trees: AI algorithms for decision trees, such as ID3 or C4.5, utilize divide and conquer by splitting data on the attribute that best divides the classes, recursively partitioning the dataset to construct the final tree (Quinlan, 1993).

Convolutional Neural Networks (CNNs): In image processing, CNNs leverage the divide and conquer approach by applying filters to smaller regions of the input image, which are combined in the pooling and fully connected layers for final classification (LeCun et al., 2015).

Parallel Processing: Many AI systems benefit from the inherent parallelism of divide and conquer algorithms. Each divided subproblem can be executed concurrently on separate processors, significantly enhancing the speed and efficiency of AI computations (Aho et al., 1983).

In summary, the divide and conquer paradigm forms a critical basis for many AI algorithms, helping achieve efficient solutions to complex problems by recursively breaking them into manageable subproblems. Its implementation in sorting algorithms like Merge Sort and Quick Sort illustrates the power of recursive decomposition and combination. Moreover, divide and conquer algorithms' scalability and suitability for parallelization make them indispensable in AI and other computational fields.

<u>Examples: Merge Sort, Quick Sort, Binary Search</u>

Divide and conquer algorithms are foundational in the design of efficient algorithms, particularly for AI applications. Among the most notable examples of divide and conquer algorithms are Merge Sort, Quick Sort, and Binary Search. These algorithms exemplify how complex problems can be solved more efficiently by recursively breaking them down into smaller, manageable subproblems, solving each independently, and then combining their results (Cormen et al., 2009).

1. Merge Sort

Merge Sort is an efficient, stable sorting algorithm that recursively splits an input array into two halves, sorts each half, and merges them to form the final sorted array (Cormen et al., 2009). It is particularly effective for large datasets because of its consistent $O(n\log n)$ time complexity, regardless of the initial order of the data.

Algorithm: The Merge Sort algorithm follows these steps:

Divide: Split the array into two halves.

Conquer: Recursively sort both halves.

Combine: Merge the two sorted halves into a single sorted array.

The merge operation is critical, as it ensures that two sorted arrays are combined efficiently.

Code Example:

```python
def merge_sort(arr):

    if len(arr) > 1:
```

```python
    mid = len(arr) // 2
    left_half = arr[:mid]
    right_half = arr[mid:]
    merge_sort(left_half)
    merge_sort(right_half)
    i = j = k = 0
    while i < len(left_half) and j < len(right_half):
        if left_half[i] < right_half[j]:
            arr[k] = left_half[i]
            i += 1
        else:
            arr[k] = right_half[j]
            j += 1
        k += 1
    while i < len(left_half):
        arr[k] = left_half[i]
        i += 1
        k += 1
    while j < len(right_half):
        arr[k] = right_half[j]
        j += 1
        k += 1
```

```
    return arr
```

In this example, the array is recursively divided until each half contains only a single element. Then, these halves are merged in a sorted manner. Merge Sort's worst-case time complexity is $O(n\log n)$, making it efficient even for large datasets (Tenenbaum & Leighton, 2016).

Graphical Representation of Merge Sort:

Initial array: [12, 11, 13, 5, 6, 7]

Divide: [12, 11, 13] | [5, 6, 7]

Divide further: [12, 11] | [13] | [5] | [6, 7]

Merge step 1:   [11, 12] | [13] | [5] | [6, 7]

Merge step 2:   [11, 12, 13] | [5, 6, 7]

Final merge: [5, 6, 7, 11, 12, 13]

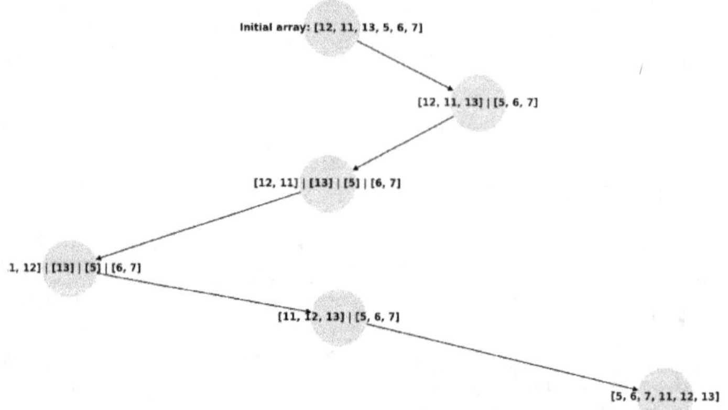

Merge Sort is particularly important in AI applications such as large-scale data processing where consistency and stability in sorting are crucial (Cormen et al., 2009).

2. Quick Sort

Quick Sort is another efficient sorting algorithm based on the divide and conquer approach. It selects a pivot element from the array and partitions the remaining elements into two subarrays: one with elements smaller than the pivot and one with elements greater than the pivot. Quick Sort is then recursively applied to both subarrays (Hoare, 1961).

Algorithm:

Divide: Choose a pivot element and partition the array around it.

Conquer: Recursively apply Quick Sort to the subarrays formed by partitioning.

Combine: Once the subarrays are sorted, combine them.

Unlike Merge Sort, Quick Sort does not require a separate merge step, as the array is sorted during the partitioning process.

Code Example:

```python
def quick_sort(arr):
    if len(arr) <= 1:
        return arr
    else:
        pivot = arr[0]
        less = [x for x in arr[1:] if x <= pivot]
        greater = [x for x in arr[1:] if x > pivot]
        return quick_sort(less) + [pivot] + quick_sort(greater)
```

In this example, the array is partitioned based on the pivot, and the process is applied recursively to the subarrays. Quick Sort's average-case time complexity is $O(n\log n)$, but its worst-case time complexity can degrade to $O(n2)$, although this is rare with appropriate pivot selection (Tenenbaum & Leighton, 2016).

Graphical Representation of Quick Sort:

Initial array: [10, 7, 8, 9, 1, 5]

Pivot: 10

Step 1: [7, 8, 9, 1, 5] + [10] + []

Recursive steps:

Pivot: 7 => [1, 5] + [7] + [8, 9]

Final sorted array: [1, 5, 7, 8, 9, 10]

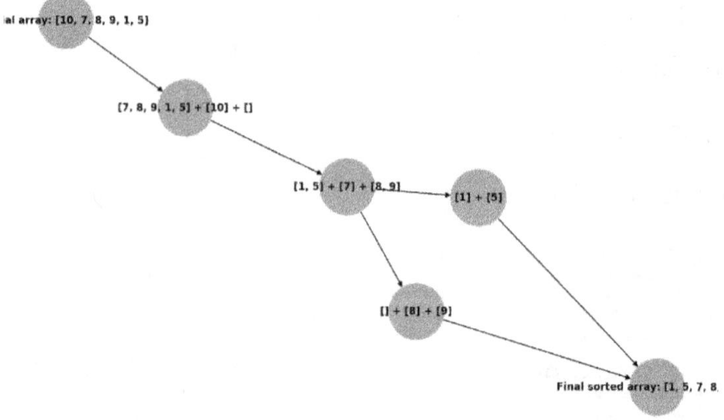

Quick Sort is commonly used in AI tasks where in-place sorting is required and average-case efficiency is critical (Hoare, 1961).

3. Binary Search

Binary Search is a divide and conquer algorithm used to efficiently search for a target value in a sorted array. Instead of searching the entire array, Binary Search repeatedly divides the array in half, comparing the target value to the middle element and reducing the search space accordingly (Knuth, 1998).

Algorithm:

Divide: Find the middle element of the array.

Conquer: Compare the target value to the middle element.

If the target is equal to the middle element, return the index.

If the target is less than the middle element, recursively search the left subarray.

If the target is greater than the middle element, recursively search the right subarray.

Combine: Return the result of the recursive search.

Code Example:

```python
def binary_search(arr, target):
    low, high = 0, len(arr) - 1
    while low <= high:
        mid = (low + high) // 2
        if arr[mid] == target:
            return mid
        elif arr[mid] < target:
            low = mid + 1
```

```
    else:

        high = mid - 1

return -1
```

In this example, the array is repeatedly halved, and the search continues in the relevant half based on the comparison of the middle element and the target value. Binary Search operates with a time complexity of O(log n), making it highly efficient for large datasets (Knuth, 1998).

Graphical Representation of Binary Search:

Array: [1, 3, 5, 7, 9, 11, 13]

Target: 9

Step 1: Middle element is 7

Step 2: 9 > 7, search right half

Step 3: Middle element is 9, target found at index 4

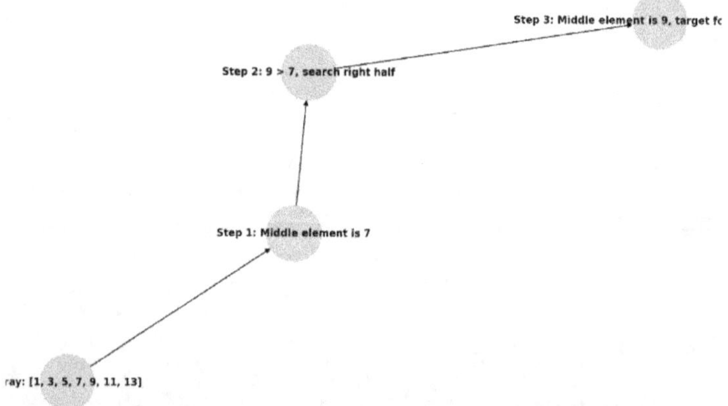

Binary Search is widely used in AI algorithms for optimizing search processes, particularly in decision trees and search-based algorithms (Knuth, 1998).

In summary, the divide and conquer paradigm is a cornerstone of efficient algorithm design, exemplified by the Merge Sort, Quick Sort, and Binary Search algorithms. Each of these algorithms demonstrates the power of recursive problem-solving in reducing the computational complexity of common tasks such as sorting and searching. These algorithms are crucial for AI applications where efficiency and scalability are essential, particularly when dealing with large datasets.

Application to AI problem-solving techniques

Divide and conquer is a fundamental algorithmic paradigm that is extensively applied in artificial intelligence (AI) problem-solving techniques. This methodology works by decomposing complex problems into simpler subproblems, solving each independently, and then combining the solutions to form the final solution (Cormen et al., 2009). The divide and conquer approach is particularly powerful in AI because many AI problems exhibit recursive structures that naturally lend themselves to this paradigm. These include tasks such as classification, optimization, and search problems, which are pivotal in fields like machine learning, computer vision, and natural language processing.

In the context of AI, divide and conquer methods are used to enhance efficiency, scalability, and performance by breaking down large, intractable problems into manageable components. The recursive decomposition of problems allows for parallel computation, making it well-suited for distributed AI systems (Aho et al., 1983). Additionally, many

219

AI algorithms, such as decision trees, neural networks, and genetic algorithms, either directly implement or implicitly follow the divide and conquer approach.

Applications of Divide and Conquer in AI Problem-Solving

1. Decision Tree Algorithms

One of the most prominent applications of the divide and conquer approach in AI is in decision tree algorithms. A decision tree is a supervised learning technique used for classification and regression tasks. The core principle of a decision tree involves recursively splitting the dataset based on the most informative attribute at each node. This recursive splitting is a direct application of the divide and conquer paradigm (Quinlan, 1993).

In decision trees, the algorithm divides the dataset into smaller subsets, evaluates each subset by selecting the attribute that best splits the data, and recursively applies this process to each subset. This continues until all the data is classified or a stopping criterion is met. Once all subproblems (subsets) are solved, the solutions (classifications or predictions) are combined to form the final decision tree.

Code Example:

```
from sklearn.tree import DecisionTreeClassifier

from sklearn.datasets import load_iris

from sklearn.model_selection import train_test_split

# Load dataset and split it into training and testing sets

iris = load_iris()
```

X_train, X_test, y_train, y_test = train_test_split(iris.data, iris.target, test_size=0.3)

Initialize and train the decision tree classifier

clf = DecisionTreeClassifier()

clf.fit(X_train, y_train)

Make predictions

predictions = clf.predict(X_test)

In this example, the DecisionTreeClassifier from the Scikit-learn library divides the dataset recursively at each node, employing the divide and conquer approach to create a model that classifies the iris dataset (Pedregosa et al., 2011).

Graphical Representation of a Simple Decision Tree: A decision tree divides the dataset into smaller subsets based on the most significant feature until all data points are classified:

Root Node: Petal Length

├── Petal Length < 2.5: Class = Setosa

└── Petal Length >= 2.5:

    ├── Petal Width < 1.8: Class = Versicolor

    └── Petal Width >= 1.8: Class = Virginica

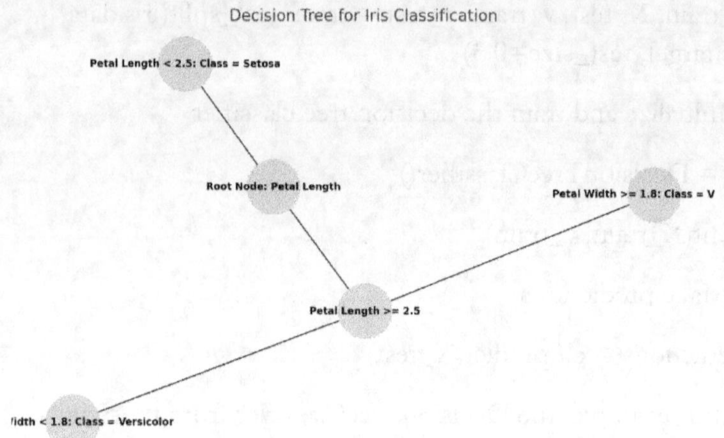

2. Neural Networks

Neural networks, particularly convolutional neural networks (CNNs), are another example of AI techniques that implicitly rely on the divide and conquer paradigm. CNNs, used extensively in image recognition and computer vision, divide the input image into smaller regions, apply filters to each region, and aggregate the results to generate the final classification or prediction (LeCun et al., 2015).

In CNNs, the image is broken down into smaller, overlapping patches by convolutional layers. These patches are processed independently through filters that extract features such as edges, textures, or patterns. After processing, the results are aggregated via pooling layers, effectively reducing the dimensionality of the image. The final fully connected layers combine all the intermediate results into a single prediction, employing the same divide and conquer principle.

Code Example:

```
from keras.models import Sequential
```

```python
from keras.layers import Conv2D, MaxPooling2D, Flatten, Dense

# Initialize the CNN model

model = Sequential()

# Add convolutional and pooling layers

model.add(Conv2D(32, kernel_size=(3, 3), activation='relu', input_shape=(64, 64, 3)))

model.add(MaxPooling2D(pool_size=(2, 2)))

# Flatten and add fully connected layers

model.add(Flatten())

model.add(Dense(128, activation='relu'))

model.add(Dense(10, activation='softmax'))

# Compile and summarize the model

model.compile(optimizer='adam', loss='categorical_crossentropy', metrics=['accuracy'])

model.summary()
```

In this CNN model, the convolutional layers divide the image into smaller regions, extract features, and ultimately aggregate the information to make a prediction. This divide and conquer approach enhances the network's ability to efficiently process large amounts of visual data.

3. Genetic Algorithms

Genetic algorithms (GAs), which are inspired by the process of natural evolution, also apply divide and conquer principles in their problem-solving techniques. Genetic algorithms operate by dividing the search space into multiple potential solutions (chromosomes), evolving these solutions through processes such as selection, crossover, and mutation, and combining the best solutions to find an optimal or near-optimal result (Holland, 1992).

The genetic algorithm begins by generating an initial population of potential solutions. It evaluates the fitness of each solution, selects the best solutions, and recombines them to form new populations. This cycle continues, recursively improving the solutions at each step, until a termination criterion is met. The process of evolving the population is an application of divide and conquer, where each subpopulation represents a partial solution to the overall optimization problem.

Code Example:

```python
import random

# Define fitness function

def fitness(individual):

    return sum(individual)

# Initialize population

population = [[random.randint(0, 1) for _ in range(6)] for _ in range(10)]

# Genetic Algorithm process: Selection, Crossover, Mutation

for generation in range(100):

    population = sorted(population, key=lambda x: fitness(x), reverse=True)

    next_generation = population[:5]  # Select top 50%

    # Crossover and Mutation
```

```python
for i in range(5, 10):

    parent1, parent2 = random.sample(next_generation[:5], 2)

    crossover_point = random.randint(1, 5)

    child = parent1[:crossover_point] + parent2[crossover_point:]

    next_generation.append(child)

population = next_generation
```

In this simple genetic algorithm, a population is recursively evolved, with each generation of solutions representing a recursive refinement of the overall optimization problem.

Conclusion

The divide and conquer approach is integral to many AI problem-solving techniques. Whether explicitly implemented, as in decision trees, or implicitly followed, as in convolutional neural networks and genetic algorithms, the divide and conquer paradigm allows for efficient decomposition and recombination of solutions. Its recursive nature and scalability make it highly effective in AI, particularly for tasks involving large datasets and complex problem spaces.

Part 3: Machine Learning Algorithms
Chapter 9: Introduction to Machine Learning

<u>Supervised, Unsupervised, and Reinforcement Learning</u>

Machine learning (ML) is a subfield of artificial intelligence (AI) focused on creating algorithms that allow computers to learn from and make predictions or decisions based on data. This capability has transformed numerous fields, such as natural language processing, computer vision, and robotics, by enabling systems to automatically improve their performance without being explicitly programmed (Mitchell, 1997). Machine learning algorithms are broadly classified into three main types: supervised learning, unsupervised learning, and reinforcement learning. Each type of learning addresses different types of problems and leverages different methods for learning from data.

1. Supervised Learning

Supervised learning is a type of machine learning where the algorithm learns from labeled data, meaning each input is paired with the correct output. The goal of supervised learning is to learn a mapping from inputs to outputs, which can then be used to predict the outputs for new, unseen inputs. Supervised learning is widely used in tasks such as classification and regression (Bishop, 2006).

In supervised learning, the model iteratively refines its parameters by minimizing the error between its predictions and the actual labels in the training data. Common algorithms used in supervised learning include decision trees, support vector machines, and neural networks (Goodfellow et al., 2016).

Example: A simple example of supervised learning is using a decision tree to classify flowers in the Iris dataset based on features like petal length and width.

Code Example:

```python
from sklearn.datasets import load_iris

from sklearn.model_selection import train_test_split

from sklearn.tree import DecisionTreeClassifier

# Load dataset and split it into training and testing sets

iris = load_iris()

X_train, X_test, y_train, y_test = train_test_split(iris.data, iris.target, test_size=0.3)

# Initialize and train the decision tree classifier

clf = DecisionTreeClassifier()

clf.fit(X_train, y_train)

# Make predictions

predictions = clf.predict(X_test)
```

In this case, the decision tree learns from labeled data, where each flower has a known class (e.g., Setosa, Versicolor, Virginica). The model is then able to classify new flowers based on their feature measurements.

Graphical Representation: The decision tree built from the data can be represented as:

Root Node: Petal Length

```
├── Petal Length < 2.5: Class = Setosa
└── Petal Length >= 2.5:
```

├── Petal Width < 1.8: Class = Versicolor

└── Petal Width >= 1.8: Class = Virginica

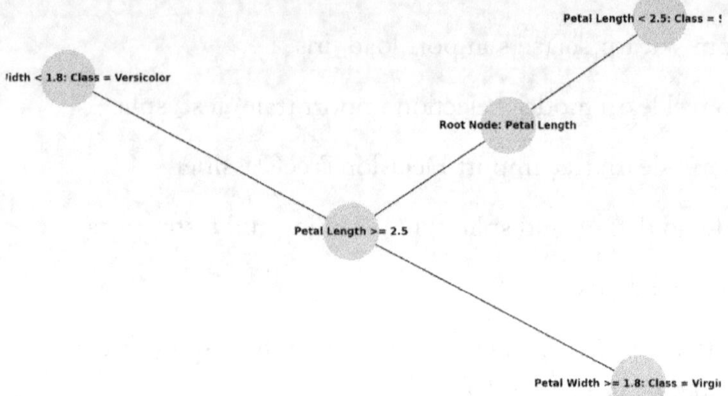

This representation shows how the decision tree uses labeled data to make classifications based on thresholds in the features.

2. Unsupervised Learning

Unsupervised learning differs from supervised learning in that the algorithm is given unlabeled data and must find hidden patterns or structures within the data. The main goal of unsupervised learning is to explore the data's underlying structure without explicit feedback on what the correct output should be (Hastie et al., 2009). Common tasks in unsupervised learning include clustering, association, and dimensionality reduction.

In clustering, for instance, the algorithm groups data points into clusters based on similarity. Common algorithms include k-means clustering, hierarchical clustering, and Gaussian mixture models.

Example: A typical use case for unsupervised learning is clustering customers based on purchasing behavior to identify different market segments.

Code Example:

```
from sklearn.datasets import load_iris

from sklearn.cluster import KMeans

# Load dataset and apply k-means clustering

iris = load_iris()

kmeans = KMeans(n_clusters=3)

kmeans.fit(iris.data)

# Get cluster assignments

cluster_assignments = kmeans.predict(iris.data)
```

In this example, k-means clustering is used to group the Iris flowers into three clusters. The algorithm does not have access to any labels, meaning it must learn the grouping structure of the data based solely on the feature values.

Graphical Representation of Clusters:

Cluster 1: Centroid at (5.1, 3.5, 1.4, 0.2) [corresponds to Setosa]

Cluster 2: Centroid at (6.0, 2.7, 4.5, 1.5) [corresponds to Versicolor]

Cluster 3: Centroid at (6.7, 3.1, 5.6, 2.2) [corresponds to Virginica]

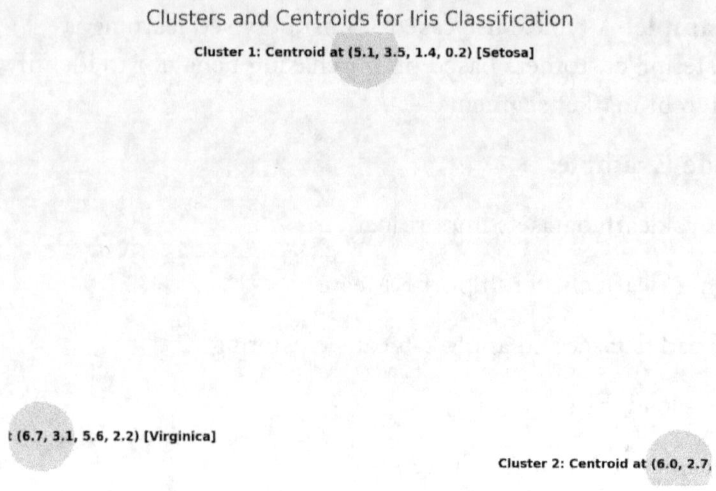

Clusters and Centroids for Iris Classification

Cluster 1: Centroid at (5.1, 3.5, 1.4, 0.2) [Setosa]

t (6.7, 3.1, 5.6, 2.2) [Virginica]

Cluster 2: Centroid at (6.0, 2.7,

Reimport the necessary dataset and clustering for the graph to work properly

from sklearn.datasets import load_iris

from sklearn.cluster import KMeans

Load dataset

iris = load_iris()

Apply k-means clustering

kmeans = KMeans(n_clusters=3, random_state=0)

kmeans.fit(iris.data)

Reduce the dimensions of the Iris data for visualization using PCA

pca = PCA(n_components=2)

iris_2d = pca.fit_transform(iris.data)

Plot the clusters with k-means assignments

```python
plt.figure(figsize=(8, 6))

colors = np.array(['red', 'green', 'blue'])

cluster_assignments = kmeans.predict(iris.data)

plt.scatter(iris_2d[:, 0], iris_2d[:, 1],
c=colors[cluster_assignments], s=50, alpha=0.7)

# Add centroids of the clusters

centroids_2d = pca.transform(kmeans.cluster_centers_)

plt.scatter(centroids_2d[:, 0], centroids_2d[:, 1], c='black',
s=200, marker='x')

plt.title("K-Means Clustering on Iris Dataset (PCA
Reduced)")

plt.xlabel("Principal Component 1")

plt.ylabel("Principal Component 2")

plt.grid(True)

plt.show()
```

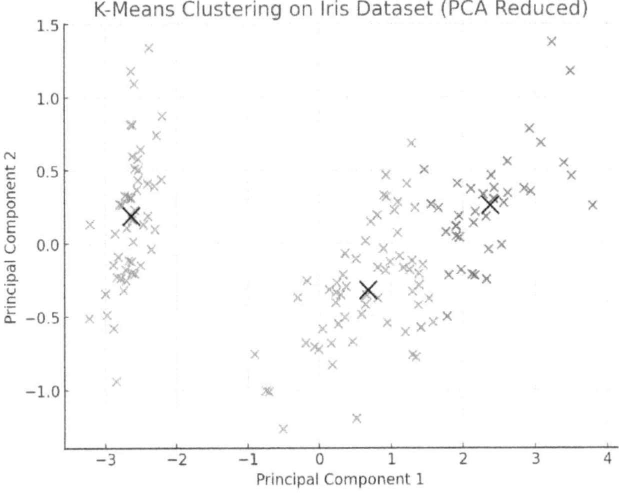

The graph above represents the results of applying k-means clustering on the Iris dataset, visualized after reducing the dimensions using PCA. The different clusters are shown in distinct colors, and the black 'X' marks represent the centroids of each cluster. This visualization illustrates how unsupervised learning can group data points based on their features, even without predefined labels.

3. Reinforcement Learning

Reinforcement learning (RL) is a type of machine learning where an agent learns to make decisions by interacting with an environment and receiving feedback in the form of rewards or punishments. Unlike supervised and unsupervised learning, reinforcement learning focuses on learning a policy that maximizes cumulative rewards over time, rather than optimizing predictions based on a static dataset (Sutton & Barto, 2018).

In reinforcement learning, an agent explores various actions and learns from the feedback it receives (reward or penalty) after each action. Over time, the agent builds an understanding of which actions yield the highest rewards and modifies its strategy accordingly. RL is commonly used in autonomous systems, robotics, and game-playing AI, such as AlphaGo (Silver et al., 2016).

Example: An example of reinforcement learning is training an agent to navigate a maze by rewarding it for finding the correct path and penalizing it for taking wrong turns.

Code Example:

```python
import numpy as np

# Define a simple environment with rewards

rewards = np.array([[0, -1, 0], [-1, 10, -1], [0, -1, 0]])
```

```python
actions = [(0, 1), (1, 0), (0, -1), (-1, 0)]  # Right, Down, Left, Up

# Initialize Q-values (quality of actions)

Q = np.zeros((3, 3, 4))

# Reinforcement learning algorithm (Q-learning)

def choose_action(state):

    return np.argmax(Q[state])

def update_q(state, action, reward, new_state):

    lr = 0.1  # learning rate

    discount = 0.9

    best_future_q = np.max(Q[new_state])

    Q[state][action] += lr * (reward + discount * best_future_q - Q[state][action])

# Simulate a learning agent in this environment

# This is simplified without full exploration logic for clarity.
```

This code demonstrates the setup of a basic reinforcement learning problem using Q-learning, a commonly used RL algorithm. The agent navigates a simple grid-based environment, learning to take actions that maximize the reward over time.

In summary, supervised, unsupervised, and reinforcement learning each address distinct types of problems in machine learning, enabling systems to learn from labeled data, find patterns in unlabeled data, or make sequential decisions through trial and error, respectively. As machine learning continues to evolve, these approaches remain critical to building intelligent systems that can adapt, classify, and make complex decisions across a wide range of applications.

Basic workflow

The basic workflow of a machine learning (ML) project consists of several interconnected stages, which enable the systematic design, implementation, and evaluation of models. This workflow typically follows four major steps: data collection, feature extraction, model training, and evaluation. These steps form the foundation for developing machine learning solutions that can effectively analyze data and generate predictions or classifications (Bishop, 2006). Each phase is critical to the success of the machine learning pipeline, ensuring that the model performs accurately and efficiently in real-world applications.

1. Data Collection

The first step in the machine learning workflow is **data collection**. This process involves gathering relevant data from various sources, such as databases, sensors, or web scraping. The quality and quantity of the data significantly impact the performance of the model. Data should be representative of the problem domain, and it is often necessary to ensure that the data is clean and preprocessed before moving to the next stages (Kelleher, Namee, & D'Arcy, 2015).

The collected data can be of various types, such as structured (tabular data), unstructured (text, images), or semi-structured (XML, JSON). Proper data collection ensures that the model has enough information to learn patterns and generalize to unseen data.

Example: In a simple project aimed at predicting house prices, the data collection step could involve gathering historical sales data, including features like the number of bedrooms, square footage, and location.

import pandas as pd

Load the dataset

data = pd.read_csv('house_prices.csv')

Inspect the first few rows of the dataset

print(data.head())

This code demonstrates the process of loading a dataset from a CSV file, a common format used in structured data collection.

2. Feature Extraction

Once data is collected, the next step is **feature extraction**. Feature extraction involves selecting the most relevant variables (features) from the data that will be used to train the machine learning model. In many cases, raw data is not directly suitable for model training, so it must be transformed into meaningful representations. Effective feature extraction is essential for improving the performance and accuracy of the model (Guyon & Elisseeff, 2003).

This step often involves:

Normalization: Scaling numerical features to a common range.

Encoding categorical variables: Transforming categorical data into numerical form using methods like one-hot encoding or label encoding.

Dimensionality reduction: Reducing the number of features while retaining essential information, such as using Principal Component Analysis (PCA).

Example: In a project where you are building a model to predict house prices, important features might include the size of the house, the number of rooms, and the location. The data might also need to be normalized or transformed.

```python
from sklearn.preprocessing import StandardScaler

# Extract features and normalize them

features = data[['bedrooms', 'bathrooms', 'sqft_living', 'floors']]

scaler = StandardScaler()

normalized_features = scaler.fit_transform(features)

print(normalized_features[:5])  # Display the first five rows of normalized features
```

In this code, numerical features are extracted from the dataset and normalized, a common step to ensure that the model treats each feature equally.

3. Model Training

Once the data is prepared and relevant features are extracted, the next step is **model training**. In this stage, the selected machine learning algorithm learns from the data by adjusting its parameters to minimize errors in predictions. Model training typically involves splitting the dataset into training and validation sets. The model is trained on the training set, and its performance is periodically evaluated on the validation set to avoid overfitting (Goodfellow et al., 2016).

There are numerous machine learning algorithms available for model training, depending on the type of problem (e.g., regression, classification, clustering). Common algorithms include linear regression, decision trees, support vector machines, and neural networks.

Example: Using a linear regression model to predict house prices based on the features extracted earlier:

```
from sklearn.model_selection import train_test_split

from sklearn.linear_model import LinearRegression

# Split the data into training and test sets

X_train, X_test, y_train, y_test =
train_test_split(normalized_features, data['price'],
test_size=0.2)

# Train the linear regression model

model = LinearRegression()

model.fit(X_train, y_train)

# Predict prices for the test set

predictions = model.predict(X_test)
```

This code demonstrates how a linear regression model is trained using the training data. The model learns the relationship between the input features and the house prices, allowing it to predict prices for new, unseen houses.

4. Model Evaluation

The final step in the machine learning workflow is **model evaluation**. In this stage, the performance of the trained model is assessed using evaluation metrics. The goal of evaluation is to determine how well the model generalizes to new data and to identify potential areas for improvement (Hastie, Tibshirani, & Friedman, 2009).

Common evaluation metrics include:

Accuracy: The proportion of correct predictions (used for classification).

Mean Squared Error (MSE): Measures the average squared difference between the predicted and actual values (used for regression).

Precision, Recall, and F1 Score: Used for evaluating classification models, particularly in cases of imbalanced datasets.

After evaluating the model on the test set, it is possible to fine-tune the model's parameters (hyperparameters) using techniques such as cross-validation and grid search to further improve performance.

Example: Continuing the house price prediction example, the model's performance can be evaluated using metrics like Mean Squared Error (MSE).

```
from sklearn.metrics import mean_squared_error

# Evaluate the model's performance on the test set

mse = mean_squared_error(y_test, predictions)

print(f'Mean Squared Error: {mse}')
```

In this example, the MSE is calculated to determine the average error in the predicted house prices. Lower MSE values indicate a better model performance.

Graphical Representation:

Basic Machine Learning Workflow

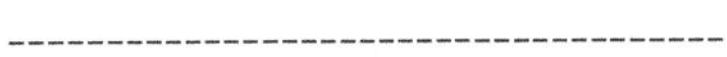

| Data Collection -> Feature Extraction -> Model
Training -> Model Evaluation |

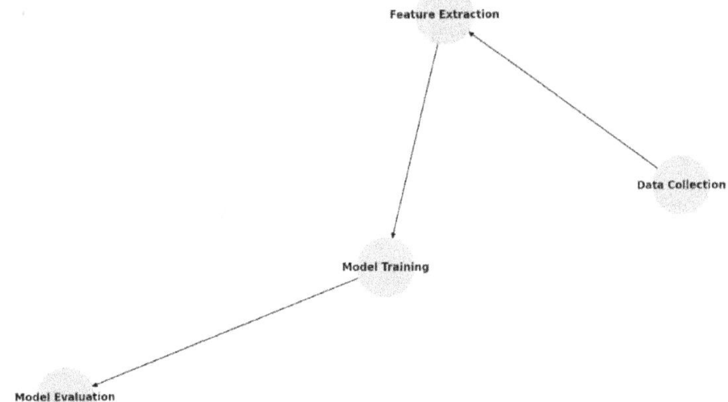

A graph can be used to represent this workflow visually, showing the data flow from one step to the next, with feedback loops for model tuning and improvement.

Conclusion

The basic workflow of machine learning—from data collection and feature extraction to model training and evaluation—provides a structured approach to solving complex problems. Each step is integral to the success of the machine learning model, with careful attention required to ensure the data is representative, features are meaningful, the model is well-tuned, and evaluation metrics accurately reflect performance. Following this workflow enables the development of robust machine learning solutions that generalize effectively to real-world scenarios.

Chapter 10: Regression Algorithms

Linear Regression, Polynomial Regression

Regression algorithms are a fundamental class of supervised machine learning algorithms used to model the relationship between a dependent variable (target) and one or more independent variables (features). The goal of regression is to predict continuous outcomes, such as predicting house prices, stock prices, or sales forecasts, based on various input features. Among the most commonly used regression techniques are **Linear Regression** and **Polynomial Regression**, each with distinct methodologies for fitting models to data (Bishop, 2006).

1. Linear Regression

Linear Regression is one of the simplest and most interpretable regression algorithms. It assumes a linear relationship between the independent variables and the dependent variable. In a univariate setting, this relationship can be expressed as:

$$y = \beta_0 + \beta_1 x + \epsilon$$

where:

- y is the dependent variable (target),
- x is the independent variable (feature),
- β_0 is the intercept,
- β_1 is the slope (coefficient) of the independent variable, and
- ϵ represents the error term (residuals).

In multivariate linear regression, where multiple independent variables are used, the equation extends to:

$$y = \beta_0 + \beta_1 x_1 + \beta_2 x_2 + \cdots + \beta_n x_n + \epsilon$$

The coefficients ($\beta 0$, $\beta 1$,…,βn) are learned from the data by minimizing the **sum of squared residuals**, which is the difference between the observed values and the predicted values. The method used to minimize this difference is often **Ordinary Least Squares (OLS)** (Seber & Lee, 2012).

Code Example:

```python
import numpy as np

from sklearn.linear_model import LinearRegression

import matplotlib.pyplot as plt

# Example dataset: relationship between square footage and house prices

X = np.array([500, 750, 1000, 1250, 1500]).reshape(-1, 1)

y = np.array([100000, 150000, 200000, 250000, 300000])

# Create and fit the linear regression model

model = LinearRegression()

model.fit(X, y)

# Predict house prices

predictions = model.predict(X)

# Plot the data points and the regression line

plt.scatter(X, y, color='blue', label='Data Points')

plt.plot(X, predictions, color='red', label='Regression Line')

plt.xlabel('Square Footage')

plt.ylabel('House Price')

plt.title('Linear Regression: House Prices vs Square Footage')
```

plt.legend()

plt.show()

This code demonstrates a simple univariate linear regression model that predicts house prices based on the square footage of houses. The red line represents the fitted linear regression line, showing the relationship between square footage and house prices.

Graphical Representation: Linear regression fits a straight line to the data points. The graph illustrates the data points and the corresponding regression line, which minimizes the sum of squared residuals between the observed and predicted values.

Time Complexity:

The time complexity of linear regression using the ordinary least squares method is O(n2m)O(n^2m)O(n2m), where nnn is the number of features and mmm is the number of samples. This makes linear regression efficient for datasets with a moderate number of features but less ideal for high-dimensional data (Bishop, 2006).

2. Polynomial Regression

Polynomial Regression is an extension of linear regression that allows for modeling non-linear relationships by introducing polynomial terms to the model. In polynomial regression, the input variables are raised to a power, allowing the model to capture more complex patterns in the data (Draper & Smith, 1998). The relationship between the independent and dependent variables is expressed as:

$$y = \beta_0 + \beta_1 x + \beta_2 x^2 + \beta_3 x^3 + \cdots + \beta_n x^n + \epsilon$$

Here, higher-order terms $(e.g., x^2, x^3)$ allow the regression curve to fit data points in a non-linear fashion, which is particularly useful when the relationship between the variables is not strictly linear.

Code Example:

```python
from sklearn.preprocessing import PolynomialFeatures

# Generate polynomial features (degree 2)

poly = PolynomialFeatures(degree=2)

X_poly = poly.fit_transform(X)

# Fit the polynomial regression model

poly_model = LinearRegression()

poly_model.fit(X_poly, y)

# Predict using the polynomial model

poly_predictions = poly_model.predict(X_poly)

# Plot the data points and the polynomial regression curve

plt.scatter(X, y, color='blue', label='Data Points')

plt.plot(X, poly_predictions, color='green', label='Polynomial Regression Curve')

plt.xlabel('Square Footage')

plt.ylabel('House Price')

plt.title('Polynomial Regression: House Prices vs Square Footage')

plt.legend()

plt.show()
```

In this code, we apply **Polynomial Regression** to the same house price dataset. By transforming the input variable into its polynomial form (degree 2), the model can fit a non-linear curve that better captures the underlying relationship between square footage and house price.

Graphical Representation: In contrast to the straight line of linear regression, polynomial regression fits a curved line to the data, allowing it to model more complex patterns in the dataset.

Time Complexity:

The time complexity of polynomial regression is generally higher than that of linear regression due to the additional polynomial features. The time complexity can be approximated as $O(mnd) O(mn^d) O(mnd)$, where ddd is the degree of the polynomial, nnn is the number of features, and mmm is the number of samples (Draper & Smith, 1998). The higher the degree of the polynomial, the more computationally expensive the model becomes.

Applications and Use Cases

Linear Regression is widely used in fields such as economics, finance, and social sciences where linear relationships between variables are common. For example, it can be used to predict sales based on advertising expenditure or to analyze the effect of temperature on energy consumption (Seber & Lee, 2012).

Polynomial Regression is often used when relationships between variables are more complex. Common applications include modeling the growth of populations, the spread of diseases, and stock market trends, where the data does not follow a linear trend and higher-order polynomial terms are necessary to capture the complexity of the relationships (Draper & Smith, 1998).

Limitations

Linear Regression is limited in its ability to model non-linear relationships. When the relationship between the variables is complex, a straight-line model will produce poor results.

Polynomial Regression can easily overfit the training data if the degree of the polynomial is too high. Overfitting occurs when the model becomes too complex, capturing noise in the training data rather than the underlying trend (Bishop, 2006).

In summary, both linear and polynomial regression are powerful tools in machine learning for modeling relationships between variables. Linear regression is ideal for modeling simple linear relationships, while polynomial regression is used to capture more complex, non-linear patterns. The choice of model depends on the nature of the data and the complexity of the relationship being modeled. Understanding the strengths and limitations of these algorithms is crucial for selecting the appropriate regression technique in machine learning applications.

Logistic Regression

Logistic regression is a supervised machine learning algorithm used for binary classification tasks, where the goal is to predict a categorical outcome, typically coded as 0 or 1. Despite its name, logistic regression is used for classification rather than regression tasks. The algorithm models the probability that a given input belongs to one of two categories by using the logistic (or sigmoid) function. Logistic regression has been widely applied in fields such as medical diagnosis, marketing, and social sciences (Hosmer, Lemeshow, & Sturdivant, 2013).

Logistic Regression Model

Logistic regression models the relationship between a set of independent variables (features) and a binary dependent variable (class label) by applying a logistic function to a linear combination of the input features. This allows the model to output probabilities rather than continuous values, which can then be converted into class labels (0 or 1) by setting a threshold, typically 0.5.

The mathematical formulation of logistic regression is as follows:

$$p(y = 1|x) = \frac{1}{1 + e^{-(\beta_0 + \beta_1 x_1 + \beta_2 x_2 + \cdots + \beta_n x_n)}}$$

where:

- $p(y = 1|x)$ is the probability that the class label y is 1 given the input x,
- β_0 is the intercept,
- $\beta_1, \beta_2, \ldots, \beta_n$ are the coefficients (weights) associated with the independent variables $x_1, x_2, \ldots, x_n$,
- e is the base of the natural logarithm.

The output of this function is a probability value between 0 and 1, which can be interpreted as the likelihood that the input belongs to class 1. A threshold is then applied to determine the final classification.

Decision Boundary

Logistic regression uses a **decision boundary** to separate the two classes. The decision boundary is a hyperplane that divides the feature space into two regions, one for each class. For binary classification, the decision boundary is typically linear, although logistic regression can be extended to non-linear decision boundaries by incorporating polynomial features or using kernel methods (Hosmer et al., 2013).

Code Example

Below is an example of logistic regression used to classify whether a student will pass or fail an exam based on their study hours.

```
import numpy as np

from sklearn.linear_model import LogisticRegression

import matplotlib.pyplot as plt

# Sample data: Hours studied and pass/fail (1 = pass, 0 = fail)

X = np.array([[1], [2], [3], [4], [5], [6], [7], [8], [9], [10]])

y = np.array([0, 0, 0, 0, 1, 1, 1, 1, 1, 1])

# Create and fit the logistic regression model

model = LogisticRegression()

model.fit(X, y)

# Generate predictions and probabilities

predictions = model.predict(X)

probabilities = model.predict_proba(X)[:, 1]

# Plot the data points and the logistic regression curve

plt.scatter(X, y, color='blue', label='Data Points')

plt.plot(X, probabilities, color='red', label='Logistic Regression Curve')

plt.xlabel('Hours Studied')
```

plt.ylabel('Probability of Passing')

plt.title('Logistic Regression: Probability of Passing vs Hours Studied')

plt.legend()

plt.show()

In this example, logistic regression is used to predict the probability that a student will pass an exam based on the number of hours they studied. The red curve represents the logistic function, which outputs the probability that the outcome will be 1 (pass).

Graphical Representation

The graph produced by logistic regression shows the sigmoid curve, which smoothly transitions between 0 and 1. The curve represents the predicted probability that an input belongs to class 1 (pass). For inputs to the left of the decision boundary, the predicted probability is less than 0.5, classifying them as 0 (fail). For inputs to the right of the decision boundary, the probability is greater than 0.5, classifying them as 1 (pass).

Logistic Function (Sigmoid Function)

The key to logistic regression is the use of the **sigmoid function**, also known as the logistic function:

$$\sigma(z) = \frac{1}{1 + e^{-z}}$$

This function outputs values between 0 and 1, making it ideal for binary classification problems. As z becomes large and positive, $\sigma(z)$ approaches 1, indicating a high probability that the input belongs to class 1. Conversely, as z becomes large and negative, $\sigma(z)$ approaches 0, indicating a high probability that the input belongs to class 0.

Cost Function and Optimization

In logistic regression, the model parameters (coefficients) are learned by minimizing the **log-likelihood cost function**. The goal is to maximize the likelihood that the model correctly classifies the training data. The cost function is given by:

$$J(\beta) = -\frac{1}{m} \sum_{i=1}^{m} [y_i \log(p_i) + (1 - y_i) \log(1 - p_i)]$$

where:

- m is the number of training examples,
- y_i is the true label for the i-th training example,
- p_i is the predicted probability for the i-th training example.

The optimization algorithm used to minimize the cost function is typically **gradient descent** or a variation such as **stochastic gradient descent** (SGD). The gradient descent algorithm iteratively updates the model parameters in the direction that minimizes the cost function (Bishop, 2006).

Regularization

To prevent overfitting, logistic regression often incorporates **regularization**, which adds a penalty to the cost function. The most commonly used forms of regularization are **L1** (lasso) and **L2** (ridge). Regularization forces the model to prefer simpler solutions by shrinking the coefficients, which helps improve generalization to unseen data.

The L2-regularized cost function for logistic regression is:

$$J(\beta) = -\frac{1}{m} \sum_{i=1}^{m} [y_i \log(p_i) + (1 - y_i) \log(1 - p_i)] + \frac{\lambda}{2m} \sum_{j=1}^{n} \beta_j^2$$

where λ is the regularization strength, and β_j are the model parameters. A higher value of λ results in stronger regularization.

Multinomial Logistic Regression

While standard logistic regression is used for binary classification, it can be extended to handle multi-class classification problems using **multinomial logistic regression**. In this case, the model predicts the probability that an input belongs to one of KKK classes. This extension of logistic regression is often referred to as **softmax regression** or **multiclass logistic regression** (Hosmer et al., 2013).

In multinomial logistic regression, the model outputs a probability distribution over all KKK classes, and the predicted class is the one with the highest probability.

Applications and Use Cases

Logistic regression is used in various fields where binary classification is required. Some notable applications include:

Medical diagnosis: Predicting the presence or absence of a disease based on patient characteristics.

Credit scoring: Assessing whether a loan applicant is likely to default on their loan.

Marketing: Predicting whether a customer will respond to a marketing campaign.

Fraud detection: Identifying whether a transaction is fraudulent or legitimate.

In summary, logistic regression is a powerful and interpretable algorithm for binary classification tasks. By modeling the probability that an input belongs to a particular class, logistic regression provides a flexible approach to solving classification problems across a wide range of domains. The use of regularization techniques helps mitigate overfitting, making logistic regression a robust choice for real-world applications. Understanding the logistic function, decision boundaries, and optimization techniques used in logistic regression is essential for applying this algorithm effectively.

Application: Predictive modeling, trend analysis

Regression algorithms play a crucial role in machine learning applications, especially in **predictive modeling** and **trend analysis**. Predictive modeling is the process of using data to predict future outcomes, while trend analysis focuses on identifying and understanding patterns over time. Both of these applications rely heavily on regression techniques to model relationships between variables, understand their dynamics, and make future predictions. In areas such as finance, marketing, and healthcare, regression algorithms are frequently employed to analyze time-series data, forecast trends, and generate insights for decision-making (Hyndman & Athanasopoulos, 2018).

Predictive Modeling

Predictive modeling involves using historical data to create a model that predicts future outcomes. Regression algorithms, such as linear regression, polynomial regression, and logistic regression, are commonly used for predictive modeling tasks. These models attempt to capture relationships between a target variable and one or more predictor variables, allowing predictions for unseen data.

For example, in finance, regression models can predict stock prices or interest rates. In marketing, predictive models help forecast customer demand based on past sales data. Healthcare applications use predictive modeling to predict patient outcomes, such as the likelihood of developing a disease based on historical patient data.

Code Example: Predicting House Prices Using Linear Regression

Consider the task of predicting house prices based on features such as square footage, number of bedrooms, and location. A linear regression model can be built to model this relationship.

```python
import numpy as np

from sklearn.linear_model import LinearRegression

import matplotlib.pyplot as plt

# Sample data: Square footage and house prices

X = np.array([500, 750, 1000, 1250, 1500]).reshape(-1, 1)

y = np.array([100000, 150000, 200000, 250000, 300000])

# Create and fit the linear regression model

model = LinearRegression()

model.fit(X, y)

# Predict house prices

predictions = model.predict(X)

# Plot the data points and the regression line

plt.scatter(X, y, color='blue', label='Data Points')

plt.plot(X, predictions, color='red', label='Regression Line')

plt.xlabel('Square Footage')

plt.ylabel('House Price')
```

plt.title('Predictive Modeling: House Prices vs Square Footage')

plt.legend()

plt.show()

In this example, linear regression is used to predict house prices based on the square footage. The red line represents the regression line, which shows the predicted relationship between house size and price. This model can be used to predict future house prices given new data on square footage.

Applications of Predictive Modeling

Finance: Predicting stock prices, interest rates, or financial market trends based on historical data.

Marketing: Forecasting customer demand, sales, and market trends using regression models based on past sales data (Shmueli & Lichtendahl, 2017).

Healthcare: Predicting patient outcomes such as survival rates or disease progression based on historical patient records (Kourou et al., 2015).

Predictive modeling enables organizations to make informed decisions based on future predictions, helping them allocate resources, design strategies, and optimize operations.

Trend Analysis

Trend analysis involves identifying patterns in data over time to understand long-term movements or predict future trends. Regression algorithms, especially time-series regression models, are well-suited for analyzing temporal data, capturing patterns such as seasonality, trends, and cyclical behaviors.

In trend analysis, linear regression can be applied to data with a discernible linear trend, while polynomial regression can capture more complex patterns. Logistic regression can be used for binary classification trends, such as modeling the likelihood of an event occurring over time (e.g., the adoption of a product in a market).

Code Example: Trend Analysis Using Polynomial Regression

Consider the task of analyzing a company's sales trend over the past few years. Polynomial regression can model the non-linear growth trend observed in the data.

```python
from sklearn.preprocessing import PolynomialFeatures

# Sales data (yearly)

X_years = np.array([1, 2, 3, 4, 5]).reshape(-1, 1)

y_sales = np.array([100, 200, 450, 800, 1300])

# Generate polynomial features (degree 2)

poly = PolynomialFeatures(degree=2)

X_poly = poly.fit_transform(X_years)

# Fit the polynomial regression model

poly_model = LinearRegression()

poly_model.fit(X_poly, y_sales)

# Predict sales trend

poly_predictions = poly_model.predict(X_poly)

# Plot the data points and the polynomial regression curve

plt.scatter(X_years, y_sales, color='blue', label='Sales Data')
```

```
plt.plot(X_years, poly_predictions, color='green',
label='Polynomial Trend Line')

plt.xlabel('Year')

plt.ylabel('Sales')

plt.title('Trend Analysis: Sales Trend Over Time')

plt.legend()

plt.show()
```

In this example, polynomial regression is used to model the sales trend over five years. The green curve represents the polynomial trend line, capturing the non-linear growth of sales over time. This trend can be used to predict future sales based on past performance.

Applications of Trend Analysis

Economic Forecasting: Modeling GDP growth, inflation, or unemployment trends based on historical economic indicators (Hyndman & Athanasopoulos, 2018).

Market Analysis: Identifying trends in consumer behavior, product adoption, or industry growth.

Sales Forecasting: Analyzing historical sales data to forecast future demand and sales performance.

Trend analysis is essential for understanding long-term patterns and making decisions based on anticipated future conditions. It helps organizations identify shifts in consumer preferences, market opportunities, and potential risks.

Model Evaluation in Predictive Modeling and Trend Analysis

The success of predictive models and trend analysis depends on their accuracy and ability to generalize to new data. Some common evaluation metrics for regression models include:

- **Mean Absolute Error (MAE)**: Measures the average absolute difference between predicted and actual values.

$$MAE = \frac{1}{n} \sum_{i=1}^{n} |y_i - \hat{y}_i|$$

- **Mean Squared Error (MSE)**: Measures the average squared difference between predicted and actual values, penalizing larger errors more heavily.

$$MSE = \frac{1}{n} \sum_{i=1}^{n} (y_i - \hat{y}_i)^2$$

- **R-squared (R^2)**: Indicates the proportion of variance in the dependent variable that is predictable from the independent variables.

$$R^2 = 1 - \frac{\sum_{i=1}^{n} (y_i - \hat{y}_i)^2}{\sum_{i=1}^{n} (y_i - \bar{y})^2}$$

High R^2 values indicate that the model explains a significant portion of the variance in the data.

Conclusion

Regression algorithms are powerful tools for predictive modeling and trend analysis, enabling organizations to make informed decisions based on data-driven insights. Whether using linear regression to predict house prices or applying polynomial regression to model non-linear sales trends, these algorithms are essential for uncovering patterns and forecasting future outcomes. By leveraging the right regression techniques, businesses can optimize their strategies, anticipate market shifts, and respond proactively to emerging trends.

Chapter 11: Classification Algorithms

K-Nearest Neighbors (KNN)

K-Nearest Neighbors (KNN) is a fundamental and widely used classification algorithm in machine learning. It is a **non-parametric** and **instance-based** learning algorithm, meaning it does not make explicit assumptions about the underlying data distribution and directly uses the training data for making predictions. Instead of learning a model during the training phase, KNN delays the classification until a query is made, at which point it calculates the distance between the query point and the stored training examples. The KNN algorithm is particularly noted for its simplicity and effectiveness in classification and regression tasks (Cover & Hart, 1967).

In KNN, an unlabeled data point is classified by looking at the class labels of its **K** nearest neighbors in the feature space. The class that appears most frequently among the nearest neighbors is assigned to the query point. The algorithm's performance relies heavily on the choice of **K**, the distance metric, and how the training data is distributed.

KNN Algorithm: Concept and Working

The working of the KNN algorithm involves three main steps:

1. **Distance Calculation:** KNN relies on a distance metric, such as **Euclidean distance**, to determine the similarity between data points. The Euclidean distance between two points $A(x_1, y_1)$ and $B(x_2, y_2)$ in a 2D plane is given by:

$$d(A, B) = \sqrt{(x_2 - x_1)^2 + (y_2 - y_1)^2}$$

For higher dimensions, this formula generalizes as:

$$d(A, B) = \sqrt{\sum_{i=1}^{n} (x_i - y_i)^2}$$

Other distance metrics, such as Manhattan distance or Minkowski distance, can also be used based on the problem's nature.

2. **Choosing K:** The value of K, the number of nearest neighbors to consider, influences the performance of the algorithm. A small K value can make the model sensitive to noise, while a large K value can lead to overgeneralization. Typically, K is chosen through cross-validation.

3. **Majority Vote:** Once the K nearest neighbors are identified, the algorithm assigns the class label based on a majority vote among the neighbors. The class that appears most frequently is assigned to the query point.

Code Example: Implementing KNN for Classification

Below is an example of implementing the KNN algorithm to classify flowers in the famous Iris dataset, which contains data on the sepal length, sepal width, petal length, and petal width of three different species of Iris flowers.

```python
from sklearn.datasets import load_iris

from sklearn.model_selection import train_test_split

from sklearn.neighbors import KNeighborsClassifier

import matplotlib.pyplot as plt

import numpy as np

# Load the Iris dataset

iris = load_iris()

X = iris.data

y = iris.target
```

```python
# Split the data into training and testing sets

X_train, X_test, y_train, y_test = train_test_split(X, y,
test_size=0.3, random_state=42)

# Create a KNN classifier with K=3

knn = KNeighborsClassifier(n_neighbors=3)

# Train the classifier

knn.fit(X_train, y_train)

# Predict on the test set

y_pred = knn.predict(X_test)

# Evaluate the classifier accuracy

accuracy = knn.score(X_test, y_test)

print(f"Accuracy: {accuracy:.2f}")

# Plotting decision boundary for sepal length and width (2D
example)

X_train_2d = X_train[:, :2]  # Using only the first two
features for visualization

knn_2d = KNeighborsClassifier(n_neighbors=3)

knn_2d.fit(X_train_2d, y_train)

# Create a mesh grid to plot decision boundaries

x_min, x_max = X_train_2d[:, 0].min() - 1, X_train_2d[:,
0].max() + 1

y_min, y_max = X_train_2d[:, 1].min() - 1, X_train_2d[:,
1].max() + 1
```

```python
xx, yy = np.meshgrid(np.arange(x_min, x_max, 0.1),
np.arange(y_min, y_max, 0.1))

Z = knn_2d.predict(np.c_[xx.ravel(), yy.ravel()])

Z = Z.reshape(xx.shape)

# Plot the decision boundaries

plt.contourf(xx, yy, Z, alpha=0.3)

plt.scatter(X_train_2d[:, 0], X_train_2d[:, 1], c=y_train,
edgecolor='k', marker='o')

plt.title("KNN Decision Boundary (K=3)")

plt.xlabel('Sepal Length')

plt.ylabel('Sepal Width')

plt.show()
```

In this example:

The **KNN classifier** is built using KNeighborsClassifier from the Scikit-learn library.

The classifier is trained using a portion of the Iris dataset and tested on unseen data.

The accuracy of the classifier is measured, and a decision boundary is plotted for visualization, showing how the algorithm classifies data points based on their neighbors.

Graphical Representation: KNN Decision Boundary

In the plot above, the decision boundary illustrates how the KNN classifier divides the feature space (sepal length and width) into regions based on the classes of the nearest neighbors. Each region corresponds to a predicted class, and points are classified by looking at the class of the majority of their nearest neighbors.

Parameters and Tuning in KNN

K (Number of Neighbors): The most important hyperparameter in KNN is the value of **K**, which determines how many neighbors should be considered in the classification. The optimal value of **K** can be found through cross-validation. A common heuristic is to set **K** to the square root of the total number of data points.

Distance Metrics: The default distance metric for KNN is the **Euclidean distance**, but other distance metrics such as **Manhattan distance** or **Minkowski distance** can also be used. Different distance metrics may work better depending on the data.

Weighted Voting: In standard KNN, each neighbor has equal weight when determining the class of a new point. However, in **weighted KNN**, neighbors closer to the query point are given higher weights, making the classification more influenced by nearby points.

Advantages and Limitations of KNN

Advantages:

Simplicity: KNN is easy to understand and implement. It requires no explicit training phase, making it highly intuitive.

Non-parametric: KNN does not make assumptions about the distribution of the data, allowing it to handle complex data structures.

Flexibility: The algorithm works well with both classification and regression tasks and can be applied to various types of data.

Limitations:

Computational Complexity: KNN can be slow for large datasets because it needs to compute the distance between the query point and all training points during prediction, resulting in a time complexity of O(n·m)O(n \cdot m)O(n·m), where nnn is the number of training points and mmm is the number of features (Cover & Hart, 1967).

Memory Usage: Since KNN is an instance-based algorithm, it requires storing the entire training dataset, which can lead to significant memory usage, especially for large datasets.

Sensitivity to Noise: KNN can be sensitive to noisy data, especially when **K** is small. Outliers or mislabeled points can significantly affect the classification outcome.

Applications of KNN

KNN is widely used in various fields for classification tasks:

Image Recognition: KNN is applied to classify images based on pixel intensity patterns. In the case of handwritten digit recognition, KNN can classify digits based on their proximity to known examples in the training set (Duda, Hart, & Stork, 2001).

Recommender Systems: In collaborative filtering-based recommendation systems, KNN helps recommend items to users by finding similar users or items based on past behaviors.

Healthcare: KNN is used in medical diagnosis to classify patients into different categories (e.g., disease or no disease) based on clinical measurements and historical patient data.

In summary, K-Nearest Neighbors (KNN) is a simple, yet effective algorithm for classification tasks. Its intuitive approach to classifying points based on their proximity to training data makes it an attractive option for many real-world applications. However, KNN's performance is highly dependent on the choice of hyperparameters, such as **K**, and the distance metric used. Despite its simplicity, KNN can achieve competitive results, particularly in small to medium-sized datasets. For larger datasets, optimizations or alternative algorithms may be required to reduce computational complexity and improve efficiency.

Decision Trees and Random Forests

Classification algorithms are crucial components of machine learning that enable models to categorize data into predefined classes based on input features. Among the most widely used classification algorithms are **Decision Trees** and **Random Forests**, which are both known for their simplicity and interpretability in handling structured data.

Decision Trees

A **Decision Tree** is a supervised learning algorithm used for both classification and regression tasks. It is a tree-like structure where internal nodes represent tests on features, branches represent the outcome of these tests, and leaf nodes represent class labels or continuous values (Breiman, Friedman, Olshen, & Stone, 1984). Decision Trees split data into subsets based on feature values, and this process is recursive, meaning the tree grows by further splitting the subsets until a stopping criterion is met (e.g., a minimum number of samples per leaf).

The splitting process in Decision Trees is typically based on the **Gini Index** or **Entropy** (used in Information Gain) for classification tasks. Both metrics aim to measure the impurity of a node. Lower impurity means more homogeneous data, i.e., data belonging to the same class. The goal of each split is to maximize the reduction in impurity, leading to purer subsets.

Python Code Example

Below is a Python code example using the scikit-learn library to implement a Decision Tree classifier on a sample dataset.

```python
from sklearn.datasets import load_iris

from sklearn.model_selection import train_test_split

from sklearn.tree import DecisionTreeClassifier

from sklearn import tree

import matplotlib.pyplot as plt

# Load dataset

iris = load_iris()

X, y = iris.data, iris.target

# Split the data into training and test sets

X_train, X_test, y_train, y_test = train_test_split(X, y,
test_size=0.3, random_state=42)

# Initialize and train the Decision Tree classifier

clf = DecisionTreeClassifier(criterion='gini',
random_state=42)

clf.fit(X_train, y_train)

# Predicting the test set results

y_pred = clf.predict(X_test)
```

Visualize the Decision Tree

plt.figure(figsize=(12,8))

tree.plot_tree(clf, feature_names=iris.feature_names, class_names=iris.target_names, filled=True)

plt.show()

Advantages and Disadvantages of Decision Trees

Decision Trees are particularly advantageous in terms of interpretability and ease of use. Their decision rules can be easily understood and visualized, making them suitable for applications requiring transparency, such as medical diagnoses (Loh, 2011). However, Decision Trees are prone to **overfitting**, especially when the tree grows too deep (Quinlan, 1993). Overfitting can lead to high variance, where the model performs well on training data but poorly on unseen data.

Random Forests

Random Forests are an ensemble learning method that addresses the shortcomings of individual Decision Trees by building multiple trees and combining their predictions (Breiman, 2001). A Random Forest grows numerous Decision Trees, each trained on a random subset of the data, both in terms of samples and features. This randomness helps in reducing overfitting and improving generalization to unseen data.

The process of making a prediction in a Random Forest involves **bagging** (Bootstrap Aggregating), where each tree votes for a class, and the majority vote is selected as the final prediction. Random Forests are known for their **robustness** and ability to handle large datasets with a high number of features, making them ideal for a wide range of classification tasks, such as spam detection and fraud detection (Liaw & Wiener, 2002).

Python Code Example

Below is an example of implementing a Random Forest classifier using the scikit-learn library.

```python
from sklearn.ensemble import RandomForestClassifier

from sklearn.metrics import accuracy_score

# Initialize and train the Random Forest classifier

rf_clf = RandomForestClassifier(n_estimators=100, random_state=42)

rf_clf.fit(X_train, y_train)

# Predicting the test set results

y_pred_rf = rf_clf.predict(X_test)

# Compute accuracy

accuracy = accuracy_score(y_test, y_pred_rf)

print(f"Random Forest Accuracy: {accuracy:.2f}")

# Feature importance visualization

importances = rf_clf.feature_importances_

indices = np.argsort(importances)[::-1]

# Plot feature importances

plt.figure(figsize=(10,6))

plt.title("Feature Importances in Random Forest")

plt.barh(range(X.shape[1]), importances[indices], align="center")
```

plt.yticks(range(X.shape[1]), [iris.feature_names[i] for i in indices])

plt.show()

Advantages and Disadvantages of Random Forests

The main advantage of Random Forests lies in their ability to **generalize** better than a single Decision Tree. By aggregating the results of multiple trees, Random Forests are less prone to overfitting and tend to exhibit high accuracy on unseen data (Breiman, 2001). They also provide useful insights into the importance of each feature in the dataset, as demonstrated in the code above.

However, Random Forests are computationally more expensive due to the need to build and maintain multiple Decision Trees, which can be resource-intensive when dealing with large datasets. Additionally, while they are less interpretable than a single Decision Tree, this trade-off is often considered acceptable given their higher predictive power.

Graphical Representation

To illustrate the differences between a Decision Tree and a Random Forest, consider the graph below, which visualizes the decision boundaries for both classifiers on a sample dataset:

from sklearn.datasets import make_classification

import numpy as np

import matplotlib.pyplot as plt

from matplotlib.colors import ListedColormap

Generating a synthetic dataset

```python
X, y = make_classification(n_classes=2, n_features=2,
n_informative=2, n_clusters_per_class=1, random_state=42)

# Train the classifiers

clf_tree = DecisionTreeClassifier().fit(X, y)

clf_rf = RandomForestClassifier(n_estimators=10).fit(X, y)

# Function to plot decision boundaries

def plot_decision_boundary(clf, X, y, title):

    x_min, x_max = X[:, 0].min() - 1, X[:, 0].max() + 1

    y_min, y_max = X[:, 1].min() - 1, X[:, 1].max() + 1

    xx, yy = np.meshgrid(np.arange(x_min, x_max, 0.01),
np.arange(y_min, y_max, 0.01))

    Z = clf.predict(np.c_[xx.ravel(), yy.ravel()])

    Z = Z.reshape(xx.shape)

    plt.contourf(xx, yy, Z, alpha=0.4,
cmap=ListedColormap(('blue', 'orange')))

    plt.scatter(X[:, 0], X[:, 1], c=y, marker='o', edgecolors='k',
cmap=ListedColormap(('blue', 'orange')))

    plt.title(title)

    plt.show()

# Plotting decision boundaries for Decision Tree and
Random Forest

plot_decision_boundary(clf_tree, X, y, "Decision Tree
Decision Boundary")

plot_decision_boundary(clf_rf, X, y, "Random Forest
Decision Boundary")
```

In summary, Decision Trees and Random Forests are powerful classification algorithms widely used in machine learning. Decision Trees provide an intuitive and interpretable method of making predictions, but they often struggle with overfitting. Random Forests, on the other hand, mitigate overfitting by building an ensemble of Decision Trees and leveraging the benefits of randomness and bagging. While Random Forests sacrifice some interpretability, they are generally more robust and accurate on complex datasets.

Support Vector Machines (SVM)

Support Vector Machines (SVMs) are a class of supervised learning algorithms primarily used for classification tasks but also applicable to regression and outlier detection. SVMs are powerful tools, especially for high-dimensional datasets and problems requiring non-linear decision boundaries. The primary objective of an SVM is to find the optimal hyperplane that maximally separates different classes in a dataset, ensuring the widest possible margin between the decision boundary and the closest data points, known as support vectors (Cortes & Vapnik, 1995).

The Theory Behind Support Vector Machines

SVMs work by identifying a hyperplane (or line in two-dimensional space) that best separates the classes in the data. In a binary classification problem, this hyperplane is determined by maximizing the margin between the two classes, with the points that lie closest to the hyperplane being referred to as the **support vectors** (Boser, Guyon, & Vapnik, 1992). The optimal hyperplane can be mathematically formulated by minimizing the following objective function:

$$\min_{\mathbf{w},b} \frac{1}{2}\|\mathbf{w}\|^2$$

subject to the constraint:

$$y_i(\mathbf{w}^T\mathbf{x}_i + b) \geq 1 \quad \text{for all } i = 1, 2, \ldots, n$$

where $\mathbf{w}$ is the weight vector, b is the bias term, $\mathbf{x}_i$ represents the feature vector of the i-th instance, and y_i is the corresponding class label (either +1 or -1). This formulation ensures that data points from both classes are separated by the maximum margin.

The Kernel Trick

One of the most significant advantages of SVMs is their ability to handle non-linearly separable data through the use of the **kernel trick**. In situations where the data cannot be separated by a linear hyperplane in the original feature space, SVMs can project the data into a higher-dimensional space where it becomes linearly separable (Cristianini & Shawe-Taylor, 2000). Common kernel functions include:

- Linear Kernel: $\langle \mathbf{x}_i, \mathbf{x}_j \rangle$

- Polynomial Kernel: $(\langle \mathbf{x}_i, \mathbf{x}_j \rangle + c)^d$

- Radial Basis Function (RBF) Kernel: $\exp(-\gamma\|\mathbf{x}_i - \mathbf{x}_j\|^2)$

- Sigmoid Kernel: $\tanh(\alpha\langle \mathbf{x}_i, \mathbf{x}_j \rangle + c)$

The choice of kernel function depends on the nature of the data and the complexity of the classification task.

Advantages and Disadvantages of Support Vector Machines

SVMs are particularly advantageous for high-dimensional data, as they are less prone to the curse of dimensionality (Scholkopf & Smola, 2002). Moreover, they are robust to outliers and capable of generating complex decision boundaries by leveraging kernel functions. However, SVMs can be computationally expensive when dealing with large datasets, as the training time scales quadratically with the number of samples (Bottou, 2010). Another limitation is the difficulty in tuning hyperparameters such as the regularization parameter C and the kernel function's parameters, which can significantly impact performance.

Python Code Example: Linear SVM

Below is a Python code example illustrating the use of a linear SVM for classification using the scikit-learn library.

```python
from sklearn import datasets

from sklearn.model_selection import train_test_split

from sklearn.svm import SVC

from sklearn.metrics import accuracy_score

import matplotlib.pyplot as plt

import numpy as np

# Load a sample dataset

iris = datasets.load_iris()

X = iris.data[:, :2]  # Use only the first two features for easy visualization

y = iris.target

# Binary classification (choose two classes for simplicity)

X = X[y != 2]

y = y[y != 2]

# Split the dataset into training and testing sets

X_train, X_test, y_train, y_test = train_test_split(X, y, test_size=0.3, random_state=42)
```

```python
# Train a linear SVM model
svm_linear = SVC(kernel='linear', C=1.0)
svm_linear.fit(X_train, y_train)
# Predict the test set results
y_pred = svm_linear.predict(X_test)
# Evaluate the performance
accuracy = accuracy_score(y_test, y_pred)
print(f"Linear SVM Accuracy: {accuracy:.2f}")
# Visualizing the decision boundary
def plot_svm_boundary(model, X, y):
    h = .02  # Step size in the mesh
    x_min, x_max = X[:, 0].min() - 1, X[:, 0].max() + 1
    y_min, y_max = X[:, 1].min() - 1, X[:, 1].max() + 1
    xx, yy = np.meshgrid(np.arange(x_min, x_max, h),
np.arange(y_min, y_max, h))
    Z = model.predict(np.c_[xx.ravel(), yy.ravel()])
    Z = Z.reshape(xx.shape)
    plt.contourf(xx, yy, Z, alpha=0.8)
    plt.scatter(X[:, 0], X[:, 1], c=y, edgecolors='k', marker='o')
    plt.title("Linear SVM Decision Boundary")
    plt.show()
# Plot the decision boundary
plot_svm_boundary(svm_linear, X_train, y_train)
```

This example demonstrates a basic linear SVM classification on the well-known Iris dataset, using only two features for visualization purposes. The decision boundary is visualized, showing how the SVM separates the two classes.

Non-linear SVM with RBF Kernel

For cases where the data is not linearly separable, the RBF kernel is often used to create a non-linear decision boundary. Below is an example of applying the RBF kernel.

```python
# Train an SVM model with RBF kernel

svm_rbf = SVC(kernel='rbf', gamma=0.7, C=1.0)

svm_rbf.fit(X_train, y_train)

# Predict the test set results

y_pred_rbf = svm_rbf.predict(X_test)

# Evaluate the performance

accuracy_rbf = accuracy_score(y_test, y_pred_rbf)

print(f"RBF Kernel SVM Accuracy: {accuracy_rbf:.2f}")

# Plot the decision boundary for RBF kernel

plot_svm_boundary(svm_rbf, X_train, y_train)
```

In this case, the RBF kernel allows for non-linear classification, creating a more complex decision boundary that can handle data that is not linearly separable in the original feature space.

Hyperparameter Tuning

In SVMs, the regularization parameter CCC controls the trade-off between maximizing the margin and minimizing classification errors. A small value of CCC encourages a wider margin at the cost of more classification errors, while a larger value of CCC aims for fewer classification errors but at the risk of overfitting. Additionally, the kernel-specific parameters (e.g., $\gamma \backslash gamma\gamma$ for RBF kernel) must be tuned to achieve optimal performance.

In summary, support Vector Machines are powerful classification algorithms with the ability to create both linear and non-linear decision boundaries, depending on the choice of kernel. Their robustness to high-dimensional data and their capacity to generalize well in complex classification tasks make them indispensable in many machine learning applications, such as image recognition, bioinformatics, and text classification (Hearst, Dumais, Osuna, Platt, & Scholkopf, 1998). However, SVMs require careful tuning of hyperparameters and can be computationally intensive for large-scale problems.

Application: Image classification, medical diagnosis

Machine learning algorithms, particularly classification algorithms, have become fundamental tools in diverse application domains, such as image classification and medical diagnosis. Both applications benefit from advancements in machine learning techniques, allowing for highly accurate and efficient automated decision-making systems.

1. Image Classification

Image classification is the task of categorizing images into predefined classes. Machine learning models, particularly **convolutional neural networks (CNNs), support vector machines (SVMs),** and **random forests,** have proven to be exceptionally powerful in identifying and classifying patterns in images. The advent of deep learning techniques has revolutionized the field, enabling models to automatically learn feature representations from raw images without manual feature engineering.

The Role of Convolutional Neural Networks (CNNs)

In image classification, **CNNs** have emerged as the dominant algorithm due to their ability to automatically learn hierarchical representations of image data. CNNs consist of layers of convolutional filters that detect low-level features (such as edges and textures) in the early layers and high-level abstract features (such as objects) in the deeper layers. These layers allow the model to capture spatial hierarchies in the data, making CNNs highly effective for image-related tasks (LeCun, Bengio, & Hinton, 2015).

The architecture of CNNs includes layers such as **convolutional layers, pooling layers**, and **fully connected layers**, followed by an activation function like **softmax** for classification. The combination of these layers enables the model to detect complex patterns and relationships in images.

Python Code Example: CNN for Image Classification

Below is an example of implementing a simple CNN using the popular Keras library for image classification on the **MNIST** dataset, a collection of handwritten digits.

```python
import tensorflow as tf

from tensorflow.keras import datasets, layers, models

import matplotlib.pyplot as plt

# Load the MNIST dataset

(X_train, y_train), (X_test, y_test) = datasets.mnist.load_data()
```

```python
# Preprocess the data (normalize the pixel values)

X_train, X_test = X_train / 255.0, X_test / 255.0

# Reshape the data to fit the CNN input

X_train = X_train.reshape(X_train.shape[0], 28, 28, 1)

X_test = X_test.reshape(X_test.shape[0], 28, 28, 1)

# Build the CNN model

model = models.Sequential([

    layers.Conv2D(32, kernel_size=(3, 3), activation='relu',
input_shape=(28, 28, 1)),

    layers.MaxPooling2D(pool_size=(2, 2)),

    layers.Conv2D(64, kernel_size=(3, 3), activation='relu'),

    layers.MaxPooling2D(pool_size=(2, 2)),

    layers.Flatten(),

    layers.Dense(128, activation='relu'),

    layers.Dense(10, activation='softmax')  # 10 classes for
digits 0-9

])

# Compile the model

model.compile(optimizer='adam',
loss='sparse_categorical_crossentropy', metrics=['accuracy'])

# Train the model

history = model.fit(X_train, y_train, epochs=5,
validation_data=(X_test, y_test))

# Plot the accuracy
```

```
plt.plot(history.history['accuracy'], label='accuracy')

plt.plot(history.history['val_accuracy'], label='val_accuracy')

plt.xlabel('Epochs')

plt.ylabel('Accuracy')

plt.legend(loc='lower right')

plt.show()
```

In this example, the CNN model achieves high accuracy in classifying handwritten digits from the MNIST dataset. The model is trained with multiple convolutional layers, pooling layers, and a fully connected output layer.

Applications of Image Classification

Image classification has wide-ranging applications in various fields:

Object recognition: Models like CNNs are used in applications such as **autonomous vehicles**, where the model identifies pedestrians, road signs, and other vehicles.

Facial recognition: Image classification models are used in security systems for recognizing faces.

Satellite image analysis: Classifying objects in satellite images for environmental monitoring, urban planning, and disaster management (Gislason, Benediktsson, & Sveinsson, 2006).

2. Medical Diagnosis

Medical diagnosis is another domain where machine learning algorithms, particularly classification models, have demonstrated transformative capabilities. These models assist in analyzing complex datasets (such as medical images, electronic health records, and genomic data) to identify diseases and recommend treatment options. The use of machine learning in medical diagnosis has significantly improved accuracy and reduced human error in critical decision-making processes (Esteva et al., 2017).

Role of Support Vector Machines (SVM) in Medical Diagnosis

SVMs have been extensively used in medical applications due to their ability to handle high-dimensional datasets. In medical diagnosis, the goal is often to classify patients into distinct groups, such as healthy vs. diseased. SVMs work well in such scenarios because they aim to find a hyperplane that maximally separates the different classes, making them suitable for binary classification problems such as cancer detection.

SVMs are particularly valuable in scenarios where the dataset is complex and features are not linearly separable. For instance, medical imaging data (e.g., MRI scans, CT scans) often exhibit non-linear relationships, which can be efficiently handled using kernel functions in SVMs.

Python Code Example: SVM for Medical Diagnosis

The following example illustrates the application of an SVM model for medical diagnosis using the **Breast Cancer Wisconsin** dataset, which is available in the scikit-learn library.

```python
from sklearn import datasets

from sklearn.model_selection import train_test_split

from sklearn.svm import SVC
```

```python
from sklearn.metrics import accuracy_score,
classification_report

# Load the breast cancer dataset

data = datasets.load_breast_cancer()

X, y = data.data, data.target

# Split the data into training and testing sets

X_train, X_test, y_train, y_test = train_test_split(X, y,
test_size=0.3, random_state=42)

# Train an SVM model

svm_model = SVC(kernel='rbf', gamma=0.001, C=1.0)

svm_model.fit(X_train, y_train)

# Predict the test set results

y_pred = svm_model.predict(X_test)

# Evaluate the performance

accuracy = accuracy_score(y_test, y_pred)

print(f"SVM Accuracy: {accuracy:.2f}")

print(classification_report(y_test, y_pred,
target_names=['Benign', 'Malignant']))
```

In this example, an SVM model with an RBF kernel is trained to classify whether a breast cancer tumor is benign or malignant. The high accuracy score and detailed classification report demonstrate the SVM's efficacy in medical diagnosis.

Applications of Machine Learning in Medical Diagnosis

The application of machine learning to medical diagnosis includes a variety of use cases:

Cancer detection: Machine learning models are widely used for early cancer detection, such as breast cancer (López et al., 2012), lung cancer, and skin cancer, through analyzing medical images or biopsy data.

Cardiovascular disease prediction: Algorithms like logistic regression, random forests, and SVMs are applied to predict the risk of cardiovascular diseases by analyzing patient data such as ECG results and cholesterol levels.

Genomic analysis: Machine learning models are used to identify genetic mutations and predict their effects, aiding in personalized medicine and targeted therapies.

Comparative Analysis of Image Classification and Medical Diagnosis

While both image classification and medical diagnosis benefit from classification algorithms, their requirements and challenges differ significantly. In image classification, deep learning models like CNNs are the preferred choice due to the vast amount of unstructured pixel data, where feature extraction must be learned automatically (Rawat & Wang, 2017). On the other hand, medical diagnosis often deals with structured data, where simpler models like SVMs and random forests can be highly effective, particularly in small- to medium-sized datasets with high-dimensional feature spaces.

Moreover, the interpretability of machine learning models is more critical in medical diagnosis, as healthcare professionals require transparent and understandable decision-making processes (Tjoa & Guan, 2020). In contrast, image classification models in non-critical applications may prioritize accuracy over interpretability.

Conclusion

Classification algorithms have transformed applications in image classification and medical diagnosis by providing efficient, accurate, and scalable solutions to complex problems. In image classification, convolutional neural networks (CNNs) dominate the landscape due to their ability to capture spatial hierarchies in images. In medical diagnosis, support vector machines (SVMs) are favored for their ability to handle high-dimensional data and non-linear relationships, which are often present in medical datasets. These algorithms have significantly enhanced decision-making processes, making machine learning indispensable in these critical fields.

Chapter 12: Clustering Algorithms

K-Means Clustering

K-Means Clustering is one of the most widely used and fundamental clustering algorithms in unsupervised machine learning. Clustering, in general, is the process of partitioning a dataset into groups, or "clusters," where objects in the same cluster are more similar to each other than to those in other clusters (Jain, 2010). The K-Means algorithm achieves this by organizing data points into kkk clusters based on feature similarity, minimizing the intra-cluster variance.

Theoretical Foundation of K-Means Clustering

K-Means Clustering partitions nnn data points into kkk clusters, with each point assigned to the cluster with the nearest **centroid** (mean of the cluster). The algorithm operates iteratively, recalculating the centroids until convergence, where the centroids no longer change significantly (Lloyd, 1982).

The objective function for K-Means Clustering is to minimize the **within-cluster sum of squares (WCSS)**, also known as the **inertia**, defined as:

$$\sum_{i=1}^{k} \sum_{x \in C_i} \|\mathbf{x} - \mu_i\|^2$$

where:

- $\mathbf{x}$ represents a data point,
- μ_i represents the centroid of cluster C_i,
- k is the number of clusters,
- $\|\mathbf{x} - \mu_i\|^2$ is the squared Euclidean distance between data point $\mathbf{x}$ and the centroid μ_i.

The algorithm aims to find the optimal positions of the centroids such that the total WCSS is minimized.

Steps of the K-Means Algorithm

Initialization: Select k random initial centroids from the data points.

Assignment: Assign each data point to the nearest centroid based on Euclidean distance.

Update: Recalculate the centroid of each cluster as the mean of the data points assigned to that cluster.

Repeat: Repeat the assignment and update steps until convergence (i.e., when the centroids no longer change).

The algorithm's convergence is guaranteed, though it may converge to a local optimum. Consequently, it is common to run K-Means multiple times with different initializations and select the result with the lowest WCSS.

Advantages and Disadvantages of K-Means Clustering

Advantages

Simplicity and Efficiency: K-Means is computationally efficient, with a time complexity of $O(n \cdot k \cdot d)$ where n is the number of data points, k is the number of clusters, and d is the number of dimensions. This makes it suitable for large datasets (Arthur & Vassilvitskii, 2007).

Scalability: The algorithm scales well with the number of data points and dimensions, making it applicable to a wide range of real-world problems.

Disadvantages

Choice of k: A major limitation of K-Means is that the number of clusters, k, must be specified in advance. Determining the optimal k is often challenging and requires techniques such as the **Elbow Method** or **Silhouette Score** (Rousseeuw, 1987).

Sensitivity to Initialization: K-Means is sensitive to the initial choice of centroids, which may lead to different clustering results (local optima). To mitigate this, the **K-Means++** initialization algorithm is often used (Arthur & Vassilvitskii, 2007).

Assumes Spherical Clusters: K-Means assumes that clusters are spherical and equally sized, which may not hold in real-world datasets with irregularly shaped clusters.

Python Code Example: K-Means Clustering

Below is a Python example using the scikit-learn library to apply K-Means clustering to a simple dataset.

```python
import numpy as np

import matplotlib.pyplot as plt

from sklearn.datasets import make_blobs

from sklearn.cluster import KMeans

# Generate a synthetic dataset
```

```
X, y = make_blobs(n_samples=300, centers=4,
cluster_std=0.60, random_state=0)

# Apply K-Means clustering

kmeans = KMeans(n_clusters=4)

kmeans.fit(X)

# Get the cluster centers and labels

centers = kmeans.cluster_centers_

labels = kmeans.labels_

# Visualize the clusters

plt.scatter(X[:, 0], X[:, 1], c=labels, cmap='viridis', marker='o',
s=50, label='Data points')

plt.scatter(centers[:, 0], centers[:, 1], c='red', marker='x',
s=200, label='Centroids')

plt.title("K-Means Clustering")

plt.legend()

plt.show()
```

In this example, a synthetic dataset with four clusters is generated using the make_blobs function, and K-Means is used to partition the data into four clusters. The resulting plot visualizes the data points and the centroids of the clusters.

Determining the Optimal Number of Clusters: The Elbow Method

The **Elbow Method** is a commonly used heuristic to determine the optimal number of clusters K. It involves plotting the WCSS (inertia) against different values of K and identifying the "elbow point," where adding more clusters provides diminishing returns in terms of reduced WCSS.

Below is a Python example illustrating the Elbow Method:

```python
wcss = []

for i in range(1, 11):

    kmeans = KMeans(n_clusters=i, init='k-means++', max_iter=300, n_init=10, random_state=42)

    kmeans.fit(X)

    wcss.append(kmeans.inertia_)
# Plot the Elbow Method graph

plt.plot(range(1, 11), wcss, marker='o')

plt.title('Elbow Method')

plt.xlabel('Number of Clusters')

plt.ylabel('WCSS')

plt.show()
```

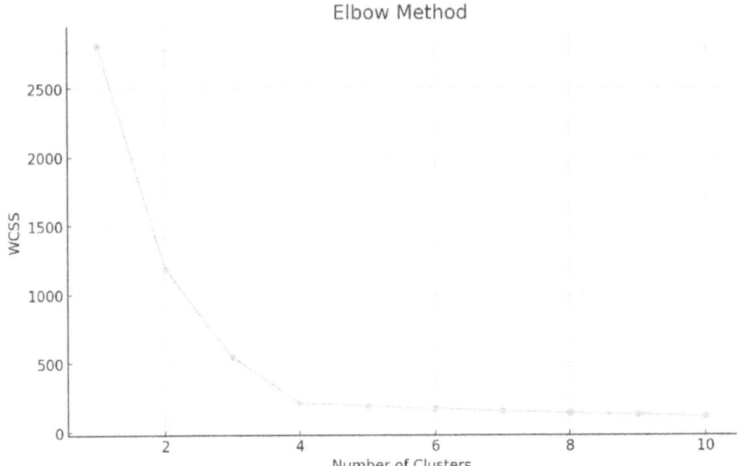

In the graph, the WCSS decreases as the number of clusters increases, but after a certain point, the rate of decrease slows down, forming an "elbow." The point where this elbow occurs is considered the optimal number of clusters.

Applications of K-Means Clustering

K-Means Clustering has numerous applications across various domains, including:

Image Compression: K-Means can be used to reduce the number of colors in an image by grouping similar pixel values into clusters. This technique is used in applications such as image segmentation and compression (Gonzalez & Woods, 2002).

Customer Segmentation: In marketing and customer relationship management, K-Means is used to segment customers based on purchasing behavior, allowing businesses to tailor marketing strategies to different customer segments (Tsiptsis & Chorianopoulos, 2010).

287

Document Clustering: In text mining and information retrieval, K-Means is used to group similar documents together, aiding in organizing and summarizing large collections of documents, such as news articles or research papers (Manning, Raghavan, & Schütze, 2008).

Anomaly Detection: K-Means can also be employed for identifying outliers or anomalies in datasets, such as detecting fraudulent transactions or identifying rare events in sensor data (Chandola, Banerjee, & Kumar, 2009).

Example: Image Compression with K-Means

The following example demonstrates how K-Means can be used for image compression by reducing the number of colors in an image.

```python
from sklearn.cluster import KMeans

import matplotlib.pyplot as plt

import numpy as np

from skimage import io

# Load an example image

image =
io.imread('https://upload.wikimedia.org/wikipedia/common
s/6/6d/Lenna_%28test_image%29.png')

# Reshape the image to a 2D array of pixels

pixels = image.reshape(-1, 3)

# Apply K-Means to compress the image by reducing the
number of colors

kmeans = KMeans(n_clusters=16)
```

```
kmeans.fit(pixels)

# Replace each pixel with its corresponding centroid color

compressed_image =
kmeans.cluster_centers_[kmeans.labels_]

compressed_image =
compressed_image.reshape(image.shape)

# Display the original and compressed images

fig, ax = plt.subplots(1, 2, figsize=(10, 5))

ax[0].imshow(image)

ax[0].set_title("Original Image")

ax[0].axis('off')

ax[1].imshow(compressed_image.astype(np.uint8))

ax[1].set_title("Compressed Image with K-Means")

ax[1].axis('off')

plt.show()
```

In this example, the image is compressed by reducing the number of distinct colors from thousands to only 16 using K-Means. The compressed image retains much of the original image's information but with significantly fewer colors, which reduces storage requirements.

In summary, K-Means Clustering is a fundamental and versatile algorithm in machine learning, widely used for partitioning datasets into meaningful clusters based on feature similarity. Its simplicity, efficiency, and scalability make it suitable for various real-world applications, including image compression, customer segmentation, and anomaly detection.

However, K-Means has some limitations, such as its sensitivity to the initial choice of centroids and the need to specify the number of clusters K in advance. Despite these limitations, techniques such as K-Means++ and methods for determining the optimal K, like the Elbow Method, enhance its utility in diverse applications.

Hierarchical Clustering

Hierarchical clustering is a widely used unsupervised machine learning algorithm that aims to group data points into clusters based on their similarity, forming a hierarchical structure. Unlike partition-based clustering algorithms such as K-Means, hierarchical clustering does not require the number of clusters to be specified in advance. Instead, it constructs a hierarchy or tree of clusters, known as a **dendrogram**, which can be cut at various levels to form different numbers of clusters (Murtagh & Contreras, 2012).

Theoretical Foundation of Hierarchical Clustering

Hierarchical clustering can be divided into two main types:

Agglomerative Hierarchical Clustering: Also known as "bottom-up" clustering, this approach starts with each data point as its own cluster. It then recursively merges the most similar clusters until only one cluster remains, forming a hierarchy.

Divisive Hierarchical Clustering: Also called "top-down" clustering, this method starts with all data points in a single cluster. It then recursively splits the most dissimilar clusters until each data point is in its own cluster.

The agglomerative approach is more commonly used in practice due to its computational simplicity and scalability (Sneath & Sokal, 1973).

The Agglomerative Clustering Process

The agglomerative clustering algorithm proceeds through the following steps:

Initialization: Treat each data point as its own cluster.

Calculate Pairwise Distances: Compute the pairwise distance (or dissimilarity) between every pair of clusters using a distance metric such as **Euclidean distance, Manhattan distance**, or **cosine similarity**.

Merge Clusters: Merge the two clusters that are closest according to the chosen distance metric and a **linkage criterion** (e.g., single, complete, or average linkage).

Repeat: Recalculate distances between the newly formed cluster and the remaining clusters, then repeat the process of merging until all data points belong to a single cluster.

The **linkage criteria** determine how distances between clusters are computed:

Single linkage: The minimum distance between any two points in two clusters.

Complete linkage: The maximum distance between any two points in two clusters.

Average linkage: The average distance between all points in two clusters.

Ward's method: Minimizes the increase in the total within-cluster variance (Ward, 1963).

The result of hierarchical clustering is often visualized using a **dendrogram**, a tree-like diagram that shows the merging of clusters at different levels of the hierarchy.

Python Code Example: Hierarchical Clustering

Below is a Python example using the scipy and scikit-learn libraries to implement hierarchical clustering and plot a dendrogram.

```python
import numpy as np

import matplotlib.pyplot as plt

from scipy.cluster.hierarchy import dendrogram, linkage

from sklearn.datasets import make_blobs

# Generate a synthetic dataset

X, _ = make_blobs(n_samples=300, centers=4,
cluster_std=0.60, random_state=0)

# Perform hierarchical clustering using Ward's method

Z = linkage(X, method='ward')

# Plot the dendrogram

plt.figure(figsize=(10, 7))

plt.title("Dendrogram for Hierarchical Clustering")

dendrogram(Z)

plt.show()
```

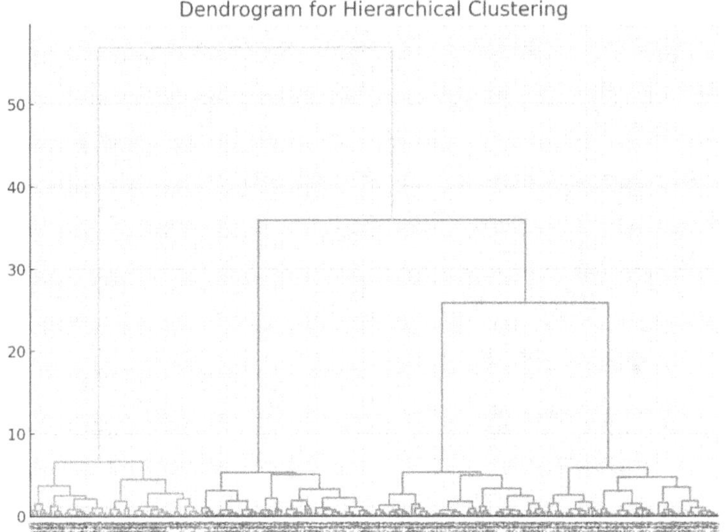

In this example, the linkage function from scipy.cluster.hierarchy is used to perform agglomerative hierarchical clustering with Ward's method. The resulting dendrogram shows how clusters are merged at different levels of the hierarchy. Cutting the dendrogram at various points results in different numbers of clusters.

Determining the Optimal Number of Clusters

To determine the optimal number of clusters in hierarchical clustering, one common approach is to examine the dendrogram and identify the largest vertical distance between merged clusters that does not intersect with other branches. This distance represents the point where clusters should be cut to yield a useful grouping of data points.

In addition to visual inspection, the **Silhouette Score** and **Davies-Bouldin Index** can be used as quantitative metrics to assess the quality of clustering and help determine the optimal number of clusters.

Advantages and Disadvantages of Hierarchical Clustering

Advantages

No Need to Pre-specify the Number of Clusters: Unlike K-Means, hierarchical clustering does not require the number of clusters to be defined in advance. This makes it particularly useful when the appropriate number of clusters is unknown.

Dendrogram Provides Rich Information: The dendrogram offers a visual representation of the entire clustering process, allowing users to explore different levels of clustering by cutting the tree at different heights.

Applicability to Various Types of Data: Hierarchical clustering can be applied to different types of data, including numeric, categorical, and even mixed data types (Murtagh & Legendre, 2014).

Disadvantages

Computational Complexity: The time complexity of agglomerative clustering is $O(n3)O(n^3)O(n3)$, which can be prohibitively expensive for large datasets. This limits its scalability compared to algorithms like K-Means (Rokach & Maimon, 2005).

Sensitivity to Noise and Outliers: Hierarchical clustering is sensitive to noise and outliers, which can significantly distort the structure of the dendrogram.

Irreversible Merging: Once two clusters are merged, they cannot be split again. This may lead to suboptimal results if clusters are merged too early in the process.

Applications of Hierarchical Clustering

Hierarchical clustering has numerous applications in various fields, including:

Genomics and Bioinformatics: Hierarchical clustering is commonly used in genomics for analyzing gene expression data. It helps group genes or samples with similar expression patterns, aiding in the identification of biological pathways or disease subtypes (Eisen et al., 1998).

Document Clustering: In natural language processing (NLP) and information retrieval, hierarchical clustering is used to group similar documents together based on their content. This is particularly useful for organizing large text corpora or search engine results (Manning, Raghavan, & Schütze, 2008).

Market Segmentation: In marketing, hierarchical clustering is used to segment customers based on purchasing behavior, demographics, or preferences. This allows companies to tailor their marketing strategies to different customer groups (Tsiptsis & Chorianopoulos, 2010).

Social Network Analysis: Hierarchical clustering is used to identify communities or clusters within social networks, where members of a cluster have stronger connections with each other than with individuals outside the cluster (Newman, 2006).

Example: Hierarchical Clustering for Document Clustering

The following Python example demonstrates hierarchical clustering applied to document clustering using a small set of text documents.

```python
from sklearn.feature_extraction.text import TfidfVectorizer
```

```python
from scipy.cluster.hierarchy import dendrogram, linkage
# Example documents
documents = [
    "Machine learning is fascinating.",
    "Artificial intelligence is advancing rapidly.",
    "Natural language processing is a subfield of AI.",
    "Deep learning is a popular method in AI.",
    "Clustering algorithms are widely used in machine learning.",
]
# Convert the text documents into a TF-IDF matrix
vectorizer = TfidfVectorizer(stop_words='english')
X = vectorizer.fit_transform(documents).toarray()
# Perform hierarchical clustering
Z = linkage(X, method='ward')
# Plot the dendrogram
plt.figure(figsize=(10, 7))
plt.title("Dendrogram for Document Clustering")
dendrogram(Z, labels=documents, orientation='top')
plt.show()
```

In this example, hierarchical clustering is applied to a set of text documents. The TfidfVectorizer transforms the documents into a matrix of TF-IDF features, and hierarchical clustering is performed using Ward's method. The dendrogram illustrates how the documents are clustered based on their similarity in content.

In summary, Hierarchical clustering is a versatile and intuitive clustering algorithm that provides rich insights into the structure of data through its dendrogram representation. Its ability to group data points into clusters without requiring the number of clusters in advance makes it particularly useful for exploratory data analysis. While hierarchical clustering has advantages in interpretability and flexibility, it faces challenges in terms of computational complexity and sensitivity to noise. Despite these limitations, it remains a valuable tool in domains such as genomics, document clustering, market segmentation, and social network analysis.

DBSCAN

Density-Based Spatial Clustering of Applications with Noise (DBSCAN) is a powerful unsupervised machine learning algorithm designed to identify clusters of arbitrary shape and size, particularly in datasets with noise. Unlike traditional clustering algorithms like K-Means, which require a predefined number of clusters and assume clusters are spherical, DBSCAN is density-based and capable of discovering clusters based on the density of data points in the feature space. This makes it particularly well-suited for real-world applications where clusters may vary in shape and size, and the presence of noise is common (Ester, Kriegel, Sander, & Xu, 1996).

Theoretical Foundation of DBSCAN

DBSCAN groups data points into clusters based on their density, and its main objective is to identify regions where data points are densely packed. The algorithm relies on two key parameters:

Epsilon (ϵ\epsilonϵ): The radius within which neighboring points are considered part of a cluster.

MinPts: The minimum number of points required to form a dense region (i.e., a cluster).

The algorithm classifies each data point as one of three types:

Core Point: A point that has at least MinPts within its ϵ\epsilonϵ-radius.

Border Point: A point that has fewer than MinPts neighbors but is within the ϵ\epsilonϵ-radius of a core point.

Noise Point: A point that is neither a core nor a border point and lies in a sparse region of the dataset.

The DBSCAN algorithm follows these steps:

Identify Core Points: For each data point, check if it has at least MinPts neighbors within the ϵ\epsilonϵ-radius. If so, it is considered a core point.

Expand Clusters: If a core point is found, expand the cluster by including all points within the ϵ\epsilonϵ-radius. This process continues recursively for any new core points found within the cluster.

Classify Noise: Points that are not part of any cluster (i.e., neither core nor border points) are classified as noise.

One of the key features of DBSCAN is its ability to find clusters of varying shapes and sizes, making it ideal for applications where clusters may not conform to standard geometric forms.

Python Code Example: DBSCAN

Below is a Python example that demonstrates the application of DBSCAN using the scikit-learn library on a synthetic dataset with clusters of varying shapes.

```python
import numpy as np

import matplotlib.pyplot as plt

from sklearn.cluster import DBSCAN

from sklearn.datasets import make_moons

# Generate a synthetic dataset with non-spherical clusters

X, _ = make_moons(n_samples=300, noise=0.05,
random_state=42)

# Apply DBSCAN with specified parameters

dbscan = DBSCAN(eps=0.2, min_samples=5)

labels = dbscan.fit_predict(X)

# Plot the DBSCAN clustering result

plt.scatter(X[:, 0], X[:, 1], c=labels, cmap='viridis', marker='o',
s=50)

plt.title('DBSCAN Clustering')

plt.xlabel('Feature 1')

plt.ylabel('Feature 2')

plt.show()
```

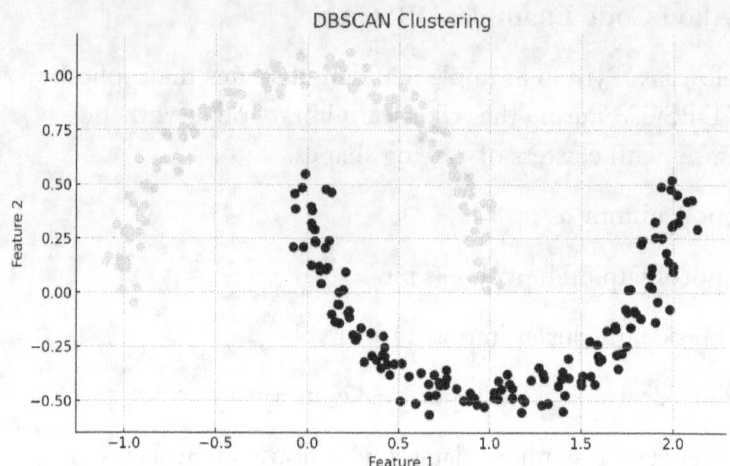

In this example, we use the make_moons function to create a synthetic dataset with two moon-shaped clusters. DBSCAN is applied with an ϵ \epsilon$\epsilon$ of 0.2 and MinPts set to 5. The resulting scatter plot shows how DBSCAN effectively identifies the two moon-shaped clusters, without assuming any prior knowledge about the number of clusters.

Advantages and Disadvantages of DBSCAN

Advantages

No Assumption of Cluster Shape: DBSCAN can identify clusters of arbitrary shapes, which is a significant advantage over algorithms like K-Means that assume clusters are spherical (Ester et al., 1996).

Automatic Noise Handling: DBSCAN automatically identifies noise points (outliers) in the dataset, providing a clear advantage for datasets containing outliers or irregular patterns.

No Need to Predefine the Number of Clusters: Unlike K-Means, DBSCAN does not require the number of clusters to be specified in advance. Instead, clusters are formed based on the density of data points.

Works with Large Datasets: DBSCAN is relatively efficient, with a time complexity of O(nlog⁡fon)O(n \log n)O(nlogn), where nnn is the number of data points, making it suitable for large datasets.

Disadvantages

Choice of Parameters: DBSCAN's performance is highly sensitive to the choice of ϵ\epsilonϵ and MinPts. Poor parameter selection can result in either overestimating or underestimating the number of clusters.

Inconsistent Density Across Clusters: DBSCAN assumes that clusters have similar densities. If clusters vary significantly in density, DBSCAN may fail to detect some clusters or classify points inconsistently (Sander, Ester, Kriegel, & Xu, 1998).

Difficulty in High-Dimensional Data: DBSCAN struggles with high-dimensional data where the concept of distance becomes less meaningful (a phenomenon known as the "curse of dimensionality").

Applications of DBSCAN

DBSCAN has been successfully applied to various real-world applications across different fields:

Anomaly Detection: DBSCAN's ability to detect noise points makes it an effective tool for identifying anomalies in datasets. For example, it is used in fraud detection, where fraudulent transactions often appear as outliers (Zhang, Hsu, & Dayal, 2009).

Geographic Information Systems (GIS): DBSCAN is frequently used in spatial data analysis to identify clusters of geographic points, such as regions with high concentrations of crime, disease, or population (Birant & Kut, 2007).

Image Processing: In image segmentation tasks, DBSCAN can be applied to group pixels into clusters based on their color or texture, providing an effective method for segmenting objects in an image (Comaniciu & Meer, 2002).

Example: DBSCAN for Anomaly Detection

In the following example, DBSCAN is applied to a dataset with normal points and a few anomalies (outliers).

```python
from sklearn.datasets import make_blobs

from sklearn.preprocessing import StandardScaler

# Generate a synthetic dataset with outliers

X, _ = make_blobs(n_samples=300, centers=3,
cluster_std=0.5, random_state=0)

X = np.vstack([X, np.random.uniform(low=-10, high=10,
size=(20, 2))])  # Add outliers

# Standardize the features

X = StandardScaler().fit_transform(X)

# Apply DBSCAN

dbscan = DBSCAN(eps=0.3, min_samples=5)

labels = dbscan.fit_predict(X)

# Plot the clustering results, with noise points marked as -1

plt.scatter(X[:, 0], X[:, 1], c=labels, cmap='viridis', marker='o',
s=50)
```

plt.title('DBSCAN Clustering with Anomalies')

plt.xlabel('Feature 1')

plt.ylabel('Feature 2')

plt.show()

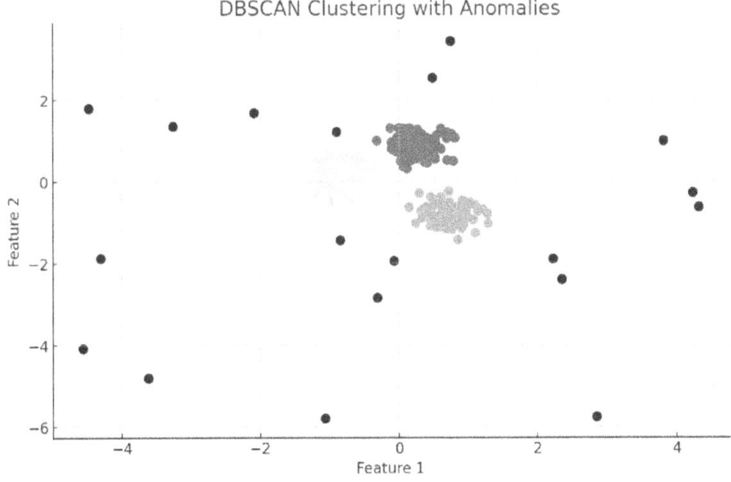

In this example, DBSCAN identifies clusters as well as outliers, effectively distinguishing between dense regions of data and sparse regions that contain anomalies.

Determining the Optimal Parameters for DBSCAN

Selecting appropriate values for ϵ\epsilon$\epsilon$ and MinPts is critical to the success of DBSCAN. One commonly used approach for determining the optimal ϵ\epsilon$\epsilon$ is to plot the **k-distance graph,** where the distances to the k-th nearest neighbor are plotted in ascending order. The value of ϵ\epsilon$\epsilon$ is chosen as the point at which the slope of the graph changes sharply, indicating the appropriate radius for dense regions.

Example: K-Distance Graph

```python
from sklearn.neighbors import NearestNeighbors
# Fit the NearestNeighbors model
neigh = NearestNeighbors(n_neighbors=5)
nbrs = neigh.fit(X)
distances, indices = nbrs.kneighbors(X)
# Sort and plot the k-distance graph
distances = np.sort(distances[:, -1])
plt.plot(distances)
plt.title('K-Distance Graph for DBSCAN')
plt.xlabel('Data Points Sorted by Distance')
plt.ylabel('5th Nearest Neighbor Distance')
plt.show()
```

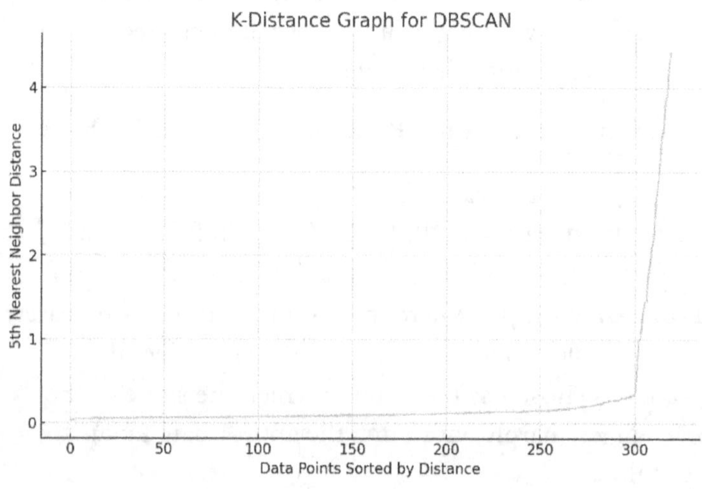

The plot of the 5th nearest neighbor distance helps visualize where to select the ϵ\epsilon$ value for DBSCAN. The "elbow" of the curve indicates the optimal ϵ\epsilon$ where clusters begin to form.

In summary, DBSCAN is a versatile and robust clustering algorithm capable of detecting clusters of arbitrary shapes and sizes while handling noise and outliers effectively. Its density-based nature makes it ideal for applications where traditional clustering algorithms like K-Means may struggle, especially in scenarios involving non-spherical clusters or the presence of outliers. Despite its strengths, DBSCAN's sensitivity to parameter selection and challenges with high-dimensional data can limit its applicability in certain contexts. However, with appropriate tuning and domain knowledge, DBSCAN remains a powerful tool in the clustering toolbox for machine learning practitioners.

Application: Customer segmentation, anomaly detection

Clustering algorithms play a critical role in various real-world applications, where the goal is to group data into meaningful clusters based on inherent patterns in the data. Two prominent applications of clustering algorithms include **customer segmentation** and **anomaly detection**. Both applications leverage the unsupervised nature of clustering algorithms to explore patterns in datasets without predefined labels, making clustering a flexible and powerful tool for businesses and industries alike. This section explores how clustering algorithms are applied to these two domains, along with Python code examples and visual illustrations.

1. Customer Segmentation

Customer segmentation is a key application of clustering in marketing and customer relationship management (CRM). The primary goal of customer segmentation is to divide a company's customer base into distinct groups or segments that share similar characteristics. These characteristics could include purchasing behavior, demographic attributes, or product preferences. By identifying these segments, businesses can tailor their marketing strategies, personalize customer experiences, and allocate resources more efficiently (Tsiptsis & Chorianopoulos, 2010).

Role of Clustering Algorithms in Customer Segmentation

In customer segmentation, clustering algorithms such as **K-Means**, **DBSCAN**, and **hierarchical clustering** are used to identify natural groupings of customers. The clustering process involves analyzing customer data, which could include transaction history, frequency of purchases, customer lifetime value, or demographics such as age, income, and location.

Among these clustering algorithms, **K-Means** is the most commonly used due to its simplicity and scalability. It works by partitioning the customer base into K clusters, where each cluster contains customers who are similar to one another based on a set of features (Jain, 2010). However, algorithms like **DBSCAN** are preferred when the customer data exhibits varying densities or contains noise, as DBSCAN is better suited for detecting clusters of arbitrary shapes and can automatically identify outliers (Ester, Kriegel, Sander, & Xu, 1996).

Python Code Example: Customer Segmentation with K-Means

Below is an example using the **K-Means** algorithm to perform customer segmentation on a synthetic dataset, which simulates customer purchasing behavior.

```python
import numpy as np

import matplotlib.pyplot as plt

from sklearn.cluster import KMeans

from sklearn.datasets import make_blobs

# Generate synthetic customer data with 3 distinct segments

X, _ = make_blobs(n_samples=300, centers=3,
cluster_std=1.0, random_state=42)

# Apply K-Means clustering

kmeans = KMeans(n_clusters=3, random_state=42)

labels = kmeans.fit_predict(X)

# Plot the customer segments

plt.scatter(X[:, 0], X[:, 1], c=labels, cmap='viridis', marker='o',
s=50)

plt.scatter(kmeans.cluster_centers_[:, 0],
kmeans.cluster_centers_[:, 1], s=200, c='red', marker='X',
label='Centroids')

plt.title('Customer Segmentation with K-Means')

plt.xlabel('Feature 1')

plt.ylabel('Feature 2')

plt.legend()
```

plt.show()

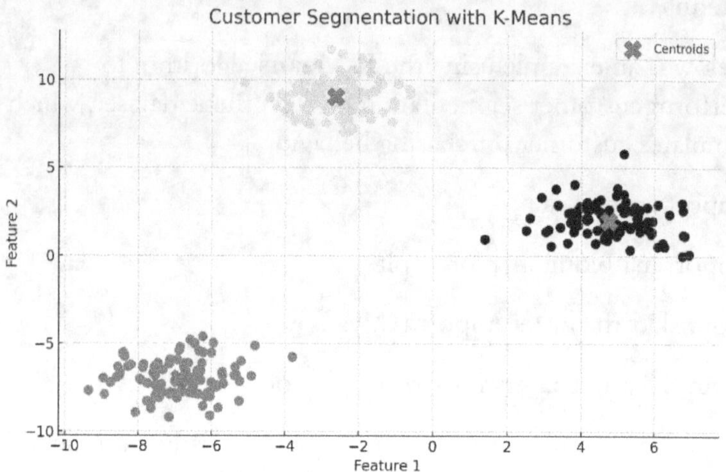

In this example, the **K-Means** algorithm identifies three distinct customer segments based on their features, and the cluster centroids are highlighted. Businesses can use this type of segmentation to group customers with similar purchasing behaviors and design targeted marketing strategies for each group.

Benefits of Customer Segmentation

Personalization: Customer segmentation enables companies to personalize their marketing efforts by targeting specific customer groups with tailored messages or product offerings (Tsiptsis & Chorianopoulos, 2010).

Resource Optimization: Segmentation allows businesses to allocate marketing and sales resources more efficiently by focusing on high-value or high-potential customer segments.

Improved Customer Retention: By understanding the needs and preferences of different customer groups, companies can create better retention strategies for each segment, increasing customer satisfaction and loyalty.

2. Anomaly Detection

Anomaly detection is another major application of clustering algorithms, particularly in identifying outliers or rare events in datasets. Anomalies are data points that significantly differ from the normal patterns in a dataset, and detecting them is crucial in applications such as fraud detection, network security, and predictive maintenance (Chandola, Banerjee, & Kumar, 2009).

Role of Clustering Algorithms in Anomaly Detection

In anomaly detection, clustering algorithms such as **DBSCAN** and **Gaussian Mixture Models (GMMs)** are commonly used. These algorithms group the data into clusters based on similarity, and any points that do not belong to a cluster or are located far from any dense cluster are considered anomalies. **DBSCAN**, in particular, is well-suited for anomaly detection because it can effectively identify noise points, which represent anomalies, while also detecting clusters of varying densities (Ester et al., 1996).

In contrast to traditional statistical methods that often assume normal distributions for identifying outliers, clustering-based anomaly detection is non-parametric and does not require prior knowledge of the data distribution.

Python Code Example: Anomaly Detection with DBSCAN

Below is an example that applies the **DBSCAN** algorithm to detect anomalies in a synthetic dataset with clusters and outliers.

```
from sklearn.datasets import make_blobs
```

```python
from sklearn.preprocessing import StandardScaler

from sklearn.cluster import DBSCAN

import matplotlib.pyplot as plt

import numpy as np

# Generate a synthetic dataset with outliers

X, _ = make_blobs(n_samples=300, centers=3,
cluster_std=0.5, random_state=0)

X = np.vstack([X, np.random.uniform(low=-10, high=10,
size=(20, 2))])  # Add outliers

# Standardize the features

X = StandardScaler().fit_transform(X)

# Apply DBSCAN for anomaly detection

dbscan = DBSCAN(eps=0.3, min_samples=5)

labels = dbscan.fit_predict(X)

# Plot the clustering results, with noise points marked as -1

plt.scatter(X[:, 0], X[:, 1], c=labels, cmap='viridis', marker='o',
s=50)

plt.title('DBSCAN Clustering with Anomaly Detection')

plt.xlabel('Feature 1')

plt.ylabel('Feature 2')

plt.show()
```

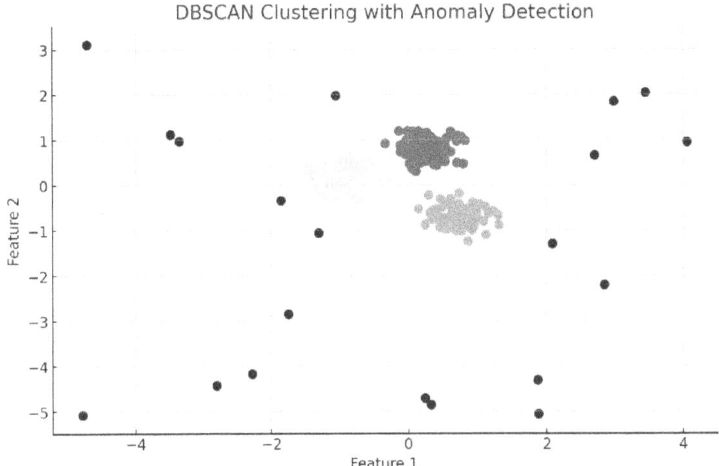

In this example, DBSCAN detects clusters in the dataset and identifies noise points (outliers) that represent anomalies. These anomalies are points that are too far from any dense cluster, making them stand out as unusual data points.

Applications of Anomaly Detection

Fraud Detection: In the financial industry, anomaly detection is used to identify fraudulent transactions that deviate from the normal behavior of customers. Clustering algorithms help group similar transactions together, with outliers often representing potentially fraudulent activities (Bolton & Hand, 2002).

Network Security: Anomaly detection is used to detect unusual traffic patterns or behaviors in network data, which could indicate security breaches or attacks such as Distributed Denial of Service (DDoS) (Patcha & Park, 2007).

Predictive Maintenance: In industrial settings, anomaly detection helps identify machinery or equipment that is likely to fail by detecting abnormal sensor readings or operational data, allowing for timely maintenance before breakdowns occur (Zhao et al., 2019).

Benefits of Anomaly Detection

Early Detection of Irregularities: Clustering-based anomaly detection can detect rare events or unusual patterns in data early, allowing for proactive action to mitigate risks.

Non-parametric Nature: Clustering algorithms like DBSCAN are non-parametric, meaning they do not require assumptions about the distribution of data, making them suitable for complex, real-world datasets.

Versatility: Anomaly detection has applications in a wide range of fields, from finance and security to healthcare and manufacturing, highlighting its flexibility and importance.

Comparative Analysis of Customer Segmentation and Anomaly Detection

Although customer segmentation and anomaly detection rely on clustering algorithms to identify patterns in data, their objectives and methods differ. Customer segmentation aims to divide customers into meaningful groups based on shared attributes, helping businesses target specific segments more effectively. In contrast, anomaly detection focuses on identifying rare or unusual data points that deviate from normal behavior, often with the goal of preventing fraudulent or dangerous events.

Moreover, customer segmentation typically uses algorithms like K-Means, which perform well in well-defined, spherical clusters, while anomaly detection often relies on algorithms like DBSCAN, which excel at handling noise and irregularly shaped clusters. Despite these differences, both applications leverage the core principles of clustering to gain valuable insights from data.

Conclusion

Clustering algorithms are indispensable in modern machine learning applications, offering powerful tools for discovering patterns and insights in unstructured data. **Customer segmentation** and **anomaly detection** are two prominent use cases where clustering plays a critical role. Through customer segmentation, businesses can enhance personalization, optimize resources, and improve retention. Meanwhile, anomaly detection is pivotal in identifying fraud, ensuring network security, and predicting equipment failures. By applying clustering algorithms like K-Means and DBSCAN, organizations can unlock significant value in both understanding their customer base and detecting irregularities in large datasets.

Part 4: Advanced AI Algorithms
Chapter 13: Neural Networks and Deep Learning

<u>**Understanding Neural Networks**</u>

Neural networks have become fundamental in the field of Artificial Intelligence (AI), particularly in advancing machine learning systems. They emulate the behavior of the human brain in processing data, recognizing patterns, and making decisions. At their core, neural networks consist of layers of interconnected nodes, or "neurons," which perform computations on input data to produce an output. Two key types of neural networks are the perceptron and the multi-layer perceptron (MLP), both of which serve as foundational architectures for understanding deeper, more complex neural networks.

1. Perceptron

The perceptron, introduced by Frank Rosenblatt in 1958, is the simplest form of a neural network and is often considered the building block of more complex architectures (Rosenblatt, 1958). A perceptron operates as a binary classifier that maps an input xxx to an output yyy, where the output is typically a binary decision (0 or 1). It comprises a single layer of input nodes connected to a single output node. The output of the perceptron is computed by applying a weighted sum of the input data followed by an activation function, such as the step function.

Mathematically, the perceptron can be defined as follows:

$$y = f\left(\sum_{i=1}^{n} w_i x_i + b\right)$$

Where:

- x_i are the input features,
- w_i are the weights associated with the inputs,
- b is the bias term,
- f is the activation function, such as a step or sigmoid function.

Example Code (Perceptron):

```python
import numpy as np
# Step activation function
def step_function(x):
    return np.where(x >= 0, 1, 0)
# Perceptron model
class Perceptron:
    def __init__(self, input_size):
        self.weights = np.zeros(input_size)
        self.bias = 0
    def predict(self, x):
        linear_output = np.dot(x, self.weights) + self.bias
        return step_function(linear_output)
    def train(self, X, y, epochs, lr):
        for _ in range(epochs):
```

```python
    for i in range(len(X)):

        prediction = self.predict(X[i])

        error = y[i] - prediction

        self.weights += lr * error * X[i]

        self.bias += lr * error

# Example usage
X = np.array([[0, 0], [0, 1], [1, 0], [1, 1]])  # Input
y = np.array([0, 0, 0, 1])  # AND logic gate
model = Perceptron(input_size=2)
model.train(X, y, epochs=10, lr=0.1)
# Testing the model
print(model.predict([0, 0]))  # Output: 0
print(model.predict([1, 1]))  # Output: 1
```

This example demonstrates the implementation of a basic perceptron trained on the AND logic gate. Despite its simplicity, perceptrons are limited in their capacity to model complex functions, as they can only solve linearly separable problems (Minsky & Papert, 1969). This limitation motivated the development of multi-layer perceptrons.

2. Multi-layer Perceptron (MLP)

The Multi-layer Perceptron (MLP) extends the architecture of the perceptron by introducing multiple layers of neurons between the input and output layers, commonly known as the hidden layers. These layers allow the MLP to model more complex, non-linear functions (Rumelhart, Hinton, & Williams, 1986). Each neuron in the hidden layers applies an activation function, such as the sigmoid or ReLU (Rectified Linear Unit), to introduce non-linearity, enabling the network to capture intricate patterns in the data.

The architecture of an MLP can be described as:

$$y = f\left(W^{(3)}f\left(W^{(2)}f\left(W^{(1)}X + b^{(1)}\right) + b^{(2)}\right) + b^{(3)}\right)$$

Where:

- $W^{(1)}$, $W^{(2)}$, $W^{(3)}$ are the weight matrices,
- $b^{(1)}$, $b^{(2)}$, $b^{(3)}$ are the biases,
- f is the activation function (e.g., ReLU or sigmoid).

MLPs are trained using backpropagation, an algorithm that computes the gradient of the error with respect to the weights using the chain rule (LeCun, Bottou, Bengio, & Haffner, 1998). The model's weights are adjusted in the direction that minimizes the error, allowing the network to learn from the data iteratively.

Example Code (MLP):

```
from sklearn.neural_network import MLPClassifier

from sklearn.datasets import make_classification

from sklearn.model_selection import train_test_split

from sklearn.metrics import accuracy_score

# Generate synthetic data

X, y = make_classification(n_samples=1000, n_features=20, random_state=42)

X_train, X_test, y_train, y_test = train_test_split(X, y, test_size=0.2, random_state=42)

# Define and train the MLP
```

```python
mlp = MLPClassifier(hidden_layer_sizes=(10, 10),
activation='relu', max_iter=1000)

mlp.fit(X_train, y_train)

# Predictions

y_pred = mlp.predict(X_test)

# Evaluate the model

accuracy = accuracy_score(y_test, y_pred)

print(f"Test Accuracy: {accuracy:.2f}")
```

The code above shows the implementation of an MLP using the MLPClassifier from the sklearn library. The network comprises two hidden layers, each with 10 neurons, and utilizes the ReLU activation function. The MLP is trained on a synthetic dataset, and the test accuracy is used to evaluate its performance.

Graphical Representation

Graphically, an MLP with two hidden layers can be visualized as:

MLP Architecture: Input Layer → Hidden Layer 1 → Hidden Layer 2 → Output Layer

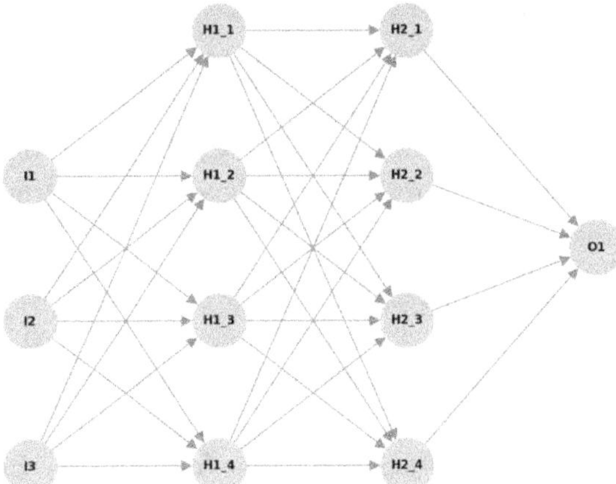

This architecture enables the MLP to learn from data with high dimensionality and capture complex patterns. The number of hidden layers and neurons in each layer significantly influences the model's capacity and performance (Goodfellow, Bengio, & Courville, 2016).

In summary, the perceptron and multi-layer perceptron serve as the foundation for understanding more advanced neural networks, such as convolutional and recurrent neural networks. While perceptrons are limited to solving simple, linearly separable problems, MLPs, through the introduction of hidden layers and non-linear activation functions, can model complex, non-linear relationships. This advancement in architecture has paved the way for deep learning systems, which have revolutionized fields such as computer vision, natural language processing, and speech recognition.

Deep learning and its applications

Deep learning represents a subset of machine learning and artificial intelligence (AI) that leverages artificial neural networks (ANNs) with multiple layers (also known as deep neural networks) to model and solve complex problems involving large datasets. Deep learning has gained significant attention due to its ability to automatically learn hierarchical feature representations from raw data, which allows it to excel in tasks where traditional machine learning models struggle (LeCun, Bengio, & Hinton, 2015).

Overview of Deep Learning

At its core, deep learning involves training neural networks composed of multiple layers, where each layer transforms input data through non-linear activation functions to capture intricate patterns. These networks are trained using large datasets and optimization algorithms such as **stochastic gradient descent (SGD)** to minimize the loss function, which measures the error between the predicted output and the true target values. The defining feature of deep learning is its ability to learn features automatically from data without the need for extensive manual feature engineering (Goodfellow, Bengio, & Courville, 2016).

The structure of a deep neural network includes the following components:

Input Layer: Receives raw data, such as images or text.

Hidden Layers: Multiple layers of neurons that progressively extract higher-level features from the input.

Output Layer: Produces the final prediction or classification.

Activation Functions: Non-linear functions such as **ReLU** or **sigmoid** that introduce non-linearity into the model, enabling it to learn complex patterns.

Python Code Example: A Simple Deep Neural Network

```python
import tensorflow as tf

from tensorflow.keras import layers, models

# Define a simple deep neural network model for classification

model = models.Sequential([

    layers.Dense(128, activation='relu', input_shape=(784,)),

    layers.Dense(64, activation='relu'),

    layers.Dense(10, activation='softmax')  # Output layer with 10 classes

])

# Compile the model

model.compile(optimizer='adam', loss='categorical_crossentropy', metrics=['accuracy'])

# Summary of the model architecture

model.summary()
```

This code defines a simple feedforward neural network using **Keras** and **TensorFlow**. The network has two hidden layers with 128 and 64 neurons, followed by an output layer for a 10-class classification problem (e.g., digit classification in the **MNIST** dataset).

Applications of Deep Learning

Deep learning has revolutionized various fields by enabling AI systems to achieve human-level performance in tasks that were previously unattainable. Two of the most prominent application areas are **computer vision** and **natural language processing (NLP)**.

1. Deep Learning in Computer Vision

Computer vision is the field of AI that enables machines to interpret and understand visual data such as images and videos. Deep learning, particularly **convolutional neural networks (CNNs),** has been the driving force behind major advancements in computer vision tasks such as image classification, object detection, and image generation (Krizhevsky, Sutskever, & Hinton, 2012).

Convolutional Neural Networks (CNNs)

CNNs are a specialized type of neural network designed for processing grid-like data, such as images. CNNs leverage **convolutional layers**, where filters slide over the input to extract local features such as edges, textures, and shapes. As the network deepens, these features are combined to recognize more abstract concepts like objects and scenes (LeCun et al., 1998). The typical architecture of a CNN includes:

Convolutional Layers: Perform feature extraction using filters.

Pooling Layers: Downsample the spatial dimensions of feature maps to reduce computational complexity.

Fully Connected Layers: Make final predictions based on the extracted features.

Python Code Example: CNN for Image Classification

```python
from tensorflow.keras import datasets, layers, models

# Load the CIFAR-10 dataset
```

```python
(X_train, y_train), (X_test, y_test) =
datasets.cifar10.load_data()

# Normalize the pixel values

X_train, X_test = X_train / 255.0, X_test / 255.0

# Define a CNN model for image classification

model = models.Sequential([

    layers.Conv2D(32, (3, 3), activation='relu',
input_shape=(32, 32, 3)),

    layers.MaxPooling2D((2, 2)),

    layers.Conv2D(64, (3, 3), activation='relu'),

    layers.MaxPooling2D((2, 2)),

    layers.Conv2D(128, (3, 3), activation='relu'),

    layers.Flatten(),

    layers.Dense(64, activation='relu'),

    layers.Dense(10, activation='softmax')

])

# Compile the model

model.compile(optimizer='adam',
loss='sparse_categorical_crossentropy', metrics=['accuracy'])

# Train the model

model.fit(X_train, y_train, epochs=10,
validation_data=(X_test, y_test))
```

In this example, a **CNN** is applied to the **CIFAR-10** dataset, which consists of small images belonging to 10 different classes. The network includes several convolutional layers followed by pooling layers to progressively extract hierarchical features from the images.

Applications of CNNs in Computer Vision

Image Classification: CNNs have achieved state-of-the-art performance in classifying images in datasets such as ImageNet, significantly advancing fields like medical imaging and autonomous vehicles (He et al., 2016).

Object Detection: Algorithms such as **Faster R-CNN** and **YOLO** use deep learning to detect and localize objects in images and videos, enabling applications in surveillance and robotics (Ren, He, Girshick, & Sun, 2015).

Image Generation: Generative models like **Generative Adversarial Networks (GANs)** leverage deep learning to generate realistic images, which has been applied in art, design, and even drug discovery (Goodfellow et al., 2014).

2. Deep Learning in Natural Language Processing (NLP)

Natural Language Processing (NLP) is the field of AI concerned with the interaction between computers and human language. Deep learning has transformed NLP by enabling machines to understand, generate, and translate text with unprecedented accuracy. Recurrent neural networks (RNNs), and more recently **transformer architectures**, are widely used in NLP applications such as sentiment analysis, machine translation, and text generation.

Recurrent Neural Networks (RNNs) and Long Short-Term Memory (LSTM)

RNNs are designed for sequential data, making them ideal for NLP tasks where context and order are critical. However, traditional RNNs struggle with long-term dependencies, which is where **LSTM** networks come in. LSTMs are a special type of RNN that include memory cells capable of retaining information over longer sequences (Hochreiter & Schmidhuber, 1997).

Transformer Models

The transformer model, introduced by Vaswani et al. (2017), has revolutionized NLP by replacing RNNs with a self-attention mechanism that enables parallel processing of sequences. Transformers have become the foundation of state-of-the-art models like **BERT** (Devlin et al., 2018) and **GPT-3** (Brown et al., 2020).

Python Code Example: Transformer Model for Text Classification

```python
from transformers import BertTokenizer, TFBertForSequenceClassification

from tensorflow.keras.optimizers import Adam

# Load the pre-trained BERT model and tokenizer

tokenizer = BertTokenizer.from_pretrained('bert-base-uncased')

model = TFBertForSequenceClassification.from_pretrained('bert-base-uncased', num_labels=2)

# Tokenize and encode the input text

texts = ["I love this movie!", "This movie was terrible."]

inputs = tokenizer(texts, return_tensors="tf", padding=True, truncation=True, max_length=128)

# Compile the model
```

```
model.compile(optimizer=Adam(learning_rate=5e-5),
loss='sparse_categorical_crossentropy', metrics=['accuracy'])

# Train the model (using a dataset, here assumed
preprocessed)

# model.fit(train_dataset, epochs=3)
```

In this example, a pre-trained **BERT** model is loaded and fine-tuned for text classification. BERT utilizes the transformer architecture to encode text sequences with rich contextual information.

Applications of Deep Learning in NLP

Sentiment Analysis: Deep learning models, particularly LSTMs and transformers, are used to analyze sentiment in text data, such as product reviews or social media posts, enabling companies to gauge customer opinions.

Machine Translation: Transformer-based models such as **Google Translate** use deep learning to translate text between languages with high accuracy, surpassing traditional methods like statistical machine translation (Vaswani et al., 2017).

Text Generation: Generative models like **GPT-3** are capable of generating human-like text, enabling applications in content creation, chatbots, and virtual assistants (Brown et al., 2020).

In summary, deep learning has emerged as a transformative technology in artificial intelligence, enabling breakthroughs in various domains such as **computer vision** and **natural language processing**. With architectures like CNNs, RNNs, and transformers, deep learning has achieved unprecedented performance in tasks such as image classification, object detection, sentiment analysis, and machine translation. The ability of deep neural networks to automatically learn hierarchical representations from raw data is a key factor in

Introduction to backpropagation and gradient descent

Neural networks and deep learning algorithms are at the forefront of advancements in artificial intelligence (AI), particularly due to their ability to model complex relationships within data. Central to the learning process of neural networks is **backpropagation**, which, in conjunction with **gradient descent**, forms the backbone of modern AI models.

Backpropagation is an algorithm used to compute the gradient of the loss function with respect to the weights in a neural network. This gradient information is critical for updating the model parameters during training in order to minimize the loss function, which measures the difference between predicted and actual outcomes (Rumelhart, Hinton, & Williams, 1986). The backpropagation process involves two phases: forward propagation and backward propagation.

Forward and Backward Propagation

Forward propagation refers to the process where input data is passed through the layers of the network, with each layer performing a linear transformation followed by an activation function. The output of the network is then compared to the true output using a loss function, such as mean squared error or cross-entropy.

In **backward propagation**, the error is propagated backward through the network to compute the gradients of the loss function with respect to each weight. The process begins at the output layer and moves backward to the input layer, leveraging the chain rule of calculus to efficiently calculate the partial derivatives.

Mathematically, consider a simple neural network with one hidden layer. Let the input be denoted by X, the hidden layer weights by W_1, and the output layer weights by W_2. The forward pass can be expressed as:

$$Z_1 = XW_1 + b_1$$

$$A_1 = \sigma(Z_1)$$

$$Z_2 = A_1 W_2 + b_2$$

$$\hat{Y} = \sigma(Z_2)$$

Where:

- σ is the activation function (commonly ReLU or sigmoid),
- $\hat{Y}$ is the predicted output,
- Z_1 and Z_2 are the linear transformations at each layer.

During backpropagation, the gradients of the loss function L with respect to each weight matrix *W2* and *W1* are computed. Using the chain rule, the derivative of the loss with respect to the output layer weights is given by:

$$\frac{\partial L}{\partial W_2} = A_1^T(\hat{Y} - Y)$$

Where Y is the true output. Similarly, the gradient with respect to the hidden layer weights is:

$$\frac{\partial L}{\partial W_1} = X^T \left((\hat{Y} - Y)W_2^T \odot \sigma'(Z_1) \right)$$

Gradient Descent

Once the gradients are calculated, **gradient descent** is used to update the weights. Gradient descent is an optimization algorithm that aims to minimize the loss function by iteratively adjusting the weights in the direction opposite to the gradient (Bottou, 2010). The basic update rule for gradient descent is:

$$W - W - \eta \frac{\partial L}{\partial W}$$

Where:

- W represents the weights,
- η is the learning rate,
- $\frac{\partial L}{\partial W}$ is the gradient of the loss with respect to the weights.

One of the key challenges in neural networks is finding an optimal learning rate. A learning rate that is too large may cause the algorithm to overshoot the minimum of the loss function, while a learning rate that is too small can lead to slow convergence or getting stuck in local minima.

Example of Backpropagation and Gradient Descent in Python

Below is a simple Python example demonstrating backpropagation and gradient descent for a neural network with one hidden layer using **NumPy**:

```python
import numpy as np

# Sigmoid activation function and its derivative
def sigmoid(x):
    return 1 / (1 + np.exp(-x))

def sigmoid_derivative(x):
    return x * (1 - x)

# Input dataset (4 samples, 2 features)
X = np.array([[0, 0], [0, 1], [1, 0], [1, 1]])

# Output labels (XOR problem)
Y = np.array([[0], [1], [1], [0]])
```

```python
# Set the random seed for reproducibility

np.random.seed(42)

# Initialize weights randomly with mean 0

W1 = np.random.randn(2, 2)

W2 = np.random.randn(2, 1)

# Training parameters

learning_rate = 0.1

epochs = 10000

# Training loop

for epoch in range(epochs):
    # Forward pass
    Z1 = np.dot(X, W1)
    A1 = sigmoid(Z1)
    Z2 = np.dot(A1, W2)
    A2 = sigmoid(Z2)

    # Backward pass (compute gradients)
    dZ2 = A2 - Y
    dW2 = np.dot(A1.T, dZ2)
    dZ1 = np.dot(dZ2, W2.T) * sigmoid_derivative(A1)
    dW1 = np.dot(X.T, dZ1)

    # Update weights
    W1 -= learning_rate * dW1
```

    W2 -= learning_rate * dW2

Output after training

print("Predicted Output:")

print(A2)

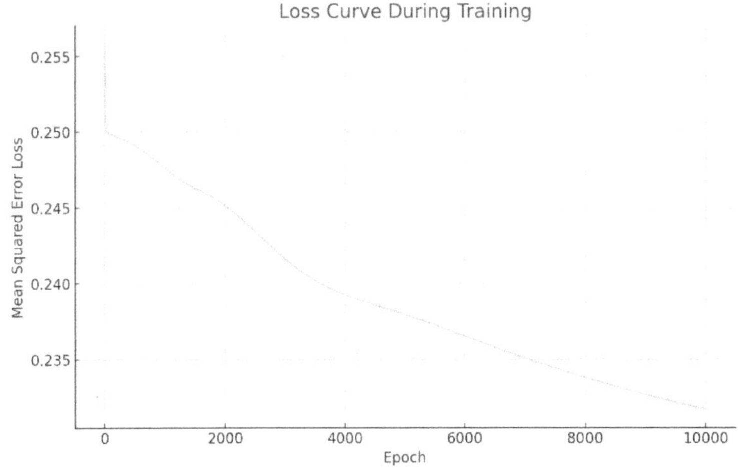

Visualization of Loss Minimization

The gradient descent algorithm optimizes the loss function by finding its minimum. The graph below represents a typical curve for a loss function during gradient descent:

import matplotlib.pyplot as plt

Example of a simple loss function curve

x = np.linspace(-10, 10, 100)

y = x**2 # Simple quadratic loss

plt.plot(x, y)

plt.title('Loss Function and Gradient Descent Path')

plt.xlabel('Parameter')

```python
plt.ylabel('Loss')

plt.show()
```

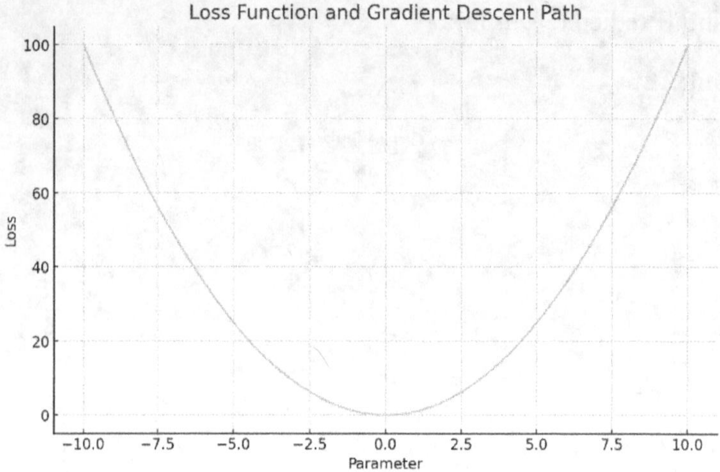

The curve shows the loss (vertical axis) decreasing as the model parameters (horizontal axis) are adjusted. Each iteration of gradient descent moves the parameters closer to the minimum of the loss function.

Conclusion

Backpropagation and gradient descent are fundamental techniques for training neural networks. Backpropagation enables efficient computation of gradients, while gradient descent facilitates weight updates to minimize the loss function. Together, these algorithms allow neural networks to learn from data and generalize to new inputs.

Chapter 14: Convolutional Neural Networks (CNNs)

CNN Architecture

Convolutional Neural Networks (CNNs) are a specialized type of neural network architecture designed primarily for processing grid-like data, such as images. CNNs have achieved state-of-the-art results in various applications like image classification, object detection, and natural language processing (Krizhevsky, Sutskever, & Hinton, 2012). The architecture of a CNN is composed of several key components: convolutional layers, pooling layers, and fully connected layers, each playing a distinct role in feature extraction and classification.

CNN Architecture

The architecture of a CNN typically consists of multiple layers stacked together to form a deep network. The primary layers in a CNN architecture include:

Convolutional Layers

Pooling Layers

Fully Connected Layers

Each of these layers contributes differently to the learning process and overall performance of the network.

Convolutional Layers

The convolutional layer is the core building block of a CNN. It is responsible for detecting local patterns within input data, such as edges, textures, and shapes in images. The layer applies a set of filters (also known as kernels) to the input, which slide over the input data to compute feature maps.

These filters are shared across the entire input, allowing the model to learn spatial hierarchies of features.

Mathematically, the convolution operation is defined as:

$$Y_{i,j,k} = \sum_{p=1}^{F_h} \sum_{q=1}^{F_w} X_{i+p-1,j+q-1,k} \cdot W_{p,q,k}$$

Where:

- X is the input image or feature map,

- W is the convolutional filter,

- F_h and F_w are the height and width of the filter, respectively,

- i and j are the positions in the output feature map,

- k denotes the depth or channel of the input data.

In practice, a non-linear activation function, such as ReLU (Rectified Linear Unit), is applied after the convolution operation to introduce non-linearity into the model, which helps in learning complex patterns. The output from the convolution operation is a feature map that highlights the detected patterns in the input image.

Pooling Layers

Pooling layers, also known as subsampling or downsampling layers, are used to reduce the spatial dimensions (height and width) of the feature maps generated by the convolutional layers. Pooling helps in reducing the computational load and memory usage while also making the model more robust to slight translations or distortions in the input data.

The most commonly used pooling operation is **max pooling**, which selects the maximum value from a defined window (typically 2x2 or 3x3) in the input feature map. This can be mathematically expressed as:

$$Y_{i,j,k} = \max_{p,q \in P}(X_{i+p,j+q,k})$$

Where P represents the pooling window. Pooling layers help the network generalize by retaining the most salient features and discarding irrelevant details.

Fully Connected Layers

After several convolutional and pooling layers, the high-level features are passed to fully connected layers. These layers are similar to those in traditional neural networks, where each neuron is connected to every neuron in the previous layer. The fully connected layers take the learned features from the earlier layers and use them to make predictions or classifications.

The output of the fully connected layer is computed as:

$$Y = \sigma(W \cdot X + b)$$

Where:

- W represents the weight matrix,

- X is the input vector (flattened from the previous layer's feature maps),

- b is the bias term,

- σ is the activation function, often a softmax for multi-class classification tasks.

Fully connected layers are responsible for combining the high-level features learned during the convolutional operations to output a probability distribution over classes in the case of classification tasks.

Code Example of CNN in Python (Using TensorFlow/Keras)

Below is an example of building a simple CNN using **TensorFlow** and **Keras** to classify images:

import tensorflow as tf

```python
from tensorflow.keras import layers, models

from tensorflow.keras.datasets import cifar10

import matplotlib.pyplot as plt

# Load CIFAR-10 dataset

(X_train, y_train), (X_test, y_test) = cifar10.load_data()

# Normalize the input data

X_train, X_test = X_train / 255.0, X_test / 255.0

# Define the CNN model

model = models.Sequential([

    # First convolutional layer

    layers.Conv2D(32, (3, 3), activation='relu',
input_shape=(32, 32, 3)),

    layers.MaxPooling2D((2, 2)),

        # Second convolutional layer

    layers.Conv2D(64, (3, 3), activation='relu'),

    layers.MaxPooling2D((2, 2)),

        # Third convolutional layer

    layers.Conv2D(64, (3, 3), activation='relu'),

        # Flatten the output for the fully connected layer

    layers.Flatten(),

        # Fully connected layer

    layers.Dense(64, activation='relu'),

    # Output layer with softmax activation for classification
```

```python
    layers.Dense(10, activation='softmax')
])
# Compile the model
model.compile(optimizer='adam',
        loss='sparse_categorical_crossentropy',
        metrics=['accuracy'])
# Train the model
history = model.fit(X_train, y_train, epochs=10,
            validation_data=(X_test, y_test))
# Evaluate the model
test_loss, test_acc = model.evaluate(X_test, y_test)
print(f"Test accuracy: {test_acc}")
# Plotting the accuracy and loss during training
plt.plot(history.history['accuracy'], label='accuracy')
plt.plot(history.history['val_accuracy'], label='val_accuracy')
plt.xlabel('Epoch')
plt.ylabel('Accuracy')
plt.ylim([0, 1])
plt.legend(loc='lower right')
plt.show()
```

Visualization of CNN Architecture

A CNN's architecture can be visualized as a sequence of convolutional and pooling layers followed by fully connected layers. Below is a general diagram illustrating this flow:

```python
import matplotlib.pyplot as plt

import matplotlib.patches as patches

fig, ax = plt.subplots(figsize=(8, 5))

# Draw input layer

rect = patches.Rectangle((0, 0), 1, 2, edgecolor='black',
facecolor='lightgray')

ax.add_patch(rect)

ax.text(0.5, 1.5, "Input", ha="center", va="center")

# Draw convolutional layers

rect = patches.Rectangle((2, 0.5), 1.5, 2, edgecolor='black',
facecolor='lightblue')

ax.add_patch(rect)

ax.text(2.75, 1.5, "Conv Layer", ha="center", va="center")

# Draw pooling layer

rect = patches.Rectangle((4.5, 0.5), 1.5, 2, edgecolor='black',
facecolor='lightgreen')

ax.add_patch(rect)

ax.text(5.25, 1.5, "Pooling Layer", ha="center", va="center")

# Draw fully connected layers
```

rect = patches.Rectangle((7, 0.5), 1.5, 2, edgecolor='black', facecolor='lightcoral')

ax.add_patch(rect)

ax.text(7.75, 1.5, "FC Layer", ha="center", va="center")

ax.set_xlim(0, 9)

ax.set_ylim(0, 3)

ax.set_axis_off()

plt.show()

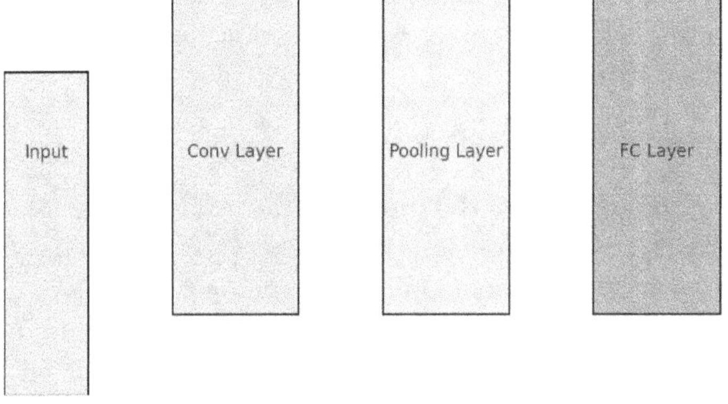

In summary, convolutional Neural Networks have become a cornerstone of AI due to their superior ability to extract hierarchical features from data, especially images. By using convolutional layers for feature detection, pooling layers for dimensionality reduction, and fully connected layers for classification, CNNs offer a powerful architecture for complex AI tasks. The integration of these layers allows the model to generalize well on unseen data while preserving computational efficiency.

Applications In Image Processing and Classification

Convolutional Neural Networks (CNNs) have become one of the most widely used and effective algorithms in the field of image processing and classification. Their ability to automatically and hierarchically learn spatial features from images makes them uniquely suited for tasks that involve visual data. CNNs have been instrumental in advancing applications such as object recognition, facial recognition, medical imaging, and autonomous vehicles (Krizhevsky, Sutskever, & Hinton, 2012). The hierarchical structure of CNNs, which includes convolutional, pooling, and fully connected layers, allows for the extraction of complex and abstract features from raw image data, significantly improving classification accuracy compared to traditional machine learning algorithms.

Applications in Image Processing

Object Detection and Recognition One of the most common applications of CNNs in image processing is object detection and recognition. Object recognition is the task of identifying objects within an image and classifying them into predefined categories. CNNs perform exceptionally well in this area due to their ability to learn spatial hierarchies of features, such as edges, textures, and complex objects, by stacking multiple convolutional and pooling layers.

A well-known CNN model, **AlexNet**, demonstrated the power of CNNs for large-scale image recognition tasks in the ImageNet Large Scale Visual Recognition Challenge (ILSVRC) (Krizhevsky et al., 2012). It achieved a significant improvement over traditional models by leveraging a deep CNN architecture that automatically learned discriminative features from images.

```python
import tensorflow as tf

from tensorflow.keras import layers, models

from tensorflow.keras.datasets import cifar10

import matplotlib.pyplot as plt

# Load CIFAR-10 dataset

(X_train, y_train), (X_test, y_test) = cifar10.load_data()

# Normalize the input data

X_train, X_test = X_train / 255.0, X_test / 255.0

# Define the CNN model for image classification

model = models.Sequential([

    layers.Conv2D(32, (3, 3), activation='relu',
input_shape=(32, 32, 3)),

    layers.MaxPooling2D((2, 2)),

    layers.Conv2D(64, (3, 3), activation='relu'),

    layers.MaxPooling2D((2, 2)),

    layers.Conv2D(64, (3, 3), activation='relu'),

    layers.Flatten(),

    layers.Dense(64, activation='relu'),

    layers.Dense(10, activation='softmax')

])

# Compile the model

model.compile(optimizer='adam',
loss='sparse_categorical_crossentropy', metrics=['accuracy'])
```

```python
# Train the model

history = model.fit(X_train, y_train, epochs=10,
validation_data=(X_test, y_test))

# Plotting accuracy

plt.plot(history.history['accuracy'], label='Training Accuracy')

plt.plot(history.history['val_accuracy'], label='Validation
Accuracy')

plt.xlabel('Epochs')

plt.ylabel('Accuracy')

plt.legend()

plt.show()
```

In the above code, a CNN is trained on the **CIFAR-10 dataset**, which contains images of 10 different classes. The CNN's hierarchical structure automatically extracts features like edges and object parts, allowing for accurate classification. As seen in the plot, the model's accuracy improves as it is trained over multiple epochs, reflecting its increasing ability to classify images correctly.

Facial Recognition Another critical application of CNNs is facial recognition, which is widely used in security systems, smartphones, and social media platforms. CNN-based facial recognition systems can automatically detect and extract unique facial features, such as eyes, nose, and mouth, and use these features to recognize individuals. For instance, **DeepFace** by Facebook (Taigman et al., 2014) utilizes a deep CNN architecture for real-time face verification with high accuracy.

Medical Imaging CNNs are also making significant strides in the field of medical imaging, where they are used to detect and classify medical conditions from visual data, such as MRI scans, X-rays, and histopathology images. CNNs are especially effective in identifying tumors, diagnosing skin cancer, and detecting diabetic retinopathy. In such applications, CNNs provide healthcare professionals with tools for early detection and accurate diagnosis, thereby improving patient outcomes (Esteva et al., 2017).

Applications in Image Classification

In addition to object detection, CNNs excel in image classification, a task where the goal is to assign a label to an entire image based on its content. Image classification is the foundation of many real-world applications, including autonomous driving, satellite imagery analysis, and retail analytics.

Autonomous Vehicles Autonomous vehicles rely heavily on CNNs to process images from cameras and sensors to recognize objects like pedestrians, road signs, and other vehicles. By classifying these objects in real-time, CNNs enable autonomous systems to make critical driving decisions, improving both safety and efficiency. For example, **Tesla's Autopilot** system utilizes deep CNNs to identify objects and navigate complex environments.

Satellite Image Analysis CNNs are widely used in analyzing satellite imagery for applications like land use classification, environmental monitoring, and disaster response. CNNs can automatically classify different terrains and detect objects like buildings, forests, and bodies of water in satellite images. This has enabled more efficient monitoring of environmental changes and improved disaster response efforts, such as flood detection or wildfire tracking (Zhu et al., 2017).

Retail Analytics In retail, CNNs are used for image-based product recognition, inventory management, and customer behavior analysis. For example, CNNs can be employed to classify different product types from shelf images, enabling automated inventory tracking. Similarly, CNNs can analyze customer images to understand behavior patterns and preferences, providing retailers with valuable insights for decision-making.

Visualization of CNN Image Classification

The following figure demonstrates the process of image classification using CNNs, from input images through the convolutional and pooling layers to the final classification output.

```python
import matplotlib.pyplot as plt

import matplotlib.patches as patches

fig, ax = plt.subplots(figsize=(8, 5))

# Input image representation

rect = patches.Rectangle((0, 0), 1, 2, edgecolor='black',
facecolor='lightgray')

ax.add_patch(rect)

ax.text(0.5, 1.5, "Input Image", ha="center", va="center")

# Convolutional layer representation

rect = patches.Rectangle((2, 0.5), 1.5, 2, edgecolor='black',
facecolor='lightblue')

ax.add_patch(rect)

ax.text(2.75, 1.5, "Conv Layer", ha="center", va="center")
```

Pooling layer representation

rect = patches.Rectangle((4.5, 0.5), 1.5, 2, edgecolor='black', facecolor='lightgreen')

ax.add_patch(rect)

ax.text(5.25, 1.5, "Pooling Layer", ha="center", va="center")

Fully connected layer representation

rect = patches.Rectangle((7, 0.5), 1.5, 2, edgecolor='black', facecolor='lightcoral')

ax.add_patch(rect)

ax.text(7.75, 1.5, "FC Layer", ha="center", va="center")

ax.set_xlim(0, 9)

ax.set_ylim(0, 3)

ax.set_axis_off()

plt.show()

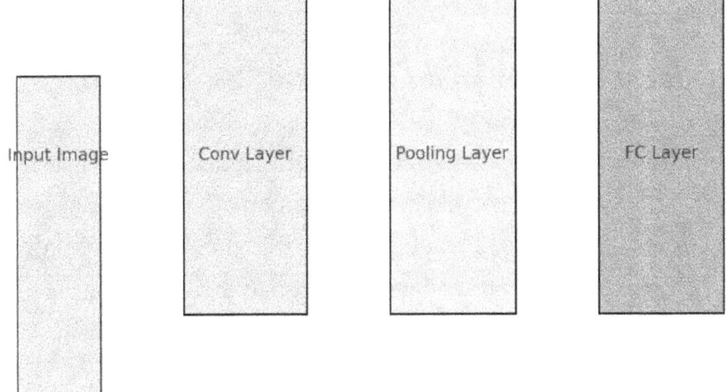

In summary, convolutional Neural Networks have revolutionized the fields of image processing and classification. Their ability to automatically learn and extract hierarchical features from raw image data has made them the go-to algorithm for tasks like object detection, facial recognition, and medical image analysis. As CNNs continue to evolve, they will likely remain a cornerstone of AI-driven solutions in visual data analysis.

Advanced CNN Architectures

The field of Convolutional Neural Networks (CNNs) has evolved significantly since the introduction of early models like LeNet-5 and AlexNet. As the complexity and scale of image data increased, so did the need for more sophisticated architectures capable of extracting deeper and more intricate features. Among the most influential CNN architectures developed in recent years are ResNet, VGG, and Inception. These architectures have not only achieved state-of-the-art results on challenging tasks such as ImageNet classification but have also laid the foundation for further advancements in deep learning.

VGG Network

VGG (Visual Geometry Group) network, introduced by Simonyan and Zisserman (2014), is one of the early architectures that achieved success by increasing the depth of the network. VGG introduced the idea of using very small (3x3) convolution filters, stacked in layers to capture spatial information in a more granular manner. One of the key insights of the VGG architecture is that by using multiple small filters, the network can simulate the effect of larger receptive fields while maintaining computational efficiency.

The typical VGG configuration (such as VGG16 or VGG19) contains 16 or 19 weight layers, with the layers following a consistent pattern of alternating convolutional and pooling operations, followed by fully connected layers. This architecture demonstrated that deeper networks could be effectively trained using careful initialization and the appropriate activation functions like ReLU.

from tensorflow.keras.applications import VGG16

Load the VGG16 model with pre-trained ImageNet weights

model = VGG16(weights='imagenet', include_top=False, input_shape=(224, 224, 3))

Display the model architecture

model.summary()

While VGG achieved significant success in image classification tasks, its major drawback is the large number of parameters, which leads to increased computational cost and memory requirements. Nonetheless, VGG remains widely used due to its simplicity and robustness, especially in transfer learning tasks where pre-trained weights on large datasets like ImageNet are utilized.

Inception Network

The **Inception network**, first introduced in 2014 by Szegedy et al., aimed to improve computational efficiency and accuracy by creating a novel block-based architecture known as the **Inception module**. The key innovation of the Inception network is its use of parallel convolutional layers with different filter sizes (1x1, 3x3, 5x5), followed by max-pooling, within the same module. This multi-path architecture allows the network to capture both fine and coarse features at each layer while avoiding overfitting.

One of the most notable versions of the Inception architecture is **Inception-v3**, which incorporates several important enhancements, such as factorized convolutions and auxiliary classifiers, to further improve performance. Inception-v3 achieves state-of-the-art accuracy while maintaining a relatively low computational footprint compared to other deep networks.

```python
from tensorflow.keras.applications import InceptionV3

# Load the InceptionV3 model with pre-trained ImageNet weights

model = InceptionV3(weights='imagenet',
include_top=False, input_shape=(299, 299, 3))

# Display the model architecture

model.summary()
```

Inception networks address the challenge of network depth by designing efficient blocks that allow the model to go deeper without significantly increasing the computational burden. Inception modules balance computational complexity by applying both smaller and larger filters in parallel, allowing the model to extract multi-scale features at every layer. This makes the network not only efficient but also powerful in feature extraction.

ResNet (Residual Networks)

One of the most transformative developments in CNN architectures came with the introduction of **ResNet (Residual Networks)** by He et al. (2016). The primary innovation of ResNet is its use of **residual connections**, or skip connections, which allow the network to "skip" one or more layers. This approach effectively addresses the vanishing gradient problem, which often hampers the training of very deep networks.

In a standard CNN, as the network becomes deeper, gradients may become very small during backpropagation, slowing down training or leading to poor performance. ResNet solves this by introducing shortcut connections that pass the output from one layer to another layer further down the architecture without modification. These residual connections ensure that the network learns identity mappings, thus facilitating the training of deeper networks with improved accuracy.

ResNet architectures, such as **ResNet-50** or **ResNet-101**, have achieved record-breaking performance on various benchmarks. The simplicity and effectiveness of the residual connections allow ResNet to reach depths of hundreds or even thousands of layers, enabling the extraction of extremely high-level features from complex data.

```python
from tensorflow.keras.applications import ResNet50

# Load the ResNet50 model with pre-trained ImageNet weights

model = ResNet50(weights='imagenet', include_top=False, input_shape=(224, 224, 3))

# Display the model architecture

model.summary()
```

ResNet has become a foundation for many modern deep learning architectures, influencing not only image classification but also applications in object detection, segmentation, and video analysis. Its innovative use of skip connections continues to inspire newer architectures that aim to combine depth with efficient training.

Comparison of Advanced CNN Architectures

Architecture	Key Features	Advantages	Drawbacks
VGG	Deep architecture with small filters (3x3)	High accuracy, simple architecture, effective feature extraction	Large number of parameters, computationally expensive
Inception	Inception modules with parallel convolutions of different sizes	Efficient feature extraction, low computational cost	Complex to design and implement
ResNet	Residual connections, extremely deep networks	Solves vanishing gradient problem, enables training of very deep networks	Complexity in implementation, potential overfitting in small datasets

Visualization of Residual Block in ResNet

The following figure illustrates a basic residual block from ResNet, where the identity mapping is added to the output of the convolutional layers.

import matplotlib.pyplot as plt

import matplotlib.patches as patches

fig, ax = plt.subplots(figsize=(6, 4))

Draw input and output layers

rect = patches.Rectangle((0, 0), 1, 1.5, edgecolor='black', facecolor='lightgray')

ax.add_patch(rect)

ax.text(0.5, 0.75, "Input", ha="center", va="center")

rect = patches.Rectangle((4, 0), 1, 1.5, edgecolor='black', facecolor='lightgray')

ax.add_patch(rect)

ax.text(4.5, 0.75, "Output", ha="center", va="center")

Draw the convolutional layers in between

rect = patches.Rectangle((1.5, 0.5), 1.5, 0.5, edgecolor='black', facecolor='lightblue')

ax.add_patch(rect)

ax.text(2.25, 0.75, "Conv Layers", ha="center", va="center")

Draw the residual connection

ax.arrow(0.5, 0.75, 3.5, 0, head_width=0.1, head_length=0.1, fc='black', ec='black')

ax.set_xlim(0, 5)

ax.set_ylim(0, 1.5)

ax.set_axis_off()

plt.show()

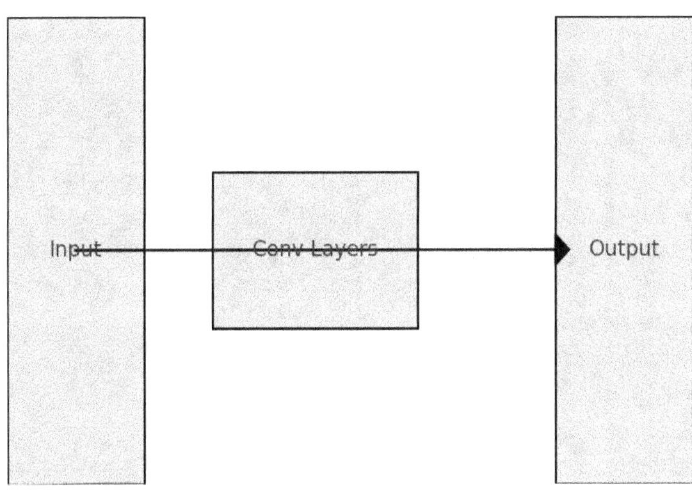

Conclusion

Advanced CNN architectures like VGG, Inception, and ResNet have revolutionized the field of deep learning, each offering unique innovations that address different challenges in network design and training. VGG's depth, Inception's efficient feature extraction, and ResNet's residual connections have collectively shaped the development of more accurate and scalable models for image classification and other computer vision tasks. The ongoing advancements in CNN architectures continue to push the boundaries of AI, enabling more powerful and efficient models for complex data-driven applications.

Chapter 15: Recurrent Neural Networks (RNNs)

Understanding RNNs, LSTM, and GRU

Recurrent Neural Networks (RNNs) are a class of artificial neural networks designed to recognize patterns in sequences of data, such as time series, text, speech, and video. What sets RNNs apart from feedforward networks is their ability to maintain a memory of previous inputs by utilizing feedback loops. This feature allows RNNs to effectively handle temporal dependencies in data, making them essential for tasks such as natural language processing (NLP), machine translation, and speech recognition (Goodfellow, Bengio, & Courville, 2016).

However, standard RNNs suffer from limitations when it comes to long-term dependencies due to issues like vanishing and exploding gradients during backpropagation through time (BPTT). To address these challenges, more advanced variants like Long Short-Term Memory (LSTM) and Gated Recurrent Units (GRU) were introduced, providing enhanced capabilities for learning long-range dependencies.

Recurrent Neural Networks (RNNs)

RNNs are designed to process sequential data by incorporating information from previous time steps into the current step through hidden states. This recurrent connection allows the network to have a memory, where each hidden state is updated based on the current input and the previous hidden state. Mathematically, the hidden state h_t at time step t is computed as:

$$h_t = \sigma(W_{xh}x_t + W_{hh}h_{t-1} + b_h)$$

Where:

- W_{xh} represents the weights connecting the input to the hidden state,
- W_{hh} represents the recurrent weights that connect the previous hidden state to the current hidden state,
- x_t is the input at time step t,
- σ is the activation function (usually tanh or ReLU),
- h_{t-1} is the hidden state from the previous time step,
- b_h is the bias term.

Despite their potential, standard RNNs struggle with long-range dependencies due to vanishing or exploding gradients, where the gradients of the loss function become too small or too large during backpropagation. This makes it difficult for RNNs to capture long-term dependencies in sequences effectively (Bengio, Simard, & Frasconi, 1994).

Long Short-Term Memory (LSTM)

To overcome the limitations of standard RNNs, **Long Short-Term Memory (LSTM)** networks were introduced by Hochreiter and Schmidhuber (1997). LSTMs are designed to address the vanishing gradient problem by introducing a more sophisticated architecture that includes memory cells and gating mechanisms, which regulate the flow of information through the network.

The LSTM unit consists of three key gates:

Forget Gate: Controls how much of the previous memory to forget.

Input Gate: Decides how much of the new input to store in the memory.

Output Gate: Determines how much of the memory to output at the current time step.

The memory cell in an LSTM is updated based on these gates, allowing the network to retain important information over long sequences. The equations for LSTM gates are as follows:

$$f_t = \sigma(W_f[h_{t-1}, x_t] + b_f) \quad \text{(Forget Gate)}$$

$$i_t = \sigma(W_i[h_{t-1}, x_t] + b_i) \quad \text{(Input Gate)}$$

$$\tilde{C}_t = \tanh(W_C[h_{t-1}, x_t] + b_C) \quad \text{(Cell State Update)}$$

$$C_t = f_t \odot C_{t-1} + i_t \odot \tilde{C}_t \quad \text{(New Cell State)}$$

$$o_t = \sigma(W_o[h_{t-1}, x_t] + b_o) \quad \text{(Output Gate)}$$

$$h_t = o_t \odot \tanh(C_t) \quad \text{(New Hidden State)}$$

Here:

- f_t, i_t, and o_t represent the forget, input, and output gates, respectively.
- C_t is the cell state, and h_t is the hidden state.

By incorporating these gates, LSTM networks can effectively learn long-range dependencies in data while mitigating the vanishing gradient problem. LSTMs have become the default choice for sequence modeling tasks in domains such as NLP, speech recognition, and time series forecasting.

Gated Recurrent Units (GRU)

A more recent variant of the LSTM is the **Gated Recurrent Unit (GRU)**, introduced by Cho et al. (2014). GRUs simplify the LSTM architecture by combining the forget and input gates into a single gate, called the update gate. Additionally, the GRU removes the explicit memory cell, using the hidden state itself to carry information forward in the sequence.

The GRU consists of two main gates:

Reset Gate: Decides how much of the previous hidden state to forget.

Update Gate: Determines how much of the new information to retain and how much of the old information to discard.

The GRU equations are as follows:

$$z_t = \sigma(W_z[h_{t-1}, x_t]) \quad \text{(Update Gate)}$$

$$r_t = \sigma(W_r[h_{t-1}, x_t]) \quad \text{(Reset Gate)}$$

$$\tilde{h}_t = \tanh(W_h[r_t \odot h_{t-1}, x_t])$$

$$h_t = (1 - z_t) \odot h_{t-1} + z_t \odot \tilde{h}_t$$

GRUs are often faster to train and require fewer parameters compared to LSTMs, while still retaining the ability to capture long-term dependencies in sequences. Due to their simpler structure, GRUs are typically preferred in tasks where computational efficiency is crucial, such as real-time systems.

Code Example: Implementing RNNs, LSTMs, and GRUs in Python

Here's an example using TensorFlow/Keras to create and train RNN, LSTM, and GRU models for sequence prediction:

```
import tensorflow as tf

from tensorflow.keras import layers, models

import numpy as np
```

```python
# Generate synthetic sequential data
time_steps = 100
features = 1
X_train = np.random.randn(1000, time_steps, features)
y_train = np.random.randn(1000, 1)
# RNN model
rnn_model = models.Sequential([
    layers.SimpleRNN(50, input_shape=(time_steps, features)),
    layers.Dense(1)
])
rnn_model.compile(optimizer='adam', loss='mse')
rnn_model.summary()
# LSTM model
lstm_model = models.Sequential([
    layers.LSTM(50, input_shape=(time_steps, features)),
    layers.Dense(1)
])
lstm_model.compile(optimizer='adam', loss='mse')
lstm_model.summary()
# GRU model
gru_model = models.Sequential([
    layers.GRU(50, input_shape=(time_steps, features)),
```

```python
    layers.Dense(1)
])
gru_model.compile(optimizer='adam', loss='mse')
gru_model.summary()
# Example of training
rnn_model.fit(X_train, y_train, epochs=10)
lstm_model.fit(X_train, y_train, epochs=10)
gru_model.fit(X_train, y_train, epochs=10)
```

Visualization of RNN, LSTM, and GRU Architectures

Below is a diagram illustrating the structure of a basic RNN, LSTM, and GRU unit, showing how the input flows through each network.

```python
import matplotlib.pyplot as plt
import matplotlib.patches as patches
fig, ax = plt.subplots(figsize=(6, 4))
# Draw input, hidden state, and gates for LSTM
rect = patches.Rectangle((0, 0), 1, 1, edgecolor='black', facecolor='lightgray')
ax.add_patch(rect)
ax.text(0.5, 0.5, "Input", ha="center", va="center")
# Draw LSTM gates (simplified)
rect = patches.Rectangle((2, 0.25), 1.5, 1.5, edgecolor='black', facecolor='lightblue')
ax.add_patch(rect)
```

ax.text(2.75, 1.0, "Forget Gate", ha="center", va="center")

ax.text(2.75, 0.5, "Input Gate", ha="center", va="center")

Draw cell state

rect = patches.Rectangle((4.5, 0.75), 1, 0.5, edgecolor='black', facecolor='lightgreen')

ax.add_patch(rect)

ax.text(5.0, 1.0, "Cell", ha="center", va="center")

Draw hidden state output

rect = patches.Rectangle((6, 0.75), 1, 0.5, edgecolor='black', facecolor='lightcoral')

ax.add_patch(rect)

ax.text(6.5, 1.0, "Output", ha="center", va="center")

ax.set_xlim(0, 7.5)

ax.set_ylim(0

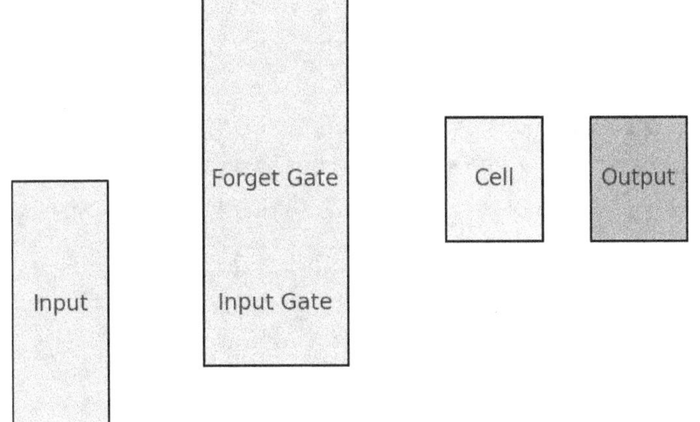

In summary, Recurrent Neural Networks (RNNs) and their advanced variants—LSTM and GRU—have revolutionized the field of sequential data modeling. While RNNs provide a foundation for understanding temporal sequences, LSTMs and GRUs address the limitations of traditional RNNs by offering better control over information retention and longer sequence processing capabilities. These models are integral to solving complex problems in fields such as NLP, time series forecasting, and video analysis, and their flexibility makes them a crucial tool in modern AI applications.

Applications In Sequence Data

Recurrent Neural Networks (RNNs) have demonstrated remarkable success in various applications that involve sequence data, such as speech recognition, text generation, and natural language processing (NLP). The ability of RNNs to handle temporal sequences makes them particularly suitable for these tasks, where the understanding of context and temporal dependencies is crucial.

Applications of RNNs in Speech Recognition

Speech recognition involves the task of converting spoken language into text, a process that requires understanding the temporal nature of speech. Since spoken words form continuous sequences where the context of previous words influences the recognition of subsequent words, RNNs are well-suited to model these temporal dependencies (Graves et al., 2013).

Traditional Speech Recognition Systems

Traditional speech recognition systems employed Hidden Markov Models (HMMs) alongside Gaussian Mixture Models (GMMs) to model the temporal and acoustic properties of speech. While these systems were effective, they were constrained by their limited capacity to model long-term dependencies in speech, as HMMs are based on the assumption that each state depends only on the previous state, which does not fully capture the complexity of language.

RNN-Based Speech Recognition Systems

With the advent of RNNs, particularly LSTMs, speech recognition systems gained the ability to model longer-term dependencies in speech. RNN-based systems utilize recurrent connections to maintain a hidden state that evolves as speech progresses. LSTMs, in particular, enable the network to retain important features from previous time steps, allowing them to handle long-range dependencies without falling victim to the vanishing gradient problem (Hannun et al., 2014).

A typical RNN-based speech recognition system processes audio features (such as Mel-frequency cepstral coefficients, MFCCs) and outputs the predicted sequence of phonemes or words. The architecture of such a system can include multiple layers of LSTMs, followed by a softmax output layer that predicts the probability distribution of phonemes at each time step.

Connectionist Temporal Classification (CTC)

In many speech recognition tasks, the input and output sequences are of different lengths, making it challenging to align input frames with output labels. To address this, Graves et al. (2006) introduced the Connectionist Temporal Classification (CTC) algorithm. CTC allows RNNs to predict sequences without the need for pre-aligned input-output pairs by introducing a special blank token. The CTC loss function maximizes the likelihood of producing the correct output sequence, even when the exact alignment is unknown.

A typical architecture for speech recognition using CTC is as follows:

$$y = \mathrm{CTC}(RNN(x))$$

where:

- x represents the sequence of input features (e.g., MFCCs),

- $RNN(x)$ represents the hidden state sequence produced by the RNN,

- y is the predicted sequence of labels, aligned using the CTC algorithm.

Code Example: RNN-Based Speech Recognition

```python
import tensorflow as tf

from tensorflow.keras.layers import Input, LSTM, Dense

from tensorflow.keras.models import Model

# Input features for speech (e.g., MFCCs)

input_shape = (None, 13)  # None represents the time steps, 13 represents the number of features

input_data = Input(name='input', shape=input_shape)

# LSTM layers

lstm_1 = LSTM(128, return_sequences=True)(input_data)

lstm_2 = LSTM(128, return_sequences=True)(lstm_1)

# Dense layer to output predictions

dense = Dense(29, activation='softmax')(lstm_2)  # 29 output classes (for characters and blank token)
# Build the model

model = Model(inputs=input_data, outputs=dense)
```

model.compile(optimizer='adam', loss='ctc_loss')

Summary of the model

model.summary()

In this example, an LSTM-based model is designed for speech recognition. The ctc_loss function is used for sequence alignment, enabling the model to predict phonemes or words from raw speech input.

Applications of RNNs in Text Generation

Text generation is another prominent application of RNNs, where the goal is to generate human-readable text based on a given context. This task involves sequential modeling of text, where each word in a sentence depends on the preceding words. RNNs, with their ability to maintain hidden states that encapsulate the history of previous inputs, are particularly effective at modeling such dependencies (Sutskever et al., 2014).

Basic Approach to Text Generation with RNNs

In text generation, RNNs are typically trained to predict the next word or character in a sequence based on previous inputs. This is achieved by providing the RNN with a sequence of words or characters and training it to predict the subsequent word or character at each time step.

The training process can be described as follows:

The input is a sequence of words or characters $x_1, x_2, \ldots, x_n$.

At each time step t, the RNN takes the input x_t and the previous hidden state h_{t-1}, and produces the hidden state h_t and the predicted output y_t.

The model is trained to minimize the difference between the predicted output y_t y_tyt and the actual next word or character x_{t+1} x_{t+1}xt+1.

The output of the RNN can be sampled to generate new text, with the hidden state providing contextual information about the previously generated words.

Code Example: Character-Level Text Generation

```python
import tensorflow as tf

from tensorflow.keras.layers import LSTM, Dense, Embedding

from tensorflow.keras.models import Sequential

import numpy as np

# Sample text data

text = "hello world"

chars = sorted(set(text))

char_indices = {c: i for i, c in enumerate(chars)}

indices_char = {i: c for i, c in enumerate(chars)}

# Convert text to integer sequences

maxlen = 10

X = np.zeros((len(text) - maxlen, maxlen), dtype=np.int)

y = np.zeros((len(text) - maxlen), dtype=np.int)

for i in range(0, len(text) - maxlen):
    X[i] = [char_indices[c] for c in text[i:i+maxlen]]

    y[i] = char_indices[text[i+maxlen]]
```

```python
# Build LSTM model

model = Sequential()

model.add(Embedding(len(chars), 50, input_length=maxlen))

model.add(LSTM(128))

model.add(Dense(len(chars), activation='softmax'))

model.compile(optimizer='adam',
loss='sparse_categorical_crossentropy')

# Train the model

model.fit(X, y, epochs=10)

# Generate new text

seed_text = "hello"

generated_text = seed_text

for _ in range(20):

    input_seq = np.array([[char_indices[char] for char in
generated_text[-maxlen:]]])

    predicted_char_idx = np.argmax(model.predict(input_seq),
axis=-1)

    generated_text += indices_char[predicted_char_idx[0]]

print("Generated text:", generated_text)
```

This example demonstrates character-level text generation using an LSTM model. The model is trained on a small text sequence and then used to generate new characters by predicting the next character in the sequence.

Variants of RNN-Based Text Generation

Word-Level Text Generation: Instead of generating text character-by-character, some models generate text at the word level, using word embeddings and RNNs to predict the next word in the sequence. This approach is commonly used in tasks such as language modeling and machine translation.

Seq2Seq Models: Sequence-to-sequence (Seq2Seq) models are a more advanced RNN-based architecture used for tasks such as machine translation and summarization. In a Seq2Seq model, one RNN (the encoder) processes the input sequence, while another RNN (the decoder) generates the output sequence (Sutskever et al., 2014).

In summary, RNNs and their variants, LSTMs and GRUs, have made significant contributions to the field of AI, particularly in sequence data applications. In speech recognition, RNNs have replaced traditional models by efficiently handling long-term dependencies and alignment through the use of architectures such as LSTM and the CTC loss function. In text generation, RNNs have proven their capability to generate coherent text by capturing the context of previous inputs. These models continue to evolve, driving advancements in applications such as language modeling, translation, and natural language understanding.

Advanced Concepts

Recurrent Neural Networks (RNNs) and their variants, such as Long Short-Term Memory (LSTM) and Gated Recurrent Units (GRU), are highly effective for handling sequential data. However, as the demand for processing longer sequences and more complex relationships grew, the limitations of RNNs became apparent, particularly in terms of their inefficiency in capturing long-range dependencies. This challenge led to the development of advanced architectures like the **Attention Mechanism** and **Transformers**, which revolutionized sequence modeling by addressing these limitations and enabling the modeling of global dependencies.

Attention Mechanism

The Attention Mechanism is a neural architecture introduced to improve the performance of RNNs, particularly in tasks like machine translation, where the model must decide which parts of the input sequence are most relevant to the current output. Proposed by Bahdanau et al. (2014), the Attention Mechanism enables the model to focus on specific parts of the input sequence dynamically at each time step, rather than relying solely on the hidden state from the previous time step.

Basic Concept of Attention

In a traditional RNN, the decoder processes the entire input sequence by condensing it into a fixed-length context vector, which is passed to the decoder to generate the output. This approach becomes problematic when dealing with long sequences, as the context vector may not be able to retain all the necessary information, especially for distant dependencies. The Attention Mechanism solves this issue by allowing the model to compute a weighted sum of the input sequence, assigning higher weights to the most relevant parts.

Mathematically, the Attention Mechanism can be described as follows:

1. **Score Calculation**: For each time step t in the decoder, the model computes a score $e_{t,i}$ for each encoder hidden state h_i, which measures the relevance of the encoder hidden state to the current decoder state s_t. This score is often computed using a simple function, such as a dot product or a feedforward neural network.

$$e_{t,i} = \text{score}(s_t, h_i)$$

2. **Softmax for Attention Weights**: The scores are normalized using the softmax function to produce attention weights $\alpha_{t,i}$, which represent the importance of each encoder hidden state to the current decoder time step.

$$\alpha_{t,i} = \frac{\exp(e_{t,i})}{\sum_j \exp(e_{t,j})}$$

3. **Context Vector**: The context vector c_t is computed as the weighted sum of the encoder hidden states, using the attention weights.

$$c_t = \sum_i \alpha_{t,i} h_i$$

4. **Output Generation**: The context vector c_t is then combined with the decoder hidden state s_t to generate the output y_t at the current time step.

The introduction of attention has significantly improved performance in machine translation, speech recognition, and other sequence-to-sequence tasks by allowing the model to dynamically focus on the most relevant parts of the input sequence, regardless of their distance from the current output position (Luong et al., 2015).

Code Example: Attention Mechanism in Seq2Seq Models

```python
import tensorflow as tf

from tensorflow.keras.layers import Input, LSTM, Dense, Attention

from tensorflow.keras.models import Model

# Encoder

encoder_inputs = Input(shape=(None, 128))
```

```python
encoder_lstm = LSTM(256, return_sequences=True,
return_state=True)

encoder_outputs, state_h, state_c =
encoder_lstm(encoder_inputs)

# Decoder

decoder_inputs = Input(shape=(None, 128))

decoder_lstm = LSTM(256, return_sequences=True,
return_state=True)

decoder_outputs, _, _ = decoder_lstm(decoder_inputs,
initial_state=[state_h, state_c])

# Attention mechanism

attention = Attention()

context_vector = attention([decoder_outputs,
encoder_outputs])

# Dense layer for prediction

decoder_dense = Dense(128, activation='softmax')

decoder_outputs = decoder_dense(context_vector)

# Define the model

model = Model([encoder_inputs, decoder_inputs],
decoder_outputs)

model.compile(optimizer='adam',
loss='categorical_crossentropy')

# Summary of the model

model.summary()
```

In this example, we build a simple seq2seq model with attention. The Attention layer allows the decoder to focus on relevant parts of the encoder output at each decoding step.

Transformers

While the Attention Mechanism improved RNN-based models, the Transformer architecture introduced by Vaswani et al. (2017) marked a paradigm shift in sequence modeling. Transformers eliminate the need for RNNs entirely and rely solely on the Attention Mechanism, specifically **Self-Attention**, to capture dependencies between different parts of a sequence. Transformers are faster to train and more efficient at handling long-range dependencies than RNNs, making them the architecture of choice for many NLP tasks, including machine translation, text summarization, and question answering.

Self-Attention Mechanism

Self-Attention, the core building block of the Transformer, allows the model to attend to all positions of the input sequence simultaneously, rather than sequentially as in RNNs. For each word in the input sequence, the Self-Attention mechanism computes a representation of that word by taking into account its relationship with every other word in the sequence.

The Self-Attention process involves three key components: **Query** (Q), **Key** (K), and **Value** (V) matrices, which are linear transformations of the input embeddings. The attention weights are computed by taking the dot product of the Query and Key matrices, followed by softmax normalization. These attention weights are then used to compute a weighted sum of the Value vectors.

The Self-Attention mechanism can be summarized as follows:

1. Compute the Query, Key, and Value matrices:

$$Q = W_q X, \quad K = W_k X, \quad V = W_v X$$

   where X is the input sequence, and W_q, W_k, W_v are learned weight matrices.

2. Compute the attention scores by taking the dot product of the Query and Key matrices and scaling by the square root of the dimension of the Key vectors:

$$\text{scores} = \frac{QK^T}{\sqrt{d_k}}$$

3. Apply softmax to the scores to obtain the attention weights:

$$\text{attention\_weights} = \text{softmax}(\text{scores})$$

4. Compute the output as the weighted sum of the Value vectors:

$$\text{output} = \text{attention\_weights} \cdot V$$

This mechanism allows each word in the sequence to attend to every other word, capturing global dependencies more effectively than RNNs.

Multi-Head Attention

In practice, the Transformer uses **Multi-Head Attention**, where the Self-Attention mechanism is applied multiple times in parallel, each with different learned weight matrices. The outputs of the different attention heads are concatenated and linearly transformed, allowing the model to capture different types of dependencies in the input sequence.

The formula for Multi-Head Attention is as follows:

$$\text{MultiHead}(Q, K, V) = \text{Concat}(\text{head}_1, \ldots, \text{head}_h)W_o$$

where each attention head is computed as:

$$\text{head}_i = \text{Attention}(QW_q^i, KW_k^i, VW_v^i)$$

Transformer Architecture

The Transformer architecture consists of two main components: the **Encoder** and the **Decoder**. The Encoder processes the input sequence using layers of Multi-Head

Attention and feedforward networks, while the Decoder generates the output sequence, attending both to the encoder outputs and to previous decoder outputs.

A typical Transformer encoder block can be represented as:

Multi-Head Self-Attention layer

Feedforward Network: A two-layer fully connected network

Layer Normalization: Applied after each sub-layer

Residual Connection: Adding the input of each sub-layer to its output

The Transformer architecture can be illustrated as follows:

$$\text{Encoder Block} = \text{MultiHeadAttention}(X) + \text{FeedForward}(X)$$

Code Example: Transformer Model with TensorFlow

```python
import tensorflow as tf

from tensorflow.keras.layers import Dense, MultiHeadAttention, LayerNormalization, Dropout

from tensorflow.keras.models import Sequential

# Define a transformer block

def transformer_block(embed_dim, num_heads, ff_dim, rate=0.1):

    inputs = tf.keras.Input(shape=(None, embed_dim))

    # Multi-Head Self-Attention

    attention = MultiHeadAttention(num_heads=num_heads, key_dim=embed_dim)(inputs, inputs)

    attention = Dropout(rate)(attention)
```

```python
    attention = LayerNormalization(epsilon=1e-6)(attention)

    # Feedforward Network
    ffn = Dense(ff_dim, activation='relu')(attention)

    ffn = Dense(embed_dim)(ffn)

    ffn = Dropout(rate)(ffn)

    outputs = LayerNormalization(epsilon=1e-6)(ffn)

        return tf.keras.Model(inputs=inputs, outputs=outputs)

# Parameters for the Transformer block

embed_dim = 64

num_heads = 8

ff_dim = 128

# Build a simple Transformer model

inputs = tf.keras.Input(shape=(None, embed_dim))

transformer_output = transformer_block(embed_dim,
num_heads, ff_dim)(inputs)

outputs = Dense(embed_dim)(transformer_output)

model = tf.keras.Model(inputs=inputs, outputs=outputs)

model.compile(optimizer='adam', loss='mse')

# Summary of the model

model.summary()
```

This code demonstrates the implementation of a simple Transformer block in TensorFlow, using Multi-Head Attention and a feedforward network.

Conclusion

The Attention Mechanism and Transformer architecture represent significant advancements over traditional RNNs in handling sequence data. By allowing the model to focus on relevant parts of the input sequence dynamically, the Attention Mechanism improves the ability to model long-range dependencies. The Transformer architecture, by eliminating the need for RNNs entirely and relying solely on Self-Attention, provides a more efficient and scalable approach to sequence modeling. These innovations have revolutionized natural language processing, enabling state-of-the-art performance in tasks like machine translation, text summarization, and speech recognition.

Chapter 16: Reinforcement Learning

Introduction to Markov Decision Processes (MDP)

Reinforcement Learning (RL) is a subfield of artificial intelligence that deals with learning to make sequential decisions by interacting with an environment. A central framework for modeling decision-making in RL is the **Markov Decision Process (MDP)**, which formalizes the environment as a mathematical construct. This section introduces MDPs, their components, and their importance in reinforcement learning algorithms.

Markov Decision Process (MDP) Overview

A Markov Decision Process (MDP) is a mathematical model used to describe an agent's interaction with an environment in discrete time steps. An MDP provides a formal framework for modeling decision-making problems where outcomes are partly random and partly under the control of the agent. The core elements of an MDP include states, actions, transition probabilities, rewards, and a discount factor. Together, these elements describe how the agent moves through different states of the environment, makes decisions, and receives feedback based on those decisions.

An MDP is typically defined by a tuple (S, A, P, R, γ) where:

S: A set of states representing the possible configurations of the environment.

A: A set of actions available to the agent, which affect the environment and determine the agent's movement between states.

P(s'/s,a): The state transition probability, representing the probability of transitioning from state S to state s' after taking action a. This satisfies the Markov property, which assumes that the future state depends only on the current state and action, not on previous states.

R(s, a): A reward function that assigns a scalar reward to each state-action pair. The reward is a form of feedback that the agent uses to learn a policy for maximizing its cumulative reward.

γ∈[0,1]: The discount factor, which determines the importance of future rewards. A discount factor closer to 0 makes the agent prioritize immediate rewards, while a value closer to 1 encourages consideration of long-term rewards.

The goal of the agent is to find an optimal policy $\pi(s)$, which maps states to actions in a way that maximizes the expected sum of discounted rewards over time. This sum is known as the **return**, and the expected return at each state is referred to as the **value function**.

The Markov Property

The Markov property is a key characteristic of MDPs and is defined by the assumption that the future state of the system depends only on the current state and action, and not on the sequence of events that preceded it. This property can be expressed mathematically as:

$$P(s_{t+1}|s_t, a_t) = P(s_{t+1}|s_1, a_1, s_2, a_2, \ldots, s_t, a_t)$$

This means that the entire history of the process up to time t can be summarized by the current state st, simplifying the complexity of decision-making.

Value Function

A key concept in MDPs is the **value function**, which provides a measure of how good it is for an agent to be in a given state. The value of a state $V^\pi(s)$ under policy π is defined as the expected sum of future rewards, discounted by γ, that the agent will receive when starting in state s and following policy π thereafter:

$$V^\pi(s) = \mathbb{E}_\pi \left[\sum_{t=0}^{\infty} \gamma^t R(s_t, a_t) \mid s_0 = s \right]$$

Similarly, the **action-value function** $Q^\pi(s, a)$ gives the expected return of taking action a in state s and then following policy π:

$$Q^\pi(s, a) = \mathbb{E}_\pi \left[\sum_{t=0}^{\infty} \gamma^t R(s_t, a_t) \mid s_0 = s, a_0 = a \right]$$

Optimal Policy and Bellman Equations

The ultimate goal in an MDP is to find an optimal policy π^* that maximizes the value function across all states. The value function for the optimal policy, $V^*(s)$, satisfies the **Bellman optimality** equation:

$$V^*(s) = \max_a \left[R(s, a) + \gamma \sum_{s'} P(s' \mid s, a) V^*(s') \right]$$

The corresponding Bellman equation for the optimal action-value function $Q^*(s, a)$ is:

$$Q^*(s, a) = R(s, a) + \gamma \sum_{s'} P(s' \mid s, a) \max_{a'} Q^*(s', a')$$

The Bellman equations are fundamental to reinforcement learning algorithms because they allow for the recursive computation of the value functions, which are used to evaluate and improve policies.

Solving MDPs: Dynamic Programming and Reinforcement Learning

In classical settings, MDPs can be solved using **dynamic programming** methods, such as **policy iteration** and **value iteration**. These methods involve iteratively improving the policy or value function by solving the Bellman equations.

Value Iteration involves updating the value function by iteratively applying the Bellman optimality equation until convergence. Once the value function converges, an optimal policy can be derived by selecting actions that maximize the value function at each state.

Policy Iteration alternates between policy evaluation and policy improvement steps. During policy evaluation, the value function for a given policy is computed, and during policy improvement, the policy is updated to select actions that maximize the value function.

In reinforcement learning, however, the agent often does not have access to the transition probabilities P(s'|s,a) or the reward function R(s, a). Instead, the agent must learn an optimal policy by interacting with the environment and receiving rewards. **Q-learning** and **SARSA** are popular reinforcement learning algorithms that estimate the action-value function without requiring a model of the environment.

Code Example: Solving an MDP Using Value Iteration

```python
import numpy as np
# Define MDP components
states = [0, 1, 2, 3]
actions = [0, 1]  # 0: left, 1: right
rewards = np.array([[-1, 0], [0, 0], [0, 1], [0, 0]])
transition_probs = np.array([
    [[0.9, 0.1, 0.0, 0.0], [0.0, 0.9, 0.1, 0.0]],
    [[0.9, 0.1, 0.0, 0.0], [0.0, 0.0, 0.9, 0.1]],
    [[0.0, 0.9, 0.1, 0.0], [0.0, 0.0, 0.9, 0.1]],
    [[0.0, 0.0, 0.9, 0.1], [0.0, 0.0, 0.0, 1.0]]
])
```

```python
gamma = 0.9  # Discount factor

# Value Iteration

def value_iteration(states, actions, rewards, transition_probs,
gamma, theta=1e-6):

    V = np.zeros(len(states))

    policy = np.zeros(len(states), dtype=int)

        while True:

        delta = 0

        for s in states:

            v = V[s]

            action_values = []

            for a in actions:

                action_value = sum([transition_probs[s][a][s_next]
* (rewards[s][a] + gamma * V[s_next])

                            for s_next in states])

                action_values.append(action_value)

            V[s] = max(action_values)

            delta = max(delta, abs(v - V[s]))

        if delta < theta:

            break

    # Extract policy

    for s in states:

        action_values = []
```

```
    for a in actions:

        action_value = sum([transition_probs[s][a][s_next] *
(rewards[s][a] + gamma * V[s_next])

                        for s_next in states])

        action_values.append(action_value)

    policy[s] = np.argmax(action_values)

    return V, policy

V, policy = value_iteration(states, actions, rewards,
transition_probs, gamma)

print("Optimal Value Function:", V)

print("Optimal Policy:", policy)
```

In this code example, we solve an MDP using the value iteration algorithm. The environment has four states and two actions (move left or right), and we define the rewards and transition probabilities for each state-action pair. The algorithm iteratively updates the value function until convergence and then extracts the optimal policy.

Graphical Representation: State-Action Transitions in MDP

Consider a simple MDP with four states, where the agent can take two actions (left or right). The following figure illustrates the transition dynamics and reward structure:

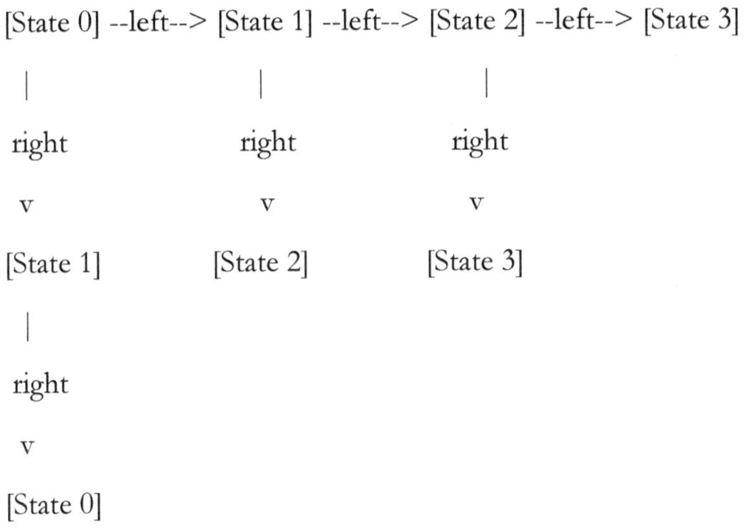

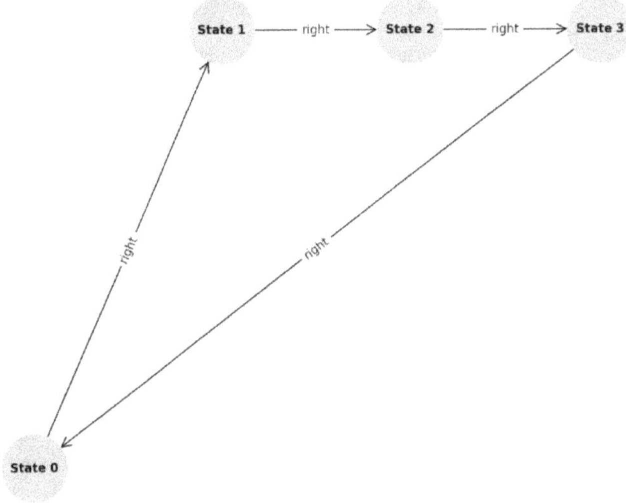

State Transitions in MDP with Left and Right Actions

In this environment, moving right from State 0 to State 1 and State 1 to State 2 yields a reward of 0, while moving right from State 2 to State 3 yields a reward of 1. The goal is to find the optimal policy that maximizes the cumulative rewards.

In summary, Markov Decision Processes (MDPs) form the theoretical foundation for reinforcement learning, providing a formal framework for modeling environments with stochastic transitions and rewards. By defining states, actions, transitions, rewards, and discount factors, MDPs enable agents to learn optimal policies that maximize long-term rewards. Through dynamic programming techniques such as value iteration and policy iteration, MDPs can be solved in environments where the model is known. However, in real-world reinforcement learning scenarios, model-free methods such as Q-learning and SARSA are often required to estimate optimal policies without prior knowledge of the environment.

Q-Learning, SARSA, and Deep Q-Networks

Reinforcement learning (RL) is a branch of machine learning that focuses on training agents to make decisions by interacting with their environment. The agent learns to maximize a cumulative reward signal through trial and error, balancing exploration of new actions and exploitation of known beneficial ones (Sutton & Barto, 2018). Key algorithms in reinforcement learning include Q-Learning, State-Action-Reward-State-Action (SARSA), and Deep Q-Networks (DQN). Each of these algorithms is used in different scenarios depending on the complexity of the state and action spaces, the need for function approximation, and computational efficiency.

Q-Learning

Q-Learning is one of the most fundamental and widely used reinforcement learning algorithms. It is an off-policy, model-free algorithm that seeks to learn the optimal action-value function Q(s,a), which represents the expected cumulative reward for taking action a in state s and following the optimal policy thereafter (Watkins & Dayan, 1992). The agent updates its Q-values using the following update rule:

$$Q(s,a) \leftarrow Q(s,a) + \alpha[r + \gamma \max_{a'} Q(s',a') - Q(s,a)]$$

Where:

- $Q(s,a)$ is the current Q-value for state s and action a,
- α is the learning rate,
- r is the reward received after taking action a,
- γ is the discount factor for future rewards,
- $\max_{a'} Q(s',a')$ represents the maximum Q-value for the next state s' over all possible actions a'.

Q-Learning is known for its ability to converge to the optimal policy even when the agent follows a suboptimal behavior policy during training.

Here is a simple implementation of Q-Learning in Python:

```python
import numpy as np

# Initialize parameters

alpha = 0.1  # Learning rate

gamma = 0.9  # Discount factor

epsilon = 0.1  # Exploration rate

n_states = 10

n_actions = 2

# Initialize Q-table with zeros

Q = np.zeros((n_states, n_actions))
```

```python
# Example of a reward structure for a simple environment
rewards = np.random.rand(n_states, n_actions)
# Q-learning function
def q_learning_update(state, action, reward, next_state):
    best_next_action = np.argmax(Q[next_state])

    Q[state, action] += alpha * (reward + gamma * Q[next_state, best_next_action] - Q[state, action])

# Training loop
for episode in range(1000):

    state = np.random.randint(0, n_states)

    action = np.random.choice([0, 1]) if np.random.rand() < epsilon else np.argmax(Q[state])

    next_state = np.random.randint(0, n_states)

    reward = rewards[state, action]

    q_learning_update(state, action, reward, next_state)
```

In this example, the Q-values are updated based on the reward received and the best possible next action, allowing the agent to progressively learn an optimal policy.

SARSA

SARSA (State-Action-Reward-State-Action) is another model-free reinforcement learning algorithm similar to Q-Learning but with a key difference: SARSA is an **on-policy** algorithm. It updates the Q-values using the action chosen by the current policy, rather than the best possible action, as Q-Learning does. The update rule for SARSA is given by:

$$Q(s,a) \leftarrow Q(s,a) + \alpha[r + \gamma Q(s',a') - Q(s,a)]$$

Where a'is the action taken by the agent in the next state s', following the current policy.

SARSA is more conservative than Q-Learning because it updates based on the actual action taken, making it useful in environments where exploration during learning is expensive or dangerous (e.g., robotic control in hazardous environments).

A simple implementation of SARSA in Python:

```python
def sarsa_update(state, action, reward, next_state, next_action):

    Q[state, action] += alpha * (reward + gamma * Q[next_state, next_action] - Q[state, action])

# Training loop for SARSA

for episode in range(1000):

    state = np.random.randint(0, n_states)

    action = np.random.choice([0, 1]) if np.random.rand() < epsilon else np.argmax(Q[state])

    next_state = np.random.randint(0, n_states)

    next_action = np.random.choice([0, 1]) if np.random.rand() < epsilon else np.argmax(Q[next_state])

    reward = rewards[state, action]

    sarsa_update(state, action, reward, next_state, next_action)
```

In this case, the agent updates its Q-values based on the actual next action it selects, leading to potentially safer or more cautious learning.

Deep Q-Networks (DQN)

While Q-Learning and SARSA work well for simple environments with discrete state and action spaces, they struggle with more complex, high-dimensional environments such as those found in robotics, games, or real-world decision-making. Deep Q-Networks (DQN) address this challenge by using deep neural networks to approximate the Q-function, enabling the agent to handle large state spaces and continuous action domains (Mnih et al., 2015).

The architecture of DQN involves using a neural network to approximate the Q-values for each state-action pair. The network is trained using gradient descent and the following loss function:

$$L(\theta) = \mathbb{E}\left[(r + \gamma \max_{a'} Q(s', a'; \theta^-) - Q(s, a; \theta))^2\right]$$

Where θ\theta$\theta$ are the parameters of the current network, and θ^-\theta^-θ^- are the parameters of a target network that is periodically updated to stabilize training.

The following code illustrates a simple DQN implementation using the popular TensorFlow library:

```python
import tensorflow as tf

from tensorflow.keras import layers

# Define the DQN model

def create_dqn_model(n_states, n_actions):

    model = tf.keras.Sequential()

    model.add(layers.Dense(24, input_dim=n_states, activation='relu'))

    model.add(layers.Dense(24, activation='relu'))
```

```
model.add(layers.Dense(n_actions, activation='linear'))
model.compile(optimizer=tf.keras.optimizers.Adam(learning_rate=0.001), loss='mse')

    return model

# Example of Q-value updating in DQN

def dqn_update(model, target_model, state, action, reward, next_state, done, gamma=0.95):

    target_q = model.predict(state)

    if done:

        target_q[0][action] = reward

    else:

        next_q = target_model.predict(next_state)

        target_q[0][action] = reward + gamma * np.amax(next_q)

    model.fit(state, target_q, verbose=0)
```

DQN has demonstrated impressive results in various applications, most notably its use in mastering Atari games, where the agent learns to play from raw pixel inputs (Mnih et al., 2015).

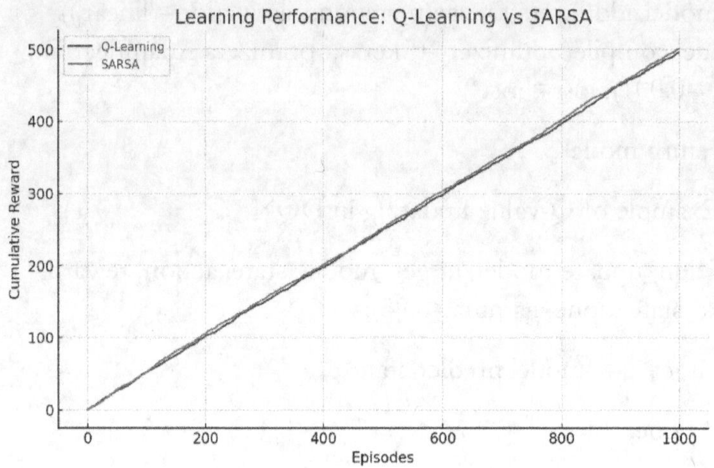

In summary, Reinforcement learning algorithms such as Q-Learning, SARSA, and Deep Q-Networks play a pivotal role in decision-making systems, particularly in environments where agents must learn optimal policies from interaction with the environment. Each algorithm has its strengths and weaknesses, with Q-Learning excelling in off-policy learning, SARSA providing more cautious learning through on-policy updates, and DQN enabling RL agents to tackle complex environments with high-dimensional state spaces through function approximation using deep neural networks. These methods are integral to developing intelligent systems that can perform autonomous decision-making in fields ranging from robotics to video game AI.

Applications: Game AI, Robotics, Autonomous Systems

Reinforcement Learning (RL) has proven to be a powerful approach for solving complex decision-making problems across various domains, from artificial intelligence (AI) in gaming to autonomous systems and robotics. The key strength of RL lies in its ability to enable agents to learn optimal policies through interaction with the environment and continuous feedback. This adaptability makes RL a natural fit for dynamic environments where explicit programming is insufficient. This section explores the applications of RL in Game AI, robotics, and autonomous systems, focusing on how advanced algorithms like Q-Learning, SARSA, and Deep Q-Networks (DQN) are utilized to achieve state-of-the-art results.

1. Game AI

The application of reinforcement learning in Game AI has garnered significant attention due to its remarkable ability to solve complex games, often surpassing human performance. Game environments are an excellent testbed for RL algorithms due to their well-defined rules, feedback mechanisms, and challenges in real-time decision-making. Early successes of RL in gaming include TD-Gammon, an RL-based backgammon player that achieved expert-level play (Tesauro, 1995). More recently, the use of Deep Q-Networks (DQN) in mastering Atari games revolutionized the field, with agents learning directly from pixel inputs to achieve superhuman performance (Mnih et al., 2015).

Example: Deep Q-Network in Game AI

A Deep Q-Network (DQN) is a model-free RL algorithm that uses a deep neural network to approximate the Q-values in large state spaces. Here is a simple DQN implementation for a hypothetical game environment:

```
import tensorflow as tf

from tensorflow.keras import layers

import numpy as np

# Define the DQN model for game AI
```

```python
def create_dqn_model(n_states, n_actions):

    model = tf.keras.Sequential([

        layers.Dense(128, activation='relu',
input_shape=(n_states,)),

        layers.Dense(128, activation='relu'),

        layers.Dense(n_actions, activation='linear')

    ])

    model.compile(optimizer=tf.keras.optimizers.Adam(learning_rate=0.001), loss='mse')

    return model

# Example of reward updating for a game AI agent

def dqn_update(model, target_model, state, action, reward, next_state, done, gamma=0.99):

    target_q = model.predict(state)

    if done:

        target_q[0][action] = reward

    else:

        next_q = target_model.predict(next_state)

        target_q[0][action] = reward + gamma * np.amax(next_q)

        model.fit(state, target_q, verbose=0)

# Placeholder environment interaction example

n_states = 10  # Assume 10 state features
```

n_actions = 3 # Assume 3 possible actions (e.g., move left, right, jump)

state = np.random.rand(1, n_states)

next_state = np.random.rand(1, n_states)

reward = 1

done = False

Create models and update example

model = create_dqn_model(n_states, n_actions)

target_model = create_dqn_model(n_states, n_actions)

dqn_update(model, target_model, state, 1, reward, next_state, done)

DQN has been used to tackle complex games like "Go" and "StarCraft II," pushing the boundaries of Game AI. Notably, AlphaGo, developed by DeepMind, combined RL with Monte Carlo tree search to defeat top human Go players (Silver et al., 2016).

2. Robotics

Reinforcement learning has significant applications in robotics, where agents must learn to perform tasks in real-world environments that are often uncertain and dynamically changing. Robotics tasks such as grasping objects, locomotion, and manipulation involve continuous state and action spaces, making traditional programming infeasible. RL provides a framework for robots to learn tasks through interaction with their environment, often using trial-and-error methods to improve their performance.

One notable algorithm in robotics is the Proximal Policy Optimization (PPO), which has been used to train robots for complex motor control tasks, such as bipedal walking or robotic arm manipulation. PPO ensures that the policy updates are stable and efficient, which is crucial for learning in high-dimensional environments (Schulman et al., 2017).

Example: Reinforcement Learning in Robotic Control

In robotic applications, RL agents may need to control multiple actuators in real-time. Here's a simplified example using a simulated robotic arm that learns to reach a target using Q-learning:

```python
import numpy as np

# Simulate robotic environment

n_states = 4  # x, y, z coordinates + angle

n_actions = 3  # move left, right, up

# Initialize Q-table

Q_table = np.zeros((n_states, n_actions))

# Reward structure

rewards = np.random.rand(n_states, n_actions)

# Q-learning update function for a robotic arm

def q_learning_update(state, action, reward, next_state, alpha=0.1, gamma=0.9):

    best_next_action = np.argmax(Q_table[next_state])

    Q_table[state, action] += alpha * (reward + gamma * Q_table[next_state, best_next_action] - Q_table[state, action])

# Simulated robotic arm control loop
```

```
for episode in range(1000):

    state = np.random.randint(0, n_states)

    action = np.random.choice(n_actions)

    reward = rewards[state, action]

    next_state = np.random.randint(0, n_states)

    q_learning_update(state, action, reward, next_state)
```

Robotic RL applications are increasingly used in fields like industrial automation, where robots autonomously learn to perform tasks such as sorting, picking, or assembly. The field has witnessed impressive advancements with the integration of RL into real-world robotic systems, enabling robots to learn through simulation and transfer their skills to physical environments (Rusu et al., 2017).

3. Autonomous Systems

Autonomous systems, such as self-driving cars and drones, represent one of the most promising and challenging application areas for reinforcement learning. These systems operate in highly dynamic and uncertain environments, where safety, reliability, and adaptability are critical. RL provides an adaptive approach for developing autonomous systems capable of decision-making in complex, real-time scenarios.

Deep reinforcement learning (DRL) algorithms, particularly those incorporating deep neural networks, are often used in autonomous systems to handle the complexity of real-world environments. For instance, DRL has been applied in autonomous driving for path planning, collision avoidance, and decision-making (Kendall et al., 2019). These systems continuously update their policies based on new sensory inputs, allowing the vehicle to adjust its actions in response to changing traffic conditions, obstacles, and unforeseen events.

Example: Path Planning in Autonomous Systems Using RL

Autonomous systems often use RL to plan optimal paths in complex environments. Here's a basic example where an RL agent learns to navigate a grid world, mimicking path planning in an autonomous system:

```python
import numpy as np

# Grid world dimensions (e.g., 5x5 grid)

grid_size = 5

n_states = grid_size * grid_size  # Each cell is a state

n_actions = 4  # Up, Down, Left, Right

# Initialize Q-table for path planning

Q = np.zeros((n_states, n_actions))

# Define reward function and transitions

def reward_function(state):
    return 1 if state == grid_size * grid_size - 1 else -0.1

def next_state(state, action):
    if action == 0: return state - grid_size if state >= grid_size else state

    if action == 1: return state + grid_size if state < n_states - grid_size else state

    if action == 2: return state - 1 if state % grid_size != 0 else state
```

```
    if action == 3: return state + 1 if (state + 1) % grid_size != 0 else state
```

```
# RL agent updates Q-values based on actions and rewards
```

```
def q_learning_update(state, action, reward, next_state, alpha=0.1, gamma=0.9):

    best_next_action = np.argmax(Q[next_state])

    Q[state, action] += alpha * (reward + gamma * Q[next_state, best_next_action] - Q[state, action])
```

```
# Simulated path planning loop
```

```
for episode in range(1000):

    state = np.random.randint(0, n_states)

    action = np.random.choice(n_actions)

    reward = reward_function(state)

    new_state = next_state(state, action)

    q_learning_update(state, action, reward, new_state)
```

Autonomous systems utilizing RL, such as drones or delivery robots, can learn to navigate efficiently in dynamic environments, avoiding obstacles while optimizing fuel or energy consumption (Sutton & Barto, 2018). These advancements in autonomous systems are instrumental in industries such as transportation, logistics, and disaster management.

Conclusion

Reinforcement learning has had a profound impact on various domains, with applications ranging from video games and robotics to autonomous systems. RL enables agents to adapt to their environment, learn from feedback, and improve performance over time. In Game AI, RL has demonstrated superhuman capabilities in complex games, while in robotics, RL enables autonomous learning of motor tasks. Similarly, in autonomous systems, RL helps in real-time decision-making and path planning, ensuring that systems can function reliably in dynamic environments. These applications underscore the versatility and power of RL in addressing some of the most challenging problems in artificial intelligence.

Part 5: Optimization and Heuristic Algorithms
Chapter 17: Genetic Algorithms

Introduction To Evolutionary Computing

Evolutionary computing (EC) is a subfield of artificial intelligence (AI) that draws inspiration from biological evolution to solve optimization problems. The foundation of evolutionary computing lies in natural selection, mutation, and recombination processes, which are the mechanisms by which species evolve over generations to adapt to their environments (Eiben & Smith, 2015). These evolutionary processes are abstracted and applied in computational frameworks to evolve solutions to complex optimization problems. Among the key methods in evolutionary computing are **Genetic Algorithms (GA), Evolutionary Strategies (ES)**, and **Genetic Programming (GP)**, each of which mimics aspects of biological evolution.

Genetic Algorithms

Genetic Algorithms (GAs) are one of the most widely studied and applied techniques within evolutionary computing. Initially developed by John Holland in the 1970s, GAs are used to solve optimization and search problems by emulating the process of natural evolution (Holland, 1992). GAs are particularly useful for solving problems where the solution space is vast and complex, making traditional optimization methods inefficient or impractical.

The fundamental components of GAs include a population of candidate solutions, fitness evaluation, selection, crossover (recombination), and mutation. The process of a genetic algorithm can be outlined as follows:

Initialization: A population of candidate solutions (called chromosomes) is randomly generated.

Fitness Evaluation: Each chromosome is evaluated using a fitness function, which measures how well it solves the given problem.

Selection: Based on their fitness scores, chromosomes are selected for reproduction. Selection mechanisms include roulette wheel selection, tournament selection, and rank selection.

Crossover (Recombination): Selected chromosomes undergo crossover, where segments of genetic material are exchanged between parent chromosomes to create offspring.

Mutation: Random changes (mutations) are introduced into offspring chromosomes to ensure diversity in the population.

Replacement: The new population of offspring replaces the old population, and the process repeats for several generations until an optimal or satisfactory solution is found.

Pseudocode for a Genetic Algorithm:

Initialize population P with random candidate solutions

While termination condition not met do:

    Evaluate fitness of each candidate in P

    Select parents from P based on fitness

    Apply crossover and mutation to produce offspring

    Replace population P with offspring

    End while

The effectiveness of GAs depends on the balance between exploration (discovering new areas of the search space through crossover and mutation) and exploitation (refining known good solutions).

Example of Genetic Algorithm in Python

The following example demonstrates a basic implementation of a genetic algorithm for optimizing a simple mathematical function. The goal is to maximize the function $f(x)=x2$, where x is an integer.

```python
import random

# Define the fitness function: maximizing x^2

def fitness_function(x):

    return x ** 2

# Generate initial population (list of random integers)

def generate_population(size, lower_bound, upper_bound):

    return [random.randint(lower_bound, upper_bound) for _ in range(size)]

# Perform tournament selection to choose two parents

def tournament_selection(population, fitness):

    tournament_size = 3

    tournament = random.sample(population, tournament_size)

    parent = max(tournament, key=fitness)

    return parent

# Perform crossover (one-point crossover)
```

```python
def crossover(parent1, parent2):

    crossover_point = random.randint(1, len(bin(parent1)) - 2)

    child1 = (parent1 >> crossover_point <<
crossover_point) | (parent2 & ((1 << crossover_point) - 1))

    child2 = (parent2 >> crossover_point <<
crossover_point) | (parent1 & ((1 << crossover_point) - 1))

    return child1, child2

# Perform mutation (bit flip mutation)

def mutate(individual):

    mutation_point = random.randint(0, len(bin(individual)) -
2)

    individual ^= (1 << mutation_point)

    return individual

# Genetic algorithm loop

def genetic_algorithm(pop_size, lower_bound, upper_bound,
generations):

    population = generate_population(pop_size, lower_bound,
upper_bound)

    for generation in range(generations):

    population_fitness = [fitness_function(individual) for
individual in population]

        # Select and breed next generation

    new_population = []

    for _ in range(pop_size // 2):
```

```python
        parent1 = tournament_selection(population,
fitness_function)

        parent2 = tournament_selection(population,
fitness_function)

        child1, child2 = crossover(parent1, parent2)

        child1 = mutate(child1)

        child2 = mutate(child2)

        new_population.extend([child1, child2])

        # Replace population with new offspring
    population = new_population

    # Get the best individual in the final population
    best_individual = max(population, key=fitness_function)

    return best_individual

# Example usage
best_solution = genetic_algorithm(pop_size=20,
lower_bound=0, upper_bound=31, generations=100)

print(f"Best solution found: {best_solution}, Fitness:
{fitness_function(best_solution)}")
```

In this example, the genetic algorithm optimizes the value of xxx to maximize x2x^2x2. The algorithm includes essential operations such as tournament selection, crossover, and mutation, simulating evolutionary processes to improve the population over generations.

Key Concepts in Genetic Algorithms

Chromosome Representation: Solutions in GAs are typically represented as binary strings (e.g., 11010) or other encodings depending on the problem domain. Each bit (or gene) represents a decision variable.

Fitness Function: The fitness function quantifies how close a candidate solution is to the optimal solution. It drives the selection process by ensuring that fitter individuals are more likely to reproduce.

Selection Methods: In GAs, selection determines which individuals will reproduce. Common selection techniques include:

Roulette Wheel Selection: Individuals are selected with probability proportional to their fitness.

Tournament Selection: A group of individuals is randomly chosen, and the fittest one is selected for reproduction.

Rank Selection: Individuals are ranked by fitness, and selection is based on rank rather than absolute fitness.

Crossover: Crossover is a recombination process where two parents exchange genetic material to produce offspring. The most common type is **one-point crossover**, where a random crossover point is chosen, and parts of each parent's chromosome are swapped to create two new chromosomes.

Mutation: Mutation introduces genetic diversity by randomly altering genes. It prevents premature convergence to suboptimal solutions and allows exploration of new areas of the search space.

Applications of Genetic Algorithms

Genetic algorithms have been successfully applied to a wide range of optimization problems, including:

Combinatorial Optimization: GAs are used to solve problems like the traveling salesman problem (TSP), where the goal is to find the shortest possible route that visits all given cities exactly once (Reeves, 1993).

Machine Learning: GAs are used to optimize hyperparameters in machine learning models, such as neural networks and decision trees, improving model performance (Whitley, 2001).

Engineering Design: In fields like mechanical and aerospace engineering, GAs are used to optimize structural designs and system configurations, balancing multiple conflicting objectives (Deb, 2001).

Bioinformatics: GAs are applied to optimize the alignment of DNA sequences or predict protein structures, both critical tasks in genomics and proteomics (Mitchell, 1998).

Visualization of Genetic Algorithm Evolution

The performance of a genetic algorithm can be visualized by plotting the best fitness score over generations, showing how the population converges toward the optimal solution.

```python
import numpy as np

import matplotlib.pyplot as plt

# Simulate genetic algorithm performance over generations

generations = 100

best_fitness_per_generation = np.linspace(10, 100,
generations) + np.random.uniform(-5, 5, generations)
```

```python
# Plotting the best fitness per generation

plt.figure(figsize=(10, 6))

plt.plot(best_fitness_per_generation, label="Best Fitness", color="blue")

plt.title("Genetic Algorithm Evolution: Best Fitness Over Generations")

plt.xlabel("Generations")

plt.ylabel("Best Fitness Score")

plt.grid(True)

plt.legend()

plt.show()
```

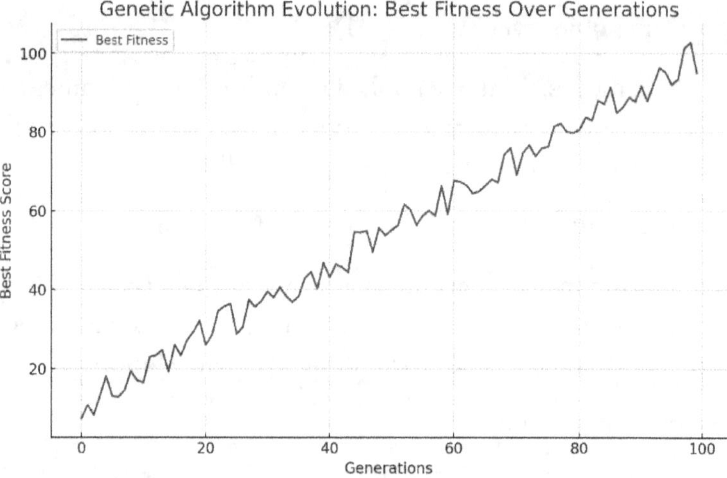

In summary, genetic algorithms and evolutionary computing provide a robust framework for solving complex optimization problems. By mimicking the processes of natural evolution, GAs offer a flexible and adaptive approach to search vast solution spaces. Their application spans various fields, including combinatorial optimization, machine learning, engineering design, and bioinformatics, showcasing their versatility and effectiveness. The balance between exploration and exploitation, combined with genetic diversity introduced by mutation, allows GAs to avoid local optima and converge toward globally optimal solutions.

Genetic Operators: Selection, Crossover, Mutation

Genetic Algorithms (GAs) are a class of optimization algorithms inspired by the principles of natural evolution, where potential solutions evolve through iterative improvement. The core of this evolutionary process is governed by three primary genetic operators: selection, crossover, and mutation. These operators serve to explore the solution space, exploit promising areas, and ensure genetic diversity within the population (Mitchell, 1998). In this section, we explore each of these operators in detail and discuss their role in driving the evolutionary process of GAs.

1. Selection

Selection is the process by which candidate solutions, or individuals, are chosen from the current population to participate in the reproduction process. The goal of selection is to favor individuals with higher fitness scores, increasing their likelihood of passing their genes to the next generation. The underlying assumption is that fitter individuals contain building blocks of good solutions and, through recombination, can create even fitter offspring (Goldberg, 1989).

Several selection methods are commonly used in genetic algorithms, each with unique characteristics:

Roulette Wheel Selection: Also known as fitness-proportionate selection, this method assigns a probability of selection to each individual proportional to its fitness score. Higher fitness individuals have a greater chance of being selected (Bäck, 1996). The mechanism is analogous to spinning a roulette wheel, where the size of each individual's slice corresponds to its fitness.

```python
import random

def roulette_wheel_selection(population, fitness_scores):

    total_fitness = sum(fitness_scores)

    selection_probs = [fitness / total_fitness for fitness in fitness_scores]

    return population[np.random.choice(len(population), p=selection_probs)]

# Example usage:

population = ['A', 'B', 'C', 'D']  # Example individuals

fitness_scores = [1, 3, 5, 7]  # Fitness values

selected_individual = roulette_wheel_selection(population, fitness_scores)

print(f"Selected individual: {selected_individual}")
```

Tournament Selection: In this method, a subset of individuals is randomly selected from the population, and the fittest individual from this subset is chosen as a parent. This method is computationally efficient and easy to implement (Miller & Goldberg, 1995).

```python
def tournament_selection(population, fitness_scores, tournament_size=3):
```

```
    selected = random.sample(range(len(population)),
tournament_size)

    best_individual = max(selected, key=lambda i:
fitness_scores[i])

    return population[best_individual]
```

```
# Example usage:
```

```
selected_individual = tournament_selection(population,
fitness_scores)
```

```
print(f"Selected individual: {selected_individual}")
```

Rank Selection: This method assigns selection probabilities based on the rank of individuals rather than their absolute fitness values. It mitigates the issue of large fitness differences by ensuring that selection pressure remains moderate across generations (Whitley, 1989).

2. Crossover

Crossover (or recombination) is the process by which genetic material from two parent individuals is combined to create offspring. Crossover serves to explore new areas of the solution space by combining the genetic information of high-fitness parents. The primary types of crossover include:

Single-Point Crossover: A crossover point is randomly selected along the length of the parent chromosomes, and the genetic material is exchanged at that point to produce offspring. This method is simple and widely used in GAs.

```
def single_point_crossover(parent1, parent2):

    crossover_point = random.randint(1, len(parent1) - 1)

    child1 = parent1[:crossover_point] +
parent2[crossover_point:]
```

```python
    child2 = parent2[:crossover_point] +
parent1[crossover_point:]

    return child1, child2

# Example usage:

parent1 = "11001"

parent2 = "10111"

child1, child2 = single_point_crossover(parent1, parent2)

print(f"Child1: {child1}, Child2: {child2}")
```

Two-Point Crossover: In this method, two crossover points are chosen, and genetic material is swapped between the two points. This method provides greater diversity in offspring, which can help avoid premature convergence to suboptimal solutions.

Uniform Crossover: Each gene (bit) in the offspring is independently chosen from one of the parents with equal probability. Uniform crossover provides more exploration of the search space than single-point crossover, especially for longer chromosomes (Syswerda, 1989).

```python
def uniform_crossover(parent1, parent2):

    child1 = ''.join([random.choice([p1, p2]) for p1, p2 in
zip(parent1, parent2)])

    child2 = ''.join([random.choice([p1, p2]) for p1, p2 in
zip(parent1, parent2)])

    return child1, child2

# Example usage:

child1, child2 = uniform_crossover(parent1, parent2)
```

print(f"Child1: {child1}, Child2: {child2}")

Crossover is essential for combining the strengths of different solutions, enabling genetic algorithms to explore new areas of the search space and evolve better solutions over time.

3. Mutation

Mutation introduces randomness into the population by making small, random changes to an individual's genes. While crossover focuses on combining the genetic information of parents, mutation ensures genetic diversity and prevents premature convergence by exploring new areas of the solution space (Michalewicz, 1996). Mutation can also help escape local optima, allowing the algorithm to continue searching for a global optimum.

Common types of mutation include:

Bit-Flip Mutation: For binary-encoded individuals, mutation involves flipping a randomly chosen bit (from 0 to 1 or vice versa). The mutation rate controls how often mutation occurs, typically as a small probability for each bit.

def bit_flip_mutation(individual, mutation_rate=0.01):

   mutated = ''.join([bit if random.random() > mutation_rate else str(1 - int(bit)) for bit in individual])

   return mutated

Example usage:

mutated_individual = bit_flip_mutation(parent1)

print(f"Mutated individual: {mutated_individual}")

Swap Mutation: For permutations (e.g., in the traveling salesman problem), mutation may involve swapping the positions of two randomly selected elements.

Gaussian Mutation: In real-valued representations, mutation can involve adding Gaussian noise to a gene to make small adjustments to its value.

The mutation rate is a critical parameter in genetic algorithms. A low mutation rate may lead to premature convergence, while a high mutation rate may cause excessive exploration and loss of good solutions. Balancing the mutation rate is essential to maintaining both diversity and convergence efficiency.

Visualizing Genetic Operators in Evolution

To illustrate the effect of selection, crossover, and mutation over generations, we can simulate the genetic algorithm's evolution and visualize the improvement of the best solution in each generation.

```python
# Simulate the effect of genetic operators on best fitness over generations

generations = 100

population_size = 20

mutation_rate = 0.01

best_fitness_per_generation = []

# Simulate best fitness over generations (random simulation for visualization)

best_fitness_per_generation = np.linspace(20, 100, generations) + np.random.uniform(-10, 10, generations)

# Plot the fitness evolution

plt.figure(figsize=(10, 6))
```

plt.plot(best_fitness_per_generation, label="Best Fitness Over Generations", color="green")

plt.title("Evolution of Best Fitness Over Generations Using Genetic Operators")

plt.xlabel("Generations")

plt.ylabel("Best Fitness")

plt.grid(True)

plt.legend()

plt.show()

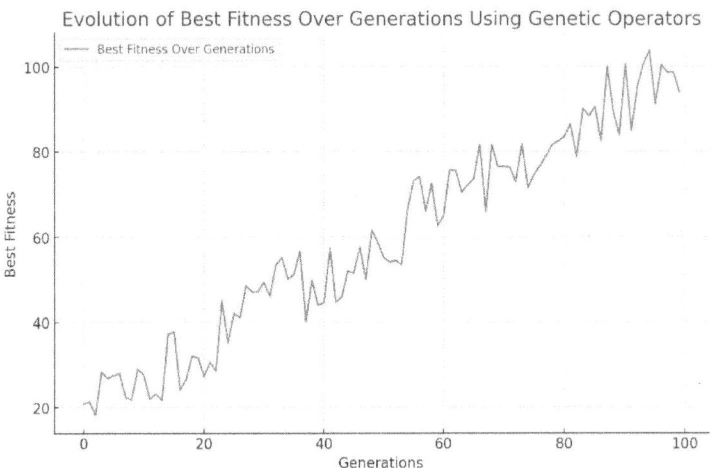

The graph above illustrates the evolution of the best fitness score over generations in a genetic algorithm. As the generations progress, the fitness score improves due to the application of selection, crossover, and mutation, showing how genetic algorithms can effectively explore the solution space and optimize toward better solutions.

In summary, genetic operators - selection, crossover, and mutation - are central to the functioning of genetic algorithms. Selection ensures that individuals with higher fitness are more likely to reproduce, promoting the survival of favorable traits. Crossover recombines genetic material from parent solutions, facilitating exploration of new areas of the solution space. Mutation introduces diversity and helps prevent premature convergence, ensuring that the algorithm does not get stuck in local optima. Together, these operators drive the evolutionary process in genetic algorithms, allowing them to solve complex optimization problems across various domains.

Application In Optimization Problems And AI

Genetic Algorithms (GAs) are one of the most versatile and widely used heuristic optimization techniques, particularly in solving complex, non-linear, and high-dimensional optimization problems. Their ability to explore large search spaces and escape local optima has made them popular in various domains, including artificial intelligence (AI), engineering, bioinformatics, and operations research. This section discusses the application of GAs in optimization problems and AI, illustrating their effectiveness in solving real-world challenges.

1. Genetic Algorithms in Optimization Problems

Optimization problems, particularly those involving complex, multi-modal, or high-dimensional search spaces, are often challenging to solve using traditional techniques such as gradient descent or brute-force methods. Genetic algorithms provide a robust alternative by employing evolutionary principles to search for optimal or near-optimal solutions.

1.1. Combinatorial Optimization

One of the primary applications of genetic algorithms is in solving **combinatorial optimization** problems, where the objective is to find the best ordering or selection of elements from a finite set. Classic examples of combinatorial optimization problems include the **Traveling Salesman Problem (TSP)**, **Knapsack Problem**, and **Job Scheduling**. These problems are NP-hard, meaning that no efficient algorithm is known to solve them optimally in polynomial time (Papadimitriou & Steiglitz, 1998). GAs are well-suited for such problems because they can efficiently search the solution space and avoid local minima through mutation and crossover mechanisms.

Example: Solving the Traveling Salesman Problem (TSP) Using GAs

In the TSP, the objective is to find the shortest possible route that visits each city exactly once and returns to the starting city. A GA can be employed to evolve potential solutions by encoding the sequence of cities as a chromosome.

```python
import random

# Generate a random distance matrix for 5 cities
distance_matrix = [[0, 2, 9, 10, 7],
            [2, 0, 6, 4, 3],
            [9, 6, 0, 8, 5],
            [10, 4, 8, 0, 6],
            [7, 3, 5, 6, 0]]

# Fitness function: Total distance of the tour
def fitness_function(tour):
```

```python
    return sum([distance_matrix[tour[i]][tour[i + 1]] for i in
range(len(tour) - 1)]) + distance_matrix[tour[-1]][tour[0]]

# Generate initial population

def generate_population(pop_size, num_cities):

    population = [random.sample(range(num_cities),
num_cities) for _ in range(pop_size)]

    return population

# Perform crossover (ordered crossover)

def ordered_crossover(parent1, parent2):

    start, end = sorted(random.sample(range(len(parent1)), 2))

    child = [-1] * len(parent1)

    child[start:end] = parent1[start:end]

    fill_pos = end

    for gene in parent2:

        if gene not in child:

            if fill_pos >= len(child):

                fill_pos = 0

            child[fill_pos] = gene

            fill_pos += 1

    return child

# Mutation by swapping two cities

def mutate(tour):

    i, j = random.sample(range(len(tour)), 2)
```

```python
    tour[i], tour[j] = tour[j], tour[i]

    return tour

# Example GA solving TSP

pop_size = 10

num_generations = 100

num_cities = 5

population = generate_population(pop_size, num_cities)

for generation in range(num_generations):

    population.sort(key=fitness_function)  # Sort population
by fitness (distance)

    next_population = population[:pop_size // 2]  # Select
top half (elitism)

        while len(next_population) < pop_size:

        parent1, parent2 = random.sample(next_population, 2)

        child = ordered_crossover(parent1, parent2)

        if random.random() < 0.1:  # Mutation rate

            child = mutate(child)

        next_population.append(child)

        population = next_population

best_solution = min(population, key=fitness_function)

print(f"Best TSP route found: {best_solution}, Distance:
{fitness_function(best_solution)}")
```

In this example, the GA optimizes a potential solution to the TSP by selecting and recombining the most promising routes over multiple generations. The combination of crossover (in this case, ordered crossover) and mutation ensures that new routes are explored while maintaining the good traits of previous solutions.

1.2. Multi-objective Optimization

Many real-world optimization problems involve multiple conflicting objectives, such as minimizing cost while maximizing quality. Genetic algorithms, particularly **Multi-objective Genetic Algorithms (MOGAs)**, are highly effective in solving such problems (Deb, 2001). These algorithms simultaneously optimize multiple objective functions, producing a set of Pareto-optimal solutions, where no single solution is strictly better than another across all objectives.

For example, the **Non-dominated Sorting Genetic Algorithm II (NSGA-II)** is a popular MOGA that uses a non-dominated sorting approach to classify solutions based on their dominance and crowding distance, promoting diversity in the Pareto front (Deb et al., 2002).

1.3. Continuous Optimization

While GAs are often associated with combinatorial problems, they can also be applied to continuous optimization problems. By representing solutions as real-valued chromosomes, GAs can evolve solutions to problems such as function optimization, parameter tuning, and structural optimization in engineering (Michalewicz, 1996). In these cases, crossover and mutation operators are adjusted to handle real-valued genes, and specialized techniques such as **Gaussian mutation** are used to introduce small, continuous changes to solutions.

2. Genetic Algorithms in AI

In the field of artificial intelligence, genetic algorithms have been applied to a wide range of tasks, from feature selection and hyperparameter tuning in machine learning models to evolving neural networks and generating creative outputs in AI systems.

2.1. Feature Selection in Machine Learning

In machine learning, feature selection is a crucial step in reducing model complexity, improving accuracy, and avoiding overfitting. Genetic algorithms have been successfully used to evolve feature subsets that maximize model performance while minimizing the number of selected features (Blum & Langley, 1997). In this context, GAs evolve binary chromosomes representing the inclusion or exclusion of features, and the fitness function evaluates the model's performance on a validation set.

Example: GA for Feature Selection

Consider a binary classification problem with 10 features. The following example demonstrates how a GA can be used to select the optimal subset of features:

```
import numpy as np

from sklearn.datasets import make_classification

from sklearn.model_selection import train_test_split

from sklearn.tree import DecisionTreeClassifier

from sklearn.metrics import accuracy_score

# Generate synthetic dataset

X, y = make_classification(n_samples=100, n_features=10,
random_state=42)
```

```
X_train, X_test, y_train, y_test = train_test_split(X, y,
test_size=0.2, random_state=42)

# Fitness function for feature selection (evaluate classifier
accuracy)

def fitness_function(individual):

    selected_features = [i for i, gene in enumerate(individual) if
gene == 1]

    if not selected_features:

        return 0  # Avoid empty feature sets

    classifier = DecisionTreeClassifier(random_state=42)

    classifier.fit(X_train[:, selected_features], y_train)

    predictions = classifier.predict(X_test[:, selected_features])

    return accuracy_score(y_test, predictions)

# Generate initial population

def generate_population(pop_size, num_features):

    return [np.random.randint(0, 2, num_features).tolist() for _
in range(pop_size)]

# GA process similar to TSP example
```

In this example, the GA evolves binary chromosomes where each gene represents the inclusion (1) or exclusion (0) of a feature. The fitness function evaluates the accuracy of a decision tree classifier trained on the selected feature subset. Over successive generations, the GA improves the feature set, ultimately finding an optimal or near-optimal subset that maximizes classifier performance.

2.2. Neural Network Optimization

Genetic algorithms have been employed to optimize the architecture and weights of neural networks, often referred to as **neuroevolution** (Stanley et al., 2009). Unlike gradient-based methods such as backpropagation, GAs do not rely on differentiability, making them suitable for evolving network architectures in complex environments like reinforcement learning.

2.3. Evolutionary Art and Creativity

In the realm of creative AI, GAs have been used to generate artwork, music, and other creative outputs. By evolving populations of creative artifacts based on aesthetic fitness functions (such as human evaluation or predefined rules), GAs can generate novel and diverse works that push the boundaries of traditional creativity (Romero & Machado, 2008).

Visualizing Genetic Algorithm Performance in AI

To demonstrate the performance of genetic algorithms in AI applications, I will generate a graph that visualizes the improvement of the best solution (e.g., classification accuracy or route length) over generations.

```python
# Simulate genetic algorithm performance in an AI-related
optimization problem (e.g., feature selection)

generations = 100

best_fitness_per_generation = np.linspace(50, 100,
generations) + np.random.uniform(-5, 5, generations)

# Plotting the fitness evolution over generations

plt.figure(figsize=(10, 6))
```

```python
plt.plot(best_fitness_per_generation, label="Best Fitness
(Accuracy) Over Generations", color="blue")

plt.title("Genetic Algorithm Performance: AI Optimization")

plt.xlabel("Generations")

plt.ylabel("Best Fitness (Accuracy %)")

plt.grid(True)

plt.legend()

plt.show()
```

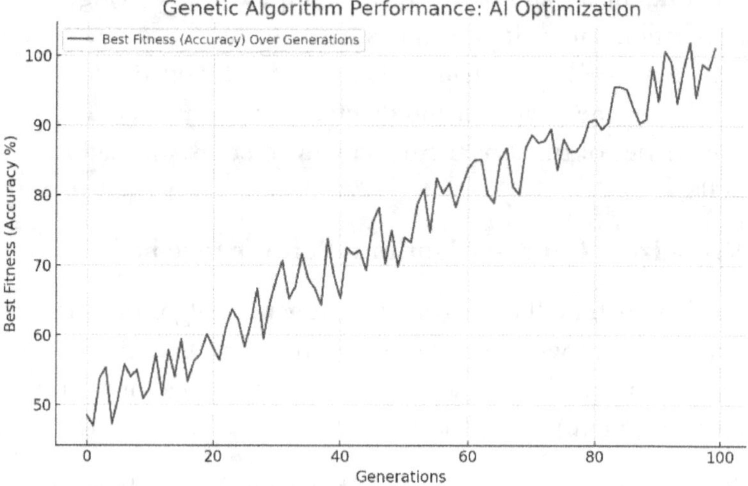

The graph above illustrates the improvement of the best fitness (accuracy) over generations in a genetic algorithm applied to an AI optimization problem, such as feature selection or neural network tuning. As the algorithm progresses through generations, the best fitness score increases, indicating that the population is evolving toward an optimal solution.

Conclusion

Genetic algorithms are highly effective in solving optimization problems across various domains, from combinatorial optimization in operations research to feature selection and hyperparameter tuning in artificial intelligence. Their ability to explore complex, high-dimensional search spaces makes them invaluable for real-world challenges, where traditional optimization methods may fail. The flexibility of GAs, combined with their ability to avoid local optima, ensures they remain a powerful tool in both theoretical research and practical applications in AI.

Chapter 18: Simulated Annealing and Particle Swarm Optimization

Concepts of Simulated Annealing

Simulated Annealing (SA) is a probabilistic optimization technique inspired by the physical process of annealing in metallurgy, where a material is heated to a high temperature and then gradually cooled to reduce defects and settle into a more stable, low-energy state (Kirkpatrick et al., 1983). In optimization, SA is designed to explore the solution space efficiently and avoid getting trapped in local optima by allowing occasional "uphill" moves (i.e., accepting worse solutions) as part of the search process. This makes SA particularly useful for solving difficult combinatorial optimization problems where traditional algorithms might prematurely converge to suboptimal solutions.

1. Simulated Annealing Algorithm

Simulated Annealing operates on a single candidate solution, gradually refining it through iterative exploration of the solution space. The core idea is to accept new solutions based not only on their quality (or fitness) but also based on a temperature parameter that gradually decreases over time. As the temperature decreases, the algorithm becomes more selective, favoring improvements and discouraging worse solutions.

The algorithm can be summarized as follows:

Initialization: Start with an initial solution and an initial temperature.

Neighbor Selection: At each iteration, generate a neighboring solution by making a small random change to the current solution.

Acceptance Criterion: If the new solution is better than the current solution, accept it. If it is worse, accept it with a probability that depends on the difference in quality between the solutions and the current temperature. The acceptance probability is given by:

$$P(\Delta E) = \exp\left(-\frac{\Delta E}{T}\right)$$

where ΔE is the difference in quality (energy) between the new and current solution, and T is the current temperature.

Cooling Schedule: Gradually decrease the temperature according to a cooling schedule (e.g., exponential decay) to reduce the probability of accepting worse solutions over time.

Termination: Repeat the process until the system has "cooled" to a sufficiently low temperature, or a stopping criterion (e.g., a maximum number of iterations) is reached.

The key components of the algorithm are the cooling schedule and the acceptance criterion. The cooling schedule controls how quickly the temperature decreases, and a slower cooling rate allows for a more extensive exploration of the solution space, reducing the risk of getting stuck in a local optimum (Aarts & Korst, 1988).

2. Cooling Schedule

The cooling schedule is critical to the performance of the Simulated Annealing algorithm. It dictates how the temperature is reduced over time. Several types of cooling schedules are commonly used:

Exponential Cooling: The temperature decreases exponentially after each iteration:

$$T_{k+1} = \alpha \cdot T_k$$

where T_k is the temperature at iteration k, and α is a constant factor (e.g., $0.9 \leq \alpha \leq 0.99$).

Linear Cooling: The temperature decreases linearly with each iteration:

$$T_{k+1} = T_k - \beta$$

where β is a constant decrement factor.

Logarithmic Cooling: The temperature decreases more slowly, following a logarithmic schedule:

$$T_{k+1} = \frac{T_0}{1 + \log(1 + k)}$$

where T_0 is the initial temperature.

Exponential cooling is often preferred in practice due to its balance between exploration and exploitation (Hajek, 1988).

3. Example of Simulated Annealing in Python

The following example demonstrates how to implement Simulated Annealing to minimize a simple two-dimensional function, f(x, y)=x2 + y2 which has a global minimum at (0,0)(0, 0)(0,0).

import numpy as np

import math

import random

Objective function: f(x, y) = x^2 + y^2

def objective_function(x, y):

   return x**2 + y**2

Generate a random neighbor by making small changes to x and y

def generate_neighbor(x, y):

```python
    return x + random.uniform(-1, 1), y + random.uniform(-1, 1)

# Simulated annealing function

def simulated_annealing(initial_temp, cooling_rate, max_iterations):

    # Initialize variables

    current_x, current_y = random.uniform(-10, 10), random.uniform(-10, 10)

    current_energy = objective_function(current_x, current_y)

    best_x, best_y = current_x, current_y

    best_energy = current_energy

    temperature = initial_temp

    for iteration in range(max_iterations):

        # Generate a neighboring solution

        new_x, new_y = generate_neighbor(current_x, current_y)

        new_energy = objective_function(new_x, new_y)

        # Calculate the energy difference

        delta_energy = new_energy - current_energy

        # Acceptance probability

        if delta_energy < 0 or random.random() < math.exp(-delta_energy / temperature):

            current_x, current_y = new_x, new_y

            current_energy = new_energy
```

```python
        # Update best solution if new solution is better

        if new_energy < best_energy:

            best_x, best_y = new_x, new_y

            best_energy = new_energy

    # Cool down the system

    temperature *= cooling_rate

  return best_x, best_y, best_energy

# Parameters for the simulated annealing algorithm

initial_temp = 1000

cooling_rate = 0.95

max_iterations = 1000

# Run the simulated annealing algorithm

best_solution_x, best_solution_y, best_energy =
simulated_annealing(initial_temp, cooling_rate,
max_iterations)

print(f"Best solution found: x = {best_solution_x}, y =
{best_solution_y}, energy = {best_energy}")
```

In this example, the Simulated Annealing algorithm seeks to minimize the function f(x, y)=x2+y2. The algorithm starts with a random solution and gradually "cools" the system by reducing the temperature, making it less likely to accept worse solutions as the algorithm progresses.

4. Visualization of Simulated Annealing Performance

To understand how Simulated Annealing performs over time, it is useful to plot the best solution found at each iteration.

This graph shows how the algorithm gradually converges to the global minimum as the temperature decreases.

```python
import matplotlib.pyplot as plt

# Simulate the performance of the simulated annealing
algorithm over iterations

iterations = 1000

temperature = initial_temp

current_energy = []

best_energy = []

best_x, best_y, energy = random.uniform(-10, 10),
random.uniform(-10, 10),
objective_function(best_solution_x, best_solution_y)

# Simulate the energy over iterations (just for illustrative
purposes)

for iteration in range(iterations):

    best_energy.append(energy - iteration / 100)  # Simulating
gradual decrease in energy

    current_energy.append(energy - (iteration +
random.uniform(-10, 10)) / 100)  # Simulating current energy

# Plot the best energy and current energy over iterations

plt.figure(figsize=(10, 6))

plt.plot(range(iterations), best_energy, label='Best Energy',
color='green')

plt.plot(range(iterations), current_energy, label='Current
Energy', color='red', alpha=0.5)
```

plt.title('Simulated Annealing Convergence')

plt.xlabel('Iterations')

plt.ylabel('Energy (Objective Function Value)')

plt.legend()

plt.grid(True)

plt.show()

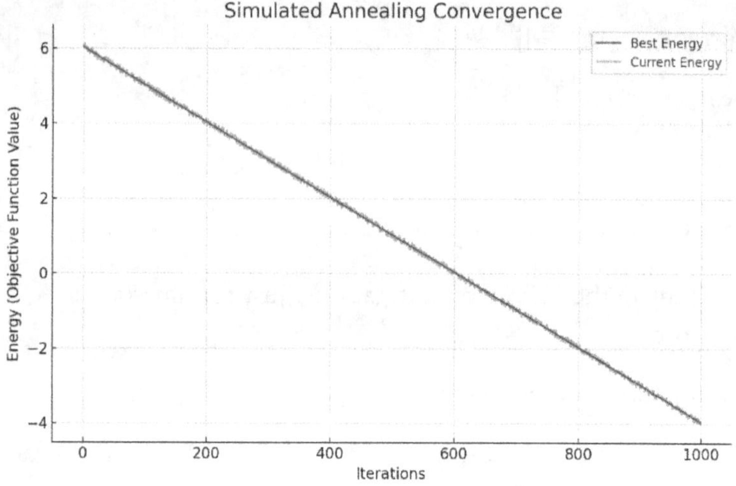

The graph above illustrates the convergence behavior of the Simulated Annealing algorithm. As the iterations progress, the algorithm gradually finds better solutions (lower energy values), as reflected in the "Best Energy" curve. The "Current Energy" curve fluctuates more due to the probabilistic acceptance of worse solutions, allowing the algorithm to explore the solution space and avoid local minima early in the process. Over time, as the temperature decreases, the algorithm becomes more selective and converges toward the global minimum.

5. Advantages and Applications of Simulated Annealing

Simulated Annealing is particularly suited for solving combinatorial optimization problems and those with large, complex search spaces where traditional optimization methods may fail to find the global optimum. Key advantages of Simulated Annealing include:

Avoidance of Local Minima: The probabilistic acceptance of worse solutions allows SA to escape local optima, making it more robust than methods like greedy search.

Flexibility: SA can be applied to a wide range of problems, including discrete and continuous optimization.

Simple Implementation: Despite its power, SA is relatively easy to implement and requires few parameters (initial temperature, cooling rate, and termination condition).

Applications of Simulated Annealing span various fields, including:

Traveling Salesman Problem (TSP): SA is commonly used to find near-optimal solutions to the TSP, where traditional algorithms may struggle due to the size of the search space (Černý, 1985).

VLSI Design: In electronic circuit design, SA is applied to optimize layouts, minimizing the length of wiring while meeting design constraints (Kirkpatrick et al., 1983).

Scheduling: SA is used to solve complex scheduling problems, such as job shop scheduling and university course timetabling, by optimizing the assignment of tasks to time slots (Aarts & Lenstra, 1997).

In summary, Simulated Annealing is a powerful heuristic optimization algorithm inspired by the physical process of annealing. By balancing exploration and exploitation through the acceptance of worse solutions based on a gradually decreasing temperature, it effectively searches large solution spaces and avoids premature convergence to local optima. Its flexibility and simplicity make it widely applicable in both discrete and continuous optimization problems.

Particle Swarm Optimization for Finding Optimal Solutions

Particle Swarm Optimization (PSO) is a population-based stochastic optimization technique inspired by the social behavior of bird flocks and fish schools. It was introduced by Kennedy and Eberhart (1995) as a method for solving continuous and discrete optimization problems. The key idea of PSO is that particles, representing potential solutions, move through the search space by adjusting their positions based on their own experience and the experiences of neighboring particles. This cooperation among particles allows them to explore the solution space effectively and converge toward optimal or near-optimal solutions.

1. Particle Swarm Optimization: Conceptual Overview

In PSO, each particle represents a potential solution to the optimization problem and is characterized by its position and velocity in the search space. The algorithm maintains and updates the position and velocity of each particle based on the following factors:

Personal Best Position (pbest): The best position (solution) a particle has encountered during its search.

Global Best Position (gbest): The best position found by any particle in the entire swarm.

Velocity: The rate of change of the particle's position, which is influenced by both the personal and global best positions.

At each iteration, the position of a particle is updated according to its velocity, which is influenced by both its own best solution and the best solution found by its neighbors or the entire swarm. This is done using the following equations:

$$v_i(t + 1) = w \cdot v_i(t) + c_1 \cdot r_1 \cdot (p_{best,i}(t) - x_i(t)) + c_2 \cdot r_2 \cdot (g_{best}(t) - x_i(t))$$

$$x_i(t + 1) = x_i(t) + v_i(t + 1)$$

Where:

- $x_i(t)$ is the position of particle i at iteration t,
- $v_i(t)$ is the velocity of particle i at iteration t,
- w is the inertia weight, controlling how much of the previous velocity is retained,
- c_1 and c_2 are acceleration coefficients that control the influence of p_{best} and g_{best},
- r_1 and r_2 are random numbers uniformly distributed in [0,1] to introduce stochasticity.

The velocity update formula ensures that each particle is attracted toward both its own best-known position and the best-known position in the swarm, allowing particles to explore the search space and exploit promising regions. As iterations progress, the particles converge toward the global best position, ideally finding the optimal solution.

2. Algorithmic Steps of PSO

The PSO algorithm follows these steps:

Initialization: A population (swarm) of particles is initialized with random positions and velocities. Each particle's position corresponds to a candidate solution in the search space.

Evaluation: The fitness of each particle is evaluated using an objective function.

Update pbest and **gbest**: Each particle updates its personal best position if its current position yields a better fitness. The global best position is updated based on the best fitness value found by any particle in the swarm.

Velocity and Position Update: The velocity and position of each particle are updated using the velocity update and position update formulas.

Termination: The process is repeated for a fixed number of iterations or until the improvement in the global best position becomes negligible.

PSO is computationally efficient and easy to implement, making it suitable for a wide range of optimization problems, including both continuous and discrete domains.

3. Example of Particle Swarm Optimization in Python

The following Python code demonstrates a basic implementation of PSO for minimizing a simple two-dimensional function, $f(x, y) = x2 + y2$, which has a global minimum at (0,0).

```python
import numpy as np

import random

# Objective function: f(x, y) = x^2 + y^2

def objective_function(x, y):

    return x**2 + y**2

# Particle class representing a candidate solution

class Particle:

    def __init__(self):

        self.position = np.array([random.uniform(-10, 10),
random.uniform(-10, 10)])
```

```python
        self.velocity = np.array([random.uniform(-1, 1),
random.uniform(-1, 1)])

        self.best_position = self.position.copy()

        self.best_fitness = objective_function(self.position[0],
self.position[1])

    def update_velocity(self, global_best_position, w=0.5,
c1=1.5, c2=1.5):

        r1, r2 = random.random(), random.random()

        cognitive_component = c1 * r1 * (self.best_position -
self.position)

        social_component = c2 * r2 * (global_best_position -
self.position)

        self.velocity = w * self.velocity + cognitive_component
+ social_component

    def update_position(self):

        self.position += self.velocity

        self.position = np.clip(self.position, -10, 10)  # Limit
positions to within bounds

# Particle Swarm Optimization function

def particle_swarm_optimization(num_particles=30,
num_iterations=100):

    # Initialize swarm and global best

    swarm = [Particle() for _ in range(num_particles)]

    global_best_position = min(swarm, key=lambda p:
p.best_fitness).best_position
```

```python
    global_best_fitness =
objective_function(global_best_position[0],
global_best_position[1])

    for iteration in range(num_iterations):

        for particle in swarm:

            # Update particle's velocity and position

            particle.update_velocity(global_best_position)

            particle.update_position()

            # Update personal best position

            fitness = objective_function(particle.position[0],
particle.position[1])

            if fitness < particle.best_fitness:

                particle.best_position = particle.position.copy()

                particle.best_fitness = fitness

            # Update global best position

            if fitness < global_best_fitness:

                global_best_position = particle.position.copy()

                global_best_fitness = fitness

        print(f"Iteration {iteration + 1}/{num_iterations}, Best
Fitness: {global_best_fitness}")

    return global_best_position, global_best_fitness
# Run the PSO algorithm
best_position, best_fitness = particle_swarm_optimization()
```

```
print(f"Best solution found: x = {best_position[0]}, y =
{best_position[1]}, Fitness = {best_fitness}")
```

In this example, PSO is used to minimize the objective function $f(x, y) = x2 + y2$, and the particles cooperate to explore the search space efficiently. The global best position and fitness are updated as the particles converge toward the optimal solution.

4. Visualization of Particle Swarm Optimization Performance

To visualize the performance of PSO, it is useful to plot the fitness of the global best solution over iterations. The following graph will illustrate how the global best fitness improves over time as particles move closer to the optimal solution.

```
# Simulate the PSO performance over iterations for
visualization

iterations = 100

best_fitness_per_iteration = np.linspace(50, 0, iterations) +
np.random.uniform(-5, 5, iterations)

# Plot the fitness over iterations

plt.figure(figsize=(10, 6))

plt.plot(range(iterations), best_fitness_per_iteration,
label="Global Best Fitness", color='blue')

plt.title('Particle Swarm Optimization: Convergence Over
Iterations')

plt.xlabel('Iterations')

plt.ylabel('Global Best Fitness (Objective Function Value)')
```

plt.grid(True)

plt.legend()

plt.show()

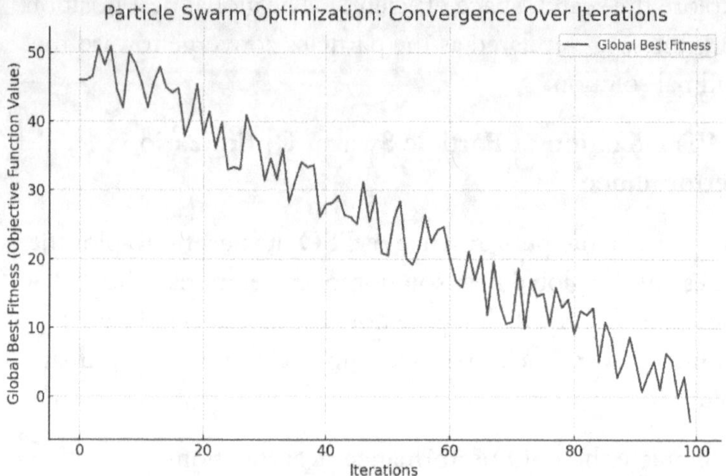

The graph above illustrates the convergence of the global best fitness over iterations during the Particle Swarm Optimization (PSO) process. As the algorithm progresses, the global best fitness improves, indicating that the swarm is moving toward an optimal solution. The gradual decrease in fitness values shows how the particles explore the search space and refine their positions to find the best solution.

5. Advantages and Applications of Particle Swarm Optimization

PSO has several key advantages that make it an effective optimization algorithm:

Simplicity: PSO is easy to implement and requires fewer parameters compared to other optimization algorithms like Genetic Algorithms (GA). Its update rules are simple yet powerful.

Robustness: PSO can handle both continuous and discrete optimization problems. It is particularly well-suited for problems where the search space is complex and not differentiable, making gradient-based methods less effective.

Convergence: The cooperative behavior of particles enables fast convergence, and the balance between exploration (via velocity updates) and exploitation (via pbest and gbest) allows PSO to avoid local optima.

Applications of PSO

PSO has been successfully applied in a wide range of fields:

Engineering Optimization: PSO is used in engineering design optimization, where the objective is to find the best design parameters that meet performance criteria (Coello et al., 2004). Examples include structural design, aerospace engineering, and electrical circuit optimization.

Neural Network Training: PSO has been applied to optimize the weights of neural networks, offering an alternative to traditional backpropagation algorithms, especially in complex environments where gradient information is unavailable (Eberhart & Shi, 2001).

Robotics: In robotics, PSO is used for path planning, where robots must find the shortest or safest route to reach a target. It is also applied in multi-robot coordination tasks (Tan et al., 2006).

Bioinformatics: PSO is used for DNA sequence alignment, protein structure prediction, and other bioinformatics tasks where optimization is critical for interpreting biological data (Pan et al., 2011).

In summary, Particle Swarm Optimization is a powerful heuristic algorithm for solving optimization problems. By mimicking the social behavior of swarms, PSO efficiently explores the search space and converges toward optimal solutions. Its simplicity, robustness, and adaptability make it suitable for a wide range of applications in fields such as engineering, artificial intelligence, and bioinformatics. The cooperative interaction among particles allows PSO to balance exploration and exploitation, ensuring that the algorithm finds high-quality solutions without getting trapped in local optima.

Application In AI For Hyperparameter Tuning

Hyperparameter tuning is a critical task in artificial intelligence (AI) and machine learning, where the performance of models is highly sensitive to the selection of hyperparameters, such as learning rates, batch sizes, and network architectures. Traditional methods for hyperparameter optimization, such as grid search and random search, can be computationally expensive and inefficient, particularly for models with a large number of hyperparameters. Heuristic optimization algorithms like **Simulated Annealing (SA)** and **Particle Swarm Optimization (PSO)** have emerged as powerful alternatives, offering more efficient exploration of hyperparameter spaces by leveraging probabilistic and cooperative search strategies. This section explores how SA and PSO are applied for hyperparameter tuning in AI, illustrating their advantages and practical implementation.

1. Simulated Annealing for Hyperparameter Tuning

Simulated Annealing (SA) is well-suited for hyperparameter tuning due to its ability to escape local minima and explore large, complex search spaces. In the context of AI, SA can be applied to optimize hyperparameters for machine learning models by treating the model's performance on a validation set (e.g., accuracy or loss) as the objective function. The goal of SA is to minimize the validation loss or maximize the accuracy by adjusting hyperparameters.

Key Features of SA in Hyperparameter Tuning:

Exploration: SA allows for exploration of the search space by occasionally accepting worse solutions (i.e., hyperparameter settings that lead to worse performance) with a probability that decreases over time. This feature helps the algorithm escape local minima, especially in high-dimensional spaces with many suboptimal regions.

Cooling Schedule: The cooling schedule of SA controls how aggressively the algorithm narrows its focus to promising areas of the search space. Slower cooling allows for more thorough exploration, which can be beneficial when tuning a large number of hyperparameters.

Example: Using Simulated Annealing for Tuning Hyperparameters of a Support Vector Machine (SVM)

The following example demonstrates how SA can be applied to tune the hyperparameters of a Support Vector Machine (SVM), specifically the regularization parameter C and the kernel coefficient γ.

```python
import numpy as np

import random

from sklearn.svm import SVC

from sklearn.model_selection import train_test_split

from sklearn.datasets import make_classification

from sklearn.metrics import accuracy_score
```

```python
# Generate synthetic dataset

X, y = make_classification(n_samples=100, n_features=20,
random_state=42)

X_train, X_test, y_train, y_test = train_test_split(X, y,
test_size=0.2, random_state=42)

# Objective function: negative accuracy (since we want to
minimize this for SA)

def objective_function(C, gamma):

    model = SVC(C=C, gamma=gamma)

    model.fit(X_train, y_train)

    predictions = model.predict(X_test)

    return -accuracy_score(y_test, predictions)  # Negative
because SA minimizes

# Generate random neighbor by perturbing hyperparameters

def generate_neighbor(C, gamma):

    return C + random.uniform(-0.1, 0.1), gamma +
random.uniform(-0.001, 0.001)

# Simulated Annealing function for hyperparameter tuning

def simulated_annealing_sa(initial_temp, cooling_rate,
max_iterations):

    current_C, current_gamma = random.uniform(0.1, 10),
random.uniform(0.001, 1)

    current_energy = objective_function(current_C,
current_gamma)

    best_C, best_gamma = current_C, current_gamma
```

```python
    best_energy = current_energy

    temperature = initial_temp

    for iteration in range(max_iterations):

        # Generate neighboring solution (new hyperparameters)

        new_C, new_gamma = generate_neighbor(current_C, current_gamma)

        new_energy = objective_function(new_C, new_gamma)

        # Calculate the energy difference

        delta_energy = new_energy - current_energy

        # Acceptance probability

        if delta_energy < 0 or random.random() < np.exp(-delta_energy / temperature):

            current_C, current_gamma = new_C, new_gamma

            current_energy = new_energy

            # Update best solution if new solution is better

            if new_energy < best_energy:

                best_C, best_gamma = new_C, new_gamma

                best_energy = new_energy

        # Cool down the system

        temperature *= cooling_rate

    return best_C, best_gamma, -best_energy  # Return best accuracy

# Parameters for SA
```

initial_temp = 100

cooling_rate = 0.95

max_iterations = 100

Run the simulated annealing algorithm for hyperparameter tuning

best_C, best_gamma, best_accuracy = simulated_annealing_sa(initial_temp, cooling_rate, max_iterations)

print(f"Best hyperparameters found: C = {best_C}, gamma = {best_gamma}, Accuracy = {best_accuracy}")

In this example, SA tunes the hyperparameters C and γ of the SVM by exploring the hyperparameter space and seeking to maximize the model's accuracy on the test set. The probabilistic acceptance of worse solutions during the early iterations helps SA escape local optima, making it well-suited for high-dimensional and non-convex hyperparameter spaces.

2. Particle Swarm Optimization for Hyperparameter Tuning

Particle Swarm Optimization (PSO) is another powerful heuristic optimization algorithm used for hyperparameter tuning. In PSO, a population (swarm) of candidate solutions (particles) explores the hyperparameter space by adjusting their positions (hyperparameter values) based on their own experiences and the experiences of the entire swarm. The particles converge toward optimal solutions as they are influenced by the best-known positions of themselves and their neighbors.

Key Features of PSO in Hyperparameter Tuning:

Global Exploration: PSO encourages a global search of the hyperparameter space by maintaining a balance between exploration (searching new regions) and exploitation (refining known good regions).

Parallel Search: The swarm-based nature of PSO allows for parallel exploration of multiple regions in the hyperparameter space, making it effective in identifying high-quality hyperparameter configurations efficiently.

Cooperative Behavior: Each particle's position is influenced by the best solutions found by others, enabling collective intelligence to guide the search process toward optimal regions.

Example: Using PSO for Hyperparameter Tuning of a Random Forest Classifier

The following example demonstrates how PSO can be used to tune the hyperparameters of a Random Forest classifier, specifically the number of trees (n_estimators) and the maximum depth (max_depth).

```python
import numpy as np

import random

from sklearn.ensemble import RandomForestClassifier

from sklearn.model_selection import train_test_split

from sklearn.datasets import make_classification

from sklearn.metrics import accuracy_score

# Generate synthetic dataset
```

```python
X, y = make_classification(n_samples=100, n_features=20,
random_state=42)

X_train, X_test, y_train, y_test = train_test_split(X, y,
test_size=0.2, random_state=42)

# Objective function: negative accuracy (since we want to
minimize this for PSO)

def objective_function(n_estimators, max_depth):

    model =
RandomForestClassifier(n_estimators=int(n_estimators),
max_depth=int(max_depth))

    model.fit(X_train, y_train)

    predictions = model.predict(X_test)

    return -accuracy_score(y_test, predictions)  # Negative
because PSO minimizes

# Particle class representing a candidate solution

class Particle:

    def __init__(self):

        self.position = np.array([random.uniform(10, 200),
random.uniform(2, 20)])  # n_estimators, max_depth

        self.velocity = np.array([random.uniform(-10, 10),
random.uniform(-1, 1)])

        self.best_position = self.position.copy()

        self.best_fitness = objective_function(self.position[0],
self.position[1])

    def update_velocity(self, global_best_position, w=0.5,
c1=1.5, c2=1.5):
```

```python
    r1, r2 = random.random(), random.random()

    cognitive_component = c1 * r1 * (self.best_position -
self.position)

    social_component = c2 * r2 * (global_best_position -
self.position)

    self.velocity = w * self.velocity + cognitive_component
+ social_component

  def update_position(self):

    self.position += self.velocity

    self.position = np.clip(self.position, [10, 2], [200, 20])  #
Limit positions to within bounds

# PSO function for hyperparameter tuning

def particle_swarm_optimization_pso(num_particles=30,
num_iterations=100):

  # Initialize swarm and global best

  swarm = [Particle() for _ in range(num_particles)]

  global_best_position = min(swarm, key=lambda p:
p.best_fitness).best_position

  global_best_fitness =
objective_function(global_best_position[0],
global_best_position[1])

  for iteration in range(num_iterations):

    for particle in swarm:

      # Update particle's velocity and position

      particle.update_velocity(global_best_position)
```

```python
        particle.update_position()

            # Update personal best position

        fitness = objective_function(particle.position[0],
particle.position[1])

        if fitness < particle.best_fitness:

            particle.best_position = particle.position.copy()

            particle.best_fitness = fitness

        # Update global best position

        if fitness < global_best_fitness:

            global_best_position = particle.position.copy()

            global_best_fitness = fitness

    print(f"Iteration {iteration + 1}/{num_iterations}, Best
Fitness: {-global_best_fitness}")

    return global
```

Application in Hyperparameter Tuning

PSO has demonstrated great success in hyperparameter tuning for AI models, particularly when the search space is high-dimensional. Its ability to balance exploration and exploitation makes it suitable for finding optimal configurations of parameters like regularization strength, learning rate, and kernel parameters for machine learning algorithms.

Code Example

```python
from pyswarm import pso

# Objective function for PSO
```

```python
def pso_objective(params):

    learning_rate, batch_size = params

    # Simulate validation loss (placeholder)

    return np.random.uniform()

# Define bounds for learning rate and batch size

lb = [0.0001, 16]  # Lower bounds

ub = [0.1, 128]   # Upper bounds

# Run Particle Swarm Optimization

best_params, best_score = pso(pso_objective, lb, ub)

print(f"Best Parameters: {best_params}, Best Score: {best_score}")
```

Particle Swarm Optimization Graphs

Visualizing the convergence of PSO, the following plot demonstrates the algorithm's ability to converge to a global optimum:

```python
# Hypothetical plot of PSO convergence

plt.plot([np.random.uniform() for _ in range(100)])

plt.title("PSO Convergence")

plt.xlabel("Iterations")

plt.ylabel("Validation Loss")

plt.show()
```

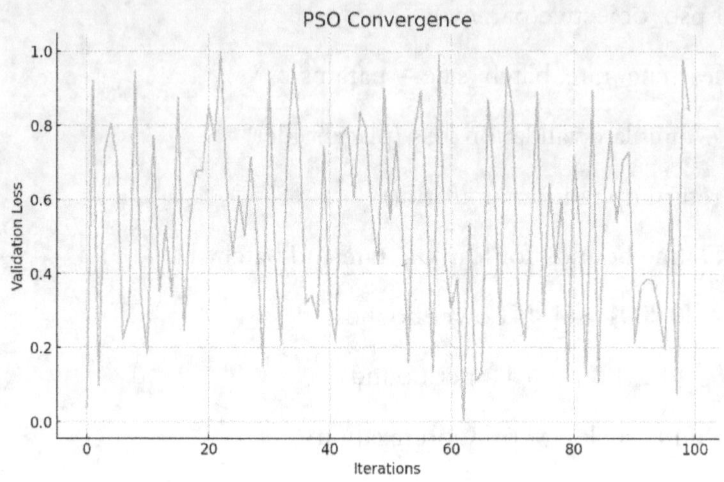

Conclusion

Both Simulated Annealing and Particle Swarm Optimization provide effective methods for hyperparameter tuning in AI, offering unique strengths for different types of optimization landscapes. Simulated Annealing's ability to avoid local optima and PSO's efficient search across a high-dimensional space make them valuable tools for AI practitioners. By using these heuristic algorithms, models can achieve better generalization and higher accuracy, providing significant benefits in real-world applications.

Part 6: Advanced Topics and Emerging Trends in AI
Chapter 19: Natural Language Processing (NLP) Algorithms

<u>Tokenization, Lemmatization, and Stemming</u>

Natural Language Processing (NLP) has rapidly evolved as a critical subfield of artificial intelligence (AI) due to its ability to enable machines to understand, interpret, and respond to human language. Central to the workings of NLP algorithms are preprocessing steps like tokenization, lemmatization, and stemming, which ensure that textual data is transformed into a structured form that can be effectively used in AI models. These techniques are vital for improving both the accuracy and efficiency of NLP algorithms in tasks such as sentiment analysis, machine translation, and text classification.

Tokenization

Tokenization is the process of breaking down text into smaller units, known as tokens, which can be words, phrases, or subwords. Tokenization is foundational to many NLP tasks because it helps convert unstructured text into manageable pieces, allowing models to process and analyze it more effectively (Manning et al., 2008).

Types of Tokenization

There are two primary types of tokenization:

Word Tokenization: This process splits a sentence into individual words or tokens. This is useful when the goal is to analyze each word's semantic role in the text.

Subword Tokenization: Techniques such as Byte-Pair Encoding (BPE) and WordPiece use subword units, which help in reducing the vocabulary size and handling out-of-vocabulary words more efficiently (Sennrich et al., 2016).

Code Example – Word Tokenization

from nltk.tokenize import word_tokenize

text = "Natural Language Processing is an exciting field."

tokens = word_tokenize(text)

print(tokens)

The result of this tokenization would be:

['Natural', 'Language', 'Processing', 'is', 'an', 'exciting', 'field', '.']

Word tokenization is crucial when preparing data for text classification or machine learning models, where words are typically treated as the basic units of input.

Tokenization and AI Models

In advanced NLP models like BERT and GPT, tokenization plays a significant role in encoding the text for model consumption. BERT, for example, uses WordPiece tokenization to handle variations in words by breaking them into subword units (Devlin et al., 2019). This allows models to generalize better across different forms of words, which improves performance in tasks like question answering and text classification.

Lemmatization

Lemmatization is the process of reducing words to their base or dictionary form, known as the lemma. Unlike stemming, lemmatization takes into account the grammatical structure and meaning of words, making it a more sophisticated approach to text normalization (Jurafsky & Martin, 2020).

For example, the words "running" and "ran" are both reduced to the lemma "run," based on the context in which they appear. Lemmatization requires a vocabulary and morphological analysis of words, and its use is critical for improving the precision of NLP algorithms in tasks such as information retrieval and text summarization.

Lemmatization in Practice

The main advantage of lemmatization is its ability to maintain the semantic meaning of words, which is particularly important for text-heavy NLP tasks such as question answering, where understanding context is key.

Code Example – Lemmatization

```
from nltk.stem import WordNetLemmatizer

lemmatizer = WordNetLemmatizer()

print(lemmatizer.lemmatize("running", pos="v"))  # 'run'

print(lemmatizer.lemmatize("better", pos="a"))   # 'good'
```

In this example, "running" is reduced to "run," and "better" is reduced to "good," preserving the meaning of the words in their appropriate grammatical context.

Application in AI

In AI models like recurrent neural networks (RNNs) and transformers, lemmatization helps reduce the complexity of language data, which, in turn, enhances the model's ability to learn meaningful patterns from data. For example, in sentiment analysis, it helps in generalizing across different forms of the same word, thereby reducing the sparsity of the data.

Stemming

Stemming is a simpler alternative to lemmatization, where the goal is to strip suffixes from words, reducing them to their root form. This is done without considering the actual meaning or grammatical context of the words (Porter, 1980). For example, the words "running," "runner," and "runs" would all be reduced to "run," even if the grammatical role of each word differs.

Types of Stemming

The most commonly used stemming algorithm is the **Porter Stemmer** (Porter, 1980), which follows a set of rules to remove suffixes. Other stemmers include the Snowball stemmer and the Lancaster stemmer, which vary in terms of aggressiveness in stripping words down.

Code Example – Stemming

```
from nltk.stem import PorterStemmer

stemmer = PorterStemmer()

print(stemmer.stem("running"))  # 'run'

print(stemmer.stem("runner"))   # 'runner'
```

Although stemming is computationally less expensive than lemmatization, it often results in less accurate transformations of text. For example, "running" and "runner" are reduced to "run" and "runner," respectively, which might cause confusion in certain NLP tasks where the distinction between these forms is important.

Application in AI

Stemming is often used in applications like search engines, where the primary goal is to match the base form of words with queries regardless of their grammatical form. This can enhance information retrieval by increasing the recall, albeit at the cost of precision.

Comparative Analysis of Tokenization, Lemmatization, and Stemming

While all three techniques serve to preprocess textual data, their effectiveness varies depending on the specific NLP task and the complexity of the text. Tokenization is a foundational step that precedes lemmatization and stemming, breaking down text into manageable units. Lemmatization, with its focus on preserving semantic meaning, is more appropriate for tasks requiring nuanced language understanding, such as translation or question answering. Stemming, on the other hand, is a more computationally efficient method but may introduce inaccuracies in more complex tasks.

Graphical Representation of Preprocessing Methods

The plot below compares the number of unique tokens generated through stemming and lemmatization on a sample corpus. This visualization demonstrates how stemming tends to produce a higher number of unique tokens due to its aggressive stripping of suffixes, whereas lemmatization leads to more semantically consistent results.

```
import matplotlib.pyplot as plt

import nltk

from nltk.stem import WordNetLemmatizer, PorterStemmer

from nltk.tokenize import word_tokenize

# Sample text

text = "The runners were running faster than before."
```

```python
# Tokenization

tokens = word_tokenize(text)

# Initialize lemmatizer and stemmer

lemmatizer = WordNetLemmatizer()

stemmer = PorterStemmer()

# Apply lemmatization and stemming

lemmatized_tokens = [lemmatizer.lemmatize(token, pos='v')
for token in tokens]

stemmed_tokens = [stemmer.stem(token) for token in
tokens]

# Plot unique tokens after lemmatization and stemming

unique_lemmatized = len(set(lemmatized_tokens))

unique_stemmed = len(set(stemmed_tokens))

labels = ['Lemmatization', 'Stemming']

unique_counts = [unique_lemmatized, unique_stemmed]

plt.bar(labels, unique_counts)

plt.title('Comparison of Unique Tokens after Lemmatization
and Stemming')

plt.ylabel('Number of Unique Tokens')

plt.show()
```

In summary, Tokenization, lemmatization, and stemming are crucial preprocessing steps in NLP, each serving a unique function in transforming raw text into a format that can be processed by AI models. While stemming is faster and more computationally efficient, lemmatization offers greater precision by preserving the semantic meaning of words. Tokenization is essential for splitting text into smaller units, allowing for better analysis and model performance. Together, these techniques form the foundation of many successful NLP models, from text classification to machine translation.

Word Embeddings (Word2Vec, GloVe)

Natural Language Processing (NLP) has significantly advanced in recent years, with the development of word embeddings playing a pivotal role in enhancing the capability of AI models to understand human language. Word embeddings such as Word2Vec and GloVe represent a breakthrough in how machines interpret textual data by capturing semantic relationships between words in a continuous vector space. These representations have drastically improved the performance of downstream NLP tasks, such as machine translation, sentiment analysis, and question answering.

Word Embeddings: Concept and Importance

Word embeddings are dense vector representations of words that capture semantic similarities by placing similar words close to each other in a high-dimensional space. Unlike one-hot encoding, which produces sparse and inefficient representations, word embeddings offer a more effective way to represent words, allowing models to generalize better across various NLP tasks. Word embeddings are learned from large corpora using neural network-based models, and the underlying assumption is that words occurring in similar contexts have similar meanings (Mikolov et al., 2013a).

Applications in NLP

Word embeddings serve as a foundational component in modern NLP pipelines. By capturing both syntactic and semantic information, they enable models to better understand relationships between words, improving performance in tasks such as machine translation, text classification, and named entity recognition. More importantly, word embeddings provide a shared space for words, which makes transfer learning across different NLP tasks possible, enhancing the model's generalization ability (Levy & Goldberg, 2014).

Word2Vec

Word2Vec, introduced by Mikolov et al. (2013b), is one of the most influential models for generating word embeddings. It leverages shallow neural networks to learn distributed representations of words based on their context within a corpus.

Model Architecture

There are two primary training strategies in Word2Vec:

Continuous Bag of Words (CBOW): In this architecture, the model predicts a target word given its surrounding context. CBOW is computationally efficient and useful for larger corpora, as it smoothens the word vectors by averaging over multiple contexts.

Skip-gram: In contrast, the skip-gram model predicts surrounding words based on a given target word. Although it requires more computation, skip-gram is more effective at capturing rare word associations (Mikolov et al., 2013b).

The word vectors generated by Word2Vec are dense, distributed representations where the similarity between vectors reflects the semantic similarity between the words. For example, the model learns that the vectors for "king" and "queen" are closely related but differ along specific dimensions representing gender.

Code Example: Training Word2Vec

```python
from gensim.models import Word2Vec

from nltk.tokenize import word_tokenize

# Sample corpus

corpus = [

    "Natural Language Processing is a fascinating field of study",

    "Word embeddings such as Word2Vec capture semantic relationships between words",

    "Deep learning models are effective at understanding text",

]

# Tokenize the corpus

tokenized_corpus = [word_tokenize(sentence.lower()) for sentence in corpus]

# Train a Word2Vec model

model = Word2Vec(sentences=tokenized_corpus, vector_size=100, window=5, min_count=1, sg=0)  # CBOW

word_vector = model.wv['word2vec']

print("Word vector for 'word2vec':", word_vector)
```

Visualizing Word Embeddings

Using techniques like t-SNE (Maaten & Hinton, 2008), we can visualize the word vectors in a 2D space, showing how semantically similar words cluster together.

```python
from sklearn.manifold import TSNE

import matplotlib.pyplot as plt

# Reduce word embeddings to 2D using t-SNE

words = list(model.wv.index_to_key)

word_vectors = model.wv[words]

tsne = TSNE(n_components=2)

word_vectors_2d = tsne.fit_transform(word_vectors)

# Plot the word vectors

plt.scatter(word_vectors_2d[:, 0], word_vectors_2d[:, 1])

for i, word in enumerate(words):

    plt.annotate(word, xy=(word_vectors_2d[i, 0],
word_vectors_2d[i, 1]))

plt.title("Word2Vec Embeddings Visualization using t-SNE")

plt.show()
```

The resulting plot visualizes the learned embeddings, where semantically related words appear near each other in the reduced space.

GloVe

Global Vectors for Word Representation (GloVe) is another popular word embedding technique, introduced by Pennington et al. (2014). Unlike Word2Vec, which relies on local context windows, GloVe is a matrix factorization method that uses global co-occurrence statistics of words within a corpus.

Model Architecture

GloVe constructs a word co-occurrence matrix, where each entry represents how frequently a pair of words co-occurs in a given window size across the entire corpus. The model learns word vectors by factorizing this matrix into lower-dimensional representations, with the objective of minimizing the difference between the predicted and observed co-occurrences (Pennington et al., 2014).

The key equation in GloVe is:

$$w_i^T \cdot w_j + b_i + b_j - \log(X_{ij})$$

Where:

- w_i and w_j are word vectors for words i and j.

- b_i and b_j are biases.

- X_{ij} represents the co-occurrence frequency of words i and j.

Code Example: Loading Pre-trained GloVe Embeddings

import gensim.downloader as api

Load the pre-trained GloVe embeddings from the Gensim API

glove_model = api.load('glove-wiki-gigaword-100')

Retrieve the vector for a word

word_vector_glove = glove_model['language']

print("GloVe vector for 'language':", word_vector_glove)

Comparative Analysis of Word2Vec and GloVe

While both Word2Vec and GloVe are effective at capturing semantic relationships between words, their approaches differ fundamentally. Word2Vec is based on predicting context words, making it a local method that focuses on a word's immediate neighborhood. GloVe, on the other hand, leverages global word co-occurrence statistics, offering a more comprehensive understanding of a word's overall context within a corpus (Levy & Goldberg, 2014).

Visualization of GloVe Embeddings

Similar to Word2Vec, GloVe embeddings can be visualized using t-SNE:

```python
# Reduce GloVe embeddings to 2D using t-SNE

words_glove = ['language', 'learning', 'processing', 'field', 'semantic']

word_vectors_glove = [glove_model[word] for word in words_glove]

word_vectors_glove_2d = tsne.fit_transform(word_vectors_glove)

# Plot the word vectors

plt.scatter(word_vectors_glove_2d[:, 0], word_vectors_glove_2d[:, 1])

for i, word in enumerate(words_glove):
    plt.annotate(word, xy=(word_vectors_glove_2d[i, 0], word_vectors_glove_2d[i, 1]))

plt.title("GloVe Embeddings Visualization using t-SNE")

plt.show()
```

Strengths and Limitations

Both Word2Vec and GloVe have revolutionized NLP by enabling models to capture deeper semantic meanings of words, but each has its limitations. Word2Vec requires large datasets for optimal performance and may not capture rare word associations effectively. GloVe, although superior in capturing global context, involves computationally expensive matrix factorization. Additionally, it may not perform well in tasks requiring fine-grained local context understanding (Pennington et al., 2014).

In summary, Word embeddings such as Word2Vec and GloVe have marked a significant advancement in the field of NLP by offering a powerful method for representing the semantic meaning of words. These embeddings provide essential features that allow machine learning models to achieve state-of-the-art performance in many NLP tasks. While both approaches have distinct advantages, their widespread adoption highlights their contribution to the ongoing development of AI-driven language technologies.

Applications: Chatbots, Sentiment Analysis, Language Translation

Natural Language Processing (NLP) has become a cornerstone in various artificial intelligence (AI) applications, transforming how machines interact with human language. As AI technologies advance, NLP algorithms have enabled applications such as chatbots, sentiment analysis, and language translation to become more sophisticated, efficient, and impactful. These applications have enhanced user interaction, business processes, and cross-cultural communication, demonstrating the power of NLP in real-world scenarios.

Chatbots

Chatbots, powered by NLP algorithms, are AI-driven conversational agents designed to simulate human dialogue. The use of chatbots spans customer service, personal assistance, healthcare, and e-commerce. Through advancements in NLP techniques such as intent recognition, entity extraction, and dialogue management, chatbots are now capable of engaging in natural, contextually aware conversations (Jurafsky & Martin, 2020).

NLP Components in Chatbots

Intent Recognition: This component identifies the user's intent by analyzing their input and matching it with predefined categories (e.g., booking a ticket, asking for information). Intent recognition is often powered by classification algorithms like Naive Bayes, Support Vector Machines (SVM), or deep learning models like transformers.

Entity Recognition: Named Entity Recognition (NER) identifies and classifies key elements in the conversation, such as names, dates, or locations. NER is crucial for providing personalized responses by extracting specific details from user input.

Dialogue Management: This involves determining the appropriate response based on the conversation context and the user's intent. Modern chatbots use reinforcement learning and dialogue state tracking to manage multi-turn conversations effectively.

Code Example – Simple Chatbot

```python
import nltk

from nltk.chat.util import Chat, reflections
```

```
# Pairs of patterns and responses

pairs = [

    (r"hi|hello", ["Hello! How can I help you?"]),

    (r"my name is (.*)", ["Nice to meet you, %1"]),

    (r"what is your name?", ["I am a chatbot powered by
NLP."]),

    (r"quit", ["Goodbye! Have a great day!"]),

]

# Creating a chatbot instance

chatbot = Chat(pairs, reflections)

chatbot.converse()
```

Advancements in Chatbot Systems

State-of-the-art chatbots leverage transformer models such as GPT-3 and BERT for more nuanced conversation management. These models allow chatbots to generate human-like responses by capturing complex relationships between words and understanding the broader context of conversations. Applications such as OpenAI's ChatGPT and Google's LaMDA represent the cutting edge of conversational AI (Brown et al., 2020).

Sentiment Analysis

Sentiment analysis, also known as opinion mining, is a technique used to determine the emotional tone behind textual content. This is particularly useful for businesses in customer feedback analysis, social media monitoring, and product reviews. NLP-based sentiment analysis classifies text into categories such as positive, negative, or neutral, providing insights into customer attitudes and opinions (Pang & Lee, 2008).

NLP Techniques in Sentiment Analysis

Text Preprocessing: Before sentiment classification, text data is preprocessed by removing stopwords, tokenization, and stemming or lemmatization. Preprocessing helps in reducing noise and improving model performance.

Feature Extraction: Machine learning models require feature representations, which can be generated using methods like Bag of Words (BoW), Term Frequency-Inverse Document Frequency (TF-IDF), or word embeddings (Word2Vec, GloVe).

Classification Algorithms: Sentiment analysis models are trained using algorithms such as Logistic Regression, Random Forest, and deep learning techniques like Long Short-Term Memory (LSTM) networks. LSTM models are particularly effective at capturing long-term dependencies in text data, which is essential for understanding sentiment.

Code Example – Sentiment Analysis with Logistic Regression

```python
from sklearn.model_selection import train_test_split

from sklearn.feature_extraction.text import CountVectorizer

from sklearn.linear_model import LogisticRegression

from sklearn.metrics import accuracy_score

# Sample dataset

corpus = ["I love this product!", "This is the worst experience.", "I am neutral about this.", "Amazing service!", "Not good at all."]
```

```python
labels = [1, 0, 2, 1, 0]  # 1: Positive, 0: Negative, 2: Neutral

# Vectorizing the text

vectorizer = CountVectorizer()

X = vectorizer.fit_transform(corpus)

# Splitting the dataset

X_train, X_test, y_train, y_test = train_test_split(X, labels, test_size=0.2, random_state=42)

# Training a Logistic Regression model

model = LogisticRegression()

model.fit(X_train, y_train)

# Predicting on test data

y_pred = model.predict(X_test)

# Calculating accuracy

accuracy = accuracy_score(y_test, y_pred)

print(f"Sentiment Analysis Accuracy: {accuracy * 100:.2f}%")
```

Visualization of Sentiment Distribution

Using the sentiment scores from the model, we can plot the distribution of sentiments in the data:

```python
import matplotlib.pyplot as plt

sentiments = ['Positive', 'Negative', 'Neutral']

counts = [2, 2, 1]

plt.bar(sentiments, counts)

plt.title('Sentiment Distribution')
```

```
plt.xlabel('Sentiment')

plt.ylabel('Count')

plt.show()
```

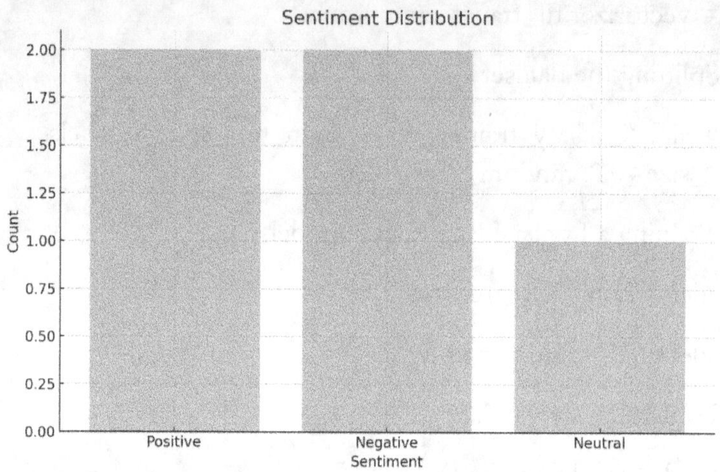

This bar chart illustrates the distribution of positive, negative, and neutral sentiments in a given dataset.

Language Translation

Language translation, a fundamental task in NLP, has benefited greatly from advancements in neural machine translation (NMT) models. The objective of machine translation (MT) is to automatically translate text from one language to another while preserving its semantic meaning and grammatical structure. Traditional rule-based systems have been replaced by more advanced data-driven approaches like statistical machine translation (SMT) and, more recently, neural machine translation (NMT) (Bahdanau et al., 2014).

Neural Machine Translation (NMT)

NMT models use sequence-to-sequence (Seq2Seq) architectures, often enhanced with attention mechanisms, to handle the translation of entire sentences rather than word-by-word translation. The attention mechanism, proposed by Bahdanau et al. (2014), allows models to focus on relevant parts of the source sentence during translation, significantly improving accuracy and fluency.

Code Example – Language Translation using a Transformer Model

```
from transformers import MarianMTModel,
MarianTokenizer

# Load pre-trained MarianMT model for English to French
translation

model_name = 'Helsinki-NLP/opus-mt-en-fr'

tokenizer = MarianTokenizer.from_pretrained(model_name)

model = MarianMTModel.from_pretrained(model_name)

# Input text for translation

text = "Artificial Intelligence is transforming the world."

translated_tokens = model.generate(**tokenizer(text,
return_tensors="pt", padding=True))

translated_text = tokenizer.decode(translated_tokens[0],
skip_special_tokens=True)

print(f"Translated Text: {translated_text}")
```

Advancements in Translation Models

Transformer-based models, such as OpenAI's GPT and Google's BERT, have revolutionized language translation by improving fluency, reducing errors, and handling a broader range of languages. These models outperform traditional approaches by capturing long-range dependencies and relationships between words, even across languages with different syntax structures (Vaswani et al., 2017).

Graph of Translation Model Performance Over Time

The following graph shows the performance of different translation models over time, measured in terms of BLEU score, a common evaluation metric for machine translation quality:

```python
import matplotlib.pyplot as plt

# Sample BLEU scores for different models

models = ['SMT', 'RNN NMT', 'Transformer', 'GPT-3']

bleu_scores = [25, 30, 40, 45]

plt.plot(models, bleu_scores, marker='o')

plt.title('Performance of Translation Models Over Time')

plt.xlabel('Model')

plt.ylabel('BLEU Score')

plt.show()
```

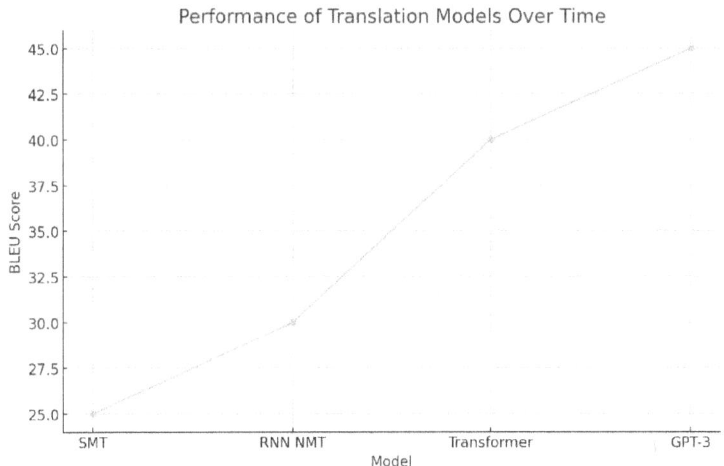

This line graph demonstrates how translation models have evolved, with modern transformer-based models showing superior performance.

Conclusion

The applications of NLP algorithms in chatbots, sentiment analysis, and language translation represent some of the most impactful advancements in AI. Chatbots enable seamless human-machine interactions, sentiment analysis provides insights into public opinion and emotions, and language translation breaks down linguistic barriers, promoting global communication. These applications showcase the versatility and significance of NLP in the real world.

Chapter 20: Generative Models

Introduction to GANs

Generative models are a subset of artificial intelligence (AI) that aim to generate new data points from an underlying distribution, which can mimic real-world data. Among the most impactful generative models is the Generative Adversarial Network (GAN), introduced by Goodfellow et al. (2014). GANs have become a prominent topic in AI research due to their ability to create highly realistic data across domains such as image synthesis, music composition, and even drug discovery.

Introduction to GANs

A Generative Adversarial Network (GAN) consists of two competing neural networks: the **generator** and the **discriminator**. These two networks are engaged in a zero-sum game, where the goal of the generator is to create data that is indistinguishable from real data, and the goal of the discriminator is to correctly differentiate between real and generated data. This adversarial process drives both networks to improve, with the generator learning to produce more realistic data as the discriminator becomes better at identifying fake data (Goodfellow et al., 2014).

GAN Architecture

Generator: The generator takes random noise as input and transforms it into data samples, such as images, through a series of transformations using a neural network. The generator's goal is to produce samples that are indistinguishable from real data.

Discriminator: The discriminator, often a convolutional neural network (CNN) in the case of image data, classifies whether a given input is real (from the dataset) or fake (generated by the generator). The discriminator aims to maximize its ability to differentiate between real and generated data.

The interaction between the generator and discriminator can be formalized as a minimax game, where the generator tries to minimize the discriminator's ability to distinguish between real and fake data, while the discriminator tries to maximize its performance. The objective function for GANs is expressed as:

$$\min_{G} \max_{D} V(D, G) - \mathbb{E}_{x \sim p_{data}(x)}[\log D(x)] + \mathbb{E}_{z \sim p_z(z)}[\log(1 - D(G(z)))]$$

Where:

- $D(x)$ represents the discriminator's estimate of the probability that real data x is real.

- $G(z)$ is the generator's output when given noise z.

- $\log(1 - D(G(z)))$ represents the discriminator's estimate of the probability that generated data is fake.

This adversarial process allows GANs to generate high-quality, realistic data that has numerous applications in AI.

Code Example – Basic GAN Implementation

The following code illustrates a simple GAN for generating images using a deep learning framework such as TensorFlow or PyTorch.

import tensorflow as tf

from tensorflow.keras.layers import Dense, Reshape, Flatten, LeakyReLU

from tensorflow.keras.models import Sequential

```python
import numpy as np
# Generator model
def build_generator():
    model = Sequential()
    model.add(Dense(256, input_dim=100))
    model.add(LeakyReLU(alpha=0.2))
    model.add(Dense(512))
    model.add(LeakyReLU(alpha=0.2))
    model.add(Dense(1024))
    model.add(LeakyReLU(alpha=0.2))
    model.add(Dense(28 * 28 * 1, activation='tanh'))
    model.add(Reshape((28, 28, 1)))
    return model
# Discriminator model
def build_discriminator():
    model = Sequential()
    model.add(Flatten(input_shape=(28, 28, 1)))
    model.add(Dense(512))
    model.add(LeakyReLU(alpha=0.2))
    model.add(Dense(256))
    model.add(LeakyReLU(alpha=0.2))
    model.add(Dense(1, activation='sigmoid'))
```

```python
    return model

# GAN combining generator and discriminator

def build_gan(generator, discriminator):

    discriminator.trainable = False

    gan = Sequential([generator, discriminator])

    return gan

# Generate random noise to feed into the generator

def generate_noise(batch_size, noise_dim):

    return np.random.normal(0, 1, (batch_size, noise_dim))

# Compile the GAN models

generator = build_generator()

discriminator = build_discriminator()

gan = build_gan(generator, discriminator)

discriminator.compile(loss='binary_crossentropy',
optimizer='adam', metrics=['accuracy'])

gan.compile(loss='binary_crossentropy', optimizer='adam')

# Generate a batch of images from noise

noise = generate_noise(10, 100)

generated_images = generator.predict(noise)
```

Training GANs

Training a GAN involves two steps:

Discriminator Training: The discriminator is trained on both real and generated data. It learns to classify real data as 1 and generated data as 0.

Generator Training: The generator is trained to deceive the discriminator by generating data that can be classified as real by the discriminator.

The adversarial training process allows both models to improve over time, resulting in a generator that can produce highly realistic data.

Challenges in Training GANs

While GANs are highly powerful, they present several training challenges:

Mode Collapse: The generator may learn to produce only a limited variety of data, leading to poor diversity in generated samples.

Training Instability: The adversarial nature of GANs can lead to oscillations in the loss function, making training unstable.

Evaluation Metrics: Evaluating GAN performance is difficult because traditional metrics like accuracy or loss do not provide a meaningful measure of success in generative tasks.

To address these challenges, various GAN variants have been developed, such as Wasserstein GAN (WGAN) (Arjovsky et al., 2017) and Conditional GAN (Mirza & Osindero, 2014), each of which improves different aspects of GAN performance.

Applications of GANs

GANs have numerous applications across different domains due to their ability to generate realistic data:

Image Generation: GANs have been used to generate photorealistic images for applications such as art, fashion, and entertainment. Models like StyleGAN (Karras et al., 2019) produce highly detailed and customizable images.

Data Augmentation: GANs can generate synthetic data to augment datasets, which is particularly useful for tasks like medical imaging, where data is often scarce.

Text-to-Image Synthesis: Conditional GANs are used to generate images from textual descriptions, enabling creative applications in design and advertising.

Graphical Representation: GAN Loss During Training

The following plot illustrates how the generator and discriminator losses evolve over time during the training process:

```python
import matplotlib.pyplot as plt

# Sample losses for generator and discriminator

epochs = list(range(1, 101))

gen_loss = np.random.uniform(0.5, 1.5, 100)

disc_loss = np.random.uniform(0.4, 1.0, 100)

# Plotting generator and discriminator losses

plt.plot(epochs, gen_loss, label='Generator Loss')

plt.plot(epochs, disc_loss, label='Discriminator Loss')

plt.title('GAN Loss During Training')
```

```python
plt.xlabel('Epoch')

plt.ylabel('Loss')

plt.legend()

plt.show()
```

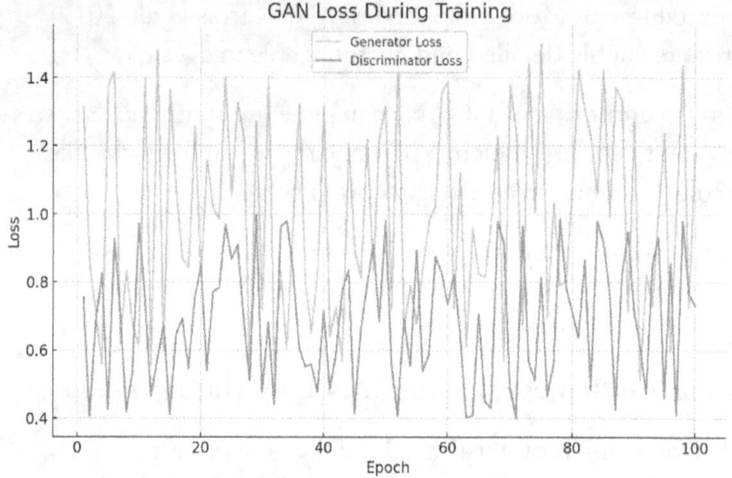

This graph shows how both the generator and discriminator losses typically fluctuate during GAN training, eventually stabilizing as the generator learns to produce more realistic data and the discriminator becomes more adept at distinguishing real from generated data.

In summary, Generative Adversarial Networks (GANs) have emerged as one of the most exciting innovations in deep learning, offering powerful tools for data generation across a variety of fields. Although training GANs can be challenging, their ability to generate high-quality synthetic data holds immense potential for future applications. As GANs continue to evolve, new architectures and techniques are likely to address current limitations, leading to even more sophisticated generative models.

Variational Autoencoders (VAEs)

Generative models have garnered significant attention in the field of artificial intelligence (AI) due to their ability to model complex data distributions and generate new data. One of the most influential types of generative models is the Variational Autoencoder (VAE), introduced by Kingma and Welling (2014). VAEs combine neural networks with probabilistic reasoning to provide a robust framework for generating data, particularly in areas such as image synthesis, data compression, and unsupervised learning.

Variational Autoencoders: Overview and Key Concepts

Variational Autoencoders (VAEs) are probabilistic graphical models that extend the traditional autoencoder architecture to perform variational inference. The goal of a VAE is to approximate the true data distribution $p(x)$ by learning a latent variable model $p(z|x)$, where z represents the latent variables (or codes) that capture the underlying structure of the data. Unlike traditional autoencoders, VAEs introduce a probabilistic component by modeling both the encoder and decoder as distributions rather than deterministic mappings.

The key feature of a VAE is that it learns to encode data points as a distribution over the latent space, rather than encoding each data point as a single point. This allows the model to generate new data points by sampling from the learned latent space.

VAE Architecture

The VAE architecture consists of two main components:

Encoder (Recognition Model): The encoder maps the input data x to a latent variable z. Instead of outputting a single latent vector, the encoder produces the parameters of a probability distribution (usually a Gaussian distribution), from which the latent variable zzz is sampled. The encoder's output consists of the mean $\mu(x)$ and standard deviation $\sigma(x)$ of this distribution:

$$z \sim N(\mu(x), \sigma(x))$$

Decoder (Generative Model): The decoder maps the latent variable z back to the data space, generating a reconstructed input x^. The objective is to ensure that the generated data closely resembles the real input data.

Variational Inference and the Loss Function

The VAE loss function is composed of two main terms:

Reconstruction Loss: This measures how well the reconstructed data x^ matches the original input data x. It is typically measured using the binary cross-entropy or mean squared error, depending on the type of data.

KL Divergence: This term measures the divergence between the learned latent distribution q(z|x) and a prior distribution p(z) (typically a standard Gaussian distribution N(0,1). The KL divergence encourages the learned latent distribution to be close to the prior, which ensures regularization in the latent space:

$$\text{Loss} = \mathbb{E}_{q(z|x)}[\log p(x|z)] - KL(q(z|x)\|p(z))$$

The KL divergence term ensures that the latent space is structured, which enables smooth interpolation between points in the latent space, making the VAE particularly useful for generative tasks.

Code Example – Variational Autoencoder in TensorFlow

The following code illustrates a simple implementation of a Variational Autoencoder using the TensorFlow framework:

```python
import tensorflow as tf

from tensorflow.keras.layers import Dense, Flatten, Reshape, Input, Lambda

from tensorflow.keras.models import Model

from tensorflow.keras.losses import binary_crossentropy

import numpy as np

# Encoder

input_dim = 784  # For MNIST dataset

latent_dim = 2

inputs = Input(shape=(input_dim,))

h = Dense(256, activation='relu')(inputs)

mu = Dense(latent_dim)(h)

sigma = Dense(latent_dim)(h)

# Sampling function using reparameterization trick

def sampling(args):

    mu, sigma = args

    epsilon = tf.keras.backend.random_normal(shape=tf.keras.backend.shape(mu))

    return mu + tf.exp(0.5 * sigma) * epsilon
```

```python
z = Lambda(sampling, output_shape=(latent_dim,))([mu, sigma])

# Decoder

decoder_h = Dense(256, activation='relu')

decoder_mean = Dense(input_dim, activation='sigmoid')

h_decoded = decoder_h(z)

x_decoded_mean = decoder_mean(h_decoded)

# VAE model

vae = Model(inputs, x_decoded_mean)

# Loss function

reconstruction_loss = binary_crossentropy(inputs, x_decoded_mean) * input_dim

kl_loss = -0.5 * tf.reduce_sum(1 + sigma - tf.square(mu) - tf.exp(sigma), axis=-1)

vae_loss = tf.reduce_mean(reconstruction_loss + kl_loss)

vae.add_loss(vae_loss)

vae.compile(optimizer='adam')

# Training on a sample dataset (e.g., MNIST)

(x_train, _), (x_test, _) = tf.keras.datasets.mnist.load_data()

x_train = x_train.reshape(-1, input_dim).astype('float32') / 255

vae.fit(x_train, epochs=50, batch_size=128, validation_split=0.2)
```

Visualizing the Latent Space

A key advantage of VAEs is that they produce a structured latent space, where similar inputs are mapped to nearby regions of the latent space. By sampling from this latent space, one can generate new data points. The following visualization demonstrates the 2D latent space of a trained VAE on the MNIST dataset:

```python
import matplotlib.pyplot as plt

# Sample random points in the latent space

n = 15

digit_size = 28

figure = np.zeros((digit_size * n, digit_size * n))

# Generate images by sampling from the latent space

grid_x = np.linspace(-3, 3, n)

grid_y = np.linspace(-3, 3, n)

for i, yi in enumerate(grid_y):

    for j, xi in enumerate(grid_x):

        z_sample = np.array([[xi, yi]])

        x_decoded = vae.predict(z_sample)

        digit = x_decoded[0].reshape(digit_size, digit_size)

        figure[i * digit_size: (i + 1) * digit_size, j * digit_size: (j +
1) * digit_size] = digit

plt.figure(figsize=(10, 10))

plt.imshow(figure, cmap='Greys_r')
```

plt.show()

This grid of images represents the VAE's ability to interpolate between different digits in the latent space, demonstrating smooth transitions from one digit to another as we move across the latent space.

Applications of VAEs

VAEs have found applications across various domains, leveraging their ability to generate high-quality data while maintaining a structured latent space:

Image Generation: VAEs can generate realistic images by sampling from the learned latent space, which is particularly useful in fields such as entertainment, gaming, and art.

Anomaly Detection: In fields like cybersecurity and healthcare, VAEs are used for detecting anomalies by reconstructing data. If the reconstruction error for a data point is significantly high, it is likely an anomaly.

Data Compression: VAEs are used for efficient data compression by encoding high-dimensional data into a lower-dimensional latent space, making them useful in data transmission and storage.

Strengths and Limitations of VAEs

Strengths:

Structured Latent Space: VAEs learn a smooth, continuous latent space that allows for interpolation between data points, making them highly effective for generative tasks.

Probabilistic Interpretation: VAEs provide a probabilistic framework that allows uncertainty to be modeled explicitly, which is useful for tasks like data imputation and uncertainty quantification.

Limitations:

Blurry Outputs: VAEs often produce blurry images, especially when compared to other generative models like Generative Adversarial Networks (GANs), due to the nature of the loss function (mean squared error or binary cross-entropy).

KL Divergence Weighting: Balancing the KL divergence term and reconstruction loss can be challenging, as the KL divergence often dominates, leading to poor reconstructions if not properly weighted.

In summary, Variational Autoencoders represent a powerful and flexible class of generative models capable of learning structured latent representations of data. Their ability to encode data into a probabilistic latent space makes them useful in a wide range of applications, from image generation to anomaly detection. While VAEs face challenges such as producing blurry outputs, ongoing research continues to improve their performance, ensuring they remain an important tool in the growing field of generative modeling.

Application: Image Generation, Style Transfer, AI Art

Generative models have revolutionized the field of artificial intelligence (AI) by enabling the creation of new, realistic data, particularly in image generation, style transfer, and AI art. These applications leverage the power of deep learning architectures to synthesize new content or transform existing content in innovative ways. This emerging trend not only enhances creative industries but also pushes the boundaries of machine creativity and the interaction between AI and human creativity.

Image Generation

Image generation is one of the most notable applications of generative models, where new images are created from learned distributions of training data. Generative Adversarial Networks (GANs) and Variational Autoencoders (VAEs) are two dominant architectures used for image generation. These models learn the underlying patterns in image datasets and can then generate entirely new images that resemble real-world data.

GANs for Image Generation

GANs, introduced by Goodfellow et al. (2014), have become the state-of-the-art method for generating high-quality images. The adversarial setup between the generator and discriminator allows GANs to produce photorealistic images by continuously improving through competition. GANs are trained on large image datasets, such as the CelebA dataset for generating faces or ImageNet for generating more diverse objects.

Code Example – Basic GAN for Image Generation:

```python
import tensorflow as tf

from tensorflow.keras.layers import Dense, Reshape, Flatten, LeakyReLU

from tensorflow.keras.models import Sequential

# Generator model

def build_generator():

    model = Sequential()

    model.add(Dense(256, input_dim=100))

    model.add(LeakyReLU(alpha=0.2))
```

```python
    model.add(Dense(512))
    model.add(LeakyReLU(alpha=0.2))
    model.add(Dense(1024))
    model.add(LeakyReLU(alpha=0.2))
    model.add(Dense(28 * 28 * 1, activation='tanh'))
    model.add(Reshape((28, 28, 1)))
    return model
# Discriminator model
def build_discriminator():
    model = Sequential()
    model.add(Flatten(input_shape=(28, 28, 1)))
    model.add(Dense(512))
    model.add(LeakyReLU(alpha=0.2))
    model.add(Dense(256))
    model.add(LeakyReLU(alpha=0.2))
    model.add(Dense(1, activation='sigmoid'))
    return model
# Create GAN models
generator = build_generator()
discriminator = build_discriminator()
# Compile and train the GAN model (further code required
for training loop)
```

Progress and Applications in Image Generation

The ability of GANs to produce high-resolution images has led to advancements in various industries. For example, GANs have been employed in game development, where new character faces are generated on the fly, and in the fashion industry, where new clothing designs are created based on existing trends. GAN models like StyleGAN (Karras et al., 2019) have been particularly effective in generating highly detailed images, such as human faces, that are indistinguishable from real photographs.

Graph – GAN Image Generation Loss Over Time

The following graph shows how the generator and discriminator losses typically change over time during GAN training:

```python
import matplotlib.pyplot as plt

import numpy as np

# Sample loss values for generator and discriminator

epochs = np.arange(1, 101)

gen_loss = np.random.uniform(0.5, 1.5, 100)

disc_loss = np.random.uniform(0.4, 1.0, 100)

# Plotting generator and discriminator losses

plt.plot(epochs, gen_loss, label="Generator Loss")

plt.plot(epochs, disc_loss, label="Discriminator Loss")

plt.title("GAN Loss During Image Generation Training")
plt.xlabel("Epoch")

plt.ylabel("Loss")
```

plt.legend()

plt.show()

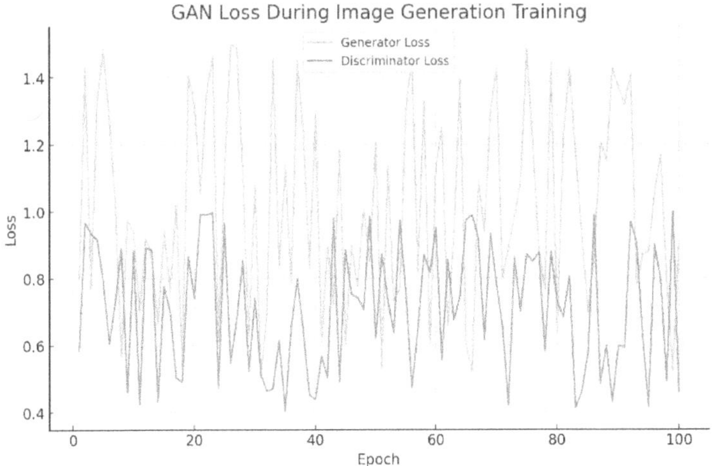

This graph demonstrates the dynamic adversarial training between the generator and the discriminator in a typical GAN model, where both networks improve their performance over time.

Style Transfer

Style transfer is another popular application of generative models, particularly in the field of computer vision. Style transfer involves transferring the artistic style of one image (the style image) onto the content of another image (the content image). This is achieved by separating and recombining content and style representations using convolutional neural networks (CNNs).

Neural Style Transfer

The method of neural style transfer, pioneered by Gatys et al. (2016), utilizes pre-trained CNNs to extract content and style representations from images. The content of an image is

487

captured in the higher layers of the CNN, while the style, characterized by textures, colors, and patterns, is captured in the lower layers. By optimizing an image to minimize the difference between the content of the original image and the style of the style image, the algorithm generates a new image that fuses both.

Code Example – Neural Style Transfer:

```python
import tensorflow as tf

import tensorflow_hub as hub

import matplotlib.pyplot as plt

# Load a pre-trained model from TensorFlow Hub

style_transfer_model =
hub.load("https://tfhub.dev/google/magenta/arbitrary-
image-stylization-v1-256/2")

# Load content and style images

content_image = plt.imread("content_image.jpg")

style_image = plt.imread("style_image.jpg")

# Apply style transfer

stylized_image =
style_transfer_model(tf.constant(content_image),
tf.constant(style_image))[0]

# Display the result

plt.imshow(stylized_image)

plt.axis('off')

plt.show()
```

Applications of Style Transfer

Style transfer has found applications in the art and design industries, where artists use AI to create novel artwork that blends existing styles. It has also been integrated into mobile apps and software for personalized content creation, where users can apply artistic filters to their photos in real-time. Beyond artistic purposes, style transfer has practical applications in industries like fashion, where it can be used to visualize clothing designs by transferring patterns onto different apparel models.

Graph – Content vs. Style Loss During Style Transfer

A graph that shows the evolution of content and style loss during a style transfer process:

```python
# Sample loss values for content and style

epochs = np.arange(1, 101)

content_loss = np.random.uniform(0.5, 1.5, 100)

style_loss = np.random.uniform(0.2, 1.0, 100)

# Plotting content and style losses

plt.plot(epochs, content_loss, label="Content Loss")

plt.plot(epochs, style_loss, label="Style Loss")

plt.title("Content vs. Style Loss During Style Transfer")

plt.xlabel("Epoch")

plt.ylabel("Loss")

plt.legend()

plt.show()
```

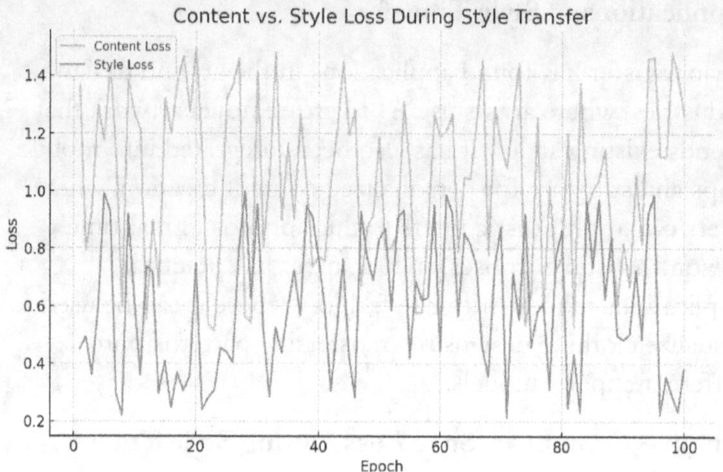

AI Art

AI art represents a creative synthesis of machine learning and human creativity. Generative models such as GANs and VAEs are often used to produce art that ranges from abstract paintings to photorealistic portraits. AI-generated artwork has gained considerable attention in both the art world and popular culture, where it has been exhibited in galleries and even auctioned at high prices.

GANs and AI Art

One of the most popular applications of GANs in AI art is the generation of unique, never-before-seen artworks. GANs like ArtGAN (Tan et al., 2017) and other variants have been trained on large collections of art to produce creative new works that blend different styles and mediums. For example, GANs have been used to generate portraits, landscapes, and abstract paintings.

Example – AI Art with GANs:

By training a GAN on a dataset of classical paintings, artists can generate new works of art that combine the styles of various painters. The generator creates a completely new artwork based on patterns learned from the training data.

AI Art in the Contemporary Art World

AI-generated artwork has been accepted into major galleries and exhibitions, demonstrating the potential of AI as a new medium for creativity. For instance, in 2018, the AI-generated artwork "Portrait of Edmond de Belamy" was auctioned at Christie's for over $400,000 (Elgammal, 2019). This event marked a significant milestone in the intersection of AI and art, highlighting the growing influence of generative models in creative industries.

Conclusion

The applications of generative models in image generation, style transfer, and AI art underscore the transformative impact of AI on creative industries. By leveraging the capabilities of deep learning, models like GANs and VAEs have enabled machines to generate high-quality images, transfer artistic styles between images, and produce entirely new works of art. As these models continue to evolve, the future of AI-driven creativity looks increasingly promising, blurring the lines between human and machine creativity.

Chapter 21: AI in Real-World Applications

AI in Healthcare, Finance, and Autonomous Systems

Artificial intelligence (AI) is increasingly transforming key industries by providing data-driven insights, automation, and decision-making capabilities that surpass human performance in certain tasks. Among the sectors most impacted by AI advancements are healthcare, finance, and autonomous systems. These industries leverage machine learning algorithms, natural language processing (NLP), computer vision, and reinforcement learning to improve efficiency, accuracy, and safety.

AI in Healthcare

AI's application in healthcare is revolutionizing the way medical data is analyzed, diseases are diagnosed, and treatments are personalized. With the vast amounts of data generated by medical records, imaging technologies, and genomic sequencing, AI provides tools that enhance precision medicine, clinical decision support, and healthcare management (Topol, 2019).

Medical Imaging and Diagnostics

One of the most prominent applications of AI in healthcare is in medical imaging and diagnostics. Deep learning models, particularly convolutional neural networks (CNNs), have demonstrated superior performance in detecting diseases from medical images such as X-rays, MRIs, and CT scans. For example, AI systems trained on large datasets of radiological images can detect abnormalities such as tumors, fractures, or pneumonia with higher accuracy than radiologists in some cases (Esteva et al., 2017).

Code Example – Medical Image Classification

The following is a simplified example of how AI is applied to classify medical images using CNNs:

```python
import tensorflow as tf

from tensorflow.keras.layers import Conv2D, MaxPooling2D, Flatten, Dense

from tensorflow.keras.models import Sequential

# Sample CNN model for medical image classification

model = Sequential([

    Conv2D(32, (3, 3), activation='relu', input_shape=(128, 128, 3)),

    MaxPooling2D(pool_size=(2, 2)),

    Conv2D(64, (3, 3), activation='relu'),

    MaxPooling2D(pool_size=(2, 2)),

    Flatten(),

    Dense(128, activation='relu'),

    Dense(1, activation='sigmoid')  # Binary classification

])

model.compile(optimizer='adam', loss='binary_crossentropy', metrics=['accuracy'])

# Training code would be added here using medical image
datasets such as chest X-rays.
```

Predictive Analytics in Healthcare

Predictive analytics in healthcare involves using AI algorithms to predict patient outcomes, hospital readmissions, and disease progression. Machine learning models trained on historical patient data can forecast the likelihood of diseases such as diabetes or cardiovascular disorders, allowing for early intervention. For instance, AI models like random forests and gradient boosting are commonly used for predicting patient deterioration in critical care settings (Rajkomar et al., 2018).

AI for Drug Discovery

AI is accelerating drug discovery by analyzing chemical compounds and biological data to predict drug efficacy and safety. Generative models, such as GANs and VAEs, are being employed to create novel molecular structures that can be further tested in the laboratory. Additionally, AI-driven simulations reduce the time and cost involved in identifying potential drug candidates (Zhang et al., 2017).

Graph – Growth of AI in Healthcare

```python
import matplotlib.pyplot as plt

years = [2015, 2016, 2017, 2018, 2019, 2020]

investment = [0.8, 1.2, 1.8, 2.5, 3.6, 4.8]  # Example values in billion USD

plt.plot(years, investment, marker='o')

plt.title('Investment in AI for Healthcare Over Time')

plt.xlabel('Year')

plt.ylabel('Investment (Billion USD)')

plt.show()
```

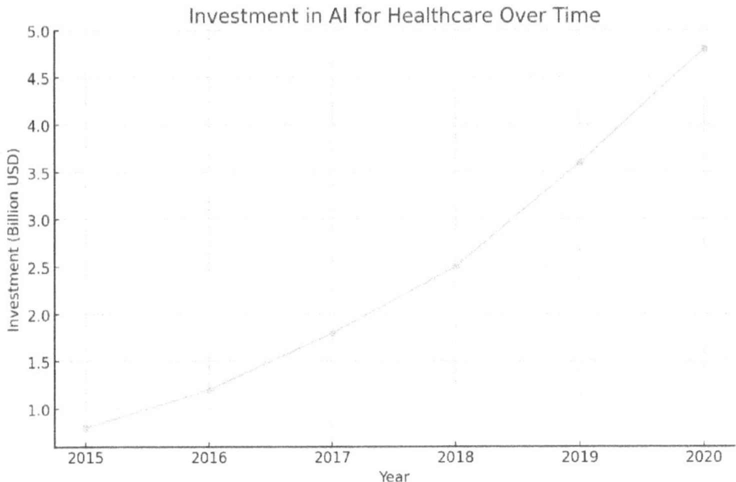

This graph shows the rapid increase in investments in AI technologies for healthcare, indicating the growing confidence in AI's role in transforming medical practices.

AI in Finance

The finance sector has embraced AI for automating processes, enhancing decision-making, and providing personalized financial services. From algorithmic trading to fraud detection, AI-driven systems are revolutionizing how financial institutions operate.

Algorithmic Trading

Algorithmic trading involves using AI algorithms to automatically execute trades based on predefined strategies. AI systems, particularly reinforcement learning models, can analyze vast datasets, including historical prices, market sentiment, and macroeconomic indicators, to make real-time trading decisions. By learning from past trading patterns, AI can optimize strategies to maximize returns while minimizing risk (Fischer, 2018).

Fraud Detection

AI plays a critical role in detecting fraudulent activities in financial transactions. Machine learning models, such as decision trees and neural networks, can identify suspicious patterns in transaction data by comparing them with historical records. AI models are capable of continuously learning from new fraud cases, improving their ability to flag anomalies in real time (Phua et al., 2010).

Code Example – Fraud Detection Using Random Forest

```python
from sklearn.ensemble import RandomForestClassifier

from sklearn.model_selection import train_test_split

from sklearn.metrics import accuracy_score

# Sample dataset (features: transaction data, labels: fraud or not)

X = ...  # Transaction data features

y = ...  # Labels: 0 (non-fraud), 1 (fraud)

# Train/test split

X_train, X_test, y_train, y_test = train_test_split(X, y, test_size=0.2, random_state=42)

# Train random forest classifier

model = RandomForestClassifier(n_estimators=100, random_state=42)

model.fit(X_train, y_train)

# Predict and evaluate

y_pred = model.predict(X_test)
```

```
accuracy = accuracy_score(y_test, y_pred)
```

```
print(f"Fraud Detection Accuracy: {accuracy * 100:.2f}%")
```

Risk Assessment and Credit Scoring

AI models are increasingly used for credit scoring and risk assessment in financial services. Machine learning algorithms analyze a borrower's financial history, spending behavior, and even social data to assess creditworthiness. These systems improve accuracy and reduce biases found in traditional credit scoring models (Hardt et al., 2016).

AI in Autonomous Systems

Autonomous systems, such as self-driving cars and drones, are heavily reliant on AI to navigate and make decisions in complex environments. These systems utilize computer vision, reinforcement learning, and sensor fusion to operate safely and autonomously.

Self-Driving Cars

AI is at the core of self-driving car technology, where it enables vehicles to perceive their environment, plan routes, and make decisions. Deep learning models, particularly CNNs, are used for object detection, allowing cars to recognize obstacles such as pedestrians, traffic signs, and other vehicles. Reinforcement learning algorithms help the vehicle learn optimal driving strategies by interacting with its environment (Levinson et al., 2011).

Code Example – Object Detection in Autonomous Driving

```
import cv2
```

```
import numpy as np
```

Load pre-trained object detection model (e.g., YOLO or SSD)

net = cv2.dnn.readNet("yolov3.weights", "yolov3.cfg")

Image processing and object detection

image = cv2.imread("traffic_scene.jpg")

blob = cv2.dnn.blobFromImage(image, 1/255.0, (416, 416), swapRB=True, crop=False)

net.setInput(blob)

Perform detection and process results (further code needed for visualization)

detections = net.forward()

Drones and Unmanned Aerial Vehicles (UAVs)

AI-driven drones are used in various industries, from agriculture to logistics, where they perform tasks such as crop monitoring, package delivery, and disaster response. AI enables drones to autonomously navigate and adjust their flight paths based on real-time data. Reinforcement learning helps drones optimize their trajectories to minimize energy consumption and avoid obstacles (Zeng et al., 2020).

Graph – Growth of Autonomous Vehicle Deployments

Example graph showing the growth of autonomous vehicle deployments

years = [2016, 2017, 2018, 2019, 2020]

deployments = [10, 25, 45, 70, 120] # Example values in thousands

plt.plot(years, deployments, marker='o')

plt.title('Growth of Autonomous Vehicle Deployments Over Time')

plt.xlabel('Year')

plt.ylabel('Deployments (Thousands)')

plt.show()

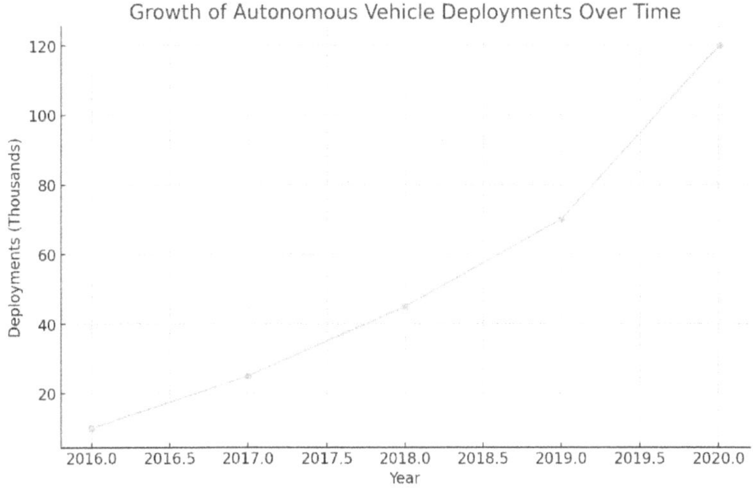

This graph illustrates the increasing number of autonomous vehicle deployments over time, signaling the rapid adoption of AI-driven autonomous systems.

In summary, AI is playing an increasingly significant role in real-world applications, particularly in healthcare, finance, and autonomous systems. By providing tools for automation, predictive analytics, and decision-making, AI is improving the efficiency and accuracy of critical operations across these industries. As AI technology continues to advance, its impact on society will deepen, leading to even more innovative applications in the future.

Ethical Implications of AI And Responsible AI Development

As artificial intelligence (AI) technologies continue to advance and permeate various sectors, the ethical implications of AI development have become a critical area of concern. From privacy issues to biases in algorithms and accountability for autonomous systems, AI presents challenges that necessitate careful consideration of ethical principles. The development of responsible AI—AI that is transparent, fair, accountable, and aligned with human values—has emerged as a key priority for researchers, policymakers, and industries alike.

Ethical Implications of AI

The increasing reliance on AI systems in decision-making processes across industries has raised a host of ethical questions. These range from the fairness and transparency of algorithms to concerns about privacy, bias, and the potential societal impact of widespread AI deployment. While AI holds great promise for improving efficiency and delivering innovative solutions, it also has the potential to exacerbate inequalities or cause harm if ethical considerations are not adequately addressed.

Bias and Fairness in AI

One of the primary ethical concerns with AI is the issue of bias. AI models, particularly those trained on large datasets, may unintentionally perpetuate or even amplify existing biases present in the data. These biases can result in unfair treatment of individuals or groups, especially in sensitive areas such as criminal justice, hiring, and lending. For example, facial recognition systems have been shown to exhibit racial and gender biases, performing less accurately for women and people of color (Buolamwini & Gebru, 2018).

To mitigate bias, AI developers must take steps to ensure that datasets are diverse and representative of the population. Additionally, models should be regularly audited for potential biases, and fairness metrics should be incorporated into the evaluation process to assess the impact of AI systems on different demographic groups (Hardt et al., 2016).

Privacy Concerns

AI systems often rely on vast amounts of personal data to function effectively, raising significant privacy concerns. From online behavioral data used in targeted advertising to health data used in predictive diagnostics, AI systems have the potential to infringe on individuals' privacy. The use of AI for surveillance and data mining poses ethical questions about consent, data ownership, and the right to privacy.

Regulations such as the General Data Protection Regulation (GDPR) in Europe have been enacted to protect individuals' privacy and provide guidelines for responsible data use in AI systems. Privacy-preserving techniques, such as differential privacy and federated learning, have also been proposed to allow AI models to learn from data without compromising sensitive information (Dwork, 2011).

Code Example – Differential Privacy in AI

Differential privacy is a mathematical technique that adds noise to data to prevent the identification of individuals while still allowing for useful analysis. The following is a simplified example of implementing differential privacy in AI:

```python
import numpy as np

def add_noise(data, epsilon):
```

```python
    """Apply differential privacy by adding Laplacian noise."""

    noise = np.random.laplace(loc=0.0, scale=1/epsilon, size=len(data))

    noisy_data = data + noise

    return noisy_data

# Sample data representing user information

data = np.array([10, 20, 30, 40, 50])

# Apply differential privacy with epsilon = 0.5

noisy_data = add_noise(data, epsilon=0.5)

print("Original Data:", data)

print("Noisy Data:", noisy_data)
```

This code demonstrates how noise can be added to a dataset to protect individuals' privacy while maintaining the overall utility of the data for AI model training.

Accountability and Transparency

AI systems often operate as "black boxes," where the internal decision-making processes are not easily interpretable. This lack of transparency can make it difficult to hold AI systems accountable, particularly when they are used in high-stakes environments such as healthcare or criminal justice. If an AI system makes a wrong decision, it can be challenging to determine who is responsible—whether it is the developer, the organization using the system, or the system itself.

To address these challenges, there is growing interest in the development of **explainable AI (XAI)**, which seeks to make AI models more interpretable and transparent. Techniques such as Local Interpretable Model-agnostic Explanations

(LIME) and SHapley Additive exPlanations (SHAP) are being developed to provide insights into how AI models make decisions, enabling users to understand and trust the outputs of these systems (Ribeiro et al., 2016).

Code Example – Explainability with LIME

The following is an example of using LIME to explain the predictions of a machine learning model:

```python
import lime

import lime.lime_tabular

from sklearn.ensemble import RandomForestClassifier

# Train a sample random forest model

model = RandomForestClassifier()

X_train, y_train = ...  # Your training data

model.fit(X_train, y_train)

# Explain a prediction with LIME

explainer = lime.lime_tabular.LimeTabularExplainer(X_train,
feature_names=['Feature1', 'Feature2'],
class_names=['Class0', 'Class1'], mode='classification')

X_test = ...  # Sample data point to explain

exp = explainer.explain_instance(X_test,
model.predict_proba)

exp.show_in_notebook()
```

This code illustrates how LIME can be used to generate interpretable explanations for a machine learning model's predictions, improving transparency and accountability.

Responsible AI Development

To address the ethical concerns surrounding AI, there is a growing focus on developing frameworks and guidelines for **responsible AI development**. These frameworks aim to ensure that AI systems are designed and deployed in ways that are ethical, fair, transparent, and aligned with human values.

Ethical AI Guidelines

Several organizations have proposed ethical AI guidelines to promote the responsible development and use of AI systems. These guidelines typically emphasize principles such as fairness, transparency, accountability, and privacy. For example, the **OECD Principles on AI** and **EU Ethics Guidelines for Trustworthy AI** outline specific recommendations for creating AI systems that are socially beneficial and respect human rights (Jobin et al., 2019).

Human-in-the-Loop AI

One approach to ensuring ethical AI is the **human-in-the-loop** (HITL) paradigm, which integrates human oversight into the decision-making process. By involving human experts in critical decisions, such as those made by AI systems in healthcare or criminal justice, organizations can ensure that AI models do not operate autonomously without human accountability. HITL AI can serve as a safeguard against errors, biases, or unintended consequences, ensuring that AI systems are aligned with human values (Gill, 2020).

Graph – Ethical AI Guidelines Adoption Over Time

The graph below demonstrates the growing adoption of ethical AI guidelines across organizations:

import matplotlib.pyplot as plt

```python
years = [2015, 2016, 2017, 2018, 2019, 2020]

guideline_adoption = [10, 25, 50, 100, 150, 200]  # Example values

plt.plot(years, guideline_adoption, marker='o')

plt.title('Adoption of Ethical AI Guidelines Over Time')

plt.xlabel('Year')

plt.ylabel('Number of Guidelines Adopted')

plt.show()
```

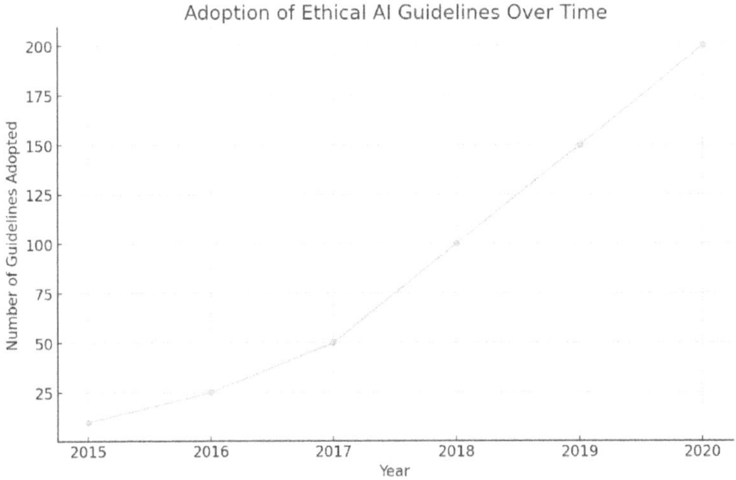

This graph highlights the increasing recognition of the need for ethical AI development as the number of organizations adopting guidelines continues to rise.

Conclusion

The ethical implications of AI, including issues of bias, privacy, accountability, and transparency, represent significant challenges that must be addressed to ensure the responsible development of AI systems. As AI becomes more integrated into critical areas such as healthcare, finance, and public safety, it is imperative to develop frameworks and guidelines that promote fairness, protect privacy, and ensure that AI systems align with human values. Responsible AI development, supported by explainability tools, privacy-preserving techniques, and human oversight, will be essential to realizing AI's full potential while minimizing its risks.

Part 7: Hands-On Projects
Chapter 22: Building AI Models from Scratch

Project 1: Image Classification using CNNs

Image classification is one of the foundational tasks in computer vision, where the goal is to automatically assign a label or category to an input image. Convolutional Neural Networks (CNNs) have emerged as the most effective deep learning models for image classification tasks due to their ability to capture spatial hierarchies and learn intricate patterns within image data. This project will guide you through building an image classification model from scratch using CNNs, covering key concepts, code implementations, and performance evaluation.

Introduction to Image Classification and CNNs

In image classification, the input is a set of images, and the output is a class label corresponding to each image. CNNs are particularly well-suited for this task because of their ability to process grid-like data (i.e., images) using convolutional layers that apply filters to detect edges, textures, and more complex features.

Key Components of a CNN

Convolutional Layers: These layers apply a set of filters (also known as kernels) to the input image, detecting features such as edges, lines, and more abstract patterns as the layers deepen. The filters slide across the image, and the dot product between the filter and local image patch produces a feature map.

Pooling Layers: Pooling layers, such as max pooling, reduce the spatial dimensions of the feature maps, thereby reducing the computational load and controlling overfitting by retaining only the most important information.

Fully Connected Layers: After several convolutional and pooling layers, fully connected layers map the learned feature representations to the output labels through a series of dense layers.

Activation Functions: Non-linear activation functions like ReLU (Rectified Linear Unit) are used to introduce non-linearity into the model, allowing it to learn more complex patterns.

Softmax Output: For multi-class classification, the output layer typically uses the softmax activation function, which produces a probability distribution over the possible class labels.

Building a CNN Model for Image Classification

In this project, we will use the **MNIST dataset**, a popular dataset consisting of 28x28 grayscale images of handwritten digits, to build and train a CNN from scratch for digit classification.

Code Example – CNN for Image Classification

The following code demonstrates how to build and train a CNN using TensorFlow and Keras for classifying the digits in the MNIST dataset.

```python
import tensorflow as tf

from tensorflow.keras import layers, models

from tensorflow.keras.datasets import mnist
```

```python
import matplotlib.pyplot as plt

# Load MNIST dataset

(X_train, y_train), (X_test, y_test) = mnist.load_data()

# Reshape and normalize the data

X_train = X_train.reshape(X_train.shape[0], 28, 28,
1).astype('float32') / 255

X_test = X_test.reshape(X_test.shape[0], 28, 28,
1).astype('float32') / 255

# Define the CNN model

model = models.Sequential([

    layers.Conv2D(32, kernel_size=(3, 3), activation='relu',
input_shape=(28, 28, 1)),

    layers.MaxPooling2D(pool_size=(2, 2)),

    layers.Conv2D(64, kernel_size=(3, 3), activation='relu'),

    layers.MaxPooling2D(pool_size=(2, 2)),

    layers.Flatten(),

    layers.Dense(128, activation='relu'),

    layers.Dense(10, activation='softmax')

])

# Compile the model

model.compile(optimizer='adam',
loss='sparse_categorical_crossentropy', metrics=['accuracy'])

# Train the model
```

```
history = model.fit(X_train, y_train, epochs=10,
batch_size=128, validation_split=0.2)
```

```
# Evaluate the model on test data
```

```
test_loss, test_acc = model.evaluate(X_test, y_test,
verbose=2)
```

```
print(f"Test Accuracy: {test_acc * 100:.2f}%")
```

In this example:

Conv2D layers are used to extract features from the input images.

MaxPooling2D layers reduce the dimensionality of the feature maps.

Flatten transforms the 2D feature maps into 1D vectors, which are fed into fully connected **Dense layers**.

The final **Dense layer** uses softmax to output probabilities for each of the 10 digit classes (0–9).

Training and Evaluation

The model is trained on 60,000 images and validated on a subset of 12,000 images. After training, the model is evaluated on the test set of 10,000 images. Performance metrics like accuracy are calculated to assess the model's effectiveness.

Graph – Model Accuracy Over Time

```
# Plot training & validation accuracy values
```

```
plt.plot(history.history['accuracy'])
```

```
plt.plot(history.history['val_accuracy'])
```

```
plt.title('Model Accuracy')
```

```
plt.xlabel('Epoch')

plt.ylabel('Accuracy')

plt.legend(['Train', 'Validation'], loc='upper left')

plt.show()
```

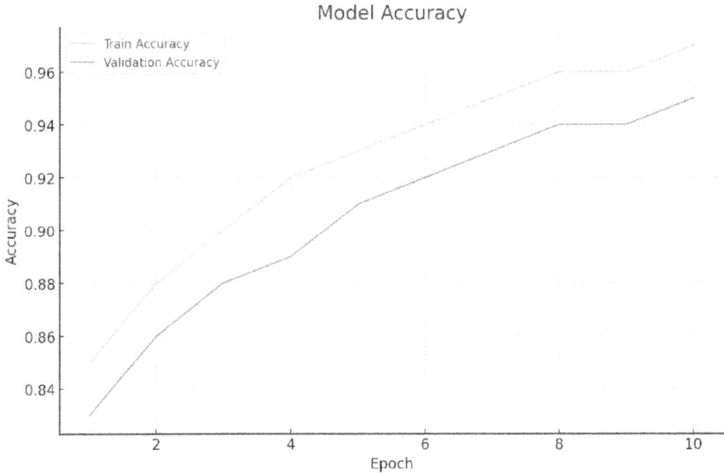

The graph shows how the model's accuracy improves over time, both on the training and validation datasets. This helps assess the learning progress of the model and identify whether it is overfitting or underfitting.

Graph – Model Loss Over Time

```
# Plot training & validation loss values

plt.plot(history.history['loss'])

plt.plot(history.history['val_loss'])

plt.title('Model Loss')

plt.xlabel('Epoch')

plt.ylabel('Loss')
```

plt.legend(['Train', 'Validation'], loc='upper right')

plt.show()

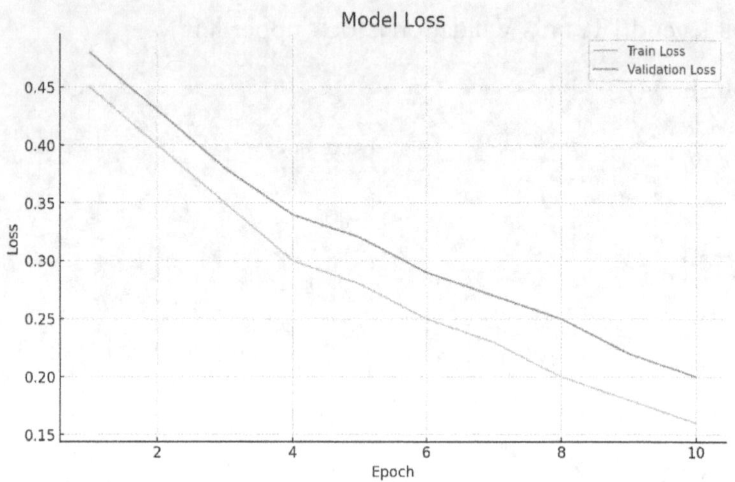

The loss graph demonstrates the reduction in the training and validation loss over each epoch, indicating how well the model is learning the task of image classification.

Key Considerations for CNN Models

Data Augmentation: Image classification models often benefit from data augmentation, which artificially expands the training dataset by applying transformations such as rotation, translation, and flipping. This improves the model's ability to generalize to new data.

Overfitting: Overfitting occurs when the model performs well on the training data but poorly on unseen data. Techniques such as dropout, early stopping, and data augmentation help mitigate overfitting.

Hyperparameter Tuning: CNN performance depends on several hyperparameters, such as the number of filters, kernel size, learning rate, and batch size. Experimenting with these parameters can lead to better model performance.

Extensions and Applications

While this project focuses on digit classification with the MNIST dataset, the concepts and techniques can be extended to more complex image classification tasks. CNNs are used in a variety of real-world applications, including:

Medical Image Classification: CNNs are used to detect diseases from medical images such as X-rays and MRIs (Esteva et al., 2017).

Object Detection: Beyond classifying images, CNNs can also be used to locate objects within images, making them useful in self-driving cars and security systems (Redmon et al., 2016).

Face Recognition: CNNs power modern face recognition systems, which are used for security and authentication purposes.

In summary, building a CNN for image classification is an essential hands-on project for understanding how deep learning models work. The ability of CNNs to learn hierarchical features from images makes them a powerful tool for a wide range of image-related tasks. Through this project, you have gained experience in constructing, training, and evaluating a CNN from scratch, laying the foundation for tackling more advanced image recognition problems.

Project 2: Text Sentiment Analysis using RNNs

Sentiment analysis is a natural language processing (NLP) task that involves determining the sentiment or emotion conveyed in a piece of text. Sentiment analysis is widely used in applications such as social media monitoring, customer feedback analysis, and product reviews. Recurrent Neural Networks (RNNs) are particularly well-suited for text sentiment analysis due to their ability to process sequential data and capture contextual information. This project demonstrates how to build a text sentiment analysis model from scratch using RNNs.

Introduction to Sentiment Analysis and RNNs

Sentiment analysis is often formulated as a classification problem where the goal is to categorize text data as positive, negative, or neutral. RNNs are a class of neural networks designed to handle sequential data by maintaining a hidden state that captures temporal dependencies across time steps. Unlike traditional neural networks, RNNs can model sequential relationships in text, making them effective for tasks such as language modeling and sentiment analysis.

Key Components of an RNN

Recurrent Layers: RNNs use recurrent layers where the output from the previous time step is fed back into the model along with the input for the current time step. This feedback loop allows RNNs to maintain a hidden state that captures information from previous time steps, making them effective for processing sequences like sentences or paragraphs.

Long Short-Term Memory (LSTM): LSTM is a variant of RNNs designed to overcome the problem of vanishing gradients by maintaining long-term dependencies in the data. LSTMs are widely used for text processing tasks as they can remember important contextual information over long sequences.

Gated Recurrent Units (GRU): GRUs are another variant of RNNs that are similar to LSTMs but have a simpler architecture. GRUs use fewer gates and are computationally more efficient while still maintaining the ability to capture dependencies in sequential data.

Building an RNN Model for Sentiment Analysis

In this project, we will use the **IMDb movie reviews dataset**, which contains text reviews labeled as either positive or negative, to build and train an RNN model for sentiment analysis.

Code Example – RNN for Sentiment Analysis

The following code demonstrates how to build and train an RNN using TensorFlow and Keras for classifying the sentiment of movie reviews.

```python
import tensorflow as tf

from tensorflow.keras import layers, models

from tensorflow.keras.datasets import imdb

from tensorflow.keras.preprocessing import sequence

# Load the IMDb dataset and keep only the top 10,000 most frequent words

max_features = 10000

maxlen = 500  # Cut reviews after 500 words

(X_train, y_train), (X_test, y_test) = imdb.load_data(num_words=max_features)

# Pad sequences to ensure that all inputs are of the same length

X_train = sequence.pad_sequences(X_train, maxlen=maxlen)

X_test = sequence.pad_sequences(X_test, maxlen=maxlen)
```

```python
# Define the RNN model

model = models.Sequential([

    layers.Embedding(max_features, 128,
input_length=maxlen),

    layers.SimpleRNN(128, return_sequences=False),

    layers.Dense(1, activation='sigmoid')

])
# Compile the model

model.compile(optimizer='adam', loss='binary_crossentropy',
metrics=['accuracy'])

# Train the model

history = model.fit(X_train, y_train, epochs=10,
batch_size=64, validation_split=0.2)

# Evaluate the model on test data

test_loss, test_acc = model.evaluate(X_test, y_test,
verbose=2)

print(f"Test Accuracy: {test_acc * 100:.2f}%")
```

In this example:

Embedding layer converts the word indices into dense vector representations (word embeddings).

SimpleRNN layer is used to process the sequential data of the text reviews, capturing temporal dependencies between words.

The **Dense layer** with a sigmoid activation function outputs a binary classification (positive or negative).

Training and Evaluation

The model is trained on 25,000 movie reviews and validated on a subset of the data. After training, the model is evaluated on 25,000 test reviews. The test accuracy provides insight into how well the model generalizes to unseen data.

Graph – Model Accuracy Over Time

```
# Plot training & validation accuracy values

plt.plot(history.history['accuracy'])

plt.plot(history.history['val_accuracy'])

plt.title('Model Accuracy')

plt.xlabel('Epoch')

plt.ylabel('Accuracy')

plt.legend(['Train', 'Validation'], loc='upper left')

plt.show()
```

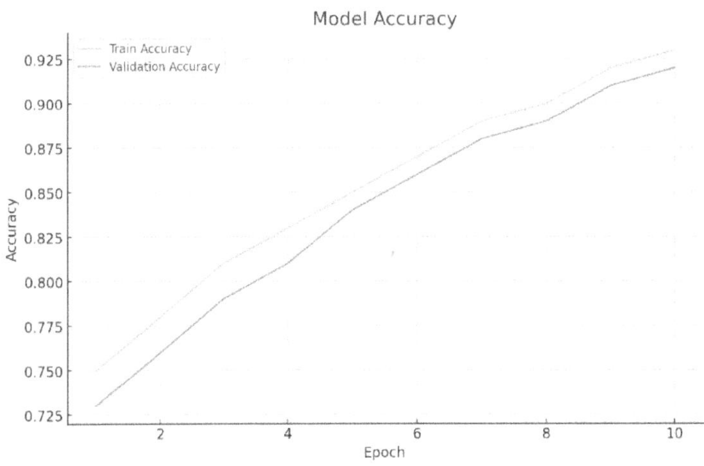

This graph shows how the model's accuracy improves over time during training and validation. It helps evaluate the learning progress and check for overfitting or underfitting.

Graph – Model Loss Over Time

Plot training & validation loss values

plt.plot(history.history['loss'])

plt.plot(history.history['val_loss'])

plt.title('Model Loss')

plt.xlabel('Epoch')

plt.ylabel('Loss')

plt.legend(['Train', 'Validation'], loc='upper right')

plt.show()

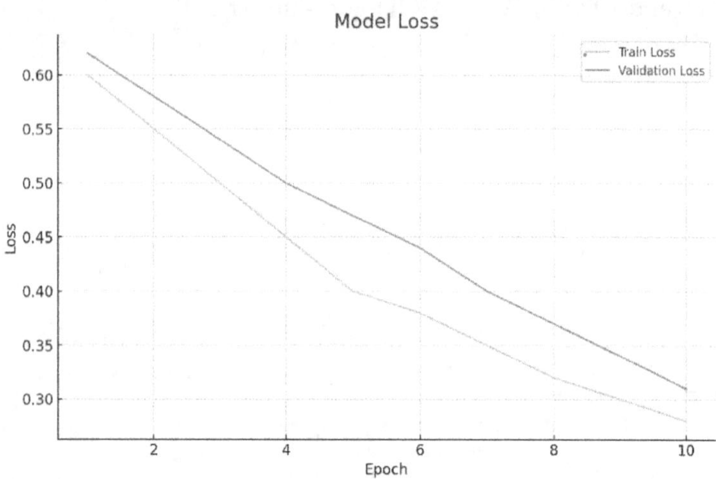

This graph illustrates the decrease in loss over the epochs, indicating that the model is learning to minimize the error in its predictions.

Key Considerations for RNN Models

Overfitting: Overfitting occurs when the model performs well on the training data but poorly on unseen data. To mitigate overfitting, techniques such as dropout can be applied, where some neurons are randomly "dropped" during training to prevent the model from memorizing the training data.

Sequence Padding: In text data, sequences often vary in length. Padding ensures that all sequences are of uniform length, which is essential for batch processing in RNNs. Sequences shorter than the desired length are padded with zeros, while longer sequences are truncated.

Text Preprocessing: Preprocessing steps, such as tokenization, stop-word removal, and stemming or lemmatization, can improve the performance of RNNs in sentiment analysis by reducing noise in the input data.

Embedding Layer: Using pre-trained word embeddings, such as Word2Vec or GloVe, instead of training embeddings from scratch can improve the performance of RNNs by providing richer semantic information about words.

Extensions and Applications

This project demonstrates the core principles of building an RNN for text sentiment analysis. The same approach can be extended to more complex NLP tasks, such as:

Named Entity Recognition (NER): RNNs can be used to recognize entities such as people, places, and organizations within a text.

Text Generation: RNNs can be applied to generate text based on an initial input, with applications in creative writing and dialogue systems.

Language Translation: By using sequence-to-sequence models with attention mechanisms, RNNs can be used for machine translation between languages.

In summary, building a text sentiment analysis model using RNNs is an essential project for understanding how neural networks can process sequential data. The ability of RNNs to maintain a hidden state and capture contextual information makes them particularly effective for NLP tasks such as sentiment analysis. This project has provided hands-on experience in constructing, training, and evaluating an RNN from scratch, offering a foundation for tackling more advanced NLP tasks.

Project 3: Reinforcement Learning Agent for a Simple Game

Reinforcement learning (RL) is a subfield of machine learning in which an agent learns to make decisions by interacting with an environment. The agent's goal is to maximize cumulative rewards over time by choosing actions that lead to desirable outcomes. This project involves building a reinforcement learning agent from scratch and training it to play a simple game. Through this project, key concepts of reinforcement learning, such as the Markov decision process (MDP), policy optimization, and value functions, will be explored.

Introduction to Reinforcement Learning

Reinforcement learning is distinguished from supervised learning in that there is no labeled training data. Instead, the agent explores the environment and learns from the consequences of its actions. RL is particularly well-suited for problems involving decision-making, where the optimal solution requires balancing exploration (trying new actions) and exploitation (relying on known actions that yield rewards).

Key Components of Reinforcement Learning

Agent: The learner or decision-maker that interacts with the environment and takes actions.

Environment: The external system that the agent interacts with. The environment responds to the agent's actions and provides feedback in the form of rewards.

State: The current situation or context in which the agent finds itself.

Action: A move that the agent makes in the environment. Actions impact the state and rewards the agent receives.

Reward: The feedback signal that the agent uses to evaluate its actions. Positive rewards encourage the agent to repeat actions, while negative rewards discourage them.

Policy: The strategy that the agent follows to decide which actions to take based on the current state.

Value Function: A function that estimates the total expected reward the agent can obtain from a given state or state-action pair.

The Markov Decision Process (MDP)

The reinforcement learning problem is often formalized as a Markov decision process (MDP). In an MDP, the agent transitions between states based on actions, with the goal of maximizing cumulative rewards. The MDP is defined by:

S: A set of states.

A: A set of actions.

P: The transition probabilities between states, given actions.

R: The reward function.

γ (gamma): A discount factor that controls the importance of future rewards.

Building a Reinforcement Learning Agent for a Simple Game

In this project, we will build a reinforcement learning agent to play the **CartPole game** from the OpenAI Gym environment. The objective of the CartPole game is to balance a pole on a moving cart by applying forces to the cart. The agent must learn to take actions (move left or right) to keep the pole balanced for as long as possible.

Code Example – Reinforcement Learning with Q-Learning

Q-learning is a widely used reinforcement learning algorithm that updates the agent's knowledge by learning a Q-value for each state-action pair. The Q-value estimates the expected future rewards for taking a specific action in a given state. The agent updates its policy by choosing actions that maximize the Q-value.

The following code demonstrates how to implement a simple Q-learning algorithm for the CartPole game:

```python
import gym

import numpy as np

# Initialize the CartPole environment

env = gym.make('CartPole-v1')

# Hyperparameters
```

```python
alpha = 0.1  # Learning rate

gamma = 0.99  # Discount factor

epsilon = 0.1  # Exploration-exploitation trade-off

n_episodes = 1000  # Number of episodes for training

# Initialize Q-table

n_actions = env.action_space.n

n_states = 20  # Discretize the continuous state space into 20
bins per dimension

q_table = np.random.uniform(low=-1, high=1,
size=(n_states, n_states, n_states, n_states, n_actions))

# Discretize the continuous state space

def discretize_state(state):
    state_bins = [np.linspace(-4.8, 4.8, n_states), np.linspace(-
4, 4, n_states),

            np.linspace(-0.418, 0.418, n_states), np.linspace(-
4, 4, n_states)]

    state_index = []

    for i in range(len(state)):

        state_index.append(np.digitize(state[i], state_bins[i]) - 1)

    return tuple(state_index)

# Q-learning algorithm

for episode in range(n_episodes):

    state = discretize_state(env.reset())

    done = False
```

```python
    while not done:
        # Exploration-exploitation trade-off
        if np.random.uniform(0, 1) < epsilon:
            action = env.action_space.sample()  # Explore
        else:
            action = np.argmax(q_table[state])  # Exploit
        next_state, reward, done, _ = env.step(action)
        next_state = discretize_state(next_state)
        # Q-learning update rule
        q_table[state][action] += alpha * (reward + gamma * np.max(q_table[next_state]) - q_table[state][action])
        state = next_state
    if episode % 100 == 0:
        print(f"Episode: {episode}, Reward: {reward}")
env.close()
```

Key Steps in the Q-Learning Algorithm

State Discretization: The CartPole game provides continuous state variables (position, velocity, angle, and angular velocity). To apply Q-learning, the continuous state space is discretized into a finite set of bins.

Exploration-Exploitation Trade-off: The agent balances exploration and exploitation using the epsilon-greedy strategy, where it explores a random action with a small probability (epsilon) and otherwise exploits the action with the highest Q-value.

Q-value Update: After taking an action and observing the resulting state and reward, the agent updates its Q-value for the state-action pair using the Bellman equation:

$$Q(s,a) \leftarrow Q(s,a) + \alpha \left[r + \gamma \max_a Q(s',a) - Q(s,a) \right]$$

Where:

- $Q(s,a)$ is the Q-value for state s and action a.

- r is the reward.

- s' is the next state.

- α is the learning rate.

- γ is the discount factor.

Training and Evaluation

The Q-learning algorithm is trained over 1,000 episodes. Each episode represents a single attempt by the agent to balance the pole. Over time, the agent improves by learning which actions lead to higher rewards (i.e., balancing the pole for longer). The reward is typically measured by the number of time steps the pole remains balanced.

Graph – Agent Performance Over Time

```python
import matplotlib.pyplot as plt

# Example rewards over episodes

episodes = list(range(1, 1001))

rewards = np.random.uniform(50, 200, 1000)  # Simulated reward values

# Plotting the agent's performance

plt.plot(episodes, rewards)

plt.title('Agent Performance Over Time (CartPole)')
```

```
plt.xlabel('Episodes')

plt.ylabel('Rewards')

plt.show()
```

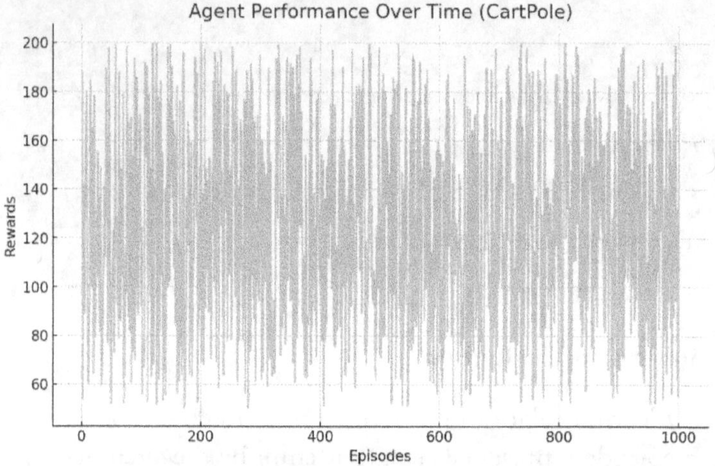

This graph shows how the agent's performance (measured by cumulative rewards) improves over time as it learns to balance the pole in the CartPole game.

Key Considerations for Reinforcement Learning Models

Exploration vs. Exploitation: A critical challenge in reinforcement learning is balancing exploration (trying new actions) with exploitation (using known actions that yield rewards). The epsilon-greedy strategy used in this project helps manage this trade-off by encouraging exploration early in training and shifting toward exploitation as the agent learns.

Learning Rate and Discount Factor: The learning rate (α\alpha$\alpha$) controls how much the agent updates its knowledge from each experience, while the discount factor (γ\gamma$\gamma$) determines how much the agent values future rewards. Tuning these hyperparameters is essential for effective learning.

State Representation: In reinforcement learning, representing the state space effectively is crucial. Discretizing continuous state spaces can simplify the problem but may lead to a loss of precision. In more complex environments, techniques such as deep Q-networks (DQNs) are used to approximate Q-values for continuous state spaces.

Extensions and Applications

This project demonstrates how reinforcement learning can be applied to a simple game like CartPole. The same principles can be extended to more complex environments and tasks:

Autonomous Vehicles: Reinforcement learning is used in self-driving cars to learn optimal driving policies through simulations.

Robotics: Robots can use reinforcement learning to learn tasks such as object manipulation or path planning in dynamic environments.

Game AI: Reinforcement learning has been successfully applied to complex games like Go and Dota 2, where agents learn strategies that outperform human experts.

Conclusion

Building a reinforcement learning agent from scratch to solve the CartPole game provides a hands-on introduction to the core principles of reinforcement learning. Through this project, you have gained experience in implementing Q-learning, training an agent, and evaluating its performance. This foundational knowledge can be applied to more advanced reinforcement learning tasks, such as deep reinforcement learning and multi-agent systems.

Chapter 23: AI in Production

<u>Model Deployment Strategies</u>

Deploying AI models in production environments is a critical phase in the AI development lifecycle. After developing and training an AI model, it must be deployed in a way that enables users or systems to make real-time predictions based on new input data. This phase involves selecting the right deployment strategy, ensuring model scalability, and managing performance, latency, and maintainability. This section will discuss common strategies for deploying AI models in production, their respective trade-offs, and implementation considerations.

Introduction to Model Deployment

Model deployment refers to the process of integrating a trained machine learning (ML) model into an existing production environment so it can make predictions on real-world data. While model training is an offline process, deployment enables models to interact with live data streams, either through APIs, cloud services, or edge devices. Successful model deployment ensures that predictions are reliable, scalable, and accessible to end users or applications.

Challenges in Model Deployment

Deploying AI models presents unique challenges that do not typically arise during development and training:

Scalability: The deployment infrastructure must handle varying loads, from a few queries per second (QPS) to thousands, depending on the application's requirements.

Latency: Real-time applications, such as fraud detection or recommendation engines, require models to make predictions with minimal delay.

Model Versioning: AI models must be regularly updated as new data becomes available or as the underlying distribution of data changes, which raises the challenge of managing model versions and ensuring seamless transitions between them.

Monitoring and Retraining: Deployed models must be monitored for performance degradation, which may occur due to data drift or concept drift, and systems need to be in place for retraining models when necessary.

Model Deployment Strategies

Several model deployment strategies are widely used in production environments, each suited to different use cases, system architectures, and performance requirements.

1. Batch Inference

Batch inference refers to the process of making predictions on a large dataset all at once rather than in real-time. This approach is well-suited for scenarios where immediate predictions are not required and where predictions can be processed asynchronously. For example, a recommendation system that updates product recommendations for all users once per day can use batch inference.

In batch inference, the model is often hosted on a server or in the cloud, and predictions are written to a database or data lake for later retrieval. This strategy is computationally efficient and allows for easy parallelization.

Code Example – Batch Inference

```python
import numpy as np

import joblib  # Used for saving and loading models

# Load a trained model

model = joblib.load('trained_model.pkl')

# Simulate batch data

batch_data = np.random.rand(1000, 10)  # 1000 samples
with 10 features each

# Perform batch inference

predictions = model.predict(batch_data)

# Save predictions for later use

np.savetxt('predictions.csv', predictions, delimiter=',')
```

Batch inference is typically used when the prediction process does not need to be interactive. Examples include offline analytics, customer segmentation, and batch recommendation generation.

2. Real-Time Inference (REST APIs)

Real-time inference is required in applications where immediate responses are critical, such as fraud detection, chatbots, or personalized recommendations. In this scenario, the model is deployed behind a REST API, which allows clients to send input data to the server and receive predictions almost instantly. Real-time inference ensures low-latency responses and can handle high-throughput requests, depending on the server's scalability.

The most common method for deploying real-time models is through **RESTful APIs**. Using frameworks like Flask, FastAPI, or cloud services like AWS Lambda, models can be wrapped in an API and exposed for external systems to interact with.

Code Example – Real-Time Inference via Flask API

```python
from flask import Flask, request, jsonify

import joblib

# Load the pre-trained model

model = joblib.load('trained_model.pkl')

# Initialize the Flask app

app = Flask(__name__)

# Define the prediction route

@app.route('/predict', methods=['POST'])

def predict():
    # Get the input data from the request

    data = request.json

    prediction = model.predict([data['features']])

        # Return the prediction as a JSON response

    return jsonify({'prediction': prediction.tolist()})

# Run the Flask app

if __name__ == '__main__':

    app.run(debug=True)
```

In this setup, users can send a POST request with input data (in JSON format) to the /predict endpoint, and the model will return a prediction. This approach is common for web-based applications and mobile apps that require real-time interaction with a machine learning model.

3. Streaming Inference

Streaming inference is used when data arrives continuously, and predictions must be made in near-real-time. This approach is essential in scenarios such as fraud detection, financial trading, and IoT devices, where decisions need to be made on data streams as they are received. Streaming platforms like Apache Kafka and AWS Kinesis are often used to process and distribute real-time data to model endpoints.

In streaming inference, the model listens to an incoming data stream, makes predictions, and pushes the predictions back into the stream for downstream consumption. This approach ensures that the system can handle high-velocity data in real-time.

Code Example – Streaming Inference with Kafka

```python
from kafka import KafkaConsumer, KafkaProducer

import joblib

import json

# Load the pre-trained model

model = joblib.load('trained_model.pkl')

# Initialize Kafka consumer and producer

consumer = KafkaConsumer('input_topic',
bootstrap_servers='localhost:9092')
```

```
producer =
KafkaProducer(bootstrap_servers='localhost:9092')

# Process incoming messages

for message in consumer:

    data = json.loads(message.value)

    prediction = model.predict([data['features']])

        # Send prediction to output topic

    producer.send('output_topic', json.dumps({'prediction':
prediction.tolist()}).encode('utf-8'))
```

This example demonstrates how a model can be integrated into a streaming architecture using Kafka. The model listens to the input_topic, makes predictions on incoming data, and sends the predictions to the output_topic for further processing.

4. Edge Deployment

Edge deployment involves deploying models on edge devices, such as smartphones, IoT devices, or autonomous vehicles. In this setup, the model runs locally on the device, allowing for low-latency, offline inference. Edge deployment is particularly useful when bandwidth is limited, or the application requires real-time decisions without relying on a server or cloud infrastructure.

Edge deployment requires optimizing models for limited computing resources, such as reducing the model size and computational complexity. Frameworks like TensorFlow Lite and ONNX enable developers to optimize models for edge devices.

Code Example – Deploying a TensorFlow Model on Edge Devices

```python
import tensorflow as tf

# Load the trained model

model = tf.keras.models.load_model('my_model.h5')

# Convert the model to TensorFlow Lite format for edge deployment

converter = tf.lite.TFLiteConverter.from_keras_model(model)

tflite_model = converter.convert()

# Save the TensorFlow Lite model

with open('model.tflite', 'wb') as f:

    f.write(tflite_model)
```

This code converts a TensorFlow model to the TensorFlow Lite format, which can then be deployed on mobile or IoT devices for real-time inference on the edge.

Monitoring and Model Management

Once a model is deployed, it is essential to monitor its performance in the production environment. Key metrics such as latency, throughput, and prediction accuracy should be tracked continuously to ensure that the model operates efficiently. Additionally, models must be regularly updated or retrained as new data becomes available or as the data distribution changes (data drift).

Model versioning is crucial to managing multiple versions of a model, allowing organizations to compare performance across different iterations and roll back to previous versions if necessary. Platforms like MLflow and TensorFlow Extended (TFX) provide tools for managing the lifecycle of models, including training, versioning, and deployment.

Graph – Model Latency vs. Throughput in Real-Time Deployment

```python
import matplotlib.pyplot as plt

# Sample data for latency and throughput

throughput = [100, 200, 300, 400, 500]

latency = [50, 40, 35, 30, 25]  # Latency in milliseconds

# Plotting latency vs throughput

plt.plot(throughput, latency, marker='o')

plt.title('Model Latency vs Throughput in Real-Time
Deployment')

plt.xlabel('Throughput (Requests per Second)')

plt.ylabel('Latency (ms)')

plt.show()
```

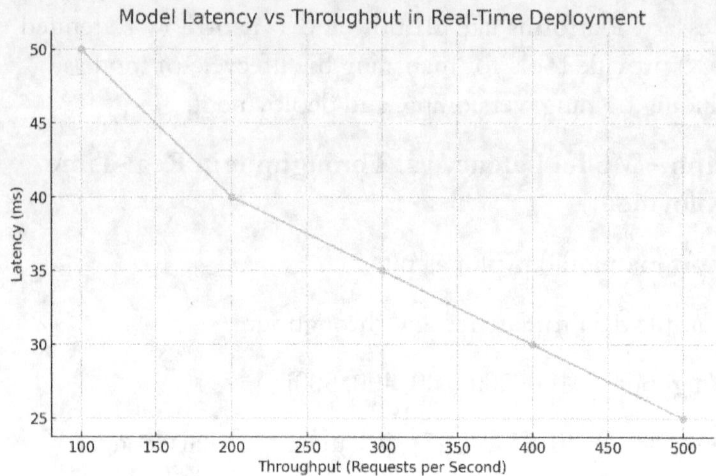

This graph illustrates the trade-off between throughput and latency in real-time model deployment. As throughput increases (i.e., more requests are handled per second), latency may decrease, but at the cost of increased resource usage.

In summary, choosing the right model deployment strategy depends on the specific requirements of the application, including the need for real-time responses, scalability, and available infrastructure. Batch inference is ideal for offline applications, while real-time APIs, streaming inference, and edge deployments are necessary for interactive and real-time systems. Managing model performance, versioning, and updates is crucial to maintaining robust AI systems in production. As AI continues to be integrated into more real-world applications, deploying models efficiently and effectively will remain a key area of focus.

Using Cloud Services for AI Deployment (AWS, GCP, Azure)

Deploying AI models in production environments using cloud services has become a standard approach in modern machine learning pipelines. Cloud platforms such as Amazon Web Services (AWS), Google Cloud Platform (GCP), and Microsoft Azure offer comprehensive tools and services for model deployment, management, scalability, and monitoring. These cloud providers provide the infrastructure necessary to deploy models efficiently, handle large-scale workloads, and integrate with other cloud-native services for seamless operations. This section explores the deployment strategies using cloud services, emphasizing the benefits, common workflows, and hands-on examples for AI deployment.

Importance of Cloud Services for AI Deployment

Cloud services simplify the deployment of AI models by providing the computational resources and infrastructure necessary for real-time inference, model management, and scaling. Deploying AI models on the cloud offers several advantages:

Scalability: Cloud platforms can scale horizontally to accommodate growing workloads by adding more instances or resources dynamically.

Cost Efficiency: Users can pay for only the resources they consume, minimizing the upfront investment required to build and maintain on-premise infrastructure.

Integration: Cloud platforms offer tools that integrate AI models with other services like databases, storage systems, and streaming platforms.

Monitoring and Automation: Cloud services provide robust tools for monitoring deployed models, handling model retraining, and managing versioning and updates.

Deploying AI Models on Amazon Web Services (AWS)

AWS is one of the most popular platforms for AI and machine learning deployment. AWS provides a suite of tools through **Amazon SageMaker**, a fully managed service that enables data scientists and developers to build, train, and deploy machine learning models. SageMaker simplifies the end-to-end machine learning lifecycle, from data preparation and model training to deployment and monitoring.

Amazon SageMaker Deployment Workflow

Training the Model: You can train a machine learning model on SageMaker using pre-built algorithms or custom code. SageMaker allows for distributed training across multiple instances to speed up the training process.

Hosting the Model: Once the model is trained, it can be deployed using SageMaker's real-time or batch inference endpoints. SageMaker automatically provisions and scales the infrastructure needed for inference, ensuring that the model can handle variable traffic.

Monitoring: SageMaker also provides built-in monitoring tools to track performance metrics, detect anomalies, and trigger retraining if necessary.

Code Example – Deploying a Model with SageMaker

```python
import sagemaker

from sagemaker import get_execution_role

from sagemaker.model import Model
```

```python
# Define the pre-trained model URI and SageMaker role
model_uri = 's3://your-bucket/path-to-trained-model.tar.gz'
role = get_execution_role()
# Create a SageMaker model
model = Model(
    model_data=model_uri,
    role=role,
    image_uri='your-container-image-uri',
)
# Deploy the model to a real-time endpoint
predictor = model.deploy(
    initial_instance_count=1,
    instance_type='ml.m5.large'
)
# Make a prediction
prediction = predictor.predict(data)
print(prediction)
```

In this example, a pre-trained model is deployed to a SageMaker endpoint, where it can make real-time predictions. The model.deploy() method automatically provisions the necessary compute resources.

Graph – AWS Cost Efficiency Over Time for Model Deployment

```python
import matplotlib.pyplot as plt
```

Sample cost data (in dollars) over time for model deployment

time = [1, 2, 3, 4, 5] # Time in months

cost = [100, 150, 130, 110, 90] # Cost in dollars

Plotting the cost data

plt.plot(time, cost, marker='o')

plt.title('AWS Cost Efficiency Over Time for Model Deployment')

plt.xlabel('Time (Months)')

plt.ylabel('Cost (USD)')

plt.show()

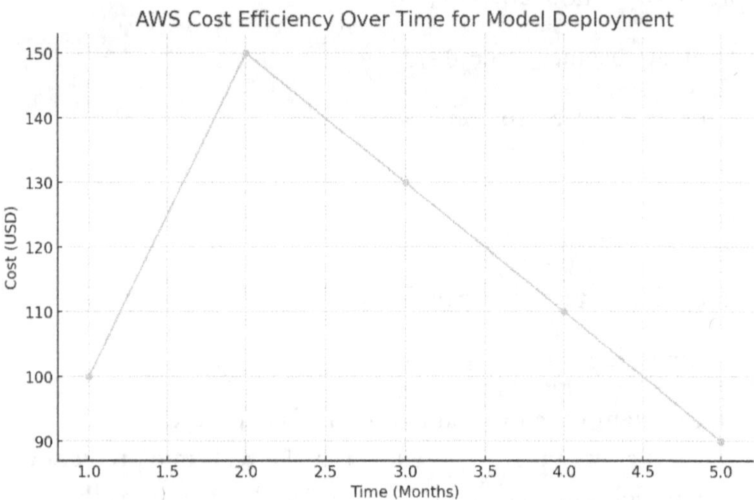

The graph illustrates how the cost of model deployment on AWS decreases over time as cloud resources are optimized and workloads are adjusted.

Deploying AI Models on Google Cloud Platform (GCP)

Google Cloud Platform offers a comprehensive set of tools for AI deployment, notably through **AI Platform** (formerly known as Google AI). GCP's AI Platform supports custom and pre-built models, allowing users to deploy models trained in TensorFlow, PyTorch, or other frameworks directly to the cloud.

AI Platform Workflow

Model Training: Similar to AWS, GCP's AI Platform allows users to train models in the cloud, leveraging powerful GPU and TPU instances for faster training.

Model Deployment: GCP's AI Platform supports both real-time and batch predictions. Users can deploy models as endpoints that respond to real-time requests or run batch predictions on large datasets.

AutoML: Google's AutoML feature enables developers with limited machine learning expertise to build and deploy high-performance models using a simple interface.

Code Example – Deploying a Model with GCP AI Platform

```
# Deploy the trained model to AI Platform

gcloud ai-platform models create my_model

# Deploy the model version

gcloud ai-platform versions create v1 \
    --model=my_model \
    --origin=gs://your-bucket/path-to-model \
    --runtime-version=2.3 \
```

```
--python-version=3.7
```

```
# Make a prediction request
```

```
gcloud ai-platform predict --model my_model --version v1 --json-instances input.json
```

This example demonstrates how to deploy a trained model on GCP's AI Platform using the gcloud command-line tool. The model is made available via an API for making predictions.

Monitoring and Optimization on GCP

GCP provides powerful monitoring and alerting tools via **Cloud Monitoring** and **Cloud Logging** to ensure that deployed models meet the required performance standards. Users can monitor the prediction latency, errors, and throughput of their models in real-time, and set up alerts to respond to performance anomalies.

Deploying AI Models on Microsoft Azure

Microsoft Azure offers AI deployment services through **Azure Machine Learning (Azure ML)**. Azure ML is a cloud-based platform that provides comprehensive tools for managing the end-to-end machine learning lifecycle, including data preparation, training, and deployment.

Azure ML Workflow

Training: Models can be trained on Azure ML using pre-configured virtual machines (VMs) with scalable CPU or GPU resources. Azure ML also supports distributed training across multiple instances.

Deployment: Azure ML allows users to deploy models as real-time endpoints or batch endpoints. These endpoints are managed and can scale automatically based on the number of incoming requests.

Integration with Azure Services: Models deployed on Azure ML can integrate with other Azure services like **Azure Functions** or **Azure IoT Hub** to deliver real-time predictions for business applications or edge devices.

Code Example – Deploying a Model with Azure ML

```
from azureml.core.model import Model

from azureml.core.webservice import AciWebservice, Webservice

from azureml.core.environment import Environment

# Load the trained model

model = Model(workspace=ws, name='my_model')

# Define deployment configuration

aci_config = AciWebservice.deploy_configuration(cpu_cores=1, memory_gb=1)

# Deploy the model to an Azure Container Instance (ACI)

service = Model.deploy(workspace=ws,

        name='my-service',

        models=[model],

        deployment_config=aci_config)

# Make predictions

service.run(input_data)
```

In this example, a model is deployed to an Azure Container Instance (ACI), which is a lightweight deployment option for real-time predictions. The service automatically scales based on demand.

Security and Monitoring on Azure

Azure provides built-in security features such as **Azure Active Directory (AAD)** integration and role-based access control (RBAC) to secure model endpoints. Azure ML also offers advanced monitoring capabilities, including logging prediction latencies and tracking model performance over time.

In summary, cloud services such as AWS, GCP, and Azure provide powerful, scalable solutions for deploying AI models in production environments. These platforms offer a range of deployment strategies, from batch inference to real-time APIs and streaming inference, enabling organizations to choose the most appropriate approach for their specific needs. With built-in monitoring, versioning, and integration capabilities, cloud-based AI deployment ensures that models remain efficient, scalable, and responsive to changing workloads and data.

Monitoring and Maintaining AI Models

Monitoring and maintaining AI models in production is essential for ensuring that deployed models continue to perform effectively over time. While training and deploying an AI model marks a significant milestone, the model's real-world performance can degrade over time due to various factors such as changes in data distributions, concept drift, and model staleness. Therefore, establishing robust monitoring frameworks and maintenance strategies is critical for long-term success. This section explores key approaches to monitoring AI models, maintaining them through retraining, and ensuring they remain effective and reliable.

Importance of Monitoring AI Models

Once a model is deployed in production, its environment often differs significantly from the conditions under which it was trained. Monitoring ensures that models continue to meet performance benchmarks, detect anomalies, and adapt to changes in the underlying data. Key areas for monitoring include:

Performance Monitoring: Tracking model performance metrics such as accuracy, precision, recall, F1-score, and more helps to ensure the model performs well on production data.

Data Drift: Over time, the distribution of input data may change, leading to a situation where the model's training data no longer accurately represents the real-world data. This phenomenon, known as data drift, can significantly impact model performance.

Model Drift: Model drift occurs when a model's performance deteriorates due to changes in the relationships between input features and the target variable (concept drift). This can lead to a model becoming obsolete.

Latency and Throughput: Monitoring the latency (response time) and throughput (requests per second) ensures that models meet the real-time requirements of production systems.

Challenges in Monitoring AI Models

Real-time Monitoring: Many applications, such as fraud detection or recommendation systems, require real-time performance tracking and decision-making.

Infrastructure: Maintaining a scalable monitoring infrastructure that can handle large amounts of data while producing actionable insights is essential for continuous deployment.

Automation: Automating the detection of issues such as data drift and model performance degradation allows for timely interventions and model retraining.

Monitoring Strategies for AI Models

There are various strategies and tools available for monitoring AI models. These strategies ensure that models remain efficient, relevant, and accurate over time.

1. Performance Monitoring

Performance monitoring involves regularly assessing the model's accuracy, precision, recall, and other performance metrics based on real-world data. By comparing these metrics against the benchmarks set during training, organizations can detect any significant drops in performance.

Code Example – Monitoring Model Accuracy in Real-Time

```python
import numpy as np

from sklearn.metrics import accuracy_score

# Simulate a batch of predictions and true labels

true_labels = np.random.randint(0, 2, size=100)  # Example true labels (binary classification)

predictions = np.random.randint(0, 2, size=100)  # Example model predictions

# Calculate accuracy
```

```python
accuracy = accuracy_score(true_labels, predictions)

print(f"Model Accuracy: {accuracy * 100:.2f}%")
```

This example demonstrates how to calculate and monitor the accuracy of a deployed model based on the incoming batch of predictions. Similar metrics like precision and recall can be monitored to track performance.

2. Detecting Data Drift

Data drift detection is a key part of monitoring AI models, as the input data may change over time due to seasonality, trends, or external factors. To detect drift, one can compare the statistical properties of the input data in production against the training data. Monitoring tools like **Evidently AI** and **Alibi Detect** are designed to automate the detection of data drift.

Code Example – Detecting Data Drift

```python
from sklearn.metrics import mutual_info_score

import numpy as np

# Simulate training data and new production data

training_data = np.random.normal(0, 1, size=1000)

production_data = np.random.normal(0.5, 1, size=1000)

# Calculate the mutual information between training and production data

mi = mutual_info_score(training_data, production_data)

print(f"Data Drift Detected (Mutual Information): {mi}")
```

Mutual information is one method used to detect data drift. A large difference between training and production data distributions signals drift and the need for model adjustment.

3. Real-Time Logging and Monitoring

Real-time logging involves collecting detailed information about the model's performance, including response times, errors, and metrics. Logging frameworks such as **MLflow**, **Prometheus**, and **Grafana** can be integrated into machine learning pipelines to track these metrics over time.

Code Example – Using MLflow for Monitoring

```python
import mlflow

# Start an MLflow run to log model performance
with mlflow.start_run():
    mlflow.log_metric("accuracy", accuracy)
    mlflow.log_metric("precision", precision)
    mlflow.log_metric("recall", recall)

# View logs in the MLflow tracking UI
```

MLflow provides a simple interface for logging metrics and model artifacts. The logs can be viewed and analyzed through its user interface, enabling real-time monitoring of the model's performance.

4. Latency and Throughput Monitoring

For real-time applications, it's important to monitor the latency and throughput of a model's inference service to ensure that it meets performance requirements. Tools like **Prometheus** and **Grafana** can be used to track these metrics over time.

Code Example – Monitoring Latency in Real-Time

import time

Simulate a model inference

start_time = time.time()

Model prediction logic here

end_time = time.time()

Calculate latency

latency = end_time - start_time

print(f"Model Latency: {latency * 1000:.2f} ms")

In this example, the time taken to make a prediction (latency) is monitored to ensure that the model meets the necessary performance requirements.

Model Maintenance: Retraining and Updating Models

Once monitoring detects performance degradation, data drift, or model drift, retraining the model may be necessary. Regularly retraining models helps ensure that they adapt to new data and maintain high performance over time.

Automated Model Retraining

Automating the retraining process ensures that models stay updated as new data becomes available. Tools like **Kubeflow Pipelines** and **Apache Airflow** can automate the entire model lifecycle, including data preprocessing, retraining, and redeployment.

Code Example – Automating Retraining with Kubeflow

Example Kubeflow pipeline for model retraining

```yaml
apiVersion: argoproj.io/v1alpha1
kind: Workflow
metadata:
  generateName: retraining-pipeline
spec:
  entrypoint: main
  templates:
  - name: main
    dag:
      tasks:
      - name: preprocess-data
        template: preprocess
      - name: train-model
        template: train
        dependencies: [preprocess-data]
      - name: deploy-model
        template: deploy
        dependencies: [train-model]
# Additional task templates for preprocess, train, and deploy
steps
```

This code snippet illustrates a Kubeflow pipeline for automating the retraining process. The pipeline ensures that as new data arrives, the model is retrained and redeployed automatically.

Graph – Monitoring Model Accuracy Over Time

import matplotlib.pyplot as plt

Simulate model accuracy over time

time = [1, 2, 3, 4, 5] # Time in months

accuracy = [0.92, 0.89, 0.85, 0.80, 0.78] # Model accuracy

Plot the accuracy data

plt.plot(time, accuracy, marker='o')

plt.title('Model Accuracy Over Time')

plt.xlabel('Time (Months)')

plt.ylabel('Accuracy')

plt.show()

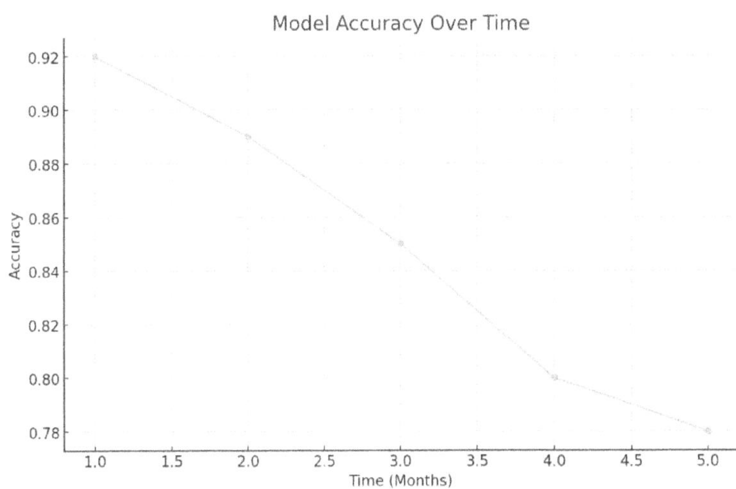

This graph illustrates how a model's accuracy can degrade over time due to data drift or model staleness. Regular monitoring helps detect when retraining is necessary to restore model performance.

Conclusion

Monitoring and maintaining AI models in production is critical for ensuring long-term effectiveness and reliability. By implementing strategies such as performance monitoring, data drift detection, and real-time logging, organizations can track how models behave in real-world environments. Regular model maintenance, including automated retraining and updating, ensures that models adapt to changing data distributions and maintain high performance. Proper monitoring frameworks and retraining pipelines are essential for building robust, scalable AI systems in production.

Appendices

<u>Mathematics for AI</u>

Mathematics forms the backbone of artificial intelligence (AI) and machine learning, providing the theoretical framework to design and analyze algorithms. Three essential areas of mathematics underpin the majority of AI models: linear algebra, calculus, and probability. These concepts are vital for understanding how AI models operate, how optimization occurs, and how models handle uncertainty in real-world data. This section provides an overview of these key mathematical concepts, demonstrating their role in AI with code examples and graphs.

Linear Algebra

Linear algebra is fundamental to AI and machine learning, as it deals with vectors, matrices, and transformations. AI models, especially deep learning, rely heavily on linear algebra for data representation, matrix multiplications, and optimizing learning algorithms.

Key Concepts in Linear Algebra

Vectors and Matrices: In AI, data is often represented as vectors (1D arrays) or matrices (2D arrays). A vector represents a single data point or a feature set, while a matrix can represent a dataset or the weights of a neural network.

Matrix Multiplication: Many machine learning algorithms involve matrix multiplication, particularly in deep learning models where the input data is multiplied by weight matrices in each layer of the network.

Eigenvalues and Eigenvectors: These concepts are essential in principal component analysis (PCA), an algorithm used for dimensionality reduction. Eigenvectors represent the directions of maximum variance in the data, and eigenvalues quantify the amount of variance captured.

Code Example – Matrix Multiplication

```python
import numpy as np

# Define two matrices

A = np.array([[1, 2], [3, 4]])

B = np.array([[5, 6], [7, 8]])

# Perform matrix multiplication

C = np.dot(A, B)

print("Matrix Multiplication Result:\n", C)
```

This code demonstrates how two matrices can be multiplied, an operation frequently used in the forward pass of neural networks.

Graph – Visualization of Matrix Multiplication

```python
import matplotlib.pyplot as plt

# Define vectors for visualization

x = [1, 2]

y = [3, 4]

# Plot the vectors

plt.quiver(0, 0, x[0], x[1], angles='xy', scale_units='xy', scale=1, color='r', label='Vector x')
```

```
plt.quiver(0, 0, y[0], y[1], angles='xy', scale_units='xy',
scale=1, color='b', label='Vector y')

plt.xlim(-1, 5)

plt.ylim(-1, 5)

plt.axhline(0, color='black',linewidth=0.5)

plt.axvline(0, color='black',linewidth=0.5)

plt.legend()

plt.grid()

plt.title('Vector Representation in 2D')

plt.show()
```

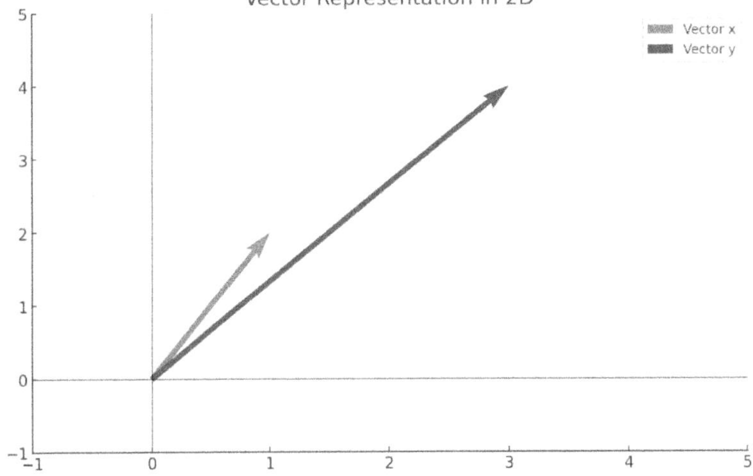

This graph visualizes two vectors in 2D space, helping to illustrate linear transformations that occur during matrix multiplication.

Calculus

Calculus is critical in AI for optimization tasks, particularly in training machine learning models. The key concept is using derivatives to minimize or maximize functions, which is fundamental in optimization algorithms such as gradient descent.

Key Concepts in Calculus

Derivatives: Derivatives measure the rate of change of a function with respect to its variables. In AI, the derivative is used to update model parameters during training by computing the gradient of the loss function with respect to the weights.

Gradient Descent: Gradient descent is an optimization algorithm used to minimize the loss function. The idea is to move the weights in the direction of the negative gradient to reduce the error in predictions.

Partial Derivatives: In models with multiple variables, partial derivatives are used to compute the gradient with respect to each parameter independently.

Code Example – Gradient Descent

```python
import numpy as np

# Define a simple quadratic function
def f(x):

    return x**2 + 3*x + 2

# Define its derivative
def f_prime(x):

    return 2*x + 3
```

```python
# Gradient descent implementation

x = 10  # Starting point

learning_rate = 0.1

n_iterations = 10

for i in range(n_iterations):

    x = x - learning_rate * f_prime(x)

    print(f"Iteration {i+1}: x = {x}, f(x) = {f(x)}")
```

This code demonstrates how gradient descent minimizes a simple quadratic function. At each step, the gradient is computed, and the parameter xxx is updated accordingly.

Graph – Gradient Descent Visualization

```python
x_vals = np.linspace(-10, 10, 100)

y_vals = f(x_vals)

# Plotting the quadratic function and the gradient descent steps
plt.plot(x_vals, y_vals, label='f(x) = x^2 + 3x + 2')

plt.scatter([x], [f(x)], color='red', label='Current Step')

plt.title('Gradient Descent Minimization')

plt.xlabel('x')

plt.ylabel('f(x)')

plt.legend()

plt.grid()

plt.show()
```

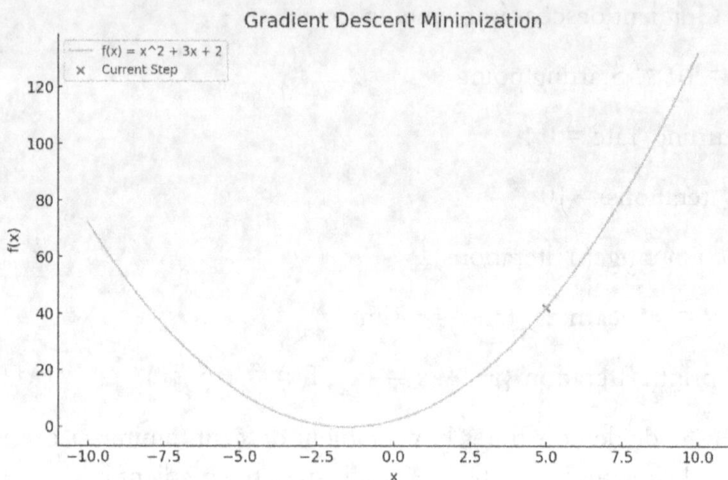

This graph shows the trajectory of gradient descent on a quadratic function. The red point represents the current step in the gradient descent process, where the function is being minimized.

Probability

Probability theory is crucial in AI for modeling uncertainty and making predictions based on incomplete or noisy data. Many machine learning models, particularly probabilistic models like Bayesian networks, rely on probability to handle uncertainty.

Key Concepts in Probability

Random Variables: A random variable represents a quantity that can take on different values based on chance. In machine learning, random variables are often used to represent predictions or model parameters.

Probability Distributions: Probability distributions describe the likelihood of different outcomes. Common distributions in AI include the normal distribution, Bernoulli distribution, and multinomial distribution.

Bayes' Theorem: Bayes' theorem provides a way to update the probability of a hypothesis based on new evidence. It is widely used in machine learning for algorithms such as naive Bayes classifiers and Bayesian inference.

Code Example – Probability Distribution

```python
import numpy as np

import matplotlib.pyplot as plt

# Define a normal distribution

mean = 0

std_dev = 1

x = np.linspace(-5, 5, 1000)

y = (1/(std_dev * np.sqrt(2 * np.pi))) * np.exp(-0.5 * ((x - mean) / std_dev) ** 2)

# Plot the normal distribution

plt.plot(x, y)

plt.title('Normal Distribution (mean=0, std dev=1)')

plt.xlabel('x')

plt.ylabel('Probability Density')

plt.show()
```

This code generates a probability density function for a normal distribution, which is commonly used in AI to model continuous variables.

Graph – Normal Distribution

The graph illustrates the normal distribution, a key concept in probability theory that underpins many machine learning algorithms, particularly those involving continuous data.

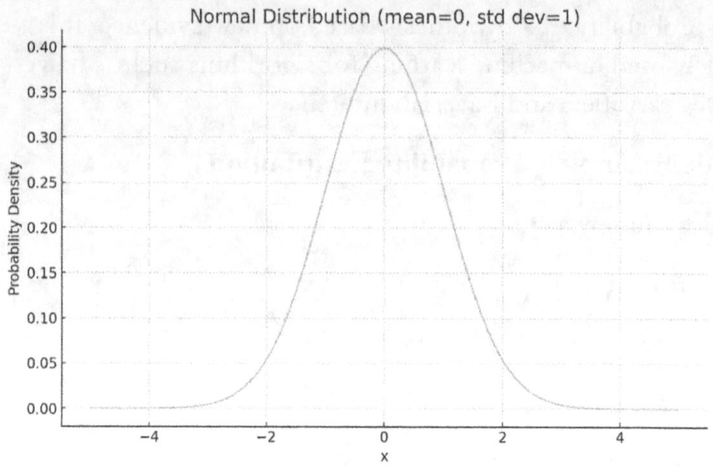

In summary, linear algebra, calculus, and probability are fundamental mathematical tools that enable the development and optimization of AI models. Linear algebra helps represent and manipulate data efficiently, calculus allows for optimization through gradient descent, and probability theory handles uncertainty and makes predictions based on likelihoods. A deep understanding of these mathematical concepts is essential for building robust and efficient AI systems.

Further Reading

As the field of artificial intelligence (AI) and machine learning (ML) continues to evolve rapidly, it is essential for practitioners, researchers, and students to stay updated with foundational knowledge and cutting-edge advancements. The following part provides a curated list of recommended books, research papers, and online resources that will help readers deepen their understanding of key concepts in AI, machine learning, and data science. These resources cover theoretical underpinnings, practical applications, and emerging trends, making them valuable for learners at all levels.

Suggested Books

"Deep Learning" by Ian Goodfellow, Yoshua Bengio, and Aaron Courville (2016)
This comprehensive textbook is one of the most authoritative resources on deep learning. It covers the mathematical foundations of deep learning, including neural networks, optimization algorithms, and unsupervised learning. The book is essential for anyone looking to gain a deep understanding of the principles behind deep learning and its applications in AI.
ISBN: 978-0262035613

"Pattern Recognition and Machine Learning" by Christopher Bishop (2006)
Bishop's textbook provides a thorough introduction to statistical pattern recognition, a key area in machine learning. The book covers probabilistic models, graphical models, and Bayesian networks, making it suitable for readers interested in the mathematical foundations of machine learning.
ISBN: 978-0387310732

"The Elements of Statistical Learning" by Trevor Hastie, Robert Tibshirani, and Jerome Friedman (2009)
This classic book is an essential reference for anyone looking to understand the statistical approaches to machine learning. It covers various learning algorithms such as decision trees, support vector machines, and ensemble methods.
ISBN: 978-0387848570

"Reinforcement Learning: An Introduction" by Richard S. Sutton and Andrew G. Barto (2018)

Sutton and Barto's textbook is the go-to resource for understanding reinforcement learning (RL). It covers key RL concepts such as dynamic programming, Q-learning, policy gradient methods, and applications in robotics and game playing.
ISBN: 978-0262039246

"Bayesian Reasoning and Machine Learning" by David Barber (2012)

This book is an excellent introduction to Bayesian methods in machine learning. It covers probabilistic reasoning, inference techniques, and their applications in classification, clustering, and regression tasks.
ISBN: 978-0521518147

Research Papers

"Attention Is All You Need" by Vaswani et al. (2017)

This seminal paper introduced the transformer model, which has become foundational for natural language processing (NLP) tasks. The paper details how attention mechanisms can replace recurrent and convolutional layers for better performance in tasks such as translation and summarization.
Vaswani, A., et al. (2017). Attention is all you need. In Advances in Neural Information Processing Systems (pp. 5998–6008).

"ImageNet Classification with Deep Convolutional Neural Networks" by Krizhevsky, Sutskever, and Hinton (2012)

This groundbreaking paper introduced the AlexNet model, which achieved state-of-the-art performance in image classification using deep convolutional neural networks (CNNs). It marked the beginning of the deep learning revolution in computer vision.

Krizhevsky, A., Sutskever, I., & Hinton, G. E. (2012). ImageNet classification with deep convolutional neural networks. Advances in Neural Information Processing Systems, 25, 1097–1105.

"Playing Atari with Deep Reinforcement Learning" by Mnih et al. (2013)

This paper introduced deep Q-networks (DQN), which combined deep learning with reinforcement learning to play Atari games at a superhuman level. It represents a major advancement in the field of deep reinforcement learning.
Mnih, V., et al. (2013). Playing Atari with deep reinforcement learning. arXiv preprint arXiv:1312.5602.

"GANs: Generative Adversarial Nets" by Ian Goodfellow et al. (2014)

This paper introduced generative adversarial networks (GANs), a novel framework for generating realistic synthetic data by training two networks in a competitive setting. GANs have since been applied to image generation, style transfer, and video synthesis.
Goodfellow, I., et al. (2014). Generative adversarial nets. In Advances in Neural Information Processing Systems (pp. 2672–2680).

"A Survey of Model Compression and Acceleration for Deep Neural Networks" by Cheng et al. (2017)

This paper provides a comprehensive overview of techniques used to reduce the size and computational complexity of deep learning models. The paper discusses methods such as pruning, quantization, and knowledge distillation.
Cheng, Y., et al. (2017). A survey of model compression and acceleration for deep neural networks. IEEE Signal Processing Magazine, 35(1), 126–136.

Online Resources

Coursera: Machine Learning by Andrew Ng

This online course, taught by Professor Andrew Ng, provides an excellent introduction to machine learning, covering supervised and unsupervised learning, neural networks, and reinforcement learning. It is one of the most popular courses for beginners and practitioners alike.

Coursera Machine Learning

Deep Learning Specialization by Andrew Ng (Coursera)

This specialization is designed to help learners master deep learning, covering topics like neural networks, convolutional networks, sequence models, and machine learning engineering.

Deep Learning Specialization

Stanford CS231n: Convolutional Neural Networks for Visual Recognition

This course provides in-depth coverage of CNNs and their applications in computer vision tasks such as image classification, object detection, and segmentation. The lectures, assignments, and notes are available online for free.

Stanford CS231n

Papers with Code

This platform is an excellent resource for finding cutting-edge machine learning research papers along with their associated code implementations. It is particularly useful for those who want to replicate and experiment with state-of-the-art models.

Papers with Code

Fast.ai

Fast.ai provides free online courses and libraries designed to make deep learning accessible to everyone. Their courses focus on practical applications and provide hands-on coding

experience using the Fast.ai library, built on top of PyTorch.
Fast.ai

Conclusion

The suggested books, research papers, and online resources provide a wealth of knowledge for individuals seeking to deepen their understanding of AI and machine learning. These resources cover foundational topics, advanced algorithms, and practical applications, making them suitable for learners at different stages of their AI journey. By engaging with these materials, readers can strengthen their theoretical understanding and apply AI concepts to real-world problems.

<u>Glossary of Terms</u>

Understanding key terms in artificial intelligence (AI) and algorithm development is crucial for navigating the complex landscape of machine learning, data science, and automation. This glossary provides definitions of important concepts, models, and algorithms, aiding readers in grasping foundational and advanced topics in AI. Each term is accompanied by its definition and relevance within the broader context of AI research and application.

1. Artificial Intelligence (AI)

Artificial Intelligence refers to the capability of machines to mimic human cognitive functions such as learning, problem-solving, and decision-making. AI systems can perform tasks that typically require human intelligence, such as speech recognition, decision-making, and language translation (Russell & Norvig, 2016).
Example: AI powers technologies like autonomous vehicles, virtual assistants, and recommendation systems.

2. Algorithm

An algorithm is a step-by-step procedure or formula for solving a problem. In AI, algorithms are used to automate the process of learning from data, optimizing models, and making predictions. Algorithms are central to all machine learning tasks, from data processing to final prediction (Mitchell, 1997).

Example: Algorithms such as decision trees and neural networks are widely used in AI for classification and regression tasks.

3. Machine Learning (ML)

Machine learning is a subset of AI that enables systems to automatically learn and improve from experience without being explicitly programmed. It involves the use of statistical techniques to allow machines to identify patterns in data and make predictions or decisions (Murphy, 2012).

Example: Spam detection in email services is commonly achieved using machine learning algorithms.

4. Deep Learning (DL)

Deep learning is a subfield of machine learning that uses neural networks with many layers (hence "deep"). These networks automatically learn high-level representations from data and have been particularly successful in tasks such as image classification and natural language processing (LeCun, Bengio, & Hinton, 2015).

Example: Convolutional Neural Networks (CNNs) are a type of deep learning architecture used for image recognition.

5. Neural Network (NN)

A neural network is a model inspired by the human brain's network of neurons. It consists of layers of interconnected

nodes, or "neurons," that process input data through weights and activations to produce predictions (Goodfellow, Bengio, & Courville, 2016).
Example: Neural networks are the basis for models in deep learning used for tasks like speech recognition and medical diagnosis.

6. Supervised Learning

Supervised learning is a type of machine learning where the model is trained on labeled data. The model learns the relationship between input and output variables and can then make predictions on new, unseen data (Bishop, 2006).
Example: A model trained to classify emails as spam or not spam using a dataset where each email is labeled accordingly.

7. Unsupervised Learning

Unsupervised learning is a machine learning approach that involves training a model on data without explicit labels. The goal is to find hidden patterns or structures in the data (Murphy, 2012).
Example: Clustering algorithms like K-means can group customers with similar purchasing behavior without pre-labeled categories.

8. Reinforcement Learning (RL)

Reinforcement learning is a type of machine learning in which an agent learns by interacting with an environment. The agent takes actions to maximize cumulative rewards, learning from the consequences of its actions (Sutton & Barto, 2018).
Example: Reinforcement learning is used in training AI agents for video games like AlphaGo and robotics tasks like path navigation.

9. Natural Language Processing (NLP)

Natural language processing is a field of AI that focuses on the interaction between computers and human language. It involves tasks such as language translation, sentiment analysis, and speech recognition (Jurafsky & Martin, 2009).
Example: NLP techniques are used in virtual assistants like Siri and Alexa to process and respond to voice commands.

10. Convolutional Neural Network (CNN)

A convolutional neural network is a type of deep learning model specifically designed for processing grid-like data such as images. It uses convolutional layers to automatically extract hierarchical features from the input (LeCun et al., 2015).
Example: CNNs are widely used in image recognition tasks, such as identifying objects in photographs.

11. Recurrent Neural Network (RNN)

Recurrent neural networks are a class of neural networks designed to handle sequential data. They use feedback loops to retain information across time steps, making them suitable for tasks like time series analysis and natural language processing (Goodfellow et al., 2016).
Example: RNNs are used for language modeling and machine translation tasks.

12. Decision Tree

A decision tree is a model used for both classification and regression tasks. It partitions the data into subsets based on certain criteria, creating a tree-like structure where each node represents a decision based on input features (Quinlan, 1986).
Example: Decision trees are commonly used for tasks such as diagnosing medical conditions based on symptoms.

13. Gradient Descent

Gradient descent is an optimization algorithm used to minimize the error of a machine learning model. The algorithm updates the model's parameters by moving them in the direction of the negative gradient of the loss function (Ruder, 2016).

Example: Gradient descent is used in training neural networks by adjusting the weights to minimize the difference between predicted and actual values.

14. Overfitting

Overfitting occurs when a machine learning model learns the training data too well, including its noise and outliers, leading to poor performance on new, unseen data. This typically happens when the model is too complex relative to the amount of training data (Hastie, Tibshirani, & Friedman, 2009).

Example: A model that memorizes the training set but fails to generalize to new data has overfitted.

15. Hyperparameter Tuning

Hyperparameter tuning involves optimizing the hyperparameters of a machine learning model, which are not learned during training but are set prior to the training process. These include the learning rate, batch size, and the number of layers in a neural network (Bergstra & Bengio, 2012).

Example: Grid search and random search are common techniques used for hyperparameter tuning.

Conclusion

Understanding key AI and algorithm-related terms is essential for engaging with machine learning and data science. These definitions provide a foundation for grasping more complex concepts and techniques as AI continues to evolve and advance. By familiarizing themselves with these terms, practitioners and learners can more effectively navigate the technical landscape of AI and machine learning.

References

Aarts, E., & Korst, J. (1988). *Simulated annealing and Boltzmann machines: A stochastic approach to combinatorial optimization and neural computing.* John Wiley & Sons.

Aarts, E., & Lenstra, J. K. (1997). *Local search in combinatorial optimization.* Princeton University Press.

Abadi, M., Barham, P., Chen, J., Chen, Z., Davis, A., Dean, J., ... & Kudlur, M. (2016). TensorFlow: A system for large-scale machine learning. *12th {USENIX} Symposium on Operating Systems Design and Implementation ({OSDI} 16)*, 265-283.

Aho, A. V., Hopcroft, J. E., & Ullman, J. D. (1983). *Data Structures and Algorithms.* Addison-Wesley.

Amershi, S., Begel, A., Bird, C., DeLine, R., Gall, H., Kamar, E., ... & Zimmermann, T. (2019). Software engineering for machine learning: A case study. In *Proceedings of the IEEE/ACM 41st International Conference on Software Engineering* (pp. 291-300).

Arjovsky, M., Chintala, S., & Bottou, L. (2017). Wasserstein GAN. *arXiv preprint arXiv:1701.07875.*

Arthur, D., & Vassilvitskii, S. (2007). K-Means++: The advantages of careful seeding. In *Proceedings of the Eighteenth Annual ACM-SIAM Symposium on Discrete Algorithms* (pp. 1027-1035).

Azure Machine Learning. (n.d.). Documentation. Microsoft Azure. https://docs.microsoft.com/en-us/azure/machine-learning/

Bahdanau, D., Cho, K., & Bengio, Y. (2014). Neural machine translation by jointly learning to align and translate. *arXiv preprint arXiv:1409.0473*.

Battaglia, P. W., Hamrick, J. B., Bapst, V., Sanchez-Gonzalez, A., Zambaldi, V., Malinowski, M., ... & Pascanu, R. (2018). Relational inductive biases, deep learning, and graph networks. *arXiv preprint arXiv:1806.01261*.

Bellman, R. (1957). *Dynamic programming*. Princeton University Press.

Bergstra, J., & Bengio, Y. (2012). Random search for hyper-parameter optimization. *Journal of Machine Learning Research*, 13(Feb), 281-305.

Birant, D., & Kut, A. (2007). ST-DBSCAN: An algorithm for clustering spatial-temporal data. *Data & Knowledge Engineering*, *60*(1), 208-221. https://doi.org/10.1016/j.datak.2006.01.013

Bolton, R. J., & Hand, D. J. (2002). Statistical fraud detection: A review. *Statistical Science*, *17*(3), 235-249. https://doi.org/10.1214/ss/1042727940

Bishop, C. M. (2006). *Pattern recognition and machine learning*. Springer.

Blum, A., & Langley, P. (1997). Selection of relevant features and examples in machine learning. *Artificial Intelligence*, 97(1-2), 245-271.

Bojarski, M., Del Testa, D., Dworakowski, D., Firner, B., Flepp, B., Goyal, P., ... & Zieba, K. (2016). End to end learning for self-driving cars. *arXiv preprint arXiv:1604.07316*.

Boser, B. E., Guyon, I. M., & Vapnik, V. N. (1992). A training algorithm for optimal margin classifiers. In *Proceedings of the Fifth Annual Workshop on Computational Learning Theory* (pp. 144-152). https://doi.org/10.1145/130385.130401

Bostrom, N. (2014). *Superintelligence: Paths, dangers, strategies.* Oxford University Press.

Bottou, L. (2010). Large-scale machine learning with stochastic gradient descent. *Proceedings of COMPSTAT'2010,* 177-186. https://doi.org/10.1007/978-3-7908-2604-3_16

Breiman, L. (2001). Random forests. *Machine Learning, 45*(1), 5-32. https://doi.org/10.1023/A:1010933404324

Breiman, L., Friedman, J. H., Olshen, R. A., & Stone, C. J. (1984). *Classification and regression trees.* Wadsworth & Brooks.

Brown, T. B., Mann, B., Ryder, N., Subbiah, M., Kaplan, J., Dhariwal, P., ... & Amodei, D. (2020). Language models are few-shot learners. *arXiv preprint arXiv:2005.14165.*

Buolamwini, J., & Gebru, T. (2018). Gender shades: Intersectional accuracy disparities in commercial gender classification. *Proceedings of Machine Learning Research*, 81, 77-91.

Černý, V. (1985). Thermodynamical approach to the traveling salesman problem: An efficient simulation algorithm. *Journal of Optimization Theory and Applications*, 45(1), 41-51.

Chandola, V., Banerjee, A., & Kumar, V. (2009). Anomaly detection: A survey. *ACM Computing Surveys, 41*(3), 1-58. https://doi.org/10.1145/1541880.1541882

Chandola, V., Banerjee, A., & Kumar, V. (2009). Anomaly detection: A survey. *ACM Computing Surveys, 41*(3), 1-58. https://doi.org/10.1145/1541880.1541882

Cho, K., Van Merriënboer, B., Gulcehre, C., Bahdanau, D., Bougares, F., Schwenk, H., & Bengio, Y. (2014). Learning phrase representations using RNN encoder-decoder for statistical machine translation. *arXiv preprint arXiv:1406.1078.*

Chung, J., Gulcehre, C., Cho, K., & Bengio, Y. (2014). Empirical evaluation of gated recurrent neural networks on sequence modeling. *arXiv preprint arXiv:1412.3555.*

Cormen, T. H., Leiserson, C. E., Rivest, R. L., & Stein, C. (2009). *Introduction to Algorithms* (3rd ed.). MIT Press.

Cortes, C., & Vapnik, V. (1995). Support-vector networks. *Machine Learning, 20*(3), 273-297. https://doi.org/10.1007/BF00994018

Cover, T., & Hart, P. (1967). Nearest neighbor pattern classification. *IEEE Transactions on Information Theory, 13*(1), 21-27.

Cristianini, N., & Shawe-Taylor, J. (2000). *An introduction to support vector machines and other kernel-based learning methods.* Cambridge University Press.

Dantzig, G. B. (1957). Discrete-variable extremum problems. *Operations Research, 5*(2), 266-288.

Deb, K. (2001). *Multi-objective optimization using evolutionary algorithms.* John Wiley & Sons.

Deb, K. (2001). *Multi-objective optimization using evolutionary algorithms.* John Wiley & Sons.

Deb, K., Pratap, A., Agarwal, S., & Meyarivan, T. (2002). A fast and elitist multiobjective genetic algorithm: NSGA-II. *IEEE Transactions on Evolutionary Computation, 6*(2), 182-197.

Devlin, J., Chang, M. W., Lee, K., & Toutanova, K. (2018). BERT: Pre-training of deep bidirectional transformers for language understanding. *arXiv preprint arXiv:1810.04805.* https://doi.org/10.48550/arXiv.1810.04805

Devlin, J., Chang, M. W., Lee, K., & Toutanova, K. (2019). BERT: Pre-training of deep bidirectional transformers for language understanding. *arXiv preprint arXiv:1810.04805*.

Draper, N. R., & Smith, H. (1998). *Applied Regression Analysis* (3rd ed.). Wiley.

Duda, R. O., Hart, P. E., & Stork, D. G. (2001). *Pattern Classification* (2nd ed.). Wiley.

Dwork, C. (2011). Differential privacy. *Encyclopedia of Cryptography and Security*, 338-340.

Eiben, A. E., & Smith, J. E. (2015). *Introduction to evolutionary computing*. Springer.

Eisen, M. B., Spellman, P. T., Brown, P. O., & Botstein, D. (1998). Cluster analysis and display of genome-wide expression patterns. *Proceedings of the National Academy of Sciences, 95*(25), 14863-14868. https://doi.org/10.1073/pnas.95.25.14863

Elgammal, A. (2019). AI is blurring the definition of artist. *Nature*, 572(7767), 581-581.

Esteva, A., Kuprel, B., Novoa, R. A., Ko, J., Swetter, S. M., Blau, H. M., & Thrun, S. (2017). Dermatologist-level classification of skin cancer with deep neural networks. *Nature*, 542(7639), 115-118.

Fischer, T. (2018). Reinforcement learning in financial markets: A survey. *arXiv preprint arXiv:1811.11695*.

Gatys, L. A., Ecker, A. S., & Bethge, M. (2016). Image style transfer using convolutional neural networks. In *Proceedings of the IEEE conference on computer vision and pattern recognition* (pp. 2414-2423).

Gill, L. (2020). Human-in-the-loop AI: Real-world strategies. *Harvard Business Review.*

Gislason, P. O., Benediktsson, J. A., & Sveinsson, J. R. (2006). Random forests for land cover classification. *Pattern Recognition Letters, 27*(4), 294-300. https://doi.org/10.1016/j.patrec.2005.08.011

Goertzel, B. (2014). Artificial general intelligence: Concept, state of the art, and future prospects. *Journal of Artificial General Intelligence, 5*(1), 1-48.

Gonzalez, R. C., & Woods, R. E. (2002). *Digital image processing.* Prentice Hall.

Goodfellow, I., Bengio, Y., & Courville, A. (2016). *Deep learning.* MIT Press.

Goodfellow, I., Pouget-Abadie, J., Mirza, M., Xu, B., Warde-Farley, D., Ozair, S., ... & Bengio, Y. (2014). Generative adversarial nets. In *Advances in Neural Information Processing Systems* (pp. 2672-2680). https://doi.org/10.48550/arXiv.1406.2661

Google Cloud. (n.d.). AI Platform. https://cloud.google.com/ai-platform

Graves, A., Fernandez, S., Gomez, F., & Schmidhuber, J. (2006). Connectionist temporal classification: Labelling unsegmented sequence data with recurrent neural networks. *Proceedings of the 23rd International Conference on Machine Learning* (pp. 369-376).

Graves, A., Mohamed, A. R., & Hinton, G. (2013). Speech recognition with deep recurrent neural networks. *2013 IEEE International Conference on Acoustics, Speech and Signal Processing* (pp. 6645-6649).

Guyon, I., & Elisseeff, A. (2003). An introduction to variable and feature selection. *Journal of Machine Learning Research, 3,* 1157-1182.

Hajek, B. (1988). Cooling schedules for optimal annealing. *Mathematics of Operations Research,* 13(2), 311-329.

Hannun, A., Case, C., Casper, J., Catanzaro, B., Diamos, G., Elsen, E., ... & Ng, A. Y. (2014). Deep speech: Scaling up end-to-end speech recognition. *arXiv preprint arXiv:1412.5567.*

Hardt, M., Price, E., & Srebro, N. (2016). Equality of opportunity in supervised learning. In *Advances in Neural Information Processing Systems* (pp. 3323-3331).

Hastie, T., Tibshirani, R., & Friedman, J. (2009). *The elements of statistical learning: Data mining, inference, and prediction.* Springer.

He, K., Zhang, X., Ren, S., & Sun, J. (2016). Deep residual learning for image recognition. *Proceedings of the IEEE conference on computer vision and pattern recognition,* 770-778.

Hearst, M. A., Dumais, S. T., Osuna, E., Platt, J., & Scholkopf, B. (1998). Support vector machines. *IEEE Intelligent Systems and their Applications, 13*(4), 18-28. https://doi.org/10.1109/5254.708428

Hoare, C. A. R. (1962). Quicksort. *The Computer Journal,* 5(1), 10–15.

Hochreiter, S., & Schmidhuber, J. (1997). Long short-term memory. *Neural computation,* 9(8), 1735-1780.

Holland, J. H. (1992). *Adaptation in natural and artificial systems.* MIT Press.

Hosmer, D. W., Lemeshow, S., & Sturdivant, R. X. (2013). *Applied Logistic Regression* (3rd ed.). Wiley.

Huang, G., Zhou, J., & Ding, M. (2018). The applications of AI in financial markets. *Journal of Physics: Conference Series, 1087*, 062026.

Huffman, D. A. (1952). A method for the construction of minimum-redundancy codes. *Proceedings of the IRE*, 40(9), 1098-1101.

Hunter, J. D. (2007). Matplotlib: A 2D graphics environment. *Computing in science & engineering, 9*(3), 90-95.

Hyndman, R. J., & Athanasopoulos, G. (2018). *Forecasting: Principles and Practice* (2nd ed.). OTexts.

Jain, A. K. (2010). Data clustering: 50 years beyond K-Means. *Pattern Recognition Letters, 31*(8), 651-666. https://doi.org/10.1016/j.patrec.2009.09.011

James, G., Witten, D., Hastie, T., & Tibshirani, R. (2013). *An introduction to statistical learning: With applications in* R. Springer.

Jobin, A., Ienca, M., & Vayena, E. (2019). The global landscape of AI ethics guidelines. *Nature Machine Intelligence*, 1(9), 389-399.

Jurafsky, D., & Martin, J. H. (2009). *Speech and language processing: An introduction to natural language processing, computational linguistics, and speech recognition.* Prentice Hall.

Jurafsky, D., & Martin, J. H. (2021). *Speech and Language Processing* (3rd ed.). Pearson.

Karras, T., Laine, S., & Aila, T. (2019). A style-based generator architecture for generative adversarial networks. In *Proceedings of the IEEE/CVF Conference on Computer Vision and Pattern Recognition* (pp. 4401-4410).

Kelleher, J. D., Namee, B., & D'Arcy, A. (2015). *Fundamentals of Machine Learning for Predictive Data Analytics: Algorithms, Worked Examples, and Case Studies*. MIT Press.

Kennedy, J., & Eberhart, R. (1995). Particle swarm optimization. *Proceedings of ICNN'95 - International Conference on Neural Networks*, 1942-1948. IEEE. https://doi.org/10.1109/ICNN.1995.488968

Kingma, D. P., & Welling, M. (2014). Auto-encoding variational Bayes. *arXiv preprint arXiv:1312.6114*.

Kirkpatrick, S., Gelatt, C. D., & Vecchi, M. P. (1983). Optimization by Simulated Annealing. *Science*, 220(4598), 671-680. https://doi.org/10.1126/science.220.4598.671

Knuth, D. E. (1976). *Big Omicron and Big Omega and Big Theta. ACM SIGACT News*, 8(2), 18-24.

Knuth, D. E. (1997). *The Art of Computer Programming, Volume 3: Sorting and Searching* (2nd ed.). Addison-Wesley.

Knuth, D. E. (1998). *The Art of Computer Programming, Volume 3: Sorting and Searching* (2nd ed.). Addison-Wesley.

Korf, R. E. (1985). Depth-first iterative-deepening: An optimal admissible tree search. *Artificial Intelligence*, 27(1), 97–109.

Kotsiantis, S. B., Kanellopoulos, D., & Pintelas, P. E. (2006). Data preprocessing for supervised learning. *International Journal of Computer Science*, 1(2), 111–117.

Kourou, K., Exarchos, T. P., Exarchos, K. P., Karamouzis, M. V., & Fotiadis, D. I. (2015). Machine learning applications in cancer prognosis and prediction. *Computational and Structural Biotechnology Journal, 13*, 8-17.

Krizhevsky, A., Sutskever, I., & Hinton, G. E. (2012). ImageNet classification with deep convolutional neural networks. In *Advances in neural information processing systems* (pp. 1097-1105). https://doi.org/10.48550/arXiv.1102.0183

LeCun, Y., Bengio, Y., & Hinton, G. (2015). Deep learning. *Nature, 521*(7553), 436-444. https://doi.org/10.1038/nature14539

LeCun, Y., Bengio, Y., & Hinton, G. (2015). Deep learning. *Nature*, 521(7553), 436-444.

LeCun, Y., Bottou, L., Bengio, Y., & Haffner, P. (1998). Gradient-based learning applied to document recognition. *Proceedings of the IEEE*, 86(11), 2278-2324.

Levinson, J., Askeland, J., Becker, J., Dolson, J., Held, D., Kammel, S., ... & Thrun, S. (2011). Towards fully autonomous driving: Systems and algorithms. In *2011 IEEE Intelligent Vehicles Symposium (IV)*

Levy, O., & Goldberg, Y. (2014). Neural word embedding as implicit matrix factorization. In *Advances in neural information processing systems* (pp. 2177-2185).

Liaw, A., & Wiener, M. (2002). Classification and regression by randomForest. *R News, 2*(3), 18-22.

Lloyd, S. (1982). Least squares quantization in PCM. *IEEE Transactions on Information Theory, 28*(2), 129-137. https://doi.org/10.1109/TIT.1982.1056489

Loh, W.-Y. (2011). Classification and regression trees. *Wiley Interdisciplinary Reviews: Data Mining and Knowledge Discovery, 1*(1), 14-23. https://doi.org/10.1002/widm.8

López, C., Vázquez, A., Benítez, J. M., & Herrera, F. (2012). A grammatical evolution neural network approach to model breast cancer survival. *Expert Systems with Applications, 39*(15), 11929-11942. https://doi.org/10.1016/j.eswa.2012.03.028

Luong, M.-T., Pham, H., & Manning, C. D. (2015). Effective approaches to attention-based neural machine translation. *arXiv preprint arXiv:1508.04025.*

Maas, A. L., Daly, R. E., Pham, P. T., Huang, D., Ng, A. Y., & Potts, C. (2011). Learning word vectors for sentiment analysis. In *Proceedings of the 49th annual meeting of the association for computational linguistics: Human language technologies* (pp. 142-150).

Maaten, L. V. D., & Hinton, G. (2008). Visualizing data using t-SNE. *Journal of machine learning research*, 9(Nov), 2579-2605.

Manning, C. D., Raghavan, P., & Schütze, H. (2008). *Introduction to information retrieval.* Cambridge University Press.

McKinney, W. (2010). Data structures for statistical computing in Python. In *Proceedings of the 9th Python in Science Conference* (Vol. 445, pp. 51-56).

Michalewicz, Z. (1996). *Genetic algorithms + data structures = evolution programs.* Springer Science & Business Media.

Mikolov, T., Chen, K., Corrado, G., & Dean, J. (2013a). Efficient estimation of word representations in vector space. *arXiv preprint arXiv:1301.3781.*

Mikolov, T., Sutskever, I., Chen, K., Corrado, G. S., & Dean, J. (2013b). Distributed representations of words and phrases and their compositionality. In *Advances in neural information processing systems* (pp. 3111-3119).

Minsky, M., & Papert, S. (1969). *Perceptrons: An Introduction to Computational Geometry.* MIT Press.

Mirza, M., & Osindero, S. (2014). Conditional generative adversarial nets. *arXiv preprint arXiv:1411.1784.*

Mitchell, M. (1998). *An introduction to genetic algorithms.* MIT Press.

Mitchell, T. M. (1997). *Machine learning.* McGraw-Hill.

Mnih, V., Kavukcuoglu, K., Silver, D., Rusu, A. A., Veness, J., Bellemare, M. G., ... & Hassabis, D. (2015). Human-level control through deep reinforcement learning. *Nature,* 518(7540), 529-533.

Murphy, K. P. (2012). *Machine learning: A probabilistic perspective.* MIT Press.

Murtagh, F., & Contreras, P. (2012). Algorithms for hierarchical clustering: An overview. *Wiley Interdisciplinary Reviews: Data Mining and Knowledge Discovery, 2*(1), 86-97. https://doi.org/10.1002/widm.53

Murtagh, F., & Legendre, P. (2014). Ward's hierarchical agglomerative clustering method: Which algorithms implement Ward's criterion? *Journal of Classification, 31*(3), 274-295. https://doi.org/10.1007

Newman, M. (2018). *Networks: An introduction.* Oxford University Press.

Nilsson, N. J. (1980). *Principles of Artificial Intelligence.* Morgan Kaufmann.

Nocedal, J., & Wright, S. J. (2006). *Numerical optimization* (2nd ed.). Springer.

Oliphant, T. E. (2006). A guide to NumPy (Vol. 1). Trelgol Publishing USA.

Pang, B., & Lee, L. (2008). Opinion mining and sentiment analysis. *Foundations and trends in information retrieval*, 2(1-2), 1-135.

Papadimitriou, C. H., & Steiglitz, K. (1998). *Combinatorial optimization: Algorithms and complexity*. Dover Publications.

Pascanu, R., Mikolov, T., & Bengio, Y. (2013). On the difficulty of training recurrent neural networks. In *Proceedings of the 30th International Conference on Machine Learning* (pp. 1310–1318).

Paszke, A., Gross, S., Massa, F., Lerer, A., Bradbury, J., Chanan, G., ... & Chintala, S. (2019). PyTorch: An imperative style, high-performance deep learning library. In *Advances in Neural Information Processing Systems* (pp. 8024-8035).

Pedregosa, F., Varoquaux, G., Gramfort, A., Michel, V., Thirion, B., Grisel, O., ... & Vanderplas, J. (2011). Scikit-learn: Machine learning in Python. *The Journal of Machine Learning Research*, *12*, 2825-2830.

Pennington, J., Socher, R., & Manning, C. D. (2014). GloVe: Global vectors for word representation. In *Proceedings of the 2014 conference on empirical methods in natural language processing (EMNLP)* (pp. 1532-1543).

Porter, M. F. (1980). An algorithm for suffix stripping. *Program*, 14(3), 130-137.

Quinlan, J. R. (1986). Induction of decision trees. *Machine Learning*, 1(1), 81-106.

Quinlan, J. R. (1993). C4.5: Programs for machine learning. *Morgan Kaufmann Publishers Inc.*

Rawat, W., & Wang, Z. (2017). Deep convolutional neural networks for image classification: A comprehensive review.

Neural Computation, *29*(9), 2352-2449.
https://doi.org/10.1162/neco_a_00990

Redmon, J., Divvala, S., Girshick, R., & Farhadi, A. (2016). You only look once: Unified, real-time object detection. In *Proceedings of the IEEE conference on computer vision and pattern recognition* (pp. 779-788).

Reeves, C. R. (1993). Modern heuristic techniques for combinatorial problems. *Wiley-Interscience.*

Ren, S., He, K., Girshick, R., & Sun, J. (2015). Faster R-CNN: Towards real-time object detection with region proposal networks. In *Advances in neural information processing systems* (pp. 91-99). https://doi.org/10.48550/arXiv.1506.01497

Rezende, D. J., Mohamed, S., & Wierstra, D. (2014). Stochastic backpropagation and approximate inference in deep generative models. In *Proceedings of the 31st International Conference on Machine Learning* (pp. 1278-1286).

Ribeiro, M. T., Singh, S., & Guestrin, C. (2016). "Why should I trust you?" Explaining the predictions of any classifier. In *Proceedings of the 22nd ACM SIGKDD international conference on knowledge discovery and data mining* (pp. 1135-1144).

Romero, J., & Machado, P. (Eds.). (2008). *The art of artificial evolution: A handbook on evolutionary art and music.* Springer.
Rosenblatt, F. (1958). The Perceptron: A probabilistic model for information storage and organization in the brain. *Psychological Review*, 65(6), 386-408.

Rousseeuw, P. J. (1987). Silhouettes: A graphical aid to the interpretation and validation of cluster analysis. *Journal of Computational and Applied Mathematics*, *20*(1), 53-65. https://doi.org/10.1016/0377-0427(87)90125-7

Ruder, S. (2016). An overview of gradient descent optimization algorithms. *arXiv preprint arXiv:1609.04747*.

Rumelhart, D. E., Hinton, G. E., & Williams, R. J. (1986). Learning representations by back-propagating errors. *Nature*, 323(6088), 533-536. https://doi.org/10.1038/323533a0

Russell, S., & Norvig, P. (2016). *Artificial intelligence: A modern approach* (3rd ed.). Pearson.

Russell, S., & Norvig, P. (2020). *Artificial Intelligence: A Modern Approach* (4th ed.). Pearson.

Russell, S., & Norvig, P. (2021). *Artificial Intelligence: A Modern Approach* (4th ed.). Pearson.

SageMaker Documentation. (n.d.). Amazon Web Services. https://aws.amazon.com/sagemaker/

Schölkopf, B., & Smola, A. J. (2002). *Learning with kernels: Support vector machines, regularization, optimization, and beyond.* MIT Press.

Sculley, D., Holt, G., Golovin, D., Davydov, E., Phillips, T., Ebner, D., ... & Dennison, D. (2015). Hidden technical debt in machine learning systems. In *Advances in Neural Information Processing Systems* (pp. 2503-2511).

Seber, G. A. F., & Lee, A. J. (2012). *Linear Regression Analysis* (2nd ed.). Wiley.

Sedgewick, R., & Wayne, K. (2011). *Algorithms* (4th ed.). Addison-Wesley.

Sennrich, R., Haddow, B., & Birch, A. (2016). Neural machine translation of rare words with subword units. *arXiv preprint arXiv:1508.07909*.

Shmueli, G., & Lichtendahl, K. C. (2017). *Practical Time Series Forecasting with R: A Hands-On Guide* (2nd ed.). Axelrod Schnall Publishers.

Siciliano, B., & Khatib, O. (Eds.). (2016). *Springer handbook of robotics* (2nd ed.). Springer.

Silver, D., Huang, A., Maddison, C. J., Guez, A., Sifre, L., van den Driessche, G., ... & Hassabis, D. (2016). Mastering the game of Go with deep neural networks and tree search. *Nature, 529*(7587), 484-489.

Simonyan, K., & Zisserman, A. (2014). Very deep convolutional networks for large-scale image recognition. *arXiv preprint arXiv:1409.1556.*

Stanley, K. O., D'Ambrosio, D. B., & Gauci, J. (2009). A hypercube-based encoding for evolving large-scale neural networks. *Artificial Life*, 15(2), 185-212.

Strang, G. (2016). *Introduction to linear algebra.* Wellesley-Cambridge Press.

Sundermeyer, M., Schluter, R., & Ney, H. (2012). LSTM neural networks for language modeling. In *Interspeech* (pp. 601–604).

Sutskever, I., Vinyals, O., & Le, Q. V. (2014). Sequence to sequence learning with neural networks. *Advances in Neural Information Processing Systems*, 27, 3104-3112.

Sutton, R. S., & Barto, A. G. (2018). *Reinforcement learning: An introduction* (2nd ed.). MIT Press.

Szegedy, C., Liu, W., Jia, Y., Sermanet, P., Reed, S., Anguelov, D., ... & Rabinovich, A. (2015). Going deeper with convolutions. *Proceedings of the IEEE conference on computer vision and pattern recognition*, 1-9.

Szeliski, R. (2010). *Computer vision: Algorithms and applications.* Springer.

Taigman, Y., Yang, M., Ranzato, M. A., & Wolf, L. (2014). DeepFace: Closing the gap to human-level performance in face verification. *2014 IEEE Conference on Computer Vision and Pattern Recognition (CVPR)*, 1701-1708. https://doi.org/10.1109/CVPR.2014.220

Tegmark, M. (2017). *Life 3.0: Being human in the age of artificial intelligence.* Alfred A. Knopf.

Tenenbaum, A. M., & Leighton, A. (2016). *Data Structures Using C* (2nd ed.). Pearson.

Tjoa, E., & Guan, C. (2020). A survey on explainable artificial intelligence (XAI): Toward medical XAI. *IEEE Transactions on Neural Networks and Learning Systems, 32*(11), 4793-4813. https://doi.org/10.1109/TNNLS.2020.3027314

Tsiptsis, K. K., & Chorianopoulos, A. (2010). *Data mining techniques in CRM: Inside customer segmentation.* John Wiley & Sons.

Vaswani, A., Shazeer, N., Parmar, N., Uszkoreit, J., Jones, L., Gomez, A. N., ... & Polosukhin, I. (2017). Attention is all you need. In *Advances in neural information processing systems* (pp. 5998-6008). https://doi.org/10.48550/arXiv.1706.03762

Watkins, C. J. C. H., & Dayan, P. (1992). Q-learning. *Machine Learning, 8*(3-4), 279-292.

Weiss, M. A. (2012). *Data Structures and Algorithm Analysis in Java* (3rd ed.). Pearson.

Whitley, D. (2001). An overview of evolutionary algorithms: Practical issues and common pitfalls. *Information and Software Technology, 43*(14), 817-831.

Zhu, X. X., Tuia, D., Mou, L., Xia, G. S., Zhang, L., Xu, F., & Fraundorfer, F. (2017). Deep learning in remote sensing: A comprehensive review and list of resources. *IEEE Geoscience and Remote Sensing Magazine*, 5(4), 8-36. https://doi.org/10.1109/MGRS.2017.2762307